HUMANISM IN RUINS

HUMANISM IN RUINS
Entangled Legacies of the
Greek-Turkish Population Exchange

Aslı Iğsız

Stanford University Press
Stanford, California

Stanford University Press
Stanford, California

©2018 by the Board of Trustees of the Leland Stanford Junior University. All rights reserved.

No part of this book may be reproduced or transmitted in any form or by any means, electronic or mechanical, including photocopying and recording, or in any information storage or retrieval system without the prior written permission of Stanford University Press.

Printed in the United States of America on acid-free, archival-quality paper

Library of Congress Cataloging-in-Publication Data

Names: Iğsız, Aslı, 1971- author.
Title: Humanism in ruins : entangled legacies of the Greek-Turkish population exchange / Aslı Iğsız
Description: Stanford, California : Stanford University Press, 2018. | Includes bibliographical references and index.
Identifiers: LCCN 2017058848 | ISBN 9781503606357 (cloth : alk. paper) | ISBN 9781503606869 (pbk. : alk. paper) | ISBN 9781503606876 (epub)
Subjects: LCSH: Population transfers—Turks—History—20th century. | Population transfers—Greeks—History—20th century. | Collective memory—Political aspects—Turkey. | Multiculturalism—Turkey. | Turkey—Cultural policy. | Turkey—Politics and government. | Humanism—History—20th century. | Biopolitics—History—20th century.
Classification: LCC DR590 .I35 2018 | DDC 304.809561/09042—dc23
LC record available at https://lccn.loc.gov/2017058848

Cover design: Black Eye Design | Michel Vrana
Cover photos: The Parthenon with scaffolding; Greek and Armenian refugee children from Anatolia standing outside one-story building, near Athens, Greece; Frank Carpenter with arms around a column, Greece. Library of Congress.
Typeset by Bruce Lundquist in 10.25/15 Adobe Caslon

Whoever has emerged victorious participates to this day in the triumphal procession in which current rulers step over those who are lying prostrate. According to traditional practice, the spoils are carried in the procession. They are called "cultural treasures," and a historical materialist views them with cautious detachment. For in every case, these treasures have a lineage which he cannot contemplate without horror. They owe their existence not only to the efforts of the great geniuses who created them, but also to the anonymous toil of others who lived in the same time period. There is no document of culture which is not at the same time a document of barbarism. And just as such a document is never free of barbarism, so barbarism taints the manner in which it was transmitted from one hand to another.

Walter Benjamin, "Theses on the Philosophy of History," 1940

CONTENTS

Acknowledgments   ix

By Way of an Introduction:
   The Entangled Legacies of a Population Exchange   1

Part I
Humanism and Its Discontents: Biopolitics,
the Politics of Expertise, and the Human Family
   Segregative Biopolitics and the Production of Knowledge   41
   Liberal Humanism, Race, and the Family of Mankind   73

Part II
Of Origins and "Men": Family History, Genealogy,
and Historicist Humanism Revisited
   Heritage and Family History   107
   Origins, Biopolitics, and Historicist Humanism   131

Part III
Unity in Diversity: Culture, Social Cohesion,
and Liberal Multiculturalism
   The Museumization of Culture and the Recognition of Alterity   173
   The Turkish-Islamic Synthesis and Coexistence
   after the 1980 Military Coup   209

In Lieu of a Conclusion:
   Cultural Analysis in an Age of Securitarianism   237

Notes   255
Index   309

ACKNOWLEDGMENTS

The present book represents a departure from my earlier research, and although the theme of the 1923 Greek-Turkish population exchange connects my earlier work to this volume, the research and sources I engage here are almost entirely new with a very few exceptions—and even then, my interpretation of them is quite different. In this process, I have benefited from the input and support of wonderful people. Although I acknowledge their specific contributions to this book in the endnotes, there are some others whose names I shall address specifically here for their input in relation to the publication of this book.

I am very grateful to Jane Burbank, Frederick Cooper, Kader Konuk, Zachary Lockman, Anton Shammas, Ella Shohat, Helga Tawil-Souri, and my former chair Zvi Ben-Dor Benite for their mentorship in the process of writing this book. My current chair Marion Katz's insights were invaluable. Aomar Boum, Aslı Gür, Farzin Vejdani, and my writing group have offered invaluable support of the writing process itself. I am forever indebted to Elif Sarı, who is an extraordinary person and research assistant. Begüm Adalet, Ismail Aji Alatas, Mikiya Koyagi, Zachary Lockman, Eduardo Matos Martín, Joanne Nucho, Ceren Özgül, Ayşe Parla, and Sara Pursley graciously read different parts and versions of the manuscript for this book and gave me remarkable comments. My students at New York University also provided wonderful feedback on different versions of my work, and I thank them all, together with Lucia Carminati at the University of Arizona. I thank Ilker Hepkaner for reading the book even though he was not in my class anymore. Their specific contributions are acknowledged in the endnotes, but suffice it to say that their intellectual rigor helped me become the best teacher and writer that I can be. I also thank Guy Barak for his generous help at the NYU library. Finally, I am most grateful to my interlocutors. Thank you for opening your archives, memories, and hearts to me.

I feel extremely fortunate to have worked with the Stanford University Press, and thank Kate Wahl for her insights, support, and feedback: it is a privilege to work with you. In addition, I am very grateful to Jessica Ling and Leah Pennywark for their exceptional work, and to Richard Gunde for being such an outstanding editor. I also would like to thank the anonymous reviewers for their excellent feedback and comments, and the time and labor they put into reading and considering my book. Thank you.

Parts of this book were presented at Princeton University, New York University, and the New School, and at meetings of the American Anthropological Association and the American Comparative Literature Association. I thank the audience for their excellent questions and helpful comments.

I am blessed with a wonderful family that has put up with so much in the process of writing this book. My brother, Hakan, always kept things in perspective. My parents rarely—if at all—agreed with anything I said, but always respected my position and supported me unconditionally. I hope one day I can be as good a parent as they have been to me. Eduardo and Marco, thank you for all the joy and happiness you brought into my life. Although Marco did not understand why his mother took so long to write a "chapter book" (when he could write so many himself), his enthusiasm motivated me beyond words. Eduardo and Marco, without you, this book could simply not exist. For this, and for everything else, I dedicate this book to you.

HUMANISM IN RUINS

BY WAY OF AN INTRODUCTION
The Entangled Legacies of a Population Exchange

"WHEN WE ARRIVED, FOÇA WAS IN RUINS" said Raşit Kemali Bonneval. Bonneval, a Muslim from Lemnos, Greece, and his family were relocated to Foça, Turkey, as part of the 1923 Greco-Turkish compulsory population exchange.[1] According to Bonneval, he and his family were descendants of a famous French nobleman who converted to Islam in the eighteenth century. The nobleman in question, Claude Alexandre, Comte de Bonneval, had been quite well known in Western Europe, including to such figures as Voltaire, Montesquieu, and Casanova.[2] Contributing to Bonneval's fame was the political turmoil that surrounded him and his subsequent conversion to Islam: that Bonneval had become a Muslim, an Ottoman Pasha with the name Humbaracı Ahmet Paşa, and later reformed the Ottoman artillery has preoccupied the European imaginary for centuries. During his life, fake memoirs addressing Bonneval's conversion were widely circulated in Europe.[3] Later, in the nineteenth century, novels and biographies were written about him—including the influential French critic Sainte Beuve's biographical essay entitled "Le Comte-Pacha Bonneval" (The Count-Pasha Bonneval).[4] With varying degrees of accuracy, these texts sought to piece together Bonneval's life.

Only fragments remain of this rich, adventurous life today: Comte de Bonneval/Humbaracı Ahmet Paşa's museumized room (the "Chamber of the Pasha" in the family chateau in France);[5] his tomb in the Galata Mevlevi Lodge in Istanbul; his letters scattered to different corners, included in different volumes and novels; and his family trajectories, each branch claiming relation to him. These family trajectories are also spread across different geographies and include the Bonneval family in France in addition to others sent to Turkey from Greece as part of the population exchange, such as Raşit Kemali.

Multi-sited research is needed to make sense of Count Bonneval's multiple lives as well as his Ottoman family. According to some French sources, Bonneval had adopted his aide in the Ottoman Empire, Süleyman Agha—another European convert to Islam.[6] According to others, he never had children or descendants.[7] Given the controversy surrounding Bonneval's life and the extent to which Western European authors went to address his conversion to Islam with exaggerated, fake, or romanticized accounts, there is reasonable doubt about the veracity of these claims.

How does one, then, approach, trace, and consider family histories, and where and when does one anchor family heritage exactly? How many languages are necessary to unlock family histories buried in the past? These questions are further complicated by forced migration. In the context of Turkey, the official adoption of the Latin alphabet in 1928 adds to this complication, as speakers of modern Turkish today need special training to read Ottoman texts, written in the Arabic script, and have limited access to family-related documents. The case of Bonneval and related family narratives exemplify the dynamics of Turkey's public domain in the 1990s and early 2000s. Tracing family histories and cultural heritage to lost maps of designated origin has marked the exchangees of that time. And as was the case with Raşit Kemali, the exchangees made decisions on where to anchor their origins—for how far one is willing to go in designating origins is a personal choice. It is also as part of this general trend that Raşit Kemali Bonneval's family history has surfaced in the public domain.

According to Raşit Kemali, his father had extensive landholdings and other property in the Greek island of Lemnos; that's how they made a living before they were forced to leave Greece. Relocated to Foça, on the Aegean coast of Turkey, the family was given property left behind by the deported Greek Orthodox—as stipulated in the 1923 exchange agreement ratified at the Lausanne conference. Upon their arrival in Foça, however, the family reportedly found most buildings in ruins and the roads full of overgrown thorny brush. Abandoned houses bore the scars of a war that led to the 1923 exchange agreement.

Today, we know the transition was not always easy for the incoming communities. Some spoke the language of the new country very well, others with an accent or not at all. While many exchanged Greek Orthodox were bourgeois merchants and tradespeople, most Muslims were farmers.[8] The property distributed to them was not always commensurate with what they left behind, nor did it necessarily match their agricultural expertise (if they had any). By way of example, a person experienced in growing olive trees could be given a property containing vineyards instead. Some so-called locals or natives in Greece addressed the incoming Greek Orthodox as "the Turkish seed" or offspring, *Turkos sporoi*.[9] Likewise some locals in Turkey called the incoming Muslims "the Greek seed," *Yunan dölü*. In all cases, such naming was meant to be an insult based on designated geographic origins, attributing a genealogical connection with the soil via the body, hence endowing the term "seed" or "offspring" with gendered implications.

The imprint of the 1923 exchange is therefore traceable beyond the buildings in ruins: it severed the physical ties of about one and a half million Muslims and Greek Orthodox to their family homes, homesteads, and pasts, and forced them to rebuild their lives elsewhere.[10] What remains today are mostly stories about different families extended to different geographies. And it is mostly through these stories, family photographs, recipes, collected family objects as pertaining to the lost geographies of "origin" that many exchangees, like Raşit Kemali Bonneval's family, seek to piece together the remains of the experiences of the exchange. Such human remains and buildings in ruins attest to the legacies of the 1923 Greek-Turkish population exchange, today addressed mostly in terms of family histories and cultural heritage. Piecing together these remains is no doubt a worthwhile endeavor in the recognition of family histories and backgrounds.

Cultural heritage and legacy, however, do not necessarily mean the same thing, nor can they be easily used interchangeably. The question of the "legacies" of the exchange, the human ruins where these legacies lie, and how they were addressed in the post-1945 world context and its aftermath, constitute the main framework of this book. Legacies of the 1923 exchange are notable in the systematization of the demographic management of alterity (cultural, religious, racial, ethnic, linguistic differences), including refugee crisis management—particularly salient in the post-1945 era. Today, the exchange may very well be engaged through cultural heritage on a personal and institutional level, but its legacies have broader political implications in the regulation of alterity. In this book, taking this regulation as a point of departure in the aftermath of the Second World War, I address the broader implications of such policies, their legacies, as well as the cultural policies developed to address the outcomes of the demographic regulation of alterity in particular, and more generally, cultural policies developed for the management of alterity. The book examines cultural frames of engaging the demographic management of alterity, including the implications of the frame of heritage. The 1923 exchange constitutes a productive case for studying these dynamics.

The 1923 Greek-Turkish Population Exchange and Its Implications for Peace

More than ninety years ago, the same route that the Syrian refugees are taking today from Turkey's Aegean seashores to Greece was the site of yet another human displacement en masse: the religious minority exchange between Greece and Turkey. Following the 1919–1922 Greco-Turkish War, which started with Greek ambitions to resuscitate a Hellenic empire on Ottoman territories,[11] the Ottoman Empire crumbled and upon its remains arose the Republic of Turkey. The new Turkish government and Greece signed the Lausanne Treaty in 1923 under the arbitration of the League of Nations. Affecting the lives of about one and a half million people, the two governments agreed to exchange Muslims in Greece and the Greek Orthodox Christians in Turkey. Those who fled during the war were also incorporated in the agreement. Excluded from the exchange were about two hundred thousand people—namely, the Muslims in Thrace, and the Greek Orthodox in the islands of Imbros/Gökçeada and Tenedos/Bozcaada, as well as in Istanbul.[12]

The Greco-Turkish population exchange was the first internationally ratified and executed compulsory population transfer between two countries. Population transfers and resettlement policies had occurred before, but the 1923 exchange was the first of its kind in that it has set an *international legal precedent* whereby forced migration was legitimized as a solution for a "greater good": peace.[13] Such legitimization implies that the segregation of different groups will restore a peaceful order. Lord Curzon, the British foreign minister who led the Military and Territorial Commission at the Lausanne conference, considered the 1923 Greek-Turkish population exchange to be a case that necessitated such measures. He thought the exchange was an instance of "unmixing peoples" and "a thoroughly bad and vicious solution for which the world will pay a heavy penalty for a hundred years to come."[14] This statement, however, did not stop Curzon from seeking to justify making the population exchange compulsory.[15]

Political figures like Lord Curzon were well aware of the hardships that a segregation implemented in the form of mass displacement would cause. Still, they justified forced migration, presumably to prevent greater harm.[16] Slogans like "never again" or "no more suffering" often accompany segregative policies such as forced migration.[17] These slogans presumably acknowledge the hardships of mass displacement through pain. Regardless, state officials have widely embraced segregation as a practical policy in the peacemaking processes. (Some exceptions do exist, such as the case of Lebanon, which did not officially undergo partition after the civil war of 1975–1990.)[18] Segregation is often justified through racialized discourses of incommensurable differences and promises of stability and peace. In general, such solutions favor segregation as if conflicts were biologically dispositioned, and obfuscate the concrete economic, political, and historical reasons behind hostilities including dispossession and appropriation. It is questionable whether officially embraced segregation as the "less bad" scenario is indeed the only viable answer.

Scholar Eyal Weizman addresses such endorsements of a scenario deemed to be "less bad" in the humanitarian context as an economy of the "lesser evil,"[19] whereby risks, bad-case and worse-case scenarios, as well as so-called proportionate measures are constantly calculated. According to Weizman, over the last few decades, the humanitarian field has operated in a manner that reinforces the status quo, justifies the exercise of power, and legitimizes decisions in the name of preventing a worse-case scenario. These decisions, he shows, do not adequately address the core problems at hand and do not lead to justice. Weizman claims that since the 1970s, an economy of lesser evil has shaped the human rights regime as we know it today.[20] As the case of the 1923 exchange reminds us, however, decisions made in the name of a greater good have long been part of finding so-called humane solutions to conflicts.

The Greek-Turkish population exchange legally presaged future population management policies based on alterity often justified in the name of humanely restoring peace and presented as a "lesser evil."[21] The very notion of the population exchange between Greece and Turkey is thus organically related to other cases informed by the same logic: the construction of walls, apartheids, partitions, and forced migrations across the world, which have marked the twentieth century and spilled into the twenty-first, leaving behind ruins, human remains, ghost towns, erased maps and memories. How does one begin to address such policies? Is it through the remains?

Legacies of the Exchange: Racialized Thinking and the Management of Alterity

The principal legacy of the 1923 exchange is its contribution to the institutionalization of the management of alterity via forced migration—a form of spatial redistribution. This management is configured in terms of numbers and space and justified as a means promoting security and stability, and with the 1923 exchange, it gained a legal framework in the international arena. For those seeking segregative solutions, the 1923 Greek-Turkish exchange not only constituted a legal precedent but also a successful case of so-called repatriation.[22] The exchange has therefore become a reference point for other cases, such as the Potsdam agreement of 1945, the partition of India in 1947, of Palestine in 1948, and of Cyprus in 1974.[23] These cases might differ in details, but they share the same segregative logic that sought either in theory or in practice to spatially redistribute different groups according to their backgrounds and "origins." Consequently, German nationals were expelled from Central Europe, India and Pakistan unofficially exchanged their Muslims and Hindus and Sikhs respectively, Arab Jews were transferred to Israel and plans to send Palestinians to Arab countries in their stead were considered, and Greek and Turkish Cypriots were redistributed in the partitioned island as the Greek south and the Turkish north. The examples can be multiplied.

If one considers Nazi eugenics and the scale of the horror of mass extermination during the Second World War, one might logically assume that in the aftermath of war, lessons would be drawn to reconsider the implications of alterity and that a natural outcome of this reconsideration would be to call such population management into question. Yet, if anything, the segregative logic was prominent in the post-1945 era marked by the establishment of the United Nations and the so-called refugee crisis. "In 1945, nations were in ruins. World War II was over, and the world wanted peace" the UN intoned.[24] And as recent scholarship on the United Nations demonstrates, minorities were widely considered to be sources of instability and potential obstacles to peace.[25] It is therefore not surprising that demographic and cultural policies were concurrently promoted to manage alterity during this time. And even in cases where race did not appear to be the primary concern, racialized thinking was very salient.

For example, in the context of the 1923 exchange, the Dönme—followers of the seventeenth-century rabbi Shabbatai Zvi who converted to Islam—in Greece wanted to be excluded from the exchange on the grounds that they always maintained their Jewish faith despite their appearance as Muslims.[26] Indeed, when the Dönme approached Dr. Rıza Nur, one of the key delegates of Turkey at the Lausanne conference, and articulated this request, he codified this community in terms of alterity.[27] Nur wrote in his memoirs that "the disaster for us [Turks] is that they [the Dönme] appear as Turks. Greeks and Armenians are better than they if for no other reason than we know they are Greeks and Armenians. This foreign element, this parasite, hides in our blood."[28] Rıza Nur's approach embodies a racialized identification embedded in the body via the bloodline.

A closer look at Rıza Nur's memoirs, however, reveals the pervasiveness of racial thinking and the importance attributed to the bloodline; racialization was certainly not limited to the case of the Dönme. The salience of racialized thinking is important because it demonstrates an embodied codification of alterity. For instance, Rıza Nur mentions how Zekâi (Aziz Zekâi Apaydın), one of the delegates from Turkey at Lausanne, sexually assaulted a chamber maid in his hotel.[29] Nur was upset that the news of the assault would get out, as was the case with a similar incident involving the Italian delegates.[30] He was concerned that other delegates would consider the assault as evidence that Turks are "savages" (*vahşi*). He quickly adds that Zekâi is not Turkish but Bosnian, but that "others would not know the difference."[31] Nur's concern resonates with eugenicist approaches to criminology—the assumption that one's bloodline determines one's criminal tendencies, which in turn implicates national character. Given that Nur was a physician by training and worked on treating syphilis,[32] his biologically informed approach to alterity and the national body in the aftermath of the Greco-Turkish War might not come as a surprise.

Overall, Nur had a clear position with regard to alterity: he was also upset that İsmet İnönü, the chief negotiator for Turkey at Lausanne, might be Kurdish,[33] and informed his readers that a potential delegate was removed from Turkey's Lausanne delegation because he was not Turkish. There seems to be no ambiguity in Nur's mind in terms of the undesirable implications of alterity, but it is also clear that he did not want to recognize these differences officially. According to him, once a group is acknowledged as different, it is likely for it to be coded as a minority. He feared that the European powers would then continue to maintain a sphere of interference in Turkey, similar to what they did in the late Ottoman era.[34]

In his memoirs, Rıza Nur explains how the Europeans identify three types of minorities (*ekalliyet*) in Turkey: racial, linguistic, and religious. He cautions his readers that, on the basis of race, there may be attempts to place Circassians, Bosnians, Kurds, and the Abhaz next to the Greek Orthodox and Armenians; with language, Muslims who speak other languages will be considered a minority; and with religion, the "two million Kızılbash," who belong to a branch of Islam other than the Sunni, will be configured as minorities. To him, the Greek Orthodox and Armenians are racially different, but he does not want to allow Kurds, Circassians, Bosnians, and others to be categorized as such.[35] As a self-declared ardent Turkish nationalist, Nur complains that these definitions are meant to divide people in Turkey and to intervene in Turkey's internal affairs. He was convinced that anyone from a different race, language, or religion needs to be surgically removed to preserve the health of the national body, because, according to him, those "foreign elements" (*ecnebî unsur*) are "germs" (*mikrop*) that lead to trouble (*belâ*).[36] Here, Nur puts race in a different category from language and religion, but this doesn't mean these modes of alterity were divorced from racialized thinking—bloodlines, origins, and lineage and the belief in an embodied, biologized essence that is transmitted from one generation to the next. Racialized thinking is therefore embedded in different categorizations of alterity, and is not limited to the hard category of race.

Nur's memoirs promote various population management policies. For those who remain in Turkey, such as the Kurds, he suggests an assimilation plan. He also proposes to redistribute villages of Circassians and Albanians and to resettle them elsewhere in Turkey, mixed (*karışık*) with Turks.[37] In short, he suggests not only assimilation and deportation, but also diluting the spatial distribution of perceived alterity in terms of numbers. Rıza Nur's approach exemplifies how the management of alterity in terms of bodies and numbers is configured simultaneously as a spatial regulation. Indeed, the core ideas of the 1934 Settlement Law (*İskân Kanunu*), implemented to presumably unify the populace of Turkey in language, culture, and blood through forced (re)settlement and depopulation in Turkey—targeting Kurds among others—are visible in Nur's statements.[38]

On the whole, Nur's memoirs hint at the pervasiveness of racialized thinking in population management. Depending on the background of a particular group, the suggested regulation of alterity ranges from deportation to assimilation, from segregation to resettlement. His thoughts are representative of the dominant views of his era and demonstrate how population management was not limited to the 1923 exchange. Further, the widespread conceptualization of the Greco-Turkish exchange as unmixing demonstrates the significance of bloodline and designated origins in the configuration of segregative policies.[39]

Lord Curzon is often quoted as referring to the 1923 Greek-Turkish population exchange in terms of unmixing.[40] Unmixing was already a notable discourse, and scholars have borrowed from Curzon, among others, to address population transfers in general, and the 1923 exchange as a particular instance.[41] Yet, unmixing is a historically charged concept also used in terms of eugenicist reproduction as mixing/degeneration and unmixing/purity.[42] This approach also surfaces in Nur's memoirs when he explains why he decided against marrying a beautiful young woman who was Albanian: he did not want to mix other blood into his unmixed lineage (*nesil*); he was determined to marry a Turk.[43] The implications of mixing here are highly racialized.

Unmixing, therefore, is a notion that necessitates unpacking: at the time when Curzon used "unmixing" to refer to the 1923 exchange, the term itself encapsulated a worldview informed by eugenics—a biologized approach to social issues in a manner that considers the populace as a site of improvement.[44] Biologized "solutions" to social matters include, for instance, approaching unemployment as a question of overpopulation that necessitates the regulation of birthrates, rather than as a consequence of economic and social policies. Often, these so-called solutions are racialized as well; it appears to matter which group's numbers should increase or be controlled.

Furthermore, Curzon's reference to unmixing implies that the groups that are supposedly not to be mixed are not diverse within themselves. Yet, the exchanged groups were in fact remarkably diverse. Consider Raşit Kemali Bonneval or the Dönme, among others. No group is monolithic, nor without hierarchies of its own. Examining a population-management technique in terms of unmixing therefore risks reinforcing emphases on bloodline and origins and falsely ascribing homogeneity; it also fails to capture the broader biologized implications of unmixing and its history.

Since at least the nineteenth century, a linear and racialized approach to human identification has marked Western European intellectual circles on multiple grounds. Unproblematized configurations of most Western Europeans as direct descendants of the ancient Greeks and Romans exemplify this approach. Linearly tracing peoples to designated origins, this system of categorization simultaneously stratifies and hierarchizes different groups, and assigns them different racialized genealogies. And race—an embodied category of classification and hierarchization through bloodline, essence, and origins—is an integral part of this intellectual history that, in this book, I identify as historicist humanism.[45]

Scientific racialism and eugenics on the one hand, and archaeology and literary histories on the other, have reinforced racialized configurations of genealogies and origins. Particularly in the nineteenth and early twentieth centuries, racial hierarchization was widely represented through the imagery of a family tree of humankind, with each branch representing racial genealogies.[46] These notions were disseminated within Western Europe and beyond: intellectuals, scientists, and politicians turned to the natural and human sciences as well as historicist humanism to trace their genealogical origins or to find proof that they belonged to favored racial branches.[47] In sum, the term "unmixing" is implicated in these histories of categorization and hierarchization—the parameters of which were then translated into population management techniques at the hands of political figures like Lord Curzon.

The 1923 exchange encapsulates the racialized alignment of different groups with designated geographies of belonging, such as the assumption that incoming Muslims from Greece belonged to Turkey and likewise that the Greek Orthodox from Turkey belonged to Greece. Such a redistribution enabled an increase in the numbers of those deemed to be desirable and a decrease in the numbers of unwanted groups without necessarily having to boost birthrates or to kill people en masse. While the regulation of birthrates or massacres did not disappear from the picture, they often coexisted with forced migration and other demographic measures, depending on the context.

All in all, the 1923 exchange signaled a modern fusion of the eugenicist logic with demography, mobilized through racialized thinking and statistics, and implemented as spatial segregation—all of which gained a legal framework in the international arena with the ratification and execution of the 1923 exchange. The Greco-Turkish population exchange, then, arguably epitomizes the international legitimization of population management in terms of numbers, bodies, and space. How, then, to approach these dynamics?

Biopolitics and the Legacies of a Population Exchange

Historian Frederick Cooper and sociologist Rogers Brubaker call attention to the important distinction between categories of analysis and practice.[48] According to them, categories of practice refer to everyday life activities of ordinary actors, whereas categories of analysis denote the analytical lens scholars use to examine those practices. The scope of practices to be examined, however, can be expanded beyond those of ordinary actors in everyday life to include statements, writings, and policies of officials like Lord Curzon or Rıza Nur, or works of other scholars and intellectuals such as eugenicists and humanists. In other words, both the policies and the intellectual histories that inform them can be considered under this rubric. As Cooper and Brubaker also point out, maintaining a critical distance between the examined sets of practices *and* the analytical lens used to study these practices is important for the production of knowledge on a topic in order to avoid conflating multiple practices, motivations, and meanings into one.

To examine the dynamics laid out, then, I propose biopolitics as a category of analysis. A term that became prominent mostly after French philosopher Michel Foucault engaged it in his lectures,[49] "biopolitics" denotes power exercised in terms of statistics, regulation of birth and death, and thus, power to manage the population as species and living beings. In terms of death, Foucault points at the fascistic extermination policies in Nazi Germany and genocide and highlights racism in that context. Foucault's work is significant in calling attention to power used to manage the population in terms of bodies and numbers. Yet, as the 1923 exchange also demonstrates, there are other ways of using this logic to manage the population without necessarily resorting to killing or boosting birthrates. Embodied categorization of humankind is central to racialized thinking, which in turn informs the segregative logic.

Foucault's references to race are important even though his primary concerns were not pressing issues like colonialism.[50] And as anthropologist Ann Stoler reminds us, when it comes to biopolitics, the racialism embedded in French colonial histories was largely ignored in the French academe at the time.[51] In Foucault's lectures, the components are there to make these connections such as the reference to regulating the population as "species," but they are not explicitly fleshed out to address the broader implications of these terms for other sites and their interconnections.

For the purposes of this book, I interpret biopolitics as the regulation of *categorized* human bodies in terms of numbers *and space*. By categorized, I mean a systematic and embodied indexing of different groups in a manner that informs demographic policies, as was the case with the 1923 exchange of populations. Configuring genealogies of bloodline and origins is instrumental in this process. Coupled with scientific racialism, cultural histories reinforce such taxonomies. This, in turn, informs the production of language and policy regarding the management of alterity—as evinced in Rıza Nur's memoirs and Lord Curzon's comments on the 1923 population exchange. It is important to note, however, that such embodied categorization does not begin and end with racialized thinking; health, hygiene, a crime-free lineage, and labor capacity are also important. As a more recent example, the International Monetary Fund's praise of the recent German policy to initially open its doors to a limited number of Syrian refugees on the grounds that Germany needs new labor to compensate for its aging population[52]—an economic move justified in terms of humanitarianism—attests to this. It clearly matters which groups are to be granted social and physical mobility and in what numbers.

In the post-1945 era, yet another large-scale refugee crisis erupted. This coincided with a wave of partitions, so-called population transfers, and the rise of the United Nations as an international body. In that context, the exchangees were still referred to as national emigrants or refugees. Presumably, the population exchange corrected a wrong as Muslims and Greek Orthodox were sent to where they supposedly actually belonged. Deeply anchored in the body, such a designation of origins configures racialized alignments with nation-states, regardless of where one might be born and raised. It is also important to remember that so-called national refugees or emigrants were not homogeneous.

A written question posed in the Turkish parliament at around the time of the population exchange further complicates this picture. On November 6, 1924, Mehmet Recep Peker, the minister of Internal Affairs as well as of Population Exchange, Property and Settlement (Dahiliye Vekili, Mübadele ve İmar İskan Vekaleti Vekili) read Zonguldak deputy Halil Bey's written question in parliament: "I would like to ask the representative of the ministry why the Kıptî [gypsies], who have neither a racial nor religious connection to Turkishness, and in particular, those who speak only Greek, have been included into the population exchange and brought to our country, and why they have been mostly settled around Zonguldak."[53] In response, Minister Peker stated that the categories set in the exchange agreement of the Lausanne Treaty were quite clear, and that if the Kıptî were to be sent to Turkey, this must have been because the committee in Greece decided that they belong among the exchangeable groups, implying that they might be Muslims. But Mehmet Recep Peker did agree that they were a different group, and added that for a population exchange of this scale, it is inevitable to include some "odd groups." Minister Peker tried to reassure deputy Halil Bey that his city, Zonguldak, was not specifically targeted to be populated with incoming gypsies. He explained that the Kıptî were offered settlement in many different places, Zonguldak being only one of them.

In addition to Rıza Nur's memoirs, this written questioning and answering in the Turkish parliament in the 1920s shows that spatial redistribution is not just a national, countrywide concern but also a micro-level question that preoccupies inhabitants and representatives of towns and cities where resettlement takes place. It is clear that religious categories are not sufficient to address racialized concerns about the origins of the exchangees and how they are hierarchized.

Segregative biopolitics, often justified as necessary for establishing order, security, and stability, crystallize the actual terms of peacemaking, also salient in the post-1945 era, when the Greco-Turkish exchange became a common reference point for population management. Such policies thus demonstrate the limits of the configuration of peace. As anthropologist Elizabeth Povinelli reminds us, limits are not the end point but instead are tools to demonstrate the anxieties and contradictions embedded in a discourse.[54] Considering limits, then, unveils the actual terms of a given discourse. And in this case, addressing the limits of the endorsement of peace—that is, presumably of harmonious coexistence to be achieved through biopolitics—clarifies the actual terms of what peace entails. For like anything else, peace is a category of practice that needs to be unpacked and carefully examined in order to address the stakes involved, especially when it comes to alterity, appropriation, and dispossession.

In sum, segregative biopolitics relies on a racialized human taxonomy, and translates this taxonomy into policies of spatial (re)distribution and (im)mobility. When implemented at an international level, waves of refugees and emigrants follow and constitute yet another terrain of population management, as was the case with the 1923 exchange or the post-1945 mass displacements. It is therefore both the process of deportation *and* the integration and assimilation of the incoming groups into the local social fabric that fall within the scope of population management.[55] Varying degrees of restrictions on physical and social mobility, discourses of order and security, and calibrated integration policies depending on the background characterize these cases. Every story of mobility in relation to segregative biopolitics is thus simultaneously a story of immobility.

In this book, I take the transnational implications of the 1923 exchange in the post-1945 era as a point of departure, and explore the interconnected biopolitical and cultural paradigms developed in the management of alterity. Different transnational organizations and social and political actors mobilized various discourses to address alterity under different circumstances. Attending to their relationality is key for this study. Such relationality includes cultural policies developed to address the legacies of segregative biopolitics as a modern population management tool, in addition to the implications of the racialized taxonomy of humankind in terms of biopolitical approaches.

Biopolitics and Historicist Humanism

Since at least the nineteenth century, historicist humanism has reinforced the human taxonomies generated in different fields such as scientific racialism, physical anthropology, and eugenics. Here, historicist humanism refers to a prominent historicist approach to human categorization—unambiguously connecting ancient peoples, their literary traditions, cultures, and arts to today. Informed by archaeology, literary history, philology, art and architectural history, among others, historicist humanism has long offered a cultural framework for biological arguments on racialized origins and genealogies. Critics Ella Shohat and Robert Stam call such categorizations that privilege a linear approach Eurocentric, as they undermine other histories and forms of identification. Shohat and Stam expose Eurocentrism as an epistemic infrastructure that reproduces such paradigms.[56]

Historicist humanism has indeed a long history embedded in especially Western European intellectual traditions that identify, categorize, and hierarchize cultures, civilizations, and race simultaneously.[57] While there is a rich archive to be exploited with regard to historicist humanism, for the purposes of this book, I am mostly interested in how, since the nineteenth century, this form of humanism has been intertwined with scientific racialism and how patterns of identification have emerged as a result. Here, I identify tracing genealogies and origins with implications of bloodlines as part of these patterns.

This mode of humanism, then, demarcates a predominantly linear identification that configures national cultures as a hierarchized constellation clustered around civilizations, presumably traceable to their civilizational "origins," with racialized implications. I return to this subject later in the book, but suffice it to say here that the major tropes of historicist humanism have been quite discernable in the methodology of some philological, literary, and intellectual works up until recently. These tropes of humanism include, but are not confined to, tracing what is believed to be a "national essence" to its civilizational origins, anchoring a civilizational identification to a historical point of origin—preferably an ancient cultural heritage—and simultaneously situating national cultures in a racially hierarchized family tree of humanity.

Likewise, since at least the late nineteenth century, Ottoman and Turkish writers, political figures, and intellectuals have engaged in a similar venture to discover their "original essence," imbued with debates on where to situate the Ottoman and Turkish core in terms of civilization: Sunni Islam, Western Europe, Central Asia, and/or Anatolia—Turkey's heartland today.[58] These debates are far from over. In contemporary Turkey, some intellectuals and political figures reject what they deem to be European manners and cultures on the grounds that they are not authentically part of the Turkish essence and call for a return to the original essence with the emblematic phrase *özümüze dönmeliyiz*—we shall return to our essence.

Ironically, this rejection does not extend to questioning how Eurocentric these very tools, concepts, and approaches to identification are to begin with, and how much searching for an original essence understood as the authentic self is a problematic venture. In addition, the very same debates about tracing authentic culture and essence occurred within European countries as well, which among themselves are far from monolithic. As with anything, cultures are the natural outcome of multiple crossings, exchanges, and borrowings, and not a matter of linearly traceable and unproblematically, historically discoverable static essence. Such an approach presumes an almost biological, embodied essence that remains unchanged throughout time and that can be transmitted from one generation to the next—implicating bloodline—that simply needs to be reactivated. When incorporated into social and cultural policy, the notion of original essence thus becomes a tool to justify social engineering with anachronistic and essentialist understandings of history, including in terms of nationalism and fascism.

For example, today, it is not a secret that tenets of historicist humanism were translated into racially informed policies in Italian and German fascism, which idealized Greek and Roman antiquity. In addition to extermination en masse, forced labor camps, and medical experiments on categorized bodies, the core of fascist biopolitics, arts, and eugenics were mobilized to reincarnate the so-called peak of Humanity, the long-gone glorious days lost to degeneration. The glorious epoch of Humanity was widely associated with ancient Greece and Rome—perceived as a static essence to be recovered. This approach selectively set a Eurocentric configuration of humanity as a universal ideal, cast as Humanity. Exclusion and hierarchization were embedded in this configuration of humanity. In Nazi Germany for instance, both culture and biology were mobilized in an attempt to revive the essence of a superior race. Important to this ideology was the notion of unmixing.

Racialized hierarchies of civilization have configured discourses of superiority beyond fascism. Such representations of different groups have also informed imperialist and colonialist expeditions and policies. As scholar Laleh Khalili shows, examples include French colonial subjugation and domination articulated in terms of a "civilizing mission," as well as the development of asymmetric warfare against the colonized. Khalili addresses how in colonial expeditions, Europeans did not consider their opponents to be civilized equals and duly developed irregular, asymmetric warfare to break them. This type of warfare, Khalili argues, was crucial in the conquest and colonization of Africa, Asia, and the Americas.[59] Anti-colonialist thinker Frantz Fanon calls this a racism that minimizes the colonized, reducing the colonial subject to the level of subhuman.[60]

In short, categorization and hierarchization of human bodies do not emerge overnight nor in a vacuum, and neither does biopolitics. Patterns of cultural representation have informed different policies, domination, and warfare. Discourses and language produced via scientific racialism, eugenics, and archives of historicist humanism have therefore broader implications for the configurations of alterity, biopolitics, and beyond. Interpreting biopolitics as a regulation of categorized bodies in terms of numbers and space also allows us to address what that systematic categorization entails in terms of biological and cultural discourses—and how archives of knowledge have generated biological and cultural frameworks conducive to such human categorization and hierarchization. Historicist humanism is an important part of this process, and offers a critical framework for analyzing the relationality between biopolitics and culture.

Segregative Biopolitics and Culture

Segregative biopolitics and fields of culture are interconnected beyond historicist humanism. Discourses of culture mobilized since the end of the Second World War with regard to alterity management constitute an additional site for examining the relationality between biopolitics and culture. These discourses include but are not confined to liberal humanism and, later, multiculturalism. In that respect, addressing such relationality helps unravel transnationally disseminated cultural policies and discourses of alterity. Moreover, other than cultural policy, there is also the very important dimension of self-identification, and thus the need to address the legacies of segregative biopolitics on a personal and institutional level via cultural heritage. With this book, therefore, I consider segregative biopolitics and culture as interrelated at multiple levels.

The use of culture here is twofold: first, to denote the fields of art and literature, including but not confined to visual arts, music, architecture, cinema, and theater. Second, to refer to the everyday practices of ordinary actors reproduced and negotiated through social exchanges and relationships, such as culinary preferences and cooking. Targeting both terrains of culture, UNESCO was arguably the most powerful international organization when it came to cultural policy in the post-1945 era. Since then, UNESCO has contributed to developing different cultural discourses and policies to address historicist humanism, question the tenets of scientific racialism, and reconfigure the implications of being human. These policies, in turn, have had their own limitations.

Further, as historian Mark Mazower shows, at its onset, the United Nations itself was instrumental in maintaining the status quo. In the name of building peace after the Second World War, the UN operated in different arenas such as population management and demographics, while UNESCO—the United Nations organization in education, science, and culture—generated policies in these fields. These dynamics are reminiscent of anthropologist Brian Silverstein's consideration of culture as a "major site of administration, governance and management," which "invites us to rethink our approaches to culture in its relation to power."[61]

What, then, were the limits of endorsing cultural policy as a message of peace, harmony, and coexistence in the post-1945 era? How did such cultural policy engage the legacies of modern segregative biopolitics—as legally sanctioned by the 1923 exchange in the international arena? More specifically, how did alterity get negotiated in such cultural policy, while biopolitics continued to inform demographic policy after 1945, generating countless instances of population displacement?

Another mode of humanism surfaced after World War II: liberal humanism, a popular cultural discourse endorsed by UNESCO.[62] Often associated with the Cold War era, liberal humanism emphasizes that, through a shared human essence, humanity is unified. Indeed, in the first decade after the end of the Second World War, which simultaneously underpinned the beginnings of the Cold War, UNESCO adopted liberal humanism as a message of peace and coexistence. Later, in the 1980s, the last decade of the Cold War, discourses of liberal humanism became instrumental for UNESCO's cultural policy of diversity. Sloganized with the phrase "we are all humans," liberal humanism calls attention to shared aspects of humanity that unify people, instead of dividing them.[63] Accordingly, despite our different genealogies and origins, we are all humans; humanity is the thread that unifies us. Hence, the emphasis on unity in diversity.

Liberal humanism has additional implications for discourses of brotherhood configured as an act of solidarity or recognition which often come with their own problematically charged meanings. In sum, versions of liberal humanism have informed UNESCO's cultural policy vis-à-vis alterity for decades. Today, the imprint of liberal humanism is visible in contemporary discourses of liberal multiculturalism—or at least, given the current global rise of neofascism and racism, what remains of it.

In Turkey, liberal humanism has been evident in narratives of Greek-Turkish brotherhood. It is important to note here that the tensions between the two countries continued after the 1923 exchange and particularly escalated with the conflicts that led to the partition of Cyprus in 1974. Brotherhood stressed the shared cultural practices such as food and music that connected Greeks and Turks beyond the political turmoil that separated them. These discourses, however, cannot be taken for granted. For example, a month before he sent Turkish troops to Cyprus during the conflict that led to the partition of the island, a poem Prime Minister Bülent Ecevit had written in the 1940s on Greek-Turkish brotherhood was brought up in the Turkish parliament. The opposition party used the poem against Ecevit to accuse him of Greek partisanship (see Part Three).

In that vein, after the 1980 military coup in Turkey, discourses of liberal humanism were mobilized to puncture the climate of oppression and hostility against alterity in Turkey. In 1983, a national culture report was commissioned under the tutelage of the junta. In it, patterns of historicist humanism reemerged as cultural policy, and the racialized origins of Turks were firmly configured as a Turkish-Islamic synthesis. The scholars who authored the report tapped into the earlier historicist humanist arguments of Ottoman and Turkish intellectuals. The report calls for the assimilation of different groups, proposes to solve class struggle by an emphasis on Islam, and is clearly hostile to minorities. Against this backdrop, some independent publishers sought to open spaces to articulate alterity via liberal humanist discourses during that time, when armed conflict with the PKK—the Partiya Karkerên Kurdistan, or the Kurdistan Workers Party—also escalated.[64] Stressing the importance of social harmony among peoples, the publishers often referred to the 1923

Greco-Turkish population exchange as a regrettable failure of coexistence. They highlighted suffering and hardships caused by the exchange as a way to reconnect with alterity in Anatolia at a human level. Overall, they calibrated liberal humanism to highlight the shared aspects of humanity in terms of the peoples of Anatolia. The political implications of such endeavors are thus different depending on the historical context. Still, even in instances where liberal humanist discourses are valuable in that they are adopted to dispel a climate of discrimination and hostility against alterity, whether they are adequate tools to raise explicit questions about social justice and dispossession remains open to question.

In sum, biopolitics and humanism have been historically intertwined in the regulation of alterity in Turkey and beyond.[65] While historicist humanism has culturally contributed to the reinforcement of ideas proposed in scientific racialism, liberal humanism has long been proposed as a remedy to both.[66] Yet, liberal humanism tends to generate an illusion of peace and coexistence, and has serious shortcomings and limitations in terms of social justice. At the heart of all peace processes lies biopolitics. How does one, then, examine the entangled biopolitical legacies of the 1923 exchange as a segregative regulation of alterity, and the *palimpsests* of language and policies—cultural and refugee and immigrant integration policies informed by the notions of humanism—that engaged these legacies in the post-1945 era?[67]

Palimpsests and the Entangled Legacies of the Exchange in the Post-1945 Era

My work draws from critic Gérard Genette's interpretation of the term "palimpsests"—originally developed as a critical tool to analyze relations between literary texts. According to Genette, a literary work is not a single entity or a closed text that exists in isolation, but always in relation to other texts.[68] This is important because any writing is in a way a rewriting, and each text draws on earlier texts that it reproduces, transforms, and reconfigures.[69] As the term "palimpsest" suggests, any new text carries the traces of older ones. It is this "transtextuality," Genette argues, "that sets the text in a relationship, whether obvious or concealed, with other texts."[70] Approaching a narrative as isolated, then, leads solely to a unitary close reading, a thick description of a specific text, whereas a transtextual approach to texts as palimpsests generates multiple readings and offers opportunities to conduct relational readings of texts.[71]

My interpretation of palimpsests here aims to consider the relationality between different discourses, practices, and policies. By way of example, rather than addressing unmixing as an isolated discourse pertaining to population transfers, engaging it as relational to racialized thinking helps to unravel this discourse's eugenicist implications and to historically and politically situate unmixing within its broader context. Likewise, considering liberal humanism as a discourse that seeks to reconfigure humanism in terms of a shared human essence—or as it is reconfigured in contemporary Turkey, via a shared human culture that speaks to human essence through sensory experience such as food and music—enables us to trace its connections to historicist humanism as well as to contemporary cultural policies of liberal multiculturalism.

Situating historicist humanism as historically relational to eugenics and scientific racialism, moreover, helps contextualizing racialized thinking as connected to segregative biopolitics through a rich archive of cultural history. Addressing the 1923 exchange as segregative biopolitics, then, offers the opportunity to consider this population exchange in relation to other forms of segregation and modern forms of population management. This relation can be explicit, with overt mention of the 1923 exchange as a legal reference point of segregative biopolitics in the international arena, or it can be more implicit, as examined in terms of logics of racialized thinking and biopolitics that have informed different practices of segregation.

A palimpsest de facto implies crossings between narratives, discourses, and conceptual frameworks such as the dissemination and pervasiveness of racialized thinking and its implications for unmixing or segregative biopolitics. Language and policies on alterity management are thus considered in relation to one another and carry the imprint of earlier discourses and practices. Considering them as relational—in palimpsests—helps put their broader political and historical implications into perspective. Hence, the significance of the 1923 Greco-Turkish population exchange in the configuration of modern-era population management techniques via spatial redistribution of different groups, and the reference to its entangled legacies.

In *Humanism in Ruins*, I consider the implications of the exchange in the post-1945 era in terms of biopolitics on the one hand, and the concurrent policies developed to engage refugees, immigrants, and alterity on the other. This relationality across time and space marks this project as transnational,[72] and its methodology, multidisciplinary. Combining archival research, interviews, visual and textual analysis, I analyze tangled modes of engagement with alterity, and address this entanglement through the palimpsests of cultural and intellectual histories as related to contemporary dynamics of biopolitics and humanism transnationally, with Turkey as a particular case. Given the terrains of culture and biopolitics that I engage as interconnected in this book, multidisciplinary analysis of palimpsests of discourses, policies, and practices in relation to alterity is key for this work. Multidisciplinarity also helps considering different archives of knowledge and demographic policies produced and mobilized at different moments of time as relational.

For a project that focuses on segregative biopolitics epitomized by the 1923 Greco-Turkish exchange of populations in the international legal arena, Turkey offers an important primary site for such analysis. Legal inheritor of the Ottoman Empire, which was deemed to be too racially mixed by some nineteenth-century race theorists, Turkey offers an excellent case to illustrate how even when race does not appear to be a primary category in population management, its paradigms are in fact salient. The entangled legacies of the 1923 exchange in alterity management attest to this phenomenon. And liberal humanism—a concept I use to refer to UNESCO-led cultural discourses and policy developed in the post-1945 era and which have continued to inform contemporary cultural discourses such as liberal multiculturalism—is significant because it helps us see how cultural policies developed in the aftermath of the Second World War were never truly intended to address the underlying logics of segregative biopolitics, and that they were rather proposed as a modality to manage alterity. Because of the importance of the 1923 exchange and its principal legacy—the institutionalization and legalization of segregative biopolitics as a population management technique—the case of Turkey is important in tracing how these policies and practices worked in a country that was never officially colonized, and which interpreted modern approaches to demography in particular terms to address alterity at different levels. While the focus is on Turkey, I bring in transnational contexts within the scope of my analysis and also address broader dynamics without generating exceptionalism for Turkey.

Turkey and the Post-1945 Transnational Context

The decades that mark the beginning and the end of the Cold War, as well its aftermath—namely, the end of the 1940s and the 1950s, and post-1980—have critical implications for contemporary Turkish politics. In Turkey, the beginning of the Cold War era coincided with the transition to multiparty democracy: in 1950, Adnan Menderes was elected as the prime minister in Turkey's first multiparty national elections. An anti-communist with authoritarian tendencies, Menderes was in power when Turkish troops were sent to the Korean War in support of the Americans and later, Turkey joined the North Atlantic Treaty Organization (NATO).[73] Following Turkey's membership in the IMF and the World Bank in 1947, the Menderes era was also marked by a transition to liberal economic policies, including privatization. Also, Menderes's policies on Sunni Islam were more open than those of earlier decades in the Turkish republic, which were characterized by imposed secularization.

During the Menderes years, Algerian decolonization begun, but Turkey appears to have largely aligned with France rather than the Algerians, despite the former's counterinsurgency brutality. Turkey, indeed, was clearly allied with the so-called free world of the Cold War era: distanced from communism and aligned with global capitalist powers, regardless of their varying degrees of illiberal policies and biopolitics at the time—such as McCarthyism and segregationism in the United States. The implications for the so-called free world are thus open to question here, as well as who qualified for liberty in that context. This is also the era when UNESCO issued its Statement on Race (1950) and promoted liberal humanism as a cultural policy.

In 1960, following a decade of being a democratically elected prime minister, Menderes was brought down by a military coup, after which he was put on trial. One of the accusations against him was his role in the orchestration of the 1955 anti-Greek pogroms that targeted the remaining Greek Orthodox community in Istanbul after the population exchange. The pogroms led to a wave of emigration of the Greek Orthodox from Istanbul to Greece. The mass migration after the pogroms may not have been the result of an international agreement on biopolitics like the 1923 exchange, but certainly achieved a similar result through state-sponsored violence: riddance of bodies codified as undesirable. At the time, Menderes's government played the Cold War card, and blamed the pogroms on the communists and arrested a large number of writers and others associated with communism. When put on trial later, Menderes was found guilty and eventually executed by the military in 1961.

As for the last decade of the Cold War, it opened with the third and arguably the bloodiest successful coup d'état in Turkish history. On September 12, 1980, following a civil war between factions of the so-called left and the right—which was never openly acknowledged to be a civil war and was referred to instead as the "years of anarchy"—the Turkish military led by General Kenan Evren overthrew the democratically elected government in the name of bringing order, social peace, and political stability to the country. The 1980 military coup is comparable to the coup that took place in Chile on September 11, 1973, which consolidated General Augusto Pinochet's power. As in Chile, factions of the left were the main target of the 1980 coup in Turkey; the junta altered the entire political, social, cultural, and legal infrastructure of the country and adopted a Turkish-Islamic interpretation of Turkishness to pacify labor unions, counter political ideals associated with the left, and oppress alterity.

During that time, Turgut Özal, the deputy prime minister of the military junta government, launched a series of neoliberal measures. This was the beginning of the rise of Özal, who had also worked in the World Bank for three years, to power. After the junta years, in 1983 Özal was the first civilian to be elected as prime minister. Later, he became the president of the republic and died while in the office in 1993. Privatization, urbanization, crippled labor unions, diminished state subsidization of agriculture, a prolonged state of emergency against the Kurds (renewed forty-six times), corruption scandals, and anti-leftist policies marked the years during which he was politically active as deputy prime minister, prime minister, and president, and the aftermath.

The political legacy of Menderes and Özal—two center-right politicians who governed the country for about a decade, one in the 1950s and the other in the 1980s and early 1990s—has important implications for the civilian political leadership in Turkey today. The current president of Turkey, Recep Tayyip Erdoğan, formerly prime minister (2003–2014), is often politically situated with Menderes and Özal. These decades have therefore broader connotations for the context of Turkey and the rise of Erdoğan's AK Party (AKP) to power. These connotations become more poignant especially considering how—so far—an unsuccessful military coup attempt was conducted against Erdoğan on July 15, 2016, by what appears to be a coalition that included the followers of Fethullah Gülen, a cleric who lives in self-imposed exile in the United States.

Since it came to power, the AKP has pursued an aggressive neoliberal agenda. In the AKP's first term (2003–2007), it encouraged liberal approaches to alterity. Gradually, it adopted neo-Ottomanism as a discourse of liberal multiculturalism, taking an imperial model to generate a limited version of cultural recognition. This model has constituted the forging of a Turkish-Sunni Islamic synthesis imbued with liberal humanist discourses of brotherhood, without necessarily translating such discourses into social, economic, and political rights. As the party gradually established its hegemony in the country, liberal discourses were eventually dropped. In the wake of the April 16, 2017, referendum, which brought an authoritarian presidential system to Turkey, effectively canceling what remained of the separation of powers, it is uncertain what direction the country will take.

In the broader context, the 1980s witnessed increasing public attention to the question of minorities and their cultural recognition in different nation-states, and the rise of the human rights regime. It is during that time that individual stories were widely publicized to make rights claims for an entire community.[74] Indeed, there was an increasing popularization of individual rights as cultural rights in the so-called memoir boom of the 1980s and 1990s.[75] The boom was arguably symptomatic of the rise of "identity" as a dominant category for discussing histories of oppression, exploitation, disparities, and displacement hardships from an individual perspective. Individual stories were, to a large extent, personified and presented as representative of a larger community and its cultural heritage.[76] In part, the public recollection of family histories like that of Raşit Kemali Bonneval or the Dönme are symptomatic of this transnational trend rearticulated in Turkey: while under the post-1980 military regime, the stories of the Dönme or Kemali Bonneval would most likely be oppressed, in the contemporary context they are naturalized without necessarily considering them a sign of diversity.

Cultural memory, in addition, has been promoted as a popular and powerful tool to discuss and challenge national historiographies.[77] In a way, this has been configured as the democratization of history: bringing individual histories to the forefront and building history from the bottom up. These shifts in engaging the past are very important, but unfortunately, they are rarely pursued to also address the social and economic aspects of disparities at a transnational level. Whether this might be, in part, an outcome of the eroding advocacy of the social and economic rights that followed the fall of the Iron Curtain is an important question worthy of exploration in a book dedicated to it on its own.

By the 2000s, state officials co-opted these laudable initiatives to develop modes of governmentality. To some, this at first might come across as a positive development. Yet, as scholars Laleh Khalili and Eyal Weizman have shown, liberal distaste for violence has made state officials more creative when it comes to governmentality. Over the last few decades, state officials have co-opted independent efforts calling for recognition in varying degrees, incorporated them into their official discourses, and instrumentalized culture to confine the recognition of rights to that field. "Culture" appears to be configured as *the* site for recognition, with relatively little attention to legal, economic, or social rights. State officials have developed policies to domesticate the demands and discourses of rights and recognition.[78]

Povinelli demonstrates that it is imperative to historicize state policies such as discrimination, colonialism, and violence. How does one, then, address history? As mentioned, one popular means is engaging the cultural memory of a community, recording its history against state-sponsored national histories. In Turkey, many works that juxtapose contemporary politics of memory with the Turkification of the Turkish republic in the 1930s have helped unravel problems with state-sponsored nationalist historiography, and how it eclipsed differences and overwrote state violence and discrimination. Whether addressing history as such helps calling power effectively into question is debatable. The reincarnation of liberal discourses, patterns of racialized thinking, changing emphases on origins and genealogies from the outset of the Cold War to today in Turkey and beyond, and how these discourses inform various modes of governmentality and cultural policies shaped under different political leadership attest to this phenomenon.

Biopolitics and liberal approaches to culture are structurally related. Depending on the time period and changing political circumstances, where the discursive emphasis on liberal values with regard to culture will be placed might be subject to change—nonetheless, their structural relation remains intact. (Liberal values addressed here are historically traceable to the white bourgeois Enlightenment configurations of the notions of liberty, fraternity, equality, and have modern-era implications such as democracy, individual rights, tolerance, and peace.[79]) Biopolitical dispossession constitutes the infrastructure of liberal discourses, which, regardless of the shape they have taken in the postwar era, including when they appeared to be critical of racialized hierarchization, have reproduced exclusion in different sites.

My goal here, then, is to offer a multidisciplinary analysis of alterity management in order to historically contextualize this relationality and to address its political implications through the entangled legacies of the 1923 exchange. With this work, I also intend to raise questions about the persistence of this relationality, and how segregative biopolitics still continues to inform minority, refugee, and immigrant management, generating ongoing ruination.[80]

Multidisciplinary Analysis and the Historicization of Ruins

Ruins are not just the leftovers or relics of war, as reportedly was the case when Raşit Kemali Bonneval's family arrived to Foça to find it in ruins or as the United Nations identifies its mission as building peace upon the ruins of war. Granted, these material remains of war and their lingering affect are very important sites for the analysis of ruination, as anthropologist Yael Navaro has shown in the context of partitioned Cyprus.[81] Ruins, however, also constitute a refiguration of what remains, as anthropologist Ann Stoler reminds us.[82] Such a refiguration might successfully obfuscate related policies, and therefore enable a favorable climate for reproducing similar policies—a process she calls ruination.

For the purposes of this book, this implies that post-1945 cultural policies and humanism created the illusion that the legacies of biopolitics were being engaged. It also means that being able to articulate cultural heritage and background can also be problematically construed as an effective way to address the legacies of segregative biopolitics like the 1923 exchange. These forms of cultural articulation are very important, but in the absence of a broader historicization of biopolitics, they remain incomplete.

The lack of historicization, then, contributes to reproducing human taxonomies and, most importantly, other policies informed by segregative biopolitics including but not confined to gentrification or the use of infrastructure to generate racialized segregation of different groups such as by building highways to separate a minority neighborhood from others or building dams to limit the mobility of a particular group—examples are multiple, both in Turkey and elsewhere.[83] The possibility of reproducing similar policies—despite the hardships they generate—might arise in part because examples of segregative biopolitics are often considered in isolation, or at best, in comparison with another case, rather than through the biopolitical logics and the palimpsests of language and policy that inform them.

As for humanism and refugees, anthropologist Liisa Malkki calls for a radical historicization that acknowledges human suffering, but also political memory, historical agency, and narrative authority, without romanticizing "giving people a voice"—which, she argues, can only lead one to find "underneath the silence not a voice waiting to be liberated but ever deeper historical layers of silencing and bitter, complicated regional struggles, over history and truth."[84] Referring to French poststructuralists Michel Foucault's and Roland Barthes's critiques of liberal humanism that seek to connect peoples via a universally shared human essence, Malkki underlines the importance of connecting people through history and historicity: "if humanism can only constitute itself on the bodies of dehistoricized, archetypal refugees and other similarly styled victims—if clinical and philanthropist modes of humanitarianism are the only options," she cautions us, then being part of the "human community itself remains curiously, indecently, outside of history."[85]

Historicization is of course important, but on its own it does not necessarily call power into question. This has important implications, as not putting the emphasis on accountability of power enables the reincarnation of similar dynamics, political formations, and discourses, conducive to the continuation of what Stoler calls ruination. How does one, then, radically historicize and politically contextualize violence, discrimination, biopolitics, and humanism, and remain critical of a local context without favoring exceptionalism?

As a scholar of Middle East studies, I am wary of the Orientalist dynamics in which Euro–North American "norms" of humanism and human rights are taken for granted, and used as a metric against which Middle Eastern countries are measured and hierarchized, as if these norms are historically and politically unproblematic. For the Middle East, exceptionalism often feeds Orientalism and problematically culturalizes and racializes violence and problems with power, as if authoritarian states are the result of a genetic disposition or a cultural trait embedded in Middle Eastern racialized genealogies, rather than a bureaucratic and legal problem. These problems do not happen overnight nor in a vacuum. There are local factors, yes, but also histories of foreign intervention, exploitation, imperialism, and colonialism fueled by economic interests.

Further, given the salience of strange bedfellows that marked Cold War–era US policies such as the support for the bloody military coups in Turkey and Chile, it is especially important to address the transnational dimensions together with the local context, so as to be able to look at the larger picture and to consider power within that context. Focusing on a local case is invaluable in uncovering the local dynamics. Equally important, however, is to attend to related histories and politics of transnational alignments and collaborations so as to raise historically informed questions about the present.

By way of example, late British prime minister Margaret Thatcher infamously supported Pinochet, and later praised him for bringing a new constitution and "democracy" to Chile, and undermined his responsibility for the loss of lives, brutality, and the forcibly disappeared.[86] More recently, after the 2013 military coup in Egypt, an editorial in the *Wall Street Journal* stated that "Egyptians would be lucky if their new ruling generals turn out to be in the mold of Chile's Augusto Pinochet" because Pinochet "took power amid chaos" and supposedly transitioned Chile to a free market economy and democracy.[87] In that respect, while critically addressing a local context, I find it crucial to keep transnational dynamics in mind—particularly with regard to issues that involve rights and liberal values. No institution or organization can be taken for granted; doing so often reproduces Euro-North American-centric critiques and Orientalism. It also risks generating blind spots favoring global economic powers and obscures the long trail of strange-bedfellow collaboration to protect capitalist interests.

In that light, my work owes much to the principles of cultural studies configured by Stuart Hall and others: addressing power, domination, and hegemony via a self-reflexive and cross-disciplinary analysis of culture. Juxtaposing palimpsests of biopolitics with approaches to culture—including racialized thinking—and humanism, opens the possibility of a multidisciplinary analysis of alterity management via the entangled legacies of the 1923 exchange. Here, self-reflexive scholarship denotes wariness of reproducing Orientalist paradigms and Euro–North American norms. As for cross-disciplinary analysis, Stuart Hall advocated interdisciplinarity in cultural studies.[88] Accordingly, interdisciplinary work makes it possible to examine and analyze complex dynamics. Hall also remarked how, from the outset, scholars of cultural studies sought to intervene in the established frameworks of sociology and literary studies—rendering their work necessarily cross-disciplinary.

Borrowing from Hall's proposed principles of analysis, I situate *Humanism in Ruins* at the intersections of anthropology, history, political critique, and cultural and literary studies. There are various reasons why I use the term "multidisciplinary." First, in my analysis, I methodologically draw from multiple disciplines: in addition to my work in a wide range of archives, I also conducted interviews, engaged in participant observation, and used tools of textual and visual culture analysis. Secondly, my sources necessitate multiple disciplinary frameworks, as some primary sources include proceedings and minutes of conferences, institutional records, memoirs, films, scholarly books, pamphlets, essays, travel accounts, personal letters, cultural policy documents, minutes of parliamentary sessions, legal regulations, official correspondence, employment records, textbooks, exhibitions, catalogs, websites, museums, fiction, poetry, newspaper columns, and photographs. Finally, multidisciplinarity becomes a necessity because the scholars and intellectuals whose works I engage in this book themselves operate in a variety of fields, including but not confined to eugenics, sociology, law, anthropology, literary and cultural history, and archaeology. In sum, the work itself is multidisciplinary at different levels.

. . .

When thinking about my research, I have found historian Michael Werner and social scientist Bénédicte Zimmermann's *histoire croisée* very productive.[89] Werner and Zimmermann propose a method of historical analysis that takes crossings into consideration, and how objects and categories of analysis can change both across time and space. Their proposed method echoes my concerns with palimpsests in this book. Werner and Zimmermann promote a self-reflexive approach, in which the scholar positions herself vis-à-vis the object of analysis (not unlike anthropologists), and considers all categories and objects in question as relational—meaning, part of a dynamic exchange, and a process of crossing and interaction. This emphasis on crossing is helpful in rethinking palimpsests of humanism, both in its historicist and liberal forms, as well as biopolitics: versions of these approaches are reproduced across time and space, they are transformed in the process, and inform different policies. *Histoire croisée*, then, is a method that helps to historically contextualize the development and transformation of various processes and discourses in time (diachrony), as well as the dynamics that occur simultaneously in different locales at a given moment in time (synchrony). It allows both historically and politically contextualizing crossings between different policies and practices across time and space. Since the palimpsests addressed in this book reveal how different discourses are produced and disseminated, and inform different practices and cultural and demographic policies in different times, crossing offers a productive framework to address the relationality between these discourses, practices, and policies across time and space.

Werner and Zimmermann's work has also helped me rethink the massive crossing that happened with the Greek-Turkish population exchange and the modalities of engagement with its legacies in the late 1940s and 1950s, and in the post-1980s, as well as their convergences and divergences. Revolving around these engagements are liberal and historicist humanism and biopolitics, as well as the politics of culture. With these dynamics in mind, I reinterpret Werner and Zimmermann's proposed method in a multidisciplinary manner to consider the entangled dynamics laid out above and to develop an analytical framework for the study of the historical as well as the social and the cultural. The diachronic and synchronic approach to palimpsests of discourses, practices, as well as the policies they inform, facilitates historicization and political contextualization without making claims of linear continuities or chronologically presented histories. Synchronic and diachronic analysis enables weaving the past into the present of alterity management from multiple perspectives.[90] I hope the palimpsests examined in this book will offer new frames for future studies, such as tracing genealogies of liberal thought in Turkey, which deserves a volume of its own.

With the book's multidisciplinary outlook, I hope to contribute to intellectual debates in different disciplines. For instance, at the time of revising this book, historians Jo Guldi and David Armitage published *The History Manifesto* advocating long-term—*longue durée*—historical research highlighting the importance of attending to, say, several centuries rather than focusing on several decades to draw conclusions from the past and consider alternatives for the future.[91] Their goal is very important: they invite historians to help make better connections with today and avoid what they call short-termism. They do not completely dismiss a smaller scale of analysis—as they reckon, both are necessary—but their call for long-term historical research is clear. I hope this book will offer yet another mode for asking historically informed questions on contemporary dynamics and weave the past into the present through a multidisciplinary synchronic and diachronic analysis, without necessarily conducting a long-term historical analysis that spans several hundred years—even though some of my own sources are from the nineteenth century.

In anthropology, at least when this book was completed, human-animal relations and environmental anthropology have become important frameworks. There are excellent studies that consider these relations in order to raise important political and ethical questions.[92] As such works demonstrate, the post-human can be interpreted as moving beyond human-centered analysis to address critical issues.[93] In yet other projects, I have witnessed how these extremely important frames of analysis are presented in depoliticized terms that seem to consider "post-human" anthropology as divorced from political context, in which post-humanism is interpreted temporally as after humanism—as if the subject were exploited enough—or as a substitute for human-centered research, rather than as transcendent and complementary to existing paradigms. The former appears apolitical and the latter could offer important insights to complicate existing notions and categories. I do not consider post-humanism as a substitute, for many categories that are beyond human have human consequences. My work seeks to reconsider humanism—both in its historicist and liberal forms—in a global context of rising neofascism and securitarian state apparatuses and raises questions about its political implications. As philosopher Michel Foucault reminds us, when a crime is committed, the offense falls within the scope of the law, but with securitarianism, it is the probability of a perceived threat that is anticipated and this anticipation informs the security apparatus.[94] Today, we witness yet another heightened racialization of this apparatus, which informs new policies of segregative biopolitics that range from erecting walls, visa and travel bans, to incarceration and dirty bids over refugees. I hope that this book's concern with different forms of humanism both transnationally and in Turkey will contribute to our understanding of the multiple implications of being human historically, culturally, and politically. Examining the past as tangled with the present in a multidisciplinary diachronic and synchronic analysis, I explore these dynamics through the lens of alterity.

In terms of cultural studies and political critique, my work seeks to develop a multidisciplinary framework for cultural analysis at a time of the return to big data in the human sciences. In many ways, big data in the social sciences mirror the longue durée in history. Just like micro- and macro-history complement each other, big data, along with qualitative cultural analysis, are essential for the human sciences. Over the last few years, multiple epistemological turns have marked the humanities and the social sciences, including those signaling shifts to biological or securitarian paradigms, especially after 9/11 and more recent developments in natural sciences and biometrics. These dynamics have generated a very productive debate on the implications of studying culture in general and cultural studies in particular. Before his death in 2014, Stuart Hall himself had started raising questions in that regard. In that light, my goal is to offer a radical cultural and historical analysis conducive to political critique. Disciplinary divides may at times lead to treating culture, politics, social and economic dimensions, and eugenics as divorced from one another and may not always allow us to see their implicit and explicit interconnections. Hence, my analysis of palimpsests in this book.

Elements of culture, biology, and the securitarian capitalist order are, furthermore, interconnected. With a radical cultural analysis that politically contextualizes alterity in the present and engages its multiple *histoires croisées*, I ask how, if at all, the world has dealt with segregative biopolitics and fascism. Indeed, the reincarnation of fascism in different parts of the world, rising walls—as a supposedly securitarian measure—and the use of culture and alterity to invite potential voters to racialize the redistribution of socioeconomic resources to win elections are a case in point. The motivations might be economically informed, but to a large extent, the consent of the public appears to be successfully mobilized through hostile discourses against alterity.

An Outline of the Book

Weaving past and present dynamics together, I thus seek to address the historical and political implications of humanist discourses and cultural policies especially in juxtaposition with biopolitics. Due to its scope, the book—aside from this introduction and the conclusion—is divided into three long parts, each consisting of two essays, instead of shorter chapters. With this organization, my goal is to read these essays together as a palimpsest in order to expand the scope of analysis of each part and to complicate the historical and political contexts analyzed in those essays.

Part One interconnects postwar scholarship on refugee integration and alterity, and initiatives to promote peace, with a photography exhibition as an embodiment of liberal humanism. The first essay of this part traces the activities, presentations, and publications of various scholars—eugenicists, sociologists, anthropologists, and legal scholars among others—and their intellectual networks to unravel a complex, transnational intellectual and cultural history to address the entangled dynamics revolving around the segregative legacy of the 1923 Greek-Turkish population exchange. Focusing on the first decade after World War II, the first essay traces how segregative biopolitics was addressed transnationally through a refugee association led by a Turkish eugenicist, Fahreddin Kerim Gökay, and founded with the contributions of an Italian eugenicist and statistician, Corrado Gini, who also was a supporter of Mussolini's fascism. The 1923 exchange was a reference point for the association, and research was conducted on the subject.

As for the story of the founding this refugee association, it crystallizes the politics of scholarly knowledge production, the institutional competition to dominate knowledge production, the fusion of fascist eugenics with demographics in refugee integration processes, and the modes of engaging alterity in the post-1945 era. Juxtaposing these dynamics with what else was concurrently happening during that decade, in the second essay I turn to the rise of UNESCO-oriented cultural policies developed to address alterity and race during that period, and analyze a photo exhibition, *The Family of Man*. The exhibition epitomizes liberal humanism par excellence and was officially endorsed by UNESCO both in the 1950s and in more recent years. This juxtaposition enables a historical and political contextualization of liberal humanist discourses and cultural policy entangled with segregative biopolitics that developed concurrently. It also helps raise questions about postwar cultural policies and from which angles they engaged alterity and the legacies of segregative biopolitics, as well as their limits and pitfalls. Through a synchronic analysis, these two essays seek to address the shortcomings of liberal discourses in terms of fraternity and equality, and raise questions about the racialized core of liberties.

Part Two turns to the notions of genealogy and origins and attends to their different uses across time and space in relation to the 1923 exchange, racialized thinking, and historicist humanism. The first essay in this part begins with post-1990s Turkey and traces how legacies of segregative biopolitics have been primarily engaged on a personal level through family histories configured as cultural heritage. Making Raşit Kemali Bonneval's family history public has also been part of this process. Engaging individual and institutional practices that configured family histories as sites of articulating different backgrounds—alterity—after the 1980 military coup, I consider the implications of engaging biopolitical ruins through individual genealogies and origins configured through the family. I also address UNESCO's cultural policy interventions with regard to alterity and interlace the broader transnational context to the local in Turkey.

Next, in the second essay of this part, I historically contextualize other forms of engaging genealogies and origins—historicist humanism and racialized thinking—which have been instrumental in categorizing peoples on the paths that have led to segregative policies in general, of which the 1923 Greco-Turkish exchange was a particular instance. Examining different examples from the nineteenth and the twentieth centuries, I also discuss a UNESCO conference on historicist humanism organized in India in 1951. The Turkish representative was philosopher and sociologist Hilmi Ziya Ülken, who was also the chair of the Turkish branch of the refugee association analyzed in Part One. From cultural history to cultural policies to individual practices of tracing genealogies and origins, the diachronic analysis of the notions of genealogies and origins across the essays in this part questions the implications of addressing biopolitics via cultural heritage, and asks whether articulating family history in terms of individual liberties is conducive to effectively addressing the ruination of segregative biopolitics and the dispossession that follows.

Part Three turns to the contemporary period, and in its two essays traces the palimpsests of cultural policy pertaining to liberal multiculturalism in Turkey and the European Union, in addition to an earlier configuration of the Turkish-Islamic synthesis. Addressing liberal and historicist humanism embedded in liberal multiculturalism narratives in Turkey and beyond, the first essay engages the discourses and cultural policies that enabled the building of the first 1923 Greco-Turkish population exchange museum in Turkey as part of the Istanbul 2010 European Capital of Culture project. Considering how UNESCO's cultural policy had an impact on the EU's policies, which then traveled to Turkey, this essay addresses the limits of liberal multiculturalism and the form it has taken in Turkey: neo-Ottomanism.

After tracing the transnational crossing of liberal multiculturalism to Turkey, in the second essay I turn to the local historical context that this discourse simultaneously draws from: post-1980 coup era cultural policy and the Turkish-Islamic synthesis. The Turkish-Islamic synthesis has broader implications for the fascistic historicist humanism mobilized during the 1980 coup era. This part also questions the efficacy of liberal values embedded in liberal cultural politics in considering the legacies of segregative biopolitics.

Overall, all parts consider the entanglement of humanism and biopolitics and the impact of this tangle on the development of a vision of "culture" significant for both today and the past. One final word with regard to liberal humanism here is necessary, especially given the securitarian turn Turkish politicians have taken against the Kurds today. At the time of writing this book, full-blown urban warfare and a campaign of violence that demolished Kurdish cities, heritage sites, and reportedly caused numerous civilian casualties were taking place. In such circumstances, one might consider liberal cultural discourses as more appealing than violence itself. In fact, I have been asked different versions of this question when I presented my research at different forums. I would like, therefore, to address it briefly, as it is important.

With its multidisciplinary cultural and historical analysis, I hope this book will contribute to our understanding of the implications of selecting the "least of all possible evils" in cultural policies supposedly developed to deal with the ruins of segregative biopolitics and configurations of alterity. That is to say, crafting cultural policies by choosing the "least of all possible evils" means choosing not to change the system nor search out a permanent solution to a cycle of problems, because it is often thought a solution simply can't be found. Having to choose between liberal cultural discourses (in the liberal humanism of the 1950s or in the liberal multiculturalism of today) and the current violence reproduces a similar dynamic. Biopolitics and liberal humanism are structurally related, even though this relation takes different forms depending on historical and geographic contexts. This is why it is important to demystify liberal humanism in all its guises and to raise questions about justice.

One of the two essays in each part excavates a liberal intervention to remedy a particular issue in relation to segregative biopolitics. Whether the purported aim of liberal cultural politics to establish liberal values truly brings equal social and political rights and mobility, a sense of solidarity informed by social justice and restitution, or liberties beyond individual claims to heritage remains questionable. The biopolitical infrastructure of liberal approaches to culture remains intact and continues to structure their limits.

If anything, the contemporary spectacles of violence crystallize the questions raised in this book: What are the broader implications of liberal humanism towering upon ruins, without having necessarily addressed the biopolitics—the tenets of which are reinforced by the paradigms of historicist humanism—in the making of those very ruins? Indeed, the fact that state policy can go (at least on the publicly visible surface, because whether state violence ever disappears is questionable) so swiftly from liberal humanism and narratives of "brotherhood" to a destructive securitarianism involving many civilian casualties and dispossession by the utter destruction of cities—now themselves in ruins—and oppression, indicates the scale of the problem. If dispossession, citizenship, and bureaucratic problems were really fixed and biopolitical implications of these dynamics were addressed at all levels of state institutions, and impunity were not a norm, would such a seemingly abrupt change in policy be possible in the first place? The problem here is not liberal humanism or multiculturalism—two forms of liberal cultural politics examined here—on their own, per se, but that they are built upon the policies of biopolitics, which are largely left unaddressed.

It is because such a matrix of power tends to obscure the fact that liberal cultural politics and segregative biopolitics are two sides of the same coin in the regulation of alterity, and because unraveling this entanglement might help us reconsider the historical and political implications of a lesser-evil scenario, that I sought to write this book.

Humanism in Ruins tells this story.

• PART I •

HUMANISM AND ITS DISCONTENTS

Biopolitics, the Politics of Expertise, and the Human Family

Anthropologists have reached general agreement in recognizing that mankind is one; that all men belong to the same species, *Homo sapiens*. . . . Biological studies lend support to the ethic of universal brotherhood; for man is born with drives toward co-operation, and unless these drives are satisfied, man and nations alike fall ill.

>Ashley Montagu, Claude Lévi-Strauss, et al., anthropologists,
>"Statement on 'Race,'" UNESCO, restricted draft, December 14, 1949

Culture, like humanity itself, is universal. It is the gradually accumulated heritage of centuries—what the mind has learnt by turning in upon itself and by contemplating the outer world. . . .

A common heritage, then—the common property of all men, from whatever civilization they spring. . . . As was pointed out by the experts who met in 1948 at Unesco House, the object of social science is . . . to improve human relationships. It has therefore a prime part to play in constructing the edifice of peace.

>"Introduction," *International Social Science Bulletin*, UNESCO,
>Summer 1950

The self-imposed task of the AER [European Association for the Study of Refugee Problems] is the study of refugee matters and of the integration process of the refugees into their reception countries. . . . By these endeavours AER, and INTEGRATION are helping to alleviate the misery among the refugees and to show ways to a better world.

>Fahreddin Kerim Gökay, Turkish psychiatrist and eugenicist,
>elected president of the AER;
>*Integration*, July 1, 1954

Segregative Biopolitics and the Production of Knowledge

ON SEPTEMBER 15-17, 1954, members of the European Association for the Study of Refugee Problems (AER) arrived in Istanbul for their fourth annual general assembly.[1] The assembly offered a platform to discuss refugee integration policies in Europe and to exchange information and present research on the subject. Renowned Turkish philosopher and sociologist Hilmi Ziya Ülken chaired the Turkish team of scholars in the AER, and during the convention in Istanbul, he gave a presentation on refugees and immigrants in Turkey, particularly covering works written on the 1923 Greek-Turkish compulsory population exchange.[2] As for the convention site of that year, Istanbul, it had a particular significance: it was the home city of the president of the AER, Fahreddin Kerim Gökay—who was also both the governor and the mayor of Istanbul (1949–1957). Gökay, formerly a professor of psychiatry at Istanbul University, was a leading eugenicist in Turkey.[3]

At first sight, it may come as a surprise that an organization whose self-declared mission was to ease the suffering of refugees and to improve the world,[4] would elect a leading eugenicist as its president. A closer look at organizations such as the AER in the 1950s and their approaches to the populace, however, reveals the limits of humanitarian discourses and the biopolitical implications of human welfare in that context. It should then be no surprise that Gökay was elected as the president of the AER. In fact, when members of the AER decided at the 1954 meeting in Istanbul to expand the geographic scope of the organization and to found a sister organization—the Association for the Study of the World Refugee Problem (AWR)—Gökay was elected president of that association as well, and served in that post for about ten years. Gökay was the only president the AER had before it officially merged with the AWR in 1961.[5] The AER/AWR's proceedings and surrounding dynamics reveal how the logic of segregative biopolitics prevailed in the most unexpected places, networks, and institutions in the post-1945 era.[6] As a matter of fact, Gökay was hardly the only eugenicist at the AER and certainly not the most controversial one.

For those familiar with the history of Turkey, there is another twist in the story: On September 6–7, 1955, exactly one year after the AER convention in Istanbul, massive violence targeted the city's remaining Greek Orthodox residents. This state-orchestrated anti-Greek pogrom destroyed previously designated shops, houses, and businesses of the Greeks of Istanbul, and cost lives. The target was the Greek Orthodox of Istanbul who had been exempt from the 1923 Greek-Turkish population exchange. Since Fahreddin Kerim Gökay was both the mayor and the governor of Istanbul, the city and the safety of its residents were his responsibility—as he himself acknowledged when he hosted the members of the AER in Istanbul the year before. According to reports, however, Gökay was complicit in the state-sponsored violence against the Greek Orthodox.[7] Despite their direct responsibility in generating this violence, Prime Minister Adnan Menderes and other Turkish officials at the time played the Cold War card and were quick to blame the pogrom on the communists.[8] A few days later, some Turkish newspapers announced that the pogrom was a disgrace and a threat to Turkey's dignified position in the "family of humankind" (*insanlık ailesi*)—or as it would have been likely put in English in the 1950s, "the family of man."[9]

The pogrom and its connection to the 1923 exchange were not addressed at the conventions of the AER. This may come as a surprise given the significance of the 1923 exchange for this refugee association: in the opening issue of *Integration*, the official publication of the AER and later also of the AWR, the 1923 Greek-Turkish exchange is cited as a key precedent in the international arena. It is also credited as one of the critical events that historically contributed to the development of the modern-day refugee problem—the very problem that, magnified after the Second World War, formed the raison d'être of the AER. In other words, the AER was founded to cope with the ripple effects and dynamics generated by segregative biopolitics, with the 1923 exchange being an important milestone in that regard. Considering the power dynamics surrounding the AER, however, the overlooking of the 1955 anti–Greek Orthodox pogrom is to be expected.

The AER proceedings also reveal how biopolitics was not addressed as part of a broader logic, but rather, through its outcomes on a case-by-case basis. Such an isolated engagement undermined the salience of segregative biopolitics implemented in different forms over time and space. The relationality between such policies and practices thus remains implicit, which makes it harder to connect them as different parts of a prevailing logic. This might be another reason why, despite having caused yet another wave of immigration, the 1955 pogrom was disregarded in international platforms such as the AER.

The relationality between different instances of segregative biopolitics, however, was not ignored altogether. It was addressed through suffering, rather than as a logic that (re)produces such suffering. Focusing on the affective outcomes, such approaches centerstaged the *human*. Highlighting pain invites the audience to connect different cases of hardship through human feelings, without considering that those ordeals are the outcome of concrete political decisions. For example, at the 1954 AER meeting in Istanbul, Turkish prime minister Adnan Menderes and Fahreddin Kerim Gökay repeated the same mantra of no more suffering and declared their wish to end all human misery, only to be involved in a plot that targeted the Greek Orthodox of Istanbul—as yet another categorized group—within a year. Menderes and Gökay were thus instrumental in reproducing exactly the same kind of human suffering they had grandly condemned the year before. Who exactly then, one might ask, qualifies as human? What is the color of the recognition of human pain?

Throughout the 1950s, biopolitical targeting of categorized populations widely continued at a local level in different parts of the world, while simultaneously, ending human suffering and finding solutions to human pain were promoted internationally as depoliticized slogans of peace and coexistence. As for the emphasis on suffering, it lends itself to liberal humanist discourses: because we are all humans and are capable of feeling pain, we should consider this capability as part of our shared humanity. Being human is a common thread that unites us despite our racialized differences. Liberal humanism thus invites an act of solidarity via a shared notion of humanity, rather than a reconsideration of politics and history. In that respect, the liberal humanist emphasis on suffering tends to divorce the affect from its political and historical contexts and thus obscures modes of relationality other than human feelings to consider the palimpsests of segregative biopolitics.

The two essays in this part focus on the divided world of the Cold War in the aftermath of the Second World War, and examine the broader implications of addressing biopolitics in liberal humanist terms against the backdrop of the foundation of the United Nations and UNESCO in 1945. The struggle of the free world—the complicated Cold War era term to designate noncommunist countries—against the communist world marked this era. The implications of being human in liberal humanist terms were therefore firmly anchored in the capitalist world.[10] As for the supposedly free world at the time, it was marked by bloody counterinsurgencies against decolonization movements such as in Algeria, mass population transfers, the partition of India and Palestine, the South African apartheid, and segregation in the United States. In this context, UNESCO and other institutions emphasized social harmony and peace as key to ensuring economic growth, configured as "development."

To that aim, the scientific and historical production of knowledge as well as terrains of culture were mobilized to consolidate social order and peace.[11] Political figures, scholars, and intellectuals, among others, have long resorted to the notions of order and social harmony to advocate peace and stability. Concerns with order—at the expense of human rights—often become more pronounced after wars, conflicts, and social upheavals.[12] In order to briefly explore how these major issues were addressed, I now turn to the AER's meetings and consider them in relation to biopolitics.

The AER:
Biopolitics, Racialized Alignment, and Displaced Populations

The inaugural issue of *Integration* configured the geographic and political scope of the AER and spelled out multiple forms of human classification in the regulation of emigration, mobility, and demography:

> As a rule, European wars during the last centuries did not basically change the composition of the resident population. Sometimes, after a lost war: a sovereign was replaced by another and people paid taxes to other lords. But the huge population increase and the growing nationalism of the 19th century finally led to the modern enforced mass migrations which we observe since the first Balkans War. About 68,000,000 persons were uprooted by this terrible process in Europe since 1912.... After World War I this movement continued. 2,200,000 Greeks, Turks and Bulgarians were resettled. *For the first time in history this population exchange took place according to a treaty between the states concerned. This Treaty of Lausanne (1923) contained already some definitions which*

were used again in the Potsdam Agreement (1945). . . . 1,200,000 Baltic people, Poles and Turks emigrated from the then established USSR. . . . 900,000 Polish, Rumanian and French "settlers" filled with state help the vacant places of the refugees. . . . A new flood of refugees was caused by fascism. . . . Between 1912 and 1939 about 14,000,600 Europeans were forced to leave their homeland. . . . World War II has multiplied their number.[13]

This introduction to the AER's official journal highlights several important points relevant to this book: First of all, it puts changes in the composition of the resident population at its center. It implies that population is a mass composed of categorized groups. Yet again, how this categorization is designated remains open to question: the reference to the Turks fleeing from the USSR attests to this, as it is not entirely clear whether Tatars, Azeris, or others are included in this ambivalent classification. Second, the urgency of demographic change that marked the first half of the twentieth century is emphasized through statistical data. Additionally, the reference to settlers, who are brought in to fill the void created by displacement, demonstrates a concern with keeping numbers at a desired level. Together, these two points amount to focusing on categorized bodies in numbers, with biopolitical implications. Indeed, the consideration of numbers as key to population improvement and power is a well-known aspect of Italian fascism promoted by race theorist, eugenicist, demographer, and statistician Corrado Gini, an active figure in the AER.[14] Third, the reason for these displacements in Europe is said to be wars, significant population increases—which point at numbers again—as well as fascism and communism.[15] Refugee integration is situated at the heart of these dynamics as a vital social problem.

Excluded from the criticized axis of power, however, is the so-called free world with its imperialist and colonial pasts and presents imbued with capitalist and settler land appropriation, systematic dispossession, and the cumulative impact of these policies on resident populations. In the 1950s, except for some remarks at the AWR—such as how the British colonizers implemented a divide-and-rule policy in India[16]—the scholars affiliated with the AER/AWR offered no substantial critique of Western Europe. Whereas major criticism targeted fascism and the communist bloc, the fascist past of some of the members of the AER, like Corrado Gini, did not seem to be questioned. For the most part, at least in the official exchanges and publications, there was no criticism of the so-called free world of the Cold War era.

A good example is Corrado Gini's presentation at the AER's 1954 convention in Istanbul. In his presentation, Gini addresses decolonization, but in terms of its consequences for the colonial powers. He highlights how, with the loss of colonies, the distribution of resources became a problem for the European colonizers. He then addresses these tensions in Eurocentric and eugenicist terms:

> The countries of Western Civilisation, and more especially those of the European Community, are indeed threatened on two fronts.
>
> On the one hand, the coloured peoples claim freedom to expand. They claim more especially the freedom to populate the colonies or other territories that are dependencies of European countries. They maintain—with arguments worthy of consideration—that the European countries are no longer able to develop adequately their dependencies since their present emigration currents are insufficient for the purpose.
>
> Therefore the coloured peoples are exercising an alarming demographic pressure on European overseas possessions, a pressure there is every reason to believe will increase in the future. As a result of their more backward starting conditions their economic progress is now relatively more rapid than that of the populations of Western Civilisation, and their numbers increase more rapidly and will probably continue to do so with the spread of hygiene and sanitation.
>
> On the other hand the white peoples behind the Iron Curtain have a rate of increase definitely higher than that of the populations of Western Civilisation. This is a factor for future political and economic strength for them. We should not blind ourselves to the danger that the two groups which, for different reasons, are antagonistic to Western Civilisation, may join in a single front against it.[17]

The concern with the birthrates of particular groups is a central issue in eugenics. Taking up this logic here, Gini configures population growth as a demographic means of land appropriation that the "coloured peoples" and the "white communists" might use against the members of "Western Civilisation." The former is considered to be a threat against European colonial land appropriation—articulated here as European overseas possession—and the latter, possibly perceived as a threat against the notion of the Western civilization itself. With this, Gini not only racializes what he calls Western civilization, but also situates it within the capitalist "free" world, by excluding the "whites" behind the Iron Curtain. He clearly perceives demographics as an issue of power and a means of land appropriation.

An outcome of this perception was the regulation of alterity in terms of numbers. To that end, partitions, mass population transfers, and forced migrations were heralded as attempts to ensure stability and social harmony.[18] Segregative biopolitics was thus configured as conducive to peace in the post-1945 era. In an environment where alterity was perceived as a potential threat against stability, emigrants were categorized and ranked in relation to the recipient country. Such categorization facilitated the process of spatial allocation of emigrants in an attempt to calibrate demographic distribution and numbers.

In a talk presented at the March 1954 AER convention in Rome, Gini explicitly addressed the issue of categorization:

> The League of Nations itself already developed a series of aid activities for refugees and not only for international refugees, as they are called to-day, i.e. the Russian refugees, but also for "national" refugees (ethnic groups) in Turkey and especially in Greece, who were involved in the exchanges of population in 1923. In 1949 the Council of Europe also acknowledged the necessity of caring for all refugees, whatever might be their nationality, religion or race.[19]

The humanitarian necessity to care for all refugees reconfigured the taxonomy of the emigrant as national and international. In the AER, "refugee" was often used as an umbrella term—interchangeably with "emigrant"—and not strictly conceived of as a legal status. In that light, the 1923 exchange was a reference point for so-called national refugees—a notion that ties the proper alignment of categorized bodies with a given country. That is, those from the desirable background are to be sent to what ought to be the country of their origin, regardless of where they were born and raised, as was the case with the 1923 exchange. To address these categorized groups, Gini uses the word "ethnic" here. But as shown above, the implications of this term cannot be divorced from racialized thinking as an embodied system of classification predicated on designated origins, genealogies, and bloodlines.

It is clear that the reallocation of so-called national refugees—as exemplified by the 1923 exchange—was considered to be a corrective demographic move. At the joint AER-AWR convention in 1956, Werner von Schmieden, the director of studies at the Council of Europe (established in 1949), similarly identified so-called national refugees as those who were located in what was considered to be their own country, even if that was not their natal home: that is, aligned with their "proper" country (*le réfugié national est le réfugié dans son propre pays*).[20] Alterity, then, was regulated by generating taxonomies of peoples and their redistribution according to designated countries of origin. Yet, as also evinced in the 1923 exchange, these categorizations were not smooth nor devoid of hierarchies.

This kind of human categorization drawn from a Eurocentric archive of knowledge undermines multiple modes of identification and hierarchization, as critic Ella Shohat also points out in her work on the Arab Jews.[21] Shohat's intervention sheds critical light on a paper presented at the AER/AWR regarding the Jews from so-called Oriental countries: Jean-Jacques Berreby, with the International Institute of Diplomatic Study and Research in Paris, discussed the case of the transfer of Jewish groups to Israel from what he called Muslim countries and addressed the possible consequences of their integration on the "character of the nation."[22]

Berreby's approach hints at the hierarchies within the groups referred to as national refugees. To him, "Oriental" Jews (*Juifs orientaux*) need to be scrutinized because they bring their so-called Oriental civilization to Israel—a country that Berreby identifies as Western. According to Berreby, Oriental Jews resemble the Arabs culturally and physically, and therefore present health and physical conditions that are distinctly defective and pose a threat to the health of the nation, because presumably they carry diseases specific to the Orient. In addition, he argues that Oriental religiosity has an impact on the growth in the numbers of Oriental Jews because they supposedly oppose birth control. The reason for this, Berreby adds, is that they are "traditional" and thus reproduce much faster than "Western Jews." He warns that in the future, Oriental Jews might overpopulate and constitute the majority of the Jewish population in Israel.[23]

Berreby's concern with numbers is reminiscent of eugenicist approaches to demography in fascist Italy. Further, his demographics resonate with the contemporary xenophobic approaches to immigrants and refugees in Europe and beyond: it implies that if the numbers of the "wrong" groups increase, they will take over the land. Birth control becomes an issue dependent on a people's designated background. Linear identifications do not suffice to address the multiple registers that inform such a designation. Arab Jews may have been sent to Israel on the grounds that they were Jewish, but they were still subjected to hierarchization. Indeed, in 1949 the Council of Europe might have very well recognized the necessity to care for all refugees regardless of their background—as Gini also points out—but the biopolitical logic is quite present in the general approach to emigration.

Given the scope of the AER's participants and their concerns, it is no wonder that the inaugural issue of *Integration* drew parallels between the task of the AER and medical research.[24] In the AER's circles in the 1950s, a Gini-style fusion of eugenics, demography, and statistics was notable in the regulation of refugees and emigrants in terms of numbers, health, and (re)productivity.[25]

Integration: Eugenicist Thought, Labor, and Demography

The fusion of eugenicist thought and demography was mobilized to address refugee integration from multiple angles. In a speech delivered at the 1953 AER convention in Strasbourg, Werner von Schmieden from the Council of Europe addressed the problem of refugees as a question of a surplus of population. Admitting that the juxtaposition of excess population and refugee problems might come across as a controversial subject, von Schmieden explains that, regardless, the Council of Europe adopted this approach because of the structural similarities between these problems: namely, unemployment and the ability to contribute productively to the economy.[26]

Overpopulation has long been an argument for implementing birth control. The comparison of refugee problems to that of overpopulation thus has broader implications. Elaborating on this question at the 1954 AER convention in Istanbul, Corrado Gini explicitly stated that the regulation of high birth rates was not fundamentally different from the regulation of emigration in that they are both solutions to problems of excess population:

> This similarity of the problem of over-population to that of refugee[s] was officially recognized in 1951 by the Committee of Ministers of the Council of

Europe, which appointed a special Committee to study them with the help of the representatives of the various international organisations concerned.

The special Committee has reached the conclusion that the problem of refugees and of over-population in view of the demographic pressure to which it gives rise, and the danger of political and economic instability that it implies is a vital and urgent one and of direct concern.... This question is of concern to the European Council and more generally speaking to "Western civilisation" as a whole. The excess of population in such countries, which under present conditions is burdensome for them and therefore indirectly for the countries which assist them—and also a cause of friction if not indeed a danger to world peace—could, if well distributed, be a source of strength, and economic progress for the international community.[27]

Likening the arrival of new communities to overpopulation, Gini associates emigration with social order and stability. The case of refugees and emigrants he therefore interprets as a question of security, and if not treated properly, as a potential threat to world peace. Eugenicist concerns with the regulation of birth rates thus appear to have been successfully mobilized by the AER and beyond to study emigration.

The biopolitical logic informs the process of deportation as well as the aftermath of arrival. Integration, in such a context, was configured as a question of security and stability. As to how integration was to be achieved, there were differing approaches. For example, Gini proposed the productive use of the displaced:

> Few realise indeed the importance of the economic contribution that immigration may make to a country when the immigrants can find adequate opportunities for employment there.
>
> This is due in part to the fact that the immigrants are, for the most part, adults and in the prime of life. They therefore represent capital, the formation of which has been a charge on the country of origin, and of which the reception country reaps the benefit without incurring any great expense.[28]

Calling attention to the beneficial sides of emigration for the host country, Gini reminds his audience that emigrants reached adulthood at the expense of their country of origin. This is not surprising, given Gini's positive approach to Italian immigration in the United States. According to him, rendering the emigrant productive for the economy might not necessitate a substantial expense for the recipient state. Hence, his configuration of the displaced as human capital. Gini and others may have articulated perceived parallels between overpopulation and emigration, but with this one broad stroke, Gini also makes a point here that does not apply to cases of overpopulation due to increased birthrates: the cost of turning the human into capital and the difference that it makes for the recipient country.

Gini's approach should not be perceived as confined to the 1950s. It in fact reflects the IMF's logic today in, for example, praising Germany for its willingness to accept a limited number of Syrian refugees to compensate for the country's declining population growth and bolster its labor force. If humanitarian assistance is justified when it serves economic interests, what does this approach tell us about the implications of humanitarianism and its limits?

Indeed, Corrado Gini's emphasis on healthy and productive bodies overshadowed other groups that might have been more vulnerable. What happens to those who do not qualify as human capital, to use Gini's terms?[29] The answer comes from Walter Schätzel, a German scholar of international law. At the 1954 AER convention in Istanbul, Schätzel addressed the case of emigrants and refugees who had no exchange value as capital and thus were deemed to be "undesirables" (*les indésirables*). He explains that this group of refugees are often called a "social burden" (*bagage social*).[30] This so-called social burden includes "the old and sickly, the orphans, criminals and the asocials, in short all those people that no State wants to receive" and who, according to Schätzel, cannot be easily employed.[31] It is indeed a primarily economic move that is materialized here: one that focuses on rendering the refugee productive, but addressed in humanitarian terms through the concurrent mobilization of discourses to alleviate pain and suffering.

Integration implies both economic productivity and cultural assimilation. To Helmut Victor Muhsam, the author of *The Genetic Origin of the Jews* and a contributor to *Eugenics Quarterly*, economic absorption is the most important aspect of integration to the recipient country.[32] Others, like Turkish sociologist Ziyaeddin Fahri Fındıkoğlu and German sociologist Karl Valentin Müller, shared this viewpoint.[33] Müller, for instance, considered the reclassification of refugees in terms of their vocation and ability to work in the recipient country as vital. That way, he claims, a refugee will stop feeling like a "deadweight on society" (*poids mort pour la société*).[34] Müller assumes that if refugees are not useful workwise, they will be a deadweight socially.

A closer look at his earlier work helps contextualizing Müller's approach to refugees and labor. As a sociologist, Müller rose to prominence during the Third Reich.[35] At the time, informed by scientific racists such as Hans F. K. Günther, Müller believed that social achievement is directly correlated with inherited racial characteristics and that social matters required a eugenic solution.[36] For example, in order to solve the problem of work, he suggested the sterilization of inferior groups and individuals and otherwise limiting their reproduction.[37] His racialist eugenics also extended to breeding quality workers. In that respect, Müller believed Nordic groups were biologically superior. He duly advocated giving better housing, job security, and hereditary titles to superior Nordic minorities.[38] After the war, he worked on refugee integration in Hanover and also chaired the German section of the AER/AWR. In the 1950s, he was on the board of the German Society for Population Sciences. He is therefore yet another figure in the AER who, after the war, transposed his eugenicist approach to the management of population with a special focus on refugee integration and labor. Considering his previous work, his suggestion to generate work-related classifications of refugees may not be surprising. One wonders to what extent such figures actually changed their previous epistemic views after the war.

In the post-1945 era, racialized taxonomies and human capital were correlated to ensure social order in biopolitical terms. Gini associated this correlation with security. The configuration of labor-ready and healthy emigrant bodies as integrable human capital was part of this process. Categorization of bodies, then, was not just about origins and background, but also about health, (re)productivity, and the ability to work. Given the pervasiveness of the biopolitical logic at the time, it may come as no surprise that eugenicist thought found a niche in the refugee and emigrant integration-related scholarship in the AER. The way the "desirable" refugee or emigrant was cast here bears an unfortunate resemblance to the logic of the survival of the fittest.

Emigrants who were sick, orphaned, asocial, or elderly—that is, for the most part, those who were in a precarious position—were considered to be a social burden, a deadweight on society. In this consideration we see the actual terms of humanitarianism at the time. Further, some, like Schätzel, aligned precarious emigrants with criminals and labeled them as undesirable. Integrability, then, was also cast as a matter of being able to care for one's self and work. In the 1950s, there seems to have been little room in the AER/AWR to discuss whether being "asocial" might actually be an outcome of experiences of hardship and discrimination,[39] or whether criminal activity arises in a climate of disparity of resources or opportunities—all of which are factors to consider in the case of forced migration. These dynamics, in turn, raise questions about the limits of humanitarian discourses to alleviate suffering: if the socially vulnerable are considered to be a nuisance, what exactly is defined and recognized as pain?

Integrability:
Affect, Assimilation, and Categorizing the Displaced

In the 1950s, assimilation was widely acknowledged as crucial for integration. In an AER report presented in Istanbul in 1954, legal specialist Walter Schätzel addressed this issue in terms of emigrants' attitudes and used it to categorize the displaced at yet another level:

> The real immigrants will try to assimilate as quickly as possible, to learn the language and to send their kids to the schools of their new country. The refugees, who will carry the memory of their lost country in their heart, are more inclined to isolate themselves, to associate with other refugees in order to preserve and cultivate the memory, the language, and the culture of their beloved country [of origin]. They will do everything they can to raise their kids born abroad in the national language of their old country and to generate in them a love for this country that they have never seen and that they only know through the enthusiastic narratives of their parents.
>
> I believe these few words are enough to show all the difference between refugees and immigrants and to show the great difficulties in the process of providing them a civic status, which corresponds simultaneously to their needs and to the interests of the implicated States.[40]

Schätzel takes the conditions of departure and arrival as key variables for integration, which he calls "the problem of the nationality of refugees."[41] Presumably, a "real" immigrant will quickly adapt to the new country, whereas a refugee will be reluctant to assimilate. Schätzel assumes that the nostalgia and longing for the lost homeland are embedded in the affect of refugeehood, which to him, complicates the process of acquiring a new citizenship. He thus makes sweeping generalizations about emigrants and refugees, and points to the importance of matching the needs of the displaced with the interests of the recipient countries.

How realistic is Schätzel's classification of refugees and emigrants with regard to integrability? The case of the 1923 exchange offers insight into this question. The exchange included those who left willingly, those who fled, and those who did not want to leave but were deported—like the Dönme. In Greece they were called "refugees," and in Turkey they were "emigrants" (*muhacir*). Despite the difference in nomenclature, to the best of our knowledge, exchangees were not officially considered to be refugees in either country as they immediately received citizenship in the recipient state. Yet, the narratives of the 1923 Greek-Turkish population exchange suggest how integration has not been a smooth process for many.[42] Many have also been discriminated against by the locals.

Just because a group is brought into a host country with the assumption that its members are *natural* citizens of the host country, does not mean that these so-called national refugees or immigrants will easily integrate into the new country. For the most part, cultural integration meant assimilation in the postwar era. Granted, in the mid-twentieth century, assimilation did not carry the same problematic implications it does today. But such a lack of problematization of the term in itself is symptomatic of the salience of these policies.

Contrary to the common belief today, exchangees' difficulties with integration were not necessarily suppressed in Turkey. They were openly addressed in the 1950s and early 1960s, in order to find more effective ways to assimilate them. For example, in an article published in *Integration* in 1961, Turkish sociologist Ziyaeddin Fahri Fındıkoğlu presented his research on the exchangees settled in the outskirts of Istanbul. All throughout the article, he refers to them as "exchangees" (*échangés*), and explains that they are mostly settled in places like the Kartal, Pendik, and Sarıyer districts of Istanbul, and that for the purposes of his study, his focus is on Bahçeköy in Sarıyer. He identifies the established community as being originally from Fouchtan, Karacaova, in Salonica:

> Despite religious ties that link our exchangees in B [Bahçeköy] to the mass of the Turkish populace, it is obvious that there is a problem of cultural assimilation in language. They consider themselves of Macedonian origin and speak Macedonian. Even today, that is after forty years [since the population exchange], it is possible to come across more or less elderly people who speak Turkish with great difficulty. A sort of bilingualism dominates the atmosphere of the village. We have, however, observed the influence of the public schools in this locale. We have also observed—if not in elderly, at least in the new generations—the accurate and fluent use of Turkish. [This is true] not only in [their] exchanges outside but also among the villagers themselves. The school and the mosque on the one hand, and the neighborhood on the other, play an effectively assimilating role.[43]

Fındıkoğlu adds another community to the remarkably diverse groups that were included in the population exchange, one that identifies itself as Macedonian. Further, the issues raised here in terms of the Turkification of the language of Muslim exchangees suggest that the population exchange was, among other things, a Turkish-Islamic synthesis project par excellence: to generate a majority of Muslims and to Turkify them.[44]

For such a project, forty years is a long time, and as Fındıkoğlu's work highlights, the assimilation of exchangees was still a concern in the 1960s:

> Even though they are glad to be settled close to Istanbul, in one of the most picturesque corners of the region, [and] despite the sympathy of the officials that surrounds them, the villagers of B [Bahçeköy] cannot forget the country from which they emigrated [Greece] and in particular its natural richness. One day, as tourists, they wish to visit the landscapes of Karacaova, the field of F [Fouchtan], and especially the tomb of Karacabey, who was one of the heroes of their national history. This nostalgia being reciprocal, a few years ago, they have hosted about ten Greek tourists who used to live in this village [Bahçeköy in Istanbul] and [who are] now settled in Greece. They cherish

the hope that one day, they will see their or their fathers' and grandfathers' places of birth. Inspired by these wishes expressed by the villagers, we hope that a special tourism will emerge in the future, one that gives satisfaction to the emigrants of 1923, [that is,] to both Greeks who emigrated from Turkey to Greece and Turks from Greece who emigrated to Turkey.[45]

The combination of the terms used here as "their" national history, in addition to his references to the exchangees as Turks and Macedonian, signals how slippery the definition of all these terms is. It is also clear that nostalgia for lost homelands does not face the same kind of Schätzelean judgment. Nostalgia does not appear to be a taboo in Fındıkoğlu's work, but rather is part of the process of integration.

Fındıkoğlu, in addition, advocates, if not anticipates, heritage tourism. Today, such heritage trips are very popular among exchangees who can afford them. But this is not the only issue that Fındıkoğlu anticipates. At the end of his article, in a footnote, Fındıkoğlu also recommends something that became equally very widespread in the late 1990s and early 2000s: collecting the stories of such visits to lost homelands and the memories of immigrants.[46] His insights into the subject would later materialize in Turkey, and become very popular during the cultural memory boom of the post–Cold War era. Overall, Fındıkoğlu's work reconfigures the affect of displacement as something worthy of being traced, recorded, and thus preserved.

An overview of the thousands of pages of proceedings and research findings presented at the AER/AWR in the 1950s and early 1960s demonstrates how these associations provided a platform for different people to exchange ideas and research findings. These included state officials like the Turkish prime minister Adnan Menderes, eugenicists like Fahreddin Kerim Gökay and Corrado Gini, sociologists like Hilmi Ziya Ülken, and various officials representing different institutions such as the UN—particularly the United Nations High Commissioner for Refugees (UNHCR)—the Red Cross, and the Council of Europe, all mingling and exchanging ideas and research on integration through the AER/AWR.

In addition to the content of these exchanges, the story of the founding of AER exposes the political and epistemological tensions in the post-1945 era. Entangled stories revolving around the foundation of the AER unmask a fierce power struggle over the production of knowledge about race, the study of the social, and the rise of UNESCO as a powerful organization in the first decade following the Second World War.

Logics of Segregative Biopolitics: Race, Fascism, and the Politics of Expertise

Corrado Gini was certainly not the only eugenicist affiliated with the AER, but without a doubt, he was the most controversial. Honored in the inaugural issue of *Integration* for his role in the founding of the AER, Gini moved across many circles and institutions in the aftermath of the Second World War. These include, but are not confined to, Istanbul University; the AER; the International Institute of Sociology; and, in the United States, the International Association for the Advancement of Ethnology and Eugenics. What to make of his crossing through different institutions within the so-called free world? The entangled history of figures like Gini and the institutions he was associated with has broader implications for the engagement with segregative biopolitics in the post-1945 era.

A well-known statistician, Corrado Gini is famous for developing the Gini coefficient to calculate income inequality. In Italy, he was a former president of the Italian Society of Genetics and Eugenics (1934). He also held honorary degrees. In 1936, after he spent a year teaching at Harvard University, the school conferred on him an honorary degree in sciences.[47] By that time, he had published "The Scientific Basis of Fascism" in English, where he sought to develop a "scientific" theory to justify fascist rule on the basis of its promise of a greater future, even if it comes at the expense of the rights and votes of the citizens in the present; contributed to the domination of social sciences by statistics in Italy; made eugenicist arguments that the larger the population the stronger it is (arguments that later became prevalent among the AER/AWR circles); focused on the degeneration of the Italian race; had a significant impact on Mussolini's political campaign; and served as president of the Central Institute of Statistics in Italy.[48] In 1950, he was invited to Turkey to found the Institute of Statistics at Istanbul University, where he would also teach a course on demography. Gini was a leading figure in the first fusion of fascism, demography, and eugenics.

A signatory of the 1925 Manifesto of Fascist Intellectuals in Italy and a prominent eugenicist before, during, and after Mussolini's fascist rule,[49] Corrado Gini later joined the executive committee of the International Association for the Advancement of Ethnology and Eugenics (IAAEE, hereafter the Association for Ethnology and Eugenics)—an organization founded in the United States in 1959, and largely viewed as supporting segregationists' views on race.[50] The Association for Ethnology and Eugenics and its semi-official journal, *Mankind Quarterly*, worked against the discourse of racial equality. At the time, under the impact of Columbia University anthropologist Franz Boas, a focus on culture instead of race had gained traction, and one of Boas's students, Ashley Montagu, was a principal author of UNESCO's first Statement on Race. Published in 1950, this document—available in UNESCO's archives—called for a shared humanity that disregarded racial differences. The notions of unity in diversity and the brotherhood of humankind resound throughout discourses of liberal humanism. The Association for Ethnology and Eugenics actively fought against such sentiments and defended the notion of racial differences.[51]

Politically, accepting racial equality implied desegregation—a demand that gained momentum with the American civil rights movement. Many scholars associated with the Association for Ethnology and Eugenics considered racial equality as "brotherhood of man" propaganda. Taking demands for racial equality to be a communist conspiracy was quite common.[52] The Association for Ethnology and Eugenics exemplifies the biologically informed racialist science of the 1950s, mobilized to advocate segregation.

In his work on segregation and science, scholar John P. Jackson Jr. examines the racialist scientists who considered advocacy of civil rights to be a major problem.[53] According to the racialists, those who demanded civil rights were naïve and deceived by social science. With this, they had in mind the work of cultural anthropologists like Boas and Montagu. Racialist scientists considered those who advocated civil rights to be agitator communists and Soviet agents. To them, these agitators took advantage of people who had the best of intentions but feeble intellects, and misled them by the "smooth language of humanitarianism."[54] In their view, opposing civil rights did not mean racism; it simply showed a preference to be associated with those of one's own race.

That racialists deemed those who called for civil rights to be misled by social science should not be taken lightly. After the Second World War, race continued to be a site of major epistemological and disciplinary conflict. For example, in a 1954 book entitled *The Story of Man,* Carleton Coon, a University of Pennsylvania anthropologist, warns his readers against

> academic debunkers and soft-peddlers who operate inside anthropology itself. Basing their ideas on the concept of the universal brotherhood of man, certain writers, who are mostly social anthropologists, consider it immoral to study race, and produce book after book exposing it as a "myth." Their argument is that because the study of race once gave ammunition to racial fascists, who misused it, we should pretend that races do not exist.... These writers are not physical anthropologists, but the public does not know the difference.[55]

Coon's warning captures the hard-line position on race at the time, and does not address the fallacy that those who "misused" race extended beyond the fascists in Europe. Again, a specific case is referenced here in isolation, without making connections to related matters such as segregation. But this too is to be expected, because while Coon would not take a public stance on the issue of segregation in the United States, his behind-the-scenes exchanges and interactions with segregationists suggest that he was, to say the least, sympathetic to them.[56] It is also important to note that in the segregationist milieu, desegregation was perceived to be *integration* which might lead to intermarriage, that is, mixing. Coon's reference to fascists in Europe implies that racism is a problem of the past. Thus he circumvents its connections to the then present—segregation. Evident here is the malaise with the social scientific intervention in the race debate, as well as with the liberal humanist implications of this intervention.

A major mission of the Association for Ethnology and Eugenics was to epistemologically defeat liberal humanist discourses of racial equality and the brotherhood of man. In this regard, the association offered an "organizational basis for the scientific attack" on *Brown v. Board of Education,*[57] the decisive 1954 Supreme Court ruling—and a landmark in the American civil rights movement—that racial segregation in the schools is unconstitutional. The politics of expertise revolving around race therefore had direct policy ramifications in the post-1945 era. Joining the executive committee of the

Association for Ethnology and Eugenics, Gini duly took a position in the epistemological struggle on the study of race.

In this context, Gini's crossing over multiple institutions has broader implications with regard to segregative biopolitics and crystallizes the terms of engagement with its legacies in the 1950s. While segregative biopolitics has been implemented in different forms depending on the context, there is a shared logic behind these differences: the regulation of categorized bodies in terms of numbers and space, limiting the spatial and social mobility of categorized groups. Race and racialized thinking are among the bases for such categorizations, together with health, labor capacity, and age, among other things. It is clear that Gini's contribution to the first fascist fusion of eugenics, demography, and statistics had direct implications for the regulation of populations—particularly in terms of segregative biopolitics—in the aftermath of the Second World War.

One of the many places that welcomed Corrado Gini was Turkey. As mentioned earlier, he was specifically targeted and invited to Istanbul in order to establish an Institute of Statistics at Istanbul University in 1950.[58] He also taught a course on demography and statistics.[59] His responsibilities as a visiting scholar included teaching four hours per week and training high school teachers and university students in statistics. He received a handsome salary in return.[60] Gini spent a total of three months—from December 1950 to March 1951—in Istanbul, and stayed in a pension with a sea view called Mano, in Moda, on the Asian side of the city.[61] In order to ensure that he met other Turkish sociologists during his stay, Hilmi Ziya Ülken—who presided over the Turkish Sociological Society (Türk Sosyoloji Cemiyeti) and chaired the Turkish section at the AER—gave a tea reception in Gini's honor.[62] To facilitate wider dissemination of his course content, Gini's university lectures were published by the Istanbul University Press in 1952 with the title *Démographie et Sociologie*—for which Hilmi Ziya Ülken also wrote a book review.[63] For the general public, Ülken separately reviewed the ideas of the book in his weekly editorial column in the Turkish daily *Yeni Sabah*.

To pave the way for Gini's arrival as a visiting scholar, the Turkish cabinet met on July 30, 1950, and issued a permit specifically tailored for him.[64] President Celal Bayar, Prime Minister Adnan Menderes, and the ministers of the cabinet, including Ottoman historian and Minister of Foreign Affairs

Fuat Köprülü, signed Gini's appointment as a visiting scholar. Only six days earlier the Turkish parliament had passed a new law regulating the travel of foreigners in Turkey and the conditions of their stay.[65]

Turkish officials were therefore familiar with Corrado Gini beyond the famous Gini coefficient. In addition, after World War II, the Turkish Prime Ministry's General Directorate of Statistics (Başbakanlık İstatistik Genel Müdürlüğü) published a Turkish translation of Gini's *Methodology of Statistics* and his earlier lectures at the University of Rome, *The Scientific Bases of the Politics of Population*.[66] The latter includes a comprehensive discussion of population displacements, in which Gini describes the 1923 Greek-Turkish population exchange as one of the great forced exoduses (*huruç*) of modern times.[67] Originally published in Italian in 1931 and representative of the fascist-era debates on race—which, as noted earlier, continued well after the Second World War—the book also addresses racial mixing and the formation of a "new race" following population displacements.[68] Today, one can easily access these two books as well as the published volume of Gini's Istanbul University lectures at the library of the Turkish Parliament. Corrado Gini was, indeed, a valued scholar in Turkey.

Gini's presence at the 1954 AER convention in Istanbul, however, is significant beyond his previous academic sojourn. He had a direct role in the founding of the AER. The inaugural issue of *Integration* explicitly mentions his name in the genealogy of the institution. In it, the idea to found the European Association for the Study of Refugee Problems is traced to another congress that Gini organized in Rome in 1950:

> The idea to found a research group for the study of refugee matters was first discussed on the XIV Congress of the International Sociological Institute (IIS). The Congress was held in Rome by invitation of its president, Prof. Dr. Corrado Gini. Different scientists treated refugee problems there, and particularly French and Dutch sociologists were of the opinion that in view of importance of this problem for Europe a special and intensified study of it was not only desirable but necessary.
>
> In December 1950 a preparatory meeting assembled experts from Belgium, Denmark, Germany, France, Italy, the Netherlands, Austria, Switzerland and the USA. On April 15, 1951 the first Assembly General of the AER

took place at Hanover. The second which gave the organization its statute came together in Munich on October 4, 1952. Experts of 15 European countries and representatives of important international organizations participated in it.... The fourth of these yearly meetings will be held in Istanbul from the 15 to 17 September 1954, the residence of the President of the AER, Prof. Dr. Fahreddin Kerim Gökay.[69]

The Fourteenth International Institute of Sociology Congress in Rome was thus crucial for the AER, as well as for the attendees who decided to found the association. The description of the meeting in Munich in 1952 highlights that the AER's sphere of influence expanded with the participation of representatives of important international organizations. Yet, this quick summary of the rapid organization of the AER following the sociology congress in Rome does not reveal what happened behind the scenes.

The institute and its president, Corrado Gini, and in fact, the very organization of that sociology congress in Rome, had their own trail of controversies.[70] This became more visible when the International Institute of Sociology held its next congress in Istanbul in 1952—the same year that the AER convened in Munich. Here, Gini clashed with some others in UNESCO. In addition to the conflict over the notion of race that continued in the fields of anthropology and biology, becoming the leading international authority in the institutionalized study of the "social" was also a highly contentious matter.

The study of the social was integral to the UNESCO-led projects in the 1950s. As mentioned, UNESCO-endorsed campaigns of racial equality and coexistence were predominantly supported with arguments drawn from the social sciences, arrayed against racialist biology and physical anthropology. In addition, UNESCO's conventions and publications at the time indicate that studying social relations was considered vital to improving human relationships and thus conducive to establishing peaceful coexistence. It is in this context that the International Sociological Association (ISA) was founded under the patronage of UNESCO.

Competing with the UNESCO-supported ISA was the International Institute of Sociology led by none other than Corrado Gini. A wide range of scholars took part in the Gini-led institute, including some who had conducted social studies in biologized terms and some with a fascist past, like

Gini himself. For example, Karl Valentin Müller served as the secretary-general of the Gini-led International Institute of Sociology (1954–1958).[71] Turkish philosopher and sociologist Hilmi Ziya Ülken was also part of this platform. It is at the sociology convention in Rome over which Gini presided, and where Ülken was also present, that the founding of the AER was proposed. Ülken, furthermore, was instrumental in bringing the next congress of Gini's International Institute of Sociology to Istanbul in 1952.

These palimpsests of scholarly activities and institutionalized knowledge production demonstrate multiple crossings of scholars over institutions and networks, and underscore the terms of engagement with biopolitical logics at multiple levels. Inasmuch as the content of the production of knowledge on notions like race, the social, integration, or being human is important, so are the institutions and people involved in producing them, unraveling the politics of expertise of the time.[72]

The Politics of Expertise and the Question of the Social

On September 5–11, 1949, a group of scholars convened in Oslo, Norway, to establish an international organization for sociological research under the auspices of UNESCO.[73] Among the officials and scholars in attendance were Hilmi Ziya Ülken, representing Turkey, and Corrado Gini representing Italy. The representative of UN secretary-general in attendance was Gustavo Durán, an exile from General Francisco Franco's fascist Spain and a friend of poet and playwright Federico García Lorca—murdered by the Francoists.[74] A pianist and composer, Durán was also a friend of Ernest Hemingway—who wrote about wars such as the Greco-Turkish War (1919–1922) that led to the population exchange and the Spanish Civil War (1936–1939).[75] Having fought in the Spanish Republican army against Franco's fascist forces during the civil war, Durán himself figured as a protagonist in Hemingway's novel *For Whom the Bell Tolls*.[76] An emigrant to the United States in 1940 and an employee in the US State Department and then the United Nations, Durán would later be ostracized by Senator Joseph McCarthy—notorious for his campaign in the House Un-American Activities Committee known as McCarthyism:

> A favorite McCarthy victim these days is Gustavo Duran. Joe flourishes a picture of Duran taken during the Spanish Civil War in what he says is "the

uniform of the S.I.M.—the counterpart of the Russian secret police." He then says that Duran's American citizenship was rushed through, that he was "promoted" by the State Department to the U.N. in 1946. "And what do you think he was doing there today? Unbelievable as it is, his task was to screen displaced persons and decide which would make good, loyal Americans!"

The true story of Duran is remarkable—but nothing like McCarthy's version. Duran was a Spanish composer of music who fought in the Spanish Republican Army, rising to command of a corps. As the Spanish Loyalists split into communist and anti-Communist factions, Duran, never a Red, was definitely and clearly anti-Communist. When defeat came, he was smuggled out of Spain on a British warship. He married an American, became a citizen in four months more than the time required by law, worked for the U.S. Government in Cuba during World War II, tracking down Axis and Communist agents. For the past five years, Duran has been working for the U.N., where he has never had anything to do with screening refugees entering the U.S. The uniform in which McCarthy shows Duran is that of the Spanish army, not of any secret police. McCarthy knows all this—but his audiences do not.[77]

Regardless of whether Durán was indeed the kind of anti-communist that *Time* depicted, his case displays some of the dynamics of the rifts of the Cold War era. McCarthy's concern with Durán's alleged monitoring of the displaced to be admitted to the United States was part and parcel of the broader issues raised by Corrado Gini at the AER: a preoccupation with the potential increase of the numbers of white communists. A concern with land appropriation through demographics—an increase of the numbers of undesirable groups deemed to be a threat—surfaces in such approaches.

Durán might not have screened refugees to enter the United States as Senator McCarthy claimed, but minorities, population displacement, and emigration were certainly on his radar. At the 1949 Oslo meeting, Durán made a series of propositions for the new and UNESCO-sponsored ISA, including establishing a commission to study the rights of minorities and a population commission to study migratory movements.[78] In response, Leopold von Wiese—the sociologist representative of Germany in Oslo—proposed that the situation of displaced peoples in foreign regions or foreign countries be studied.[79] At the inaugural meeting, at which Gini and Ülken were also present, the ISA had therefore already designated displacement and refugees as a primary site of study.

Because of Gini's fascist past, some scholars had originally objected to inviting him to ISA's meeting in Oslo.[80] They also tried to maintain a distance from him.[81] In what appears to be some networking behind the scenes, Gini still managed to take part in the Oslo meeting.[82] The minutes from the meeting show that Gini was not at all timid about openly displaying his disapproval of the ISA's newly elected executive board,[83] and clearly laying out his ambitions:

> Professor GINI spoke of the work that had been undertaken by the Italian Government and himself regarding an international conference of sociology to be held in Rome in September 1950. Preliminary steps for this conference were taken in Bucharest before the World War and after the cessation of hostilities Professor Gusti (Rumania) had written to Professor Gini requesting him to carry on with the necessary arrangements. Professor Gini pressed very strongly for the I.S.A. to combine its plans with those already set on foot in Italy and hoped that the next I.S.A. conference would be held in Rome.
>
> It was pointed out that the I.S.A. was a completely new organization and could not be bound by arrangements that had been undertaken prior to its existence.[84]

Gini's efforts to merge the new UNESCO-sponsored International Sociological Association with the International Institute of Sociology were thus rejected in Oslo. The minutes also suggest that he vigorously tried to bring the ISA under his own control. Gini's career moves indicate that he was an ambitious figure who exercised power across institutions. It appears that he tried to do the same in Oslo, but this time, at least with ISA, it didn't work.

His efforts, however, were not without support. For instance, Hilmi Ziya Ülken explains his position on the subject: "Invited by UNESCO to be one of the organizers of the International Sociological Association in Oslo in September 1949, I was the only witness present at the congress in Bucharest. I had supported the proposition of Mr. Gini to attach and affiliate the International Institute of Sociology to the new organization, but this proposal was rejected."[85] Before World War II, the International Institute of Sociology was the most important international organization for sociologists. The 1939 annual meeting in Bucharest was cancelled because of war, which also brought the activities of the institute to a halt.[86] In its active years before 1939, Gini had moved to bring the International Institute of Sociology under his power, and there he succeeded.[87] The taint of fascism marked the institute, and this stuck with it after the war.[88] The institute was idle for a decade, when Gini decided to reactivate it in what appears to have been a competition with the International Sociological Association.[89] But the competition did not end with the reactivation of the institute.

In Oslo, the ISA founding members had announced a plan to hold the first world congress of sociology in September 1950. In response to this announcement, Gini declared his own plans to organize the revived institute's international congress of sociology in Rome, which he claimed was scheduled for the same time. Later, when the Gini-led congress convened in Rome, he claimed that the UNESCO-supported International Sociological Association's meeting was purposefully scheduled at the same time as his, which is why the Gini-led institute's congress had to be moved a few days earlier.[90] The International Institute of Sociology thus met from August 30 to September 3, 1950, in Rome, and strategically ended just the day before the UNESCO-supported sociology conference began in Zürich on September 4, 1950.

Although there was tension between the two organizations, some members—including Hilmi Ziya Ülken—were active in both.[91] But from the outset, Ülken appears to have favored Gini's International Institute of Sociology. In 1950, he attended the institute's congress in Rome but was not among the participants of the UNESCO-supported sociology conference in Zürich.[92] Ülken didn't seem to mind Gini's fascist past. Indeed, in his weekly column in *Yeni Sabah*, Ülken wrote an entire piece (occupying about a quarter of a page) discussing Gini's course at Istanbul University, his work on demography, as well as the International Institute of Sociology's upcoming international congress in Istanbul.[93] We know from a later editorial column that Ülken saw no real difference between the International Institute of Sociology and the International Sociological Association.[94] Later, when he reported his impressions of the 1953 International World Congress of the UNESCO-supported ISA, Ülken wrote that the reason the International Sociological Association disregarded the International Institute of Sociology was because the institute was considered redundant after having been idle for so many years.[95]

Is it possible that he did not know the actual reason or that he was unaware of the political implications? Both seem unlikely. In his editorial, Ülken admits the founders and some of the then-current members of the Gini-led International Institute of Sociology were from the "biological" school.[96] This means they had adopted a biological approach to the study of the social. As mentioned, one of these figures was Karl Valentin Müller, who became secretary-general of the institute. At the time, such scholarship involved a scientific racialist form of eugenics, but Ülken defended this on the grounds that other approaches could coexist in the International Institute of Sociology.[97] According to him, that different approaches to the study the social could coexist constituted a good enough reason to view the Gini-led institute in a positive light. Discursively distancing oneself from the biological configuration of race or biologized approaches to social problems, however, does not necessarily mean the paradigms and logics of these approaches have disappeared from the production of knowledge.

Indeed, those who had the greatest interest in Gini's group, other than Ülken, were the German sociologists who knew him from before and had shared his political stance in the 1930s and 1940s, and who had later found themselves excluded or marginalized within the German Sociological Association and the scholarship of sociology.[98] Among many such German scholars with whom Gini and his International Institute of Sociology continued to collaborate, we can cite Carl Schmitt, who was infamously dubbed the Crown Jurist of the Third Reich.

Schmitt did not attend the conference in Rome. But his essay on "Nomos" appeared in the very first issue of the *Revue Internationale de Sociologie* (International Review of Sociology), the official publication of the International Institute of Sociology, which, in 1954, was also revived by Corrado Gini.[99] As for the other German scholars, Gini's list of scholarly collaborations included Karl Valentin Müller—who once believed social issues should be solved in eugenicist terms, and who was an active figure in both the International Institute of Sociology and the AER—as well as Hans Freyer. Both were among the very few foreigners present in the International Institute of Sociology's 1952 congress in Istanbul.[100] Müller made a short presentation,[101] but Freyer was among the prominent figures and gave an opening speech at the congress, together with Peyami Safa, a famous Turkish literary figure and reportedly a sympathizer of Nazi Germany during the Second World War.[102]

Safa, the vice-president of the Turkish Sociological Society,[103] was the author of the *East-West Synthesis* (*Doğu-Batı Sentezi*), which contributed to the configuration of the Turkish-Islamic synthesis.[104] He also wrote the famous novel *Fatih-Harbiye*, which problematizes the identification crisis associated with Turkish modernity in a spatialized manner. In the novel, Fatih is configured as a traditional Muslim neighborhood and is set against Harbiye, portrayed as a site of Europeanized style in Istanbul. Of course, in all those configurations, there is a very convenient circumvention of the fact that Fatih was integral to Fener and Balat, two historically important districts, namely Greek and Jewish, with Fener being the home to the Greek Orthodox Patriarchate in Istanbul. Likewise, the Harbiye area harbored Armenian neighborhoods and an Armenian cemetery. Dismissing the spatial demographics, the novel focuses on Fatih and Harbiye to negotiate Turkish identification. As for his speech at the 1952 Institute of Sociology conference in Istanbul, Safa gave a presentation entitled "Sociology and the Novel."[105] Therein, he promoted the novel as a genre that reconciles the universal and the particular and that has much to offer to the study of the social because each period has its own way of imagining things, which the novel can encapsulate.[106]

In short, despite the promotion of social studies as a means to improve human relationships and peaceful coexistence—an objective reasserted at the first ISA conference in Zürich—the institutionalization of sociology at the international level started off with little peace among scholars themselves.[107] Various scholars interpreted the conflict between the two organizations of sociology as springing from the issue of how to deal with the residues of fascism. Yet to what extent did this conflict actually mean fascism, racialized configurations of alterity, and the logic of biopolitics were called into question?

In my readings of scholarly and intellectual debates, newspapers, court cases, memoirs, and personal correspondence from the 1950s, the problems of fascism are mostly treated as part of particular cases associated with specific figures or institutions, rather than as part of a logic that pervasively informed approaches to population, race, and alterity. Could this be at least one of the reasons why biopolitics and racialized thinking continued to be so prevalent, as seen in the integration studies of refugees and emigrants presented at the AER?

Population displacement was designated an important topic of inquiry in Oslo in 1949. When the UN representative Gustavo Durán pointed out how such a study would be very useful to the UN, German sociologist Leopold von Wiese—disowned by Gini during the 1950 International Institute of Sociology Congress in Rome—had responded with a proposal that displaced persons in foreign countries be made a site of research. Following this, and only a few months after the two concurrent international congresses of sociology took place, a preliminary meeting was held in December 1950 to set up the AER—again under the impetus of Gini. The participants were mostly members of the network of Gini's International Institute of Sociology. Could the foundation of the AER have been a product of competition with the ISA at yet another level?

The inaugural issue of *Integration*, the official journal of the AER, states that the idea to found this organization was proposed by French and Dutch sociologists at the International Institute of Sociology Congress in Rome in 1950. In the massive volumes of the proceedings of this congress, however, it is hard to find any reference to an explicit decision to establish an association to study refugees. This includes the first volume of the proceedings in which the question-and-answer and discussion sessions following each panel were also reported.[108] There was, however, one discussion following a panel that I find important: this is a session on refugees scheduled at 9 a.m. on September 2, 1950, chaired by Karl Valentin Müller, Bernard Lahy, and Luigi Galvani.[109] One of the presentations in this session was Italian statistician Giovanni Lasorsa's "L'Assimilazione degli immigrati" (Assimilation of immigrants). Following this presentation, Alfred Sauvy,[110] the famous French demographer and director of the National Institute of Demography Studies in France spoke:

> There is only one piece of information I can add here [to this presentation]: UNESCO strongly appreciates the necessity of such studies on cultural assimilation, because the non-adaptation of individuals to a milieu is

an international and intranational cause of "tension." Under its [UNESCO] auspices, studies [on the subject] to expand [it] have been undertaken in different countries, notably in England, France, Brazil (Prof. Mortara), Israel (Prof. Bachi).[111]

Sauvy's statement on UNESCO and emigration confirms how the integration of the displaced was configured as a matter of assimilation. His words imply that assimilation is important for social harmony locally and for peace internationally. Sauvy himself opposed decontextualized control of population in terms of numbers, because to him every country had different resources to be redistributed. That notwithstanding, he considered the failure of assimilation to be a potential cause of tension. His report for UNESCO is also important here, as we learn that UNESCO encouraged studies on assimilation and that certain countries were laboratories for such research. As for the hasty founding of the AER, it is also clear from Sauvy's statement that there was an interest in and demand for research on the subject. It appears that the Gini-led institute hurried to fill that gap.

To many, not only Gini himself but also the International Institute of Sociology was tainted with fascism.[112] Tension over this issue reached a new level when, in 1952, the UNESCO-promoted ISA actively tried to prevent the annual convention of the Gini-led Institute of Sociology from taking place in Istanbul.[113] This was the second annual convention of the International Institute of Sociology since the beginning of the war in 1939. Louis Wirth,[114] the president of the ISA, reportedly put pressure on the Turkish government to cancel the congress.[115] Regardless, the Fifteenth International Institute of Sociology Congress did convene in Istanbul on September 11–17, 1952.[116] With barely fifty international presenters, participation in congress was strikingly low.[117] Furthermore, presence of but a few Turkish officials during the convention was notable.

Despite the controversy surrounding the International Institute of Sociology at the 1952 Istanbul congress, scholars and officials—including Gökay and Ülken—continued to collaborate with Gini and his like as part of the AER. It seems as though Gökay and Ülken took the hostility against the International Institute of Sociology as no more than a case of rivalry, and did not necessarily question the political logic behind the institute. This is yet another example of how problem areas appear to have been engaged in an isolated, case-by-case basis, rather than as symptomatic of a broader issue. And, indeed, when more or less the same group of people organized the 1952 AER congress in Munich and the 1954 congress in Istanbul, they did not elicit the same kind of international reaction.[118] On the contrary, we learn from *Integration* that the 1952 AER convention in Munich attracted many people from international organizations, which helped establish its statute. This raises questions about the terms of engagement with fascism and its so-called residues in the early years of the Cold War.

All in all, the very foundation of the AER and the 1954 AER convention in Istanbul are firmly situated at the intersection of institutional and epistemological tensions. These include the antagonism between the UNESCO-sponsored International Sociological Association and the Gini-led International Institute of Sociology; the UNESCO Statement on Race and its opponents—that is, those who hierarchized races or claimed that racial differences indicated different species; as well as those who supported segregation and the desegregationists. The AER was therefore positioned at the heart of competing platforms of expertise, production of knowledge, and biopolitics.

During this time, it is also clear that the racial desegregation discussed via the American civil rights movement was considered a specific case, and not part of a broader biopolitical logic related to partition, forced population exchanges, and transfers. Indeed, one could very well oppose American segregation but whole-heartedly support forced population displacements like the 1923 exchange. Of course, these cases had their differences, but they also shared a logic. In such an environment, racialized thinking continued to inform spatial divisions and the redistribution of peoples, particularly in the case of displacement.

In part, this might be because race was taken as a hard category of analysis, without much consideration of discourses and practices that were also informed by racialized paradigms even if they were articulated under different names: pedigree (*soy*), lineage, bloodline, unchanging essence that can be biologically transmitted from one generation to the next (*öz*) with claims of reactivation and origins. All of these notions allude to a racialized genealogy anchored in the body. These discourses demonstrate the pervasiveness of racialized thinking, reproduced under different rubrics. This compartmentalization might be one of the reasons why the crossing of racialized thinking over time, space, and academic platforms and institutions was so seamless. It is important to remember, therefore, that *the social* does not constitute an object of study alone, but also includes those who study it, as well as the archives and repertoires of knowledge that are resorted to in that process. Hence, the necessity of a relational reading of these dynamics as palimpsests.

Liberal Humanism, Race, and the Family of Mankind

THE 1950s were marked by institutionalized struggles to consolidate the production of knowledge on alterity and racialized diversity, *and* to unite scholars who studied the realm of the social as a matter of duty. To some, duty meant promoting human welfare and peace internationally—with all their contradictions and ambiguities; to others, it meant revealing the biological "truth" about race and the inequality of the human races. While these may come across as opposing poles, especially in the early 1950s, many scholars tended to mingle with both parties. This includes Hilmi Ziya Ülken. The palimpsests of racialized thinking and biopolitics in the post-1945 era help us put into perspective the stakes of engaging liberal humanism during that time. I now turn to the second essay of this part to reconsider UNESCO's initiatives at the time and address their broader implications in that light, with special attention to the notion of liberal humanism and its accompanying discourse: unity in diversity.

Unity in Diversity: Race, Cultural Policy, and UNESCO

> The healthiest humanity will find its realization, not through an abstract unity blind to social diversity, but in a unity within multiplicity, which can lead nations to a unique ideal of man and a unique method of education.
>
> Hilmi Ziya Ülken, *Humanisme et éducation en Orient et en Occident: entretien international organisé par l'UNESCO*, 1953

The notion of unity in diversity, with its emphasis on shared aspects of humanity as a message of peace, recognition, and coexistence, was institutionalized in the 1950s under the patronage of UNESCO. In December 1949, anthropologists Ashley Montagu and Claude Lévi-Strauss, among others, drafted the first UNESCO Statement on Race.[119] As noted above, Montagu, the principle author of the statement, was a disciple of Franz Boas—the anthropologist who spent his career fighting racialism in and through science.[120] The Statement on Race aimed at ending Nazi-style racist science, but had to be amended because of the criticisms it received. It pushed forward the idea that racial differences do not translate into a metric of mental capacity, that racial mixing does not mean degeneration, and finally, that race is less of a biological fact than a social construct.[121] It also emphasized that all humans belong to the same species, *Homo sapiens*, and therefore have the same biological origin.[122] Such interventions in the study of race were largely interpreted as emphasizing equality and brotherhood among the races. UNESCO reinforced this interpretation:

> Biological studies lend support to the ethic of universal brotherhood; for man is born with drives toward co-operation, and unless these drives are satisfied, men and nations alike fall ill. Man is born a social being, who can reach his fullest development only through interaction with his fellows. The denial at any point of this social bond between man and man brings with it disintegration. In this sense, every man is his brother's keeper. For every man is a piece of the continent, a part of the main, because he is involved in mankind.[123]

UNESCO's defense of racial equality via the social sciences mirrors its support for liberal humanism in the field of culture. Liberal humanist rhetoric of peace and brotherhood reinforced the assertions made in the Statement on Race.[124] Drawn from UNESCO's Statement on Race, however, the account above has broader implications than just humanism and brotherhood.

First of all, we see here a bodily engagement with the notions of man and nation. Accordingly, in order not to fall ill, the inborn—and therefore biologically defined—drive to cooperate must be fulfilled. Second, the social domain is considered to be a site to perform the biological disposition for cooperation. The text thus implies that being healthy and fully developed depends on cooperation at both the individual and national levels, and that this innate drive is to be gratified in the social realm. Humanity, then, is configured discursively as a site of improvement in biologized terms, and the realm of the social is configured as the site where brotherhood, unity, and collaboration will be established. It is assumed that peaceful coexistence will follow.

This configuration sheds further light on the importance attributed to the study of the social, precisely because it was construed as key to peace and harmonious coexistence. For example, in a special issue of UNESCO's *International Social Science Bulletin* based on the 1950 UNESCO General

Convention in Florence, Italy, to which Corrado Gini also contributed, the correlation between culture, peace, and social science is clearly articulated:

> Culture, like humanity itself, is universal. It is the gradually accumulated heritage of centuries—what the mind has learnt by turning in upon itself and by contemplating the outer world. . . .
>
> A common heritage, then—the common property of all men, from whatever civilization they spring—culture embraces all the ways of life and all the gifts, different and often conflicting though they may be, of every national community. The world of today is united physically, but is not yet united psychologically. Divisions still, inevitably, make themselves felt. . . . This being so, one cannot over-stress the importance of bringing about closer contact between the intellectual leaders of the world, through collaboration between the men of learning of the various countries. The only basis for the ideal of unity is a sense of "world kinship," and this can only come about if the peoples can exchange their ideas and gain a true appreciation of their various cultural traditions. This is one of the tasks to which Unesco is bending its efforts. . . . As was pointed out by the experts who met in 1948 at Unesco House, the object of social science is, in the last analysis, to improve human relationships. It has therefore a prime part to play in constructing the edifice of peace.[125]

The emphasis on world kinship here is directly related to the notions of brotherhood, common heritage, and a shared family tree for humanity even if different people presumably occupy different civilizational branches. Getting to know different cultures through literature or arts is coupled with getting to know one another via social interactions—all of which are addressed as unifying humanity and, thus, conducive to peace. Hence the emphasis on social science as a means to improve collaboration and human relationships.[126] The attempt to establish collaboration in the social sciences, however, would turn into another struggle, as was the case with the international study of sociology. Moreover, addressing cultural heritage as the shared "property" of humanity draws from historicist humanism.

These palimpsests crystallize the terms of engagement with alterity and the legacies of segregative biopolitics in the post-1945 era. As addressed, these terms of engagement had epistemological and institutional consequences, in addition to having an impact on policies of biopolitics and integration. It is important to remember that during the early decades of the Cold War, partition, apartheid, and population displacement en masse were in vogue. Here, however, we see how these engagements concurrently informed international cultural policy and cultural production, as well as the study of the social sciences. These palimpsests also shed light on UNESCO's more recent cultural policies, which build upon these ideas, construed as conducive to cultural recognition. UNESCO, like any institution, is composed of individuals with their own points of view, and hosts heated debates on different matters. That said, official positions are taken and particular approaches are encouraged under the institutional rubric and publications of UNESCO that need to be analyzed. UNESCO has long spearheaded the shaping of global cultural policy. Considering cultural policy in juxtaposition with synchronic dynamics, concerns, and power struggles—the palimpsests—reveals the limits of liberal humanism as a message of peace and coexistence.

The steps UNESCO took in the 1950s in the fields of culture have important implications for contemporary cultural policies. On January 1, 1950, the *UNESCO Courier*, an official publication of UNESCO, appeared with a front-page headline, "The Will to Peace," which accompanied a New Year's message from UNESCO's director-general:

> The wars of the Twentieth Century have, indeed, made things no better. But through suffering men have at least—and at last—learned the unity of human destiny. We have learned, by tragic experience, to believe what the philosophers had vainly attempted to teach us: that no man can save himself alone; that no class, no state, no race, no nation, can save itself alone. As Dostoievsky wrote: "We stand responsible for all things, before all men." The bullet which strikes down any man, even though he be our "enemy," strikes us too. When he is lost, a part of ourselves is lost likewise. And the family he leaves behind him has lasting claims upon us.

Like AER's references to pain, the director-general of UNESCO here emphasizes suffering as a unifying human emotion. Highlighting the shared destiny of all humanity, this statement calls for drawing lessons from wars that marked the twentieth century. Wars bring pain, and through it humanity's common destiny is to be understood: if one suffers, so does everyone else. The statement configures solidarity in terms of the well-known mantra, "We are all humans."

In the 1950s, alluding to human suffering for peace was common. From UNESCO to the AER, different international organizations offered platforms to articulate wishes to never again allow conflicts to cause suffering.[127] Calls to draw lessons from conflicts were therefore abundant. For example, at the 1953 AER convention in Rome, Fahreddin Kerim Gökay delivered a message from the president of Turkey that underlined his government's eagerness to alleviate the suffering of refugees in general, and specifically people of the Turkish "race" who emigrated to Turkey.[128] This message implied that through helping this particular group, Turkey was fulfilling its universal duty to humanity. In the years to come, human suffering continued to inform such depoliticized, abstract calls for peace, divorced from the broader implications of biopolitics.

UNESCO's earlier efforts were often paired with visual reminders of the universality of suffering in order to associate experiences of displacement and war with suffering—as a shared feature of humanity—and to turn this association into a call for peace and action. Some articles published at the time include "Press, Film, Radio to Be Mobilized for Peace" and "Unesco to Use Music as Weapon for Peace."[129] In yet another move, UNESCO turned to the innocence of childhood to further shape public opinion against war, and disseminated reminders of children's vulnerability in war.[130]

Representations and an emphasis on human suffering, then, long contributed to the visibility of ordeals. Often, these representations were conveyed as lessons of peace. In addition to UNESCO, other institutions also contributed to this endeavor. For instance, during the 1954 AER convention in Istanbul, an exhibition on refugees was organized at Istanbul University's School of Economics.[131] The exhibition consisted of literary and artistic works by refugees from different backgrounds: Greeks, Romanians, Hungarians, Germans, Finns, and so on. Dr. Ernst Schremmer, an art historian from Esslingen and a member of the AER Cultural Committee, was highly praised for organizing this exhibition on the fate of refugees.[132] The objective was to exhibit the pain of displacement. The Turkish press described the exhibition as a display of the tragic portraits of refugees' lives.[133] Addressing the outcomes of segregative biopolitics in liberal humanist terms—often with an emphasis on suffering—remains common and can be informed by different motivations and intentions.

Given the dynamics addressed here, it is not surprising that when one of the most important photography exhibitions, *The Family of Man*, was launched and toured around the world, it received the full support of UNESCO. In many ways, *The Family of Man* was a cultural representation of UNESCO's broader policy on unity in racialized diversity. With anthropologist Liisa Malkki's call for radical historicization of humanism in mind, I turn to *The Family of Man* and the debates on liberal humanism and history surrounding the exhibition.

Palimpsests of Liberal Humanism:
The Family of Man, *Race, and History*

On January 24, 1955, only a few months after the AER convened in Istanbul, one of the most famous, widely traveled, and visited photography exhibitions in history, *The Family of Man*, opened at the Museum of Modern Art (MoMA) in New York.[134] With quotes from proverbs and memoirs as well as legal, religious, and literary texts from around the world sprinkled among the photographs on display, the exhibition brought together elements that the curator Edward Steichen designated as common to humanity, such as love, birth, death, childhood, laughter, labor, dancing, singing and making music, eating, drinking, and sleeping. As the title of the exhibition also suggests, the objective was to emphasize a shared humanity, despite racial, cultural, and political differences.

The Family of Man comprised 503 photographs of 273 selected photographers from around the world, including two unrelated photographs by the famous photographer of the Spanish Civil War, Robert Capa. The exhibition highlighted the universality of humanity despite the racialized diversity of the human species, and deployed this universality on a par with equal human rights. To that end, a quote from the Charter of the United Nations and a picture of the UN decorate the closing pages of the exhibition catalog and conclude the exhibition with a message of peace and equal rights.[135] *The Family of Man* additionally contained cautionary notes on a potential nuclear war, one of the biggest fears of the Cold War era. Since 1994, the exhibition has found a permanent place and is museumized at the Château de Clervaux in Luxembourg—the place of birth and residence of the curator, Edward Steichen, before his family emigrated to the United States.

There are various reasons why this exhibition is important for this book. First, *The Family of Man* represented liberal humanism par excellence. It was an important milestone for the vision of culture and liberal humanism that UNESCO pioneered. Second, the exhibition embodied an early example of a visual culture that seeks to bring recognition through visibility—a particular mode of recognition to which I turn later in this book. Indeed, it was a landmark that anticipated future engagements with humanism via cultural works such as novels, memoirs, music albums, and film, as was the case with the recollection of the 1923 exchange via music and books in the 1990s. Overall, an overview of *The Family of Man* offers an opportunity to synchronically connect the broader framework of biopolitics to UNESCO-supported cultural politics in the 1950s, and to address the broader implications of such cultural policy for the 1950s. This in turn helps us raise historically and politically informed questions about today's cultural politics.

For instance, in 2003, the permanent exhibition was inscribed as Luxembourg's sole "registered heritage" for UNESCO's Memory of the World project. *The Family of Man* has thus found a place in UNESCO's list of "documentary heritage" along with Anne Frank's diary (Netherlands, 2009), Evliya Çelebi's "Book of Travels" manuscript recounting his peregrinations in the Ottoman Empire (Turkey, 2013),[136] and the original Declaration of the Rights of Man and of the Citizen 1789 (France, 2003), to name a few. This UNESCO initiative is meant to bring recognition to a designated heritage as an important document of humanity, worthy of preservation because of its important place in the memory of the peoples of the world. Documentary heritage is also configured as a testament of human diversity.[137] Given the description, *The Family of Man* certainly fits the criteria of UNESCO's Memory of the World project. Yet, if we were to take this endorsement literally and consider *The Family of Man* as an important milestone in the memory of the world beyond UNESCO's terms of endorsement, what would such a recollection look like?

In the first place, we would find that this contemporary recognition is not the first time that UNESCO endorsed *The Family of Man*. In February 1956, when the exhibition arrived in Paris, the headquarters of UNESCO, both the French and English issues of the *UNESCO Courier* dedicated their front page to *The Family of Man*. The opening text underlines the power of photography as a universal language that can render its message legible to different peoples. In many ways, this approach to visual culture anticipated contemporary modes of cultural recognition as a matter of visibility. Putting alterity on display is expected to make the importance of shared humanity legible to everyone. This legibility, in turn, is reductively configured as recognition.

From the outset, UNESCO's support for *The Family of Man* was in liberal humanism terms. By way of quoting Steichen himself, articles in the February 1956 issue of the *UNESCO Courier* such as American poet and author Carl Sandburg's "There Is One Man in the World, and His Name Is All Men," reinforce this support. The 1956 endorsement of the exhibition attests to this:

> [*The Family of Man*] has begun a round-the-world tour and is at present in the Paris Musée d'Art Moderne. The message of this "vast photographic symphony" has been summed up by André Maurois in these words: "We all know—or at least we should—that between all men there exists a great depth of similarity. This similarity ought to engender universal kinship and help men toward an understanding and love of one another. But preachers of hatred are at work to make us forget these similarities. Hence the scorn, the resentments, the brutal revolts and wars. That is why it is necessary, even imperative that the unity of the human family should be revealed to the sceptics. That is why this group of photographs is both useful and moving and not merely beautiful and interesting."[138]

The exhibition's emphasis on the unity of the human family was construed as a way to prevent wars. Presumably, if people are reminded of their shared humanity, hatred leading to conflicts can be prevented. This implies that hatred is the reason for wars, and not the imperialist and colonialist imperative to appropriate land. Recall that during this time, segregative biopolitics was widely deployed to supposedly avoid worse conflicts—the worst-case scenario. This means liberal humanism and biopolitics are different factors built into the equation of alterity management. While liberal humanism discursively unifies racialized genealogies around one big family of humanity, segregative biopolitics continues to classify human beings and to redistribute them spatially. In many ways, liberal humanism despatializes coexistence. It anchors brotherhood and the unity of the human family in a hypothetical human essence. The discourse of liberal humanism therefore abstracts the notion of coexistence and divorces it from its geographic context.

To consider the broader implications of UNESCO's support of liberal humanism, it is also important to keep in mind that *The Family of Man* exhibition was held only a few years after the UNESCO Statement on Race was issued.

> One exhibition entitled "The Family of Man" was cited as an example where each photograph by itself "does not tell the story" but the message is conveyed by the ensemble of photographs. In this issue a section is devoted to a presentation of "The Family of Man" a camera testament that illustrates one of the principal goals of Unesco today: the unity of all mankind within its varied diversity.[139]

Here, the *Courier* promoted the exhibition as a cultural representation of UNESCO's broader objective of achieving the unity of humankind. This objective was also articulated in UNESCO's Statement on Race in terms of humankind being a single species despite racial variance. Liberal humanism, then, was also construed as a cultural formula to protect against scientific racism. This formula smoothly blended into UNESCO's other principal goal: restoring world peace. In general, there seems to be no ambiguity that the exhibition embodies liberal humanism and that the stories and histories embedded in each photograph are less significant than the general story *The Family of Man* seeks to tell.

This interpretation is supported by curator Edward Steichen, who was also the head of the Department of Photography at MoMA at the time.[140] In the "Introduction" he wrote for *The Family of Man* exhibition catalog, Steichen claims that the exhibition "explains man to man" and that it "was conceived to be a mirror of the universal elements and emotions in the everydayness of life—as a mirror of the essential oneness of mankind throughout the world."[141] It is duly assumed that a human essence ties us all together. Our ability to have the same emotions is offered as evidence for this.

In addition, Cold War era dynamics also factor in the recollection of the exhibition as a site of the Memory of the World.[142] When it toured around the world for seven years (1955–1962), its very first stop in Europe was West Berlin: the partitioned city of the Cold War.[143] Indeed, *The Family of Man* opened in West Berlin in September 1955, at the time when the streets of Istanbul became a site of ruins because of the anti-Greek pogrom. The choice of West Berlin is widely considered to have been a strategic move to disseminate the liberal humanist agenda.[144] During that time, other institutions similarly framed the exhibition as an opportunity for the potential and actual viewers of the so-called free world to mediate a mainstream reception of the exhibition.

For example, a promotional film of *The Family of Man* was prepared by the USIS—the United States Information Service, also known as the United States Information Agency (1953–1999).[145] The 1955 film features Steichen offering a liberal humanist reading of the photographs on display. In the Cold War years, the USIS's main objective was to advocate and explain US policies in a credible and meaningful manner in foreign countries. This work was carried out by foreign service officers, who were assigned to USIS positions in almost all US embassies.[146] The promotional film was no doubt prepared as part of US public diplomacy. It appears to have been part of the efforts to mobilize the media as well as the fields of culture and arts to shape international public opinion in favor of US national interest and foreign policy.[147]

Translated into French,[148] the film additionally shows Steichen with the Republican vice president of the time—an anti-communist who had previously served in the House Un-American Activities Committee, and who, about twenty years later, would become the leading figure in the Watergate scandal: Richard Nixon. The film shows Steichen autographing a copy of the exhibition catalog for Nixon, linking it with the agenda of the USIS: to align the exhibition with the official American political line in the early years of the Cold War. Regardless of what Steichen's genuine motivations in curating the exhibition might have been, such institutional endorsement concretizes how *The Family of Man* lent itself to a particular agenda, to say the least. But external institutional endorsements are not the only important aspects to be recalled with regard to *The Family of Man* during the Cold War years. The exhibition itself also appears to have endorsed some institutions by adding them to the content of the exhibition.

A walk down memory lane helps put *The Family of Man*'s endorsement of certain institutions into historical perspective. Two of these institutions are the US Atomic Energy Commission and the United Nations. Steichen added quotes from these organizations and displayed them alongside the photos in exhibit.[149] The US Atomic Energy Commission's "statement of caution" is paired with a Sioux saying that advises that fire should be used wisely since it can otherwise do great harm. The words referenced as Sioux appear to be placed to add folkloric wisdom to the Atomic Energy Commission's statement that warns against nuclear weapons and calls for peace.[150]

The Atomic Energy Commission was involved in multiple projects. In addition to funding research on atomic energy, it also offered grants to fund ethnographic films with a similarly pedagogical intent. This includes *The Feast*, a 1970 film project of the renowned anthropologist filmmaker Timothy Asch and geneticist James V. Neel.[151] Anthropologist Faye Ginsburg describes Asch's filmmaking as a pedagogical tool to inform people about other cultures as evidence of his commitment to liberal humanism.[152] According to Ginsburg, Asch initially presumed that exposing people to images and information about other cultures would be a good tool against racism.[153] Asch's endeavor resonates with UNESCO's approach to visual culture as a universally legible language conveying a pedagogical message. *The Family of Man* might be indeed one of the most important examples of this trend, which makes it an important site for memory of the world, provided that its recollection offers a broader picture. This entails a political and historical contextualization of institutional endorsements.

For example, when Steichen added the Atomic Energy Commission's statements to his exhibition in the 1950s, he probably did not know that it was in fact conducting radiation experiments on unconsenting human beings. Not until 1993 did the American government officially acknowledge the commission's horrific experiments, which included injecting or feeding radioactive substances to uninformed human subjects—including pregnant women and people with diseases—and the disturbing violation of the dead by digging up graves without permission from the deceased's kin and loved ones in order to conduct follow-up experiments on the exposed bodies.[154] But today, we know about its unethical research on human subjects, a legacy that lies under the surface of the commission's words of peace and cooperation quoted in *The Family of Man*.

This detail was neatly tucked under the broad rubric of the Cold War when UNESCO canonized the exhibition in 2003:

> A huge undertaking, with unique cultural and artistic dimensions, it [*The Family of Man*] had a considerable influence on other exhibition organizers, stirred public interest in photography and its tremendous ability to communicate, and conveyed a personal, humanist message that was both courageous and provocative.
>
> Although *The Family of Man* has become a legend in the history of photography, it went far beyond the traditional view of what an exhibition should be. It may be regarded as the memory of an entire era, that of the Cold War and McCarthyism, in which the hopes and aspirations of millions of men and women throughout the world were focused on peace.[155]

This statement gestures toward the Cold War era's dynamics via external variables like McCarthyism, but the implications of featuring the Atomic Energy Commission as part of the exhibition are left to oblivion. It is perhaps to be expected that a registry of Memory of the World would wish to highlight the recollected in a more positive light. But then the terms of such a recollection are also questionable and raise questions about the politics of memory. If the exhibition is a memory of the Cold War, as UNESCO's statement asserts, it is not because the Cold War provided merely the historical background of the exhibition, but very much part of the exhibition itself. *The Family of Man* materializes the actual terms of peace within the so-called free world in the 1950s, as well as the terms of its recollection today.

The emphasis on democratic structures and the United Nations in UNESCO's 2003 Memory of the World statement attests to this dynamic:

> While offering infinitely diverse images of human beings living in the 1950s, it nevertheless emphatically reminds visitors that they all belong to the same big family. The 32 themes, arranged chronologically, reflect the subjects' joys and sadnesses, their satisfactions and their unhappinesses, and their longing for peace, but also the reality of bloody conflict. They emphasize the role of democratic structures and, in the exhibition's conclusion, the United Nations' role as the only body capable of saving the world from the "scourge of war, which twice in our lifetime has brought untold sorrow to mankind, and [of

reaffirming] faith in fundamental human rights, in the dignity and worth of the human person, in the equal rights of men and women and of nations large and small" (Charter of the United Nations).[156]

The democratic structures referred to here are most likely the theme of voting at the exhibition. Displaying the sole image from Turkey, the section on voting reinforced the Cold War era definition of democracy as reduced to a reasonably free and competitive electoral system. This might be the reason why Turkey is on display in this section, as it had transitioned to multiparty elections only a few years earlier; Adnan Menderes was the first prime minister elected in the multiparty electoral system.

In addition, in the 2003 UNESCO statement, the United Nations is enshrined as the ultimate peace-building body at the time *The Family of Man* was curated. In the exhibition, a photograph of the UN assembly accompanied the above quote from the UN Charter. It underlines sorrow—akin to suffering—of humankind because of war. That is this same quote that closed the exhibition, whereby all the liberal humanist content of *The Family of Man* is tied to a concluding message of peace and human rights.

We learn from historian Mark Mazower's work on the ideological foundations of the United Nations how Jan Smuts, the white supremacist South African statesman widely considered to be the architect of the apartheid regime, was instrumental in drafting the stirring preamble to the United Nations Charter and, therefore, those very lines bore his imprint.[157] Mazower calls attention to the mixed motives in drafting the UN's foundational texts.[158] His work offers important insights on how at its inception, preserving imperialist power was crucial for those who drafted the UN Charter. To a white supremacist segregationist like Jan Smuts, South Africa belonging to this international power collaboration was important, while, at home, he defended racial segregation. Different sets of discourses were thus mobilized to achieve different ends.

According to Mazower, the UN's later adoption of anticolonialism obscured "the awkward fact that like the League it [the UN] was a product of empire and indeed, at least at the outset, regarded by those with colonies to keep as a more than adequate mechanism for its defense."[159] The League of Nations was the key international body that arbitrated the Lausanne conference, where the 1923 Greek-Turkish population exchange agreement was signed. Mazower thus indicates how the founding of the UN was not a revolution, but a natural outcome of already existing institutions, ideas, and political agendas. As his work also demonstrates, despite the terrifying scale of atrocities committed during the Holocaust, the ideas and discourses that fed into it did not necessarily disappear. The brief overview of the dynamics revolving around the AER show how some of those ideas were transferred to other platforms. Meanwhile, fascism was isolated as a condemnable ideology, but largely reduced to something found in Nazi Germany and Mussolini's Italy, as a relic that belongs to the past.

In that light, the emphasis on international peace, democratic structures, and the values of liberal humanism obfuscates the modus operandi of the capitalist free world during the Cold War years and raises questions about the implications of segregative biopolitics in that context. Disregarding multiple crossings of intellectuals, images, exhibitions, ideas, and works over time and space obscures implicit and explicit connections.

In *The Family of Man*, individual photographs don't tell their own story, but need to be considered in relation to one another. This is also emphasized in the UNESCO endorsement of the exhibition. *The Family of Man* duly divorces the photographs from their original context to tell another story. This dynamic is reproduced in selective recollection, which, in the name of telling a story deemed to be important, appears to repudiate the actual content.

As for the references to the UN and human rights, that too necessitates unpacking. From the outset, the UN adopted the protection of individual rights instead of collective rights.[160] This means, despite the 1948 adoption of the Genocide Convention, the UN focused on the protection of individual rights. Reservations of member states appear to have played a role in this. For example, according to Mazower, the US Senate was worried that engaging collective rights would allow foreign meddling in US domestic affairs, especially in the biopolitical policies in the South. Indeed, the United States did not ratify the Genocide Convention until 1986.[161] The emphasis therefore remained on individual human rights and the shaping of public opinion—which, according to Mazower, was the rationale behind the Universal Declaration of Human Rights.[162]

When state-organized violence erupted in the 1950s and 1960s across the world, an international penal tribunal was not set up to bring global economic powers to justice.¹⁶³ This organized violence includes the French colonial forces' brutal suppression of the Algerian struggle for independence.¹⁶⁴ The French case is hardly aberrant. Political scientist Laleh Khalili's work demonstrates how counterinsurgencies are also interconnected; different tools and methods of oppression are exchanged between different state officials.¹⁶⁵ In the case of France, in the 1950s the authorities singled out racism and made dealing with it a public endeavor. UNESCO, during that time, also praised the French stance against racism. After all, one might think, racism violates the notion of equality embedded in the Declaration of Human Rights. Yet, as the anticolonialist thinker Frantz Fanon reminds us, it is what that equality entails—its limitations and bourgeois emphasis on individuality—that makes a difference. Further, adopting a stance against racism did not necessarily translate into policies in the colonies. One might very well have been critical of discourses of racism and simultaneously seek to assimilate alterity while crushing the decolonizers as part of broader discipline-and-punish campaigns in bloody counterinsurgencies. Likewise, let us not forget that in 1951 the Adnan Menderes government amended the penal code to ban racist organizations, in the name of fighting fascism.¹⁶⁶ This doesn't mean racism was absent from the 1955 anti-Greek pogrom nor that the officials who orchestrated the pogrom were willing to make that connection. The broader implications of race also need unpacking in that regard. Racism in Nazi terms might have been condemned, but that does not mean a racist archive of knowledge was not mobilized on other fronts.

The UN did undergo change over time. But even before it did, it still had some international weight despite the limitations embedded in its legislature. For example, France tried to keep the United Nations "from debating 'events in Algeria' (which Paris insisted were domestic problems)."¹⁶⁷ Likewise, in the Turkish parliament in 1957, the opposition Republican Peoples Party's deputy representing Kars, Mehmet Hazer, repeatedly asked the Adnan Menderes government whether, in light of what was going on in Algeria, Turkey would take a stance and bring the matter up with France or the United Nations.¹⁶⁸ His question was eventually dismissed from the parliament's agenda because it was never answered. It is clear that government officials in many countries were wary of the UN and protective of their so-called domestic policies at the expense of rights violations.

Indeed, as Mazower also points out, the prewar-era treaties signed to protect minority rights were quietly left aside in the post-1945 era: "For all the rhetoric about human rights, the mood in the General Assembly was for enforced assimilation and against any mechanisms that might retard this since new and old states alike agreed that minorities had undermined the stability of Europe."[169] The approach to minorities here is not that different from that of Dr. Rıza Nur, one of the chief negotiators for Turkey at Lausanne. In addition to the removal of "cultural genocide" from the original Genocide Convention, the avoidance of stressing minority rights in the Universal Declaration of Human Rights of 1948 focused the United Nations on individual rights. In the absence of an emphasis on minority rights, population transfers continued during that time. Forced assimilation was a common policy for dealing with remaining communities. In short, segregative biopolitics continued to be practiced, and unsurprisingly, integration, mostly understood as assimilation, became an important rubric. As Mazower shows, in order to ensure peace and social order, the Allies were promoting policies advocated by the Revisionist Zionists and the Nazis in the 1930s.[170]

Mazower also discusses how stability was set in Eurocentric terms, and that achieving stability in Europe was perceived as key among these circles.[171] If alterity was viewed as a source of instability in postwar Europe, it is not surprising that forced assimilation and population transfers became popular tools to regulate it. Hence, the prominence of international platforms like the AER. And thus, the fact that 1955 anti-Greek pogroms in Turkey were not addressed in the AER circles is not as paradoxical as one might have at first imagined. It was rather a predictable outcome of the biopolitical approaches to alterity at the time. In addition, given the dominant discourses regarding alterity, the 1955 anti-Greek pogroms might have even come across as evidence that segregative biopolitics is a necessity for ensuring stability and social order. Behind the rhetoric of stability, however, lies economic and political agendas that included confiscation of property and resources, population regulation, and, whenever applicable, settler land appropriation.

It is also in that postwar context that the 1923 Greek-Turkish population exchange was considered a promising model for an exchange of Palestinian Arabs and Jews as well as for population transfers within Europe.[172] Population exchanges needed to be rationalized and promoted,[173] as partitions were deemed insufficient to achieve social order and stability, configured as peace. It is not surprising, then, that in 1945 a minority rights protection provision—which had been significant for the League of Nations—was rejected by the United Nations. At the time, the UN endorsed national self-determination informed by segregative biopolitics as a liberating right, but as Mazower demonstrates, it was a precept that undermined the rights of others.[174] In this context, the 1923 exchange embodied a "successful" case that showed such demographic measures were possible and could be a reference point for segregative biopolitics.

Institutional histories fall beyond the scope of this book, but the fascinating history of the UN and the human rights regime unraveled by scholars like Mark Mazower and Samuel Moyn offers a stark reminder that political contextualization and historicization are crucial to complicate the general picture when it comes to liberal humanism and associated values.[175] Beyond curator Steichen's authorial intent in the exhibition, then, power was implicated in multiple ways, especially considering the entangled intellectual and cultural histories addressed in the essays in this part. This doesn't mean the United Nations does not do important work today, nor does it mean the world would be a better place without it. But at its inception, it was an ambivalent project that attracted imperialists, idealists, and pragmatists alike, and commemorating *The Family of Man* for embodying the values attributed to the UN today is anachronistic at best.

In such a context, how does one consider Steichen's limiting the treatment of the Holocaust and Second World War vis-à-vis Germany to merely three photographs? The first picture he includes is a photograph that was exhibited in the Nuremberg trials.[176] It shows the Nazis' crushing of the 1943 Warsaw ghetto uprising, and the gathering of men, women, and children at gunpoint before their deportation to the Treblinka extermination camp.[177] The second is a photograph of a German city in ruins, and the third, a photo of a gathering in a Munich beer hall—a "highly loaded expression of German nationalism in the postwar period."[178] Given the scale of the Holocaust, and its visual representation limited to these photographs in *The Family of Man* exhibition, it appears that this constellation helped keep the focus away from the issue of minorities, collective rights, and genocide. Instead, the Holocaust problematically becomes a background story of atrocities of war.

It is against all this backdrop that *The Family of Man* emphasizes liberal humanism via the shared elements of humanity such as birth, death, laughter, and love. Interestingly, labor and democracy are also included in this picture frame of shared humanity. This inclusion clearly aligns the exhibition with the capitalist free world—associated with liberal values—in which humanitarian aid is also discussed in eugenicist terms that cast the refugee as exploitable human capital. In sum, *The Family of Man* might indeed be an important site of world memory, but not exactly the way in which it is highlighted in the 2003 UNESCO statement.

Labor, Colonialism, and Liberal Humanism

On January 20, 1956, the day *The Family of Man* opened in Paris, the French newspaper *Le Monde* informed its readers that the theme of the exhibition was the unity and continuity of human life, and how "man across the world is similar to his brothers of all races, having the same attitudes about love, work, birth, suffering, dreams, [and] notions of eternity and of death. . . . The faces of workers, whether they are lumberjacks or laborers, miners or blacksmiths, captured in the accomplishment of the task at hand, all reflect the same gravity, the same religious attention."[179] The *Le Monde* editorial continues that man is the same everywhere, and that Steichen's exhibition highlights the common links that bind men as brothers.

"White men, yellow men, black men" are the same, the editorial continues, whether drinking in a beer hall in Munich—the very same photo scholar Sarah E. Young points out as being a loaded expression of German nationalism after the war—laughing in a theater, or rowing down the Ubangi River. The *Le Monde* editorial resonates with the UNESCO framing of the exhibition for audiences in France, and is very much in line with Steichen's own articulation of the project. In that respect, *Le Monde*'s presentation captures how the exhibition was mediated for wider, mainstream audiences at the time it opened in France.

Among the numerous visitors to the exhibition in Paris was none other than the French critic Roland Barthes. After his visit, Barthes wrote his famous essay on the exhibition entitled "The Great Family of Man." A short but remarkably trenchant critique of the exhibition's cultural representation of humanity, Barthes's piece objects to *The Family of Man*'s liberal humanist project on the grounds that it dehistoricizes the "human."[180] In his critique, Barthes refers to Emmett Till, the fourteen-year-old African American youth who was murdered in a hate crime in Mississippi at the end of August 1955. The murder happened about five years after UNESCO's racial equality statement, several months after *The Family of Man* opened in New York, a year after the Algerian decolonization war against the French colonizers began, almost a week before the September 6–7 anti-Greek pogroms swept Istanbul, and three months after the US Supreme Court devised a plan to proceed with its previous decision to end racial segregation in schools with *Brown v. Board of Education*,[181] the desegregation court case which prompted Corrado Gini to co-found the Association for Ethnology and Eugenics and against which his party would later launch a "scientific" attack.

In his essay, Barthes questions the tenets of liberal humanism that he detects in the exhibition. According to Barthes, history is crucial in such projects in order to consider injustices. Barthes's critique of the exhibition highlights the importance of keeping disparities—as well as the historical reasons behind them—in perspective while emphasizing unity within the diversity of humankind:

> Everything here, the content and appeal of the pictures, the discourse which justifies them, aims to suppress the determining weight of History: we are held back at the surface of an identity, prevented precisely by sentimentality from penetrating into its ulterior zone of human behaviour where historical alienation introduces some "differences" which we shall here quite simply call "injustices." . . . Examples? Here they are: those of our Exhibition. Birth, death? Yes, these are facts of nature, universal facts. But if one removes History from them, there is nothing more to say about them; any comment about them becomes purely tautological. . . . True, children are *always* born: but in the whole mass of the human problem, what does the "essence" of this process matter to us, compared to its modes which, as for them, are perfectly historical?[182]

Whether or not Barthes was exposed to the promotional film of *The Family of Man*, UNESCO's acclaim of the exhibition, and the press coverage of it in France, he certainly reacted against the cultural representation of liberal humanism on display. Birth and death might be universal phenomena, but without historicization, the essence of humanity does not convey any context for such phenomena on its own. He also reacts against the configuration of racialized diversity within unified humanity, because such a dehistoricized configuration levels differences and focuses on the human essence instead. Histories that mark these differences on display are thus obfuscated. Barthes calls these differences injustices, but without history, these stories cannot be unlocked. Some of these entangled histories with regard to alterity are addressed in this part, and I hope they help put Barthes's critique of the exhibition in perspective.

In addition, Barthes critically focuses on "work," another category on display in *The Family of Man*:

> And what can be said about work, which the Exhibition places among great universal facts, putting it on the same plane as birth and death, as if it was quite evident that it belongs to the same order of fate? That work is an age-old fact does not in the least prevent it from remaining a perfectly historical fact. Firstly, and evidently, because of its modes, its motivations, its ends, and its benefits, which matter to such an extent that it will never be fair to confuse in a purely gestural identity the colonial and the Western worker (let us ask the North African workers of the Goutte d'Or district in Paris what they think of *The Great Family of Man*). Secondly, because of the very differences in its inevitability: we know very well that work is "natural" just as long as it is "profitable" and that in modifying the inevitability of the profit, we shall perhaps one day modify the inevitability of labour. It is this entirely historified work which we should be told about, instead of an eternal aesthetics of laborious gestures.[183]

Taking note of the emphasis on "work" as a universal that binds humanity, Barthes calls attention to the problematic alignment of the colonial and what he calls the "Western worker." Placing workers from different parts of the world together erases their differences and divorces labor from its histories of colonialism and exploitation.

Recalling the AER's approach to labor in the 1950s, the eugenicist and capitalist implications of work in some so-called Western contexts becomes clearer. Addressing fit refugees as human capital and the precarious who cannot work as a social burden or deadweight on society are cases in point. In addition to the labor and productivity projects of fascist regimes in Europe, in other contexts the history of labor is fraught with hardships, exploitation, and struggles to organize. The so-called Western worker therefore further necessitates historicization and contextualization in itself, rather than being posited as an ideal. Finally, Barthes remarks that the reason labor is emphasized as a natural phenomenon alongside birth and death is the capitalist interest embedded in it to make profit. By bringing labor to the forefront, Steichen contributed to the naturalization of labor as a universal and reproduced it problematically as an apolitical binding human essence. This approach also depoliticizes labor movements.

The Family of Man displayed images of people working—in the fields, in industry, in construction, in mines, and on the sea—from across the world. The caption "the land is a mother that never dies" accompanies the section on work, and establishes a brotherhood among those who work since it is "mother" who supposedly gave birth to all humans. It includes two photographs of men from Belgian Congo.[184] In the exhibition catalog, the photos of Congolese workers—one photographed in what seems to at a construction site or a mine, and the other, exposing a missing front tooth while drinking water after doing what appears to be some manual labor—are brought together on the same two pages with a constellation of photos of male and female laborers from Germany, the United States, Bolivia, and Denmark. These photos are politically loaded, which complicates the pictures on display. For instance, the then recent history of labor in the context of Germany is imbued with fascist and eugenicist approaches that had not completely disappeared. Furthermore, the USIS promotional film of the exhibition picks up on the theme of labor, and asserts that in joining forces mankind becomes unified. The USIS thus aligned the depoliticized notion of labor on display with America's Cold War era interests. Liberal humanism here lends itself to the discursive pacification of labor movements.

This display strips labor from its historical and political context, especially given how the Belgian Congo exemplifies the horrors of colonial violence; the brutality of colonial exploitation and labor slavery appears only as a ghost to those who actually know about it and are willing to consider that history. Nothing in those images suggests the brutality of Belgian colonial rule in Congo, with amputations as a form of labor-related corporal punishment, other than the caption that identifies the locale as the Belgian Congo. Perhaps Steichen thought similar issues were already addressed in a later segment showing political dynamics and suffering.

The section on suffering and politics depicts a pensive man from South Africa who appears to have a disabled or amputated hand and underneath, a photo of a tram from Indonesia is shown. The inscription on the tram reads "All people are created equal" in English. Be that as it may, the way labor is treated and the alignment of the photos of Belgian Congolese laborers with others from Europe or the Americas appears to level them, divorcing them from their political context and from the history of ruthless colonial exploitation.[185] This does not mean everyone will read the exhibition the same way. Certainly not, and Roland Barthes, for one, appears to be one of those spectators who reads the exhibition in a non-mainstream way—unlike the way it was framed by Steichen, UNESCO, the USIS, and the media.

Considering the controversy surrounding UNESCO's Statement on Race, one could argue that even the visibility of the Belgian Congolese workers is a political statement for its time. Yet, can visibility be conflated with recognition or be unambiguously construed as an actual call for recognition? Further, in a context where collective rights were excluded from the UN's protection, labor was a subject of biopolitical integration, and civil rights and decolonization movements were gaining momentum, Barthes's resistance to conflating visibility with recognition à la liberal humanism is a valuable intervention. Reductive modes of recognition unravel the actual terms of recognition and the limits of promoted "equality."

As mentioned, in the 2003 UNESCO canonization of the exhibition, *The Family of Man* is praised for endorsing democratic structures. During the Cold War era, democracy meant reasonably fair, competitive, and transparent elections.[186] Indeed, the sole photograph of Turkey in the exhibition was taken not by a local, but by Herman Kreider and captures a scene of people voting. Kreider was an American missionary in Istanbul; he authored Turkish-language books and later became a bursar at Istanbul's Robert College, a school founded by American missionaries.[187] His photograph captioned "Turkey" in *The Family of Man* shows a woman casting her vote in a ballot box in Turkey. Turkey had recently transitioned to a multiparty system—which was equated with democracy—with the first democratically elected prime minister being Adnan Menderes. The photograph is aligned with three others of voting women in France, Japan, and China. These three countries had all granted women the right to vote in the mid and late 1940s, whereas in Turkey women had that right as early as 1930, but at the time there was only one party to vote for. Focusing on women voting in a country, this display duly emphasizes another mode of supposed representation of plurality: democracy. Given the broader issues of the 1950s, however, is it possible to argue that an electoral system is in itself sufficient to justify claims of democracy or to bring equal rights and social justice?

The Family of Man did not become a landmark in a vacuum; its canonization and institutional endorsements matter as much as its curation. As the *UNESCO Courier* states, *The Family of Man*'s "photographic essay" composed of different pictures tells a completely different story than the particular stories embedded in each picture. The curation and selection process thus brought out a new configuration of meaning, overriding the original meaning of the photos. Museums, exhibitions, anthologies, documentary film and books, biographies and archives, among others, also deploy a similar logic to ascribe new meanings to a collection. As anthropologist Penelope Papailias has pointed out in the context of archival poetics in Greece, critic Mikhail Bakhtin would call these complex genres,[188] which absorb simple genres—such as shopping lists, notes, anecdotes, and so on, to which I would also add objects—and in this process, their original meaning is translated into another platform wherein it is rewritten. While the original meaning might not be entirely lost, it matters how complex genres are scripted into the new platform and how the script configures the framing of those objects.

Rewriting is thus embedded in every act of curation, assembling, (re)collecting, and representation. When a work is canonized, its contents are framed and scripted in a particular way as well. Critic André Lefevere, for example, addresses this issue through the fields of literature and translation, and convincingly argues that there are concrete factors as to why a work is canonized.[189] This is not related to a work's intrinsic value, nor is canonization random, Lefevere argues, because how a work crosses time and space, and the meanings it acquires in the process, depend on the context. This is because there are concrete reasons that inform what is valued, when, and why.

This process includes the selection of objects and photographs for a museum or an exhibition, or the selection of one exhibition instead of others as a canonical site configured as representative of an attributed value. This is also the case of UNESCO's canonization of *The Family of Man.*

Drawing on Lefevere's work, then, we can rethink the concrete historical and political contexts in which *The Family of Man* was canonized.[190] Indeed, without the clearly conveyed message of liberal humanism, could the exhibition have become the canonical landmark that it is, traveling around the world in 1955–1962 and attracting millions of visitors across the globe? With canonization, I do not necessarily mean the contemporary recognition of *The Family of Man* in the UNESCO Memory of the World register, along with other canons such as Anne Frank's diary and Evliya Çelebi's "Book of Travels." I also mean the consolidation of the exhibition as a canonized site that visualized a liberal humanist call for peace and coexistence in the 1950s.

Today, the website of the permanent collection in Luxembourg—the Steichen Collections of *The Family of Man*—repeats that the exhibited photographs taken from their original context have been brought together in a "photographic essay" to convey a "message of peace in the midst of the Cold War."[191] As discussed, however, peace is not a notion that can be taken lightly. Its broader implications need to be carefully unpacked. The permanent collection website admits that *The Family of Man* carries some traces of the Cold War, but what that entails is not addressed.

One of the reasons *The Family of Man* is engaged anachronistically might be the changes the notion of the human rights has undergone. According to historian Samuel Moyn, human rights were reconfigured in the 1970s. This is when human rights gained the meanings we largely attribute to them today. Moyn therefore argues that human rights the way we know them today did not exist before the 1970s.[192] Could this be a vectoring factor to the anachronistic readings of the Charter of the United Nations today—the preamble of which, as we have noted, was written with the help of the white supremacist Jan Smuts—to the extent that an idealized meaning is ascribed to it that did not necessarily exist at the time?

In addition, the Universal Declaration of Human Rights highlighted individual rights—collective rights were not incorporated—and as Moyn puts it, in the absence of abiding international law, the declaration was a promise made on paper.[193] And as addressed in this part, historicization and contextualization of discourses and practices of engagement with alterity at the time reveal the actual terms of that promise. Segregative biopolitics continued to inform population displacement, and the logic of human categorization according to origins—such as historicist humanism—continued to racialize and hierarchize different groups. Upon the ruins and remains of such practices towered the much-celebrated discourse of liberal humanism in the 1950s. Liberal humanism arguably generated an illusion that there was indeed unity in racialized diversity. This illusion has no doubt contributed to the conflation of visibility with recognition. *The Family of Man* is the visual cultural representation of these dynamics par excellence. The fact that to this day there are still attempts to undermine Barthes's important intervention is evidence of how the limits of liberal humanism are not recognized. As Barthes and Malkki remind us, it also demonstrates the importance of historical contextualization.

Reconsidering the Contribution of The Family of Man

In the 1950s, UNESCO's intervention against biological racism was a significant step against Nazi-style racist science. As scholars have recently shown, however, race did not disappear from scholarly repertoires.[194] In the field of culture, the liberal humanist advocacy that all "men" are the same, because they are all *Homo sapiens*, and that they all laugh, die, eat, love, and so on, did not mean this discourse was translated into actual policy to implement equality in social rights and opportunities. As discussed in this part, racialized notions of alterity continued to inform policies of segregative biopolitics as well as refugee and emigrant integration. Even when race does not appear to be a primary category of identification, racialized categorization is very much embedded in public and scholarly repertoires—the topic of the next part. In fact, as will be addressed, while UNESCO advocated liberal humanism in the field of culture, it simultaneously promoted historicist humanism, together with all its Eurocentric tools of identification.

As for "the family of man," it is actually a trope with its own cultural history, beyond liberal humanism. Critic Anne McClintock has shown how in the nineteenth century, "a visual paradigm" emerged in some European circles to "display evolutionary progress as a measurable spectacle": the "evolutionary family Tree of Man."[195] Accordingly, the image of the tree of humankind configures evolution in a racially hierarchal manner; it embodies progress. The tree image then associates progress with the racially most "evolved": the Aryans. McClintock discusses how the image of the tree is thus paired with another image: "the Family of Man." The family of man is intertwined with the evolutionary tree of humankind, and represents evolutionary progress via a "series of distinct anatomical types, organized as a linear image of progress."[196] This visual trope has long represented historicist humanism, racialist science, and progress.

UNESCO's Statement on Race was in part an intervention against the discourses that informed this trope. A decade later, it was still contested. The notion of equality was a particular topic of contention. An article entitled "Family of Mankind: Some New Light?" published in 1961 by *Mankind Quarterly* exemplifies this. As noted earlier, *Mankind Quarterly* was the semi-official publication of the Association for Ethnology and Eugenics, the organization in which Gini served as a member of its executive committee. "Family of Mankind: Some New Light?" was written by American economist Elizabeth Hoyt at Iowa State University. In the article, she interprets a quote from a 1951 book written by paleontologist George Gaylord Simpson, who worked on evolution:

> Western Man "seems terrifyingly near the knowledge of how to destroy his planet and terrifyingly far from the self-control necessary to avoid using that knowledge." The lower alpha frequency of the brain waves of blacks, if substantiated, would at least not have led them in this direction.
>
> It may, in fact, be time for us to revise those concepts of "equality" in race which we liberals have adopted. It may be that we will serve mankind better in looking for differences in the human family in an objective spirit than by assuming all people to be alike.[197]

In this article, racialized narratives of progress are seasoned with "scientific" hypotheses. They are intertwined with the image of the "family of man" and the Cold War era fear of the destruction of the planet. Hoyt's piece illustrates how the proponents of racialism can interpret the statement of equality among the human races as well as discourses of liberal humanism.

It is perhaps in this particular context that we can in fact situate Edward Steichen's intervention. He appears to have recreated a visual representation for the "family of mankind" that reorganizes the notion of "family" as a unity in diversity, through the shared aspects of humanity, rather than as a hierarchized evolutionary tree of racialized humankind. The implications of genealogy and origins have not disappeared, but, visualized as a tree, they were not the main organizing principle of the exhibition. Steichen's reconfiguration of the family of humankind also emphasizes progress through labor, technology, and democracy interpreted within the paradigms of the Cold War.

Whether intended or not, Steichen rearticulates the European trope of the family of the humankind. *The Family of Man* intervenes in the visual representation of this trope as a racialized tree of progress, and translates the basic tenets of racial equality—as emphasized in UNESCO's Statement on Race—into liberal humanism. This might have been an important step, but as addressed here, it came with its own sets of problems. In fact, it appears that Barthes noticed the intervention that is attempted with *The Family of Man*, but found it problematic, flawed, and incomplete.[198] In his critique of the exhibition, Barthes demands a historicized, nuanced, and politically sensitive interpretation of humanism. *The Family of Man* might be an intervention to advocate liberal humanism—implying that all human races are the same and thus equal—through visual representation. If so, it is conveyed in a problematic manner, as Barthes reminds us.

In concluding this discussion, it is important to once again mention Frantz Fanon. After having worked as a psychiatrist in Algeria in the mid-1950s—where he attended to the French soldiers who conducted torture to suppress decolonization—Fanon joined the Algerian decolonization fight against the French colonial regime. He was deported in 1957. This is around the time when Turkey hosted the AER and orchestrated the anti-Greek pogroms and Paris, despite France's brutal counterinsurgency campaign in colonial Algeria, continued to be the headquarters of UNESCO, which purported to promote peace and coexistence throughout the world. It is also around that time that *The Family of Man* opened in Paris, which, as we have noted, UNESCO praised for showing humankind's unity in diversity and making people of different colors visible, with the understanding that all "men" shared human attributes.

In a work published in 1961, only a few days before his death, Fanon wrote a critical statement on such assertions of equality:

> The Western bourgeoisie, though fundamentally racist, most often manages to mask this racism by a multiplicity of nuances which will allow it to preserve intact its proclamation of mankind's outstanding dignity....
>
> ...Western bourgeois racial prejudice as regards the nigger and the Arab is a racism of contempt; it is a racism which minimizes what it hates. Bourgeois ideology, however, which is the proclamation of an essential equality between men, manages to appear logical in its own eyes by inviting the submen to become human, and to take as their prototype Western humanity as incarnated in the Western bourgeoisie....
>
> For Europe, for ourselves, and for humanity, comrades, we must turn over a new leaf, we must work out new concepts, and try to set afoot a new man.[199]

Fanon clearly demarcates the terms of equality here: that those deemed to be racially inferior and exploited—the subhuman—are invited to become human, but not on their own terms. It is an invitation to join what Fanon calls Western humanity, meaning equality relies on expanding Eurocentric norms and modes of identification—in other words, humanism. He considers this paradigm to be closely associated with the "Western bourgeoisie" as representative of concerns with capitalist production, and within the context of colonialism, positioned as the group that exploits the labor of the colonized.

Further, along with the Western bourgeoisie and equality, the 1789 French Revolution is also implicated here. With the famous declaration of human rights that followed, equality was among the stipulated notions of the 1789 revolution closely associated with the bourgeoisie. It is well known that when the slaves in the French colony of Haiti started their revolution, many French revolutionaries who had invested in the colonial economy turned around and supported the attempts to brutally suppress their decolonization struggle. After Haiti won independence in 1804, the French government forced it to pay a very large sum to compensate for the loss of its colony. Fanon's reference to bourgeois ideology and its emphasis on the equality of the humankind has therefore broader historical implications.

As for the Declaration of the Rights of Man and of the Citizen, just like *The Family of Man*, it was canonized in UNESCO's Memory of the World project in 2003. Equality, fraternity, liberty—the tenets of the French Revolution—find a different point of articulation via liberal humanism as a discourse of the brotherhood of humankind. Liberal humanism implies that despite racial differences, human beings are equal, because supposedly they are all *Homo sapiens*. The recognition of the presumably inferior races as equal is configured as emancipation, or liberty.[200]

Liberal humanism translates these discourses into cultural politics, channeling demands for equality and justice to the plane of culture. To the privileged, the recognition of the "subspecies" as human might appear to be sufficient. But this recognition, in fact, is far from egalitarian in its social scope and comes with its own limits. Meanwhile, historicist humanism continues to inform racialized thinking, human categorization, and segregative biopolitics. Frantz Fanon's work is a reminder of the importance of unmasking the actual terms of recognition. What, then, is one to make all of these palimpsests of biopolitics and liberal humanism?

Liberal Humanism, Segregative Biopolitics, and Cultural Politics

German jurist and political theorist Carl Schmitt's work helps us reconsider the implications of responding to biopolitics in liberal humanist terms. In particular, his article "Appropriation/Distribution/Production: An Attempt to Determine from *Nomos* the Basic Questions of Every Social and Economic Order," published by Corrado Gini in 1954 after the revival of *Revue Internationale de Sociologie*, is significant for this book, especially since it helps put into perspective the palimpsests we have addressed. And, in terms of the story of its publication, Schmitt's piece is entangled with the dynamics raised in this part.

In "Appropriation/Distribution/Production," Schmitt argues that at the core of all social, legal, and economic order lies land appropriation, distribution, and production.[201] Land appropriation includes property. Accordingly, prior "to every legal, economic and social order, prior to every legal, economic, and social theory" are the questions: "Where and how was it appropriated? Where and how was it divided? Where and how was it produced?"[202] The sequence of these questions, he argues, changes depending on the political agenda.²⁰³ To Schmitt, then, the emphasis on any of these issues reveals the priorities of a political context.²⁰⁴

For example, when production is given priority, addressing social justice and dispossession appear to be of lesser concern. In such circumstances, peaceful coexistence is configured as social order—necessary for economic growth—rather than a matter of social justice and egalitarian access to rights. Postwar-era liberal humanism is part of this process; it is a discourse that calibrates the regulation of alterity in terms of recognition, and not necessarily in terms of redistribution or restitution. Recognition is then construed as liberty. In the context of law, Schmitt identifies *the social* as a program of (re)distribution, the terms of which are informed by the political agenda.

The dynamics regarding order addressed in this part can be reconsidered in terms of appropriation, distribution, and production as suggested by Schmitt. Social order becomes a question of redistribution of resources and property, regulated according to the composition of the population. The process of distribution has racialized implications via segregative biopolitics. Human categorization and geographic redistribution are integral to this process. In the post-1945 era, the legacies of segregative biopolitics—epitomized and legalized in the international arena with the 1923 exchange—were engaged through the mobilization of more policies of biopolitics and liberal humanism.

Within the context of the palimpsests addressed here, there is a clear emphasis on production and turning the persons involved into productive contributors to the economy. Resonating with Adam Smith's approach that there is no functioning of economy without peace, different fields were mobilized in the aftermath of the Second War to secure peace. Yet, what that actually entailed remains open to question given the mass population transfers, partitions, and apartheid that marked the era. Steps toward securing peace within the so-called free world in the early decades of the Cold War were interpreted as progress. Self-determination was configured as emancipation, simultaneously deploying segregative biopolitics to limit the mobility of undesirable groups through partitions or population transfers, all which were steps taken to presumably secure peace and stability in Europe and beyond.

It is by exploring the limits of the endorsements of liberal humanism, human welfare, and peace that the inconsistencies embedded in these discourses become clear. Other than emphasizing suffering, these discourses, translated into transnational cultural politics, did little to engage matters of dispossession or the legacies of segregative biopolitics. Cultural policy was part of this process.

UNESCO's cultural politics in the late 1940s and 1950s thus have direct ramifications for today's cultural policies and cultural politics. At the time, UNESCO mobilized art, music, film, and the media to secure world peace. To that end, it undertook initiatives to free books, art, and films from customs charges so that they could circulate in different countries but simultaneously took steps to enforce international copyright regulations.[205] The mobility of books, film, and art brought with it the territorialization of art as property. Further, UNESCO's mobilization of terrains of culture arguably contributed to the growth of a cultural industry that has foregrounded human suffering and personal experiences of hardship as a form of cultural recognition.

Indeed, at the end of the Cold War era, this branch of the cultural industry would repeatedly raise issues of human rights via memoirs, films, and novels.[206] Just Like Ernest Hemingway's use of Gustavo Durán as a protagonist in his realist novel about the Spanish Civil War, or Turkish author Peyami Safa's call to pay more attention to sociology and the novel because fiction can realistically capture the social dynamics of an era, a culture industry that blended these approaches further developed, calling attention to human pain and suffering. That culture industry arose as a means to raise questions about violations of rights, and gradually become very visible, especially in the 1980s and afterward.

In Turkey, among notable works on the population exchange that author Kemal Yalçın has described as "documentary novels," are Yalçın's *The Entrusted Trousseau*, which tells the story of the author's search in Greece for the owner of the trousseau entrusted to his family right before their Greek Orthodox neighbors were deported as part of the 1923 exchange, as well as *The Great Separation* (*Büyük Ayrılık*) by Kemal Anadol, a former deputy from the mainstream national secularist party CHP (Cumhuriyet Halk Partisi, or Republican People's Party). During my interview with Anadol in his office in the Turkish parliament, he told me that he sought an actual family affected by the 1923 exchange in order to construct a realistic depiction of history and thereby demonstrate the human suffering caused by forced migration. In many ways, contemporary works carry out Turkish sociologist Fındıkoğlu's suggestion to record the oral history of the exchangees and to note their suffering and nostalgia for their lost homeland.

In addition, during my interviews with some documentary filmmakers from Turkey and Greece—whose names I shall keep confidential—I have been told that today special set ups are being used to illustrate the suffering and pain, because this helps increase the ratings. On the other hand, other documentary filmmakers mentioned they were so moved that their eyes teared up when discussing the suffering they encountered during the oral history interviews they conducted with exchangees. From efforts of visibility to realism, some aspects of the post-1980 Turkish culture industry resonate with the broader dynamics of mobilizing culture in the name of raising questions about displacement and rights violations, and in some cases, like those documentary filmmakers who accentuated suffering in order to raise ratings, they also commodify pain. Schmitt's "Appropriation/Distribution/Production" thus anticipates the contemporary neoliberal mode of "progress" that configures culture as a site for promoting social peace and coexistence, and simultaneously turning this promotion into a terrain of production and consumption.

· PART II ·

OF ORIGINS AND "MEN"

Family History, Genealogy,

and Historicist Humanism Revisited

Memory is not an instrument for exploring the past, but rather a medium. It is the medium of that which is experienced, just as the earth is the medium in which ancient cities are buried. He who seeks to approach his own buried past must conduct himself like a man digging. . . . Memory must therefore yield an image of the person who remembers, in the same way a good archaeological report not only informs us about the strata from which its findings originate, but also gives an account of the strata which first had to be broken through.

Walter Benjamin, "Excavation and Memory," ca. 1932

Heritage and Family History

"WHERE IS YOUR CAMERA?" asked my interlocutor, whom I shall call Fuat, as we were about to enter his home museum. Surprised, I realized he wanted me to photograph his museum—set up on the second floor of his house. I rushed back downstairs to pick up my camera and when I joined him in the room, "Here!" he said, opening his arms as if to embrace the objects on display. We were in Cunda (pronounced "Djunda"), a tiny isle connected to mainland Turkey with a bridge, and only a short ferry trip away from the Greek island of Lesbos. Happily situated in the Aegean, Cunda is home to ruins, old and new: it hosts an old church in ruins that used to belong to the now departed Greek Orthodox residents, and the region is surrounded by ancient ruins, such as the remains of Troy. I was in Cunda in 2004 and 2005, to conduct research and interview those affected by the 1923 Greek-Turkish compulsory religious minority exchange. Fuat was one of my interlocutors during that time, and he had invited me to see his home museum after my second visit.

The museum contained objects related to Fuat's family: garments, a silver tea set and silver spoons, embroidery, lace, a purse, pictures, Ottoman documents, a map of Crete, and a framed photo of a boat. Underneath the photo, a carefully typed caption explained that it was the boat that brought Muslims from Greece to Turkey during the exchange of religious minorities between Greece and Turkey. This home museum was set up as a space of recollection to inform visitors and to display the experience of the exchange through family objects and heritage.

Fuat was born in Crete but had left the island with his family as part of the 1923 Greek-Turkish population exchange. Many Muslims from Crete and Lesbos were located in Cunda and Ayvalık—the town that connects Cunda to mainland Turkey. Today, the same path between Greek islands, in particular Lesbos, and the Turkish shores are again a hotbed of displacement: this time it is Syrian refugees who try to follow the same path secretly at night—not unlike some of the Greek Orthodox who had to flee from the same spot during the war that led to the 1923 exchange.

At the time we met, Fuat had become a local celebrity because of the numerous oral history interviews he had given on the population exchange to journalists, documentary filmmakers, and scholars—including myself. His response to the then recent interest in the exchange and, duly, to the requests to meet with him had been to adopt the position of what I call the "ethnohistorical informant." Assuming this position casts elder members of a family as sources of information about familial and geographic origins and history, with implications for their cultural background. In this case, this subject position was materialized in the form of Fuat's recently set up home museum. As for the escalating number of requests to interview Fuat at the time, it is in fact symptomatic of the broader dynamics of that period.

Personal excavations of familial pasts and the discovery of different family backgrounds marked the 1990s and early 2000s.[1] These acts of recollection mobilized memory work such as memoirs, museums, and family histories. Excavated family histories were made public thanks to personal efforts or institutional projects developed by publishing houses or nongovernmental organizations (NGOs) such as the History Foundation/Tarih Vakfı and the Foundation of Lausanne Treaty Emigrants/Lozan Mübadilleri Vakfı (hereafter Emigrants' Foundation). Family backgrounds entangled in Greek-Turkish shared histories were among the most frequently revisited in that context.

Given the factors such as emigration, policies of resettlement, biopolitics, and conversions that have long left their historical imprint on Turkey—especially if we also count the Ottoman era—there are as many different backgrounds to be discovered as there are families to discover them. Consider the stories of Raşit Kemali Bonneval, the Dönme, the Kıptî, the Macedonians—as referred to by Ziyaeddin Fahri Fındıkoğlu when he conducted research on them—and Fuat among others, all of whom came from remarkably different backgrounds, attesting to the diversity of the exchangees. Such acts of recollection thus contributed to the dissemination of discourses of diversity, even if indirectly. These dynamics, however, were hardly confined to Turkey.

A so-called memoir boom marked the post–Cold War era.[2] This trend was accompanied by the international rise of neoliberalism and its emphasis on the individual, as well as the popularization of discourses of liberal multiculturalism and diversity. UNESCO-supported cultural policy at the time foregrounded diversity and thus contributed to this process. In academia, these dynamics resonated with the "cultural turn" that marked the humanities and social sciences in the 1980s and 1990s.[3] In short, in Turkey, like elsewhere, personal stories and histories were configured as cultural or collective memory.[4] For the most part, they were coded as attesting to cultural identification and as testimonials of atrocities and oppression. These are very important endeavors toward unmasking how dispossession—and different forms of violence embedded in it—affected individuals and their families. Symbolic acts of reclaiming material dispossession through family heritage, they also fit into the individual rights paradigm of the liberal human rights regime.

The oppressive aftermath of the 1980 military coup was a difficult period in which to articulate alterity or dissidence in public within the Turkish context. In such settings, reclaiming family heritage and identification was construed as emancipation, a question of liberal rights. In the 1980s, state officials sought to configure Turkishness heavily informed by an interpretation of Sunni Islam as a unifying national ideology: the Turkish-Islamic synthesis. Islam was also to be centrally controlled with a tight secularist grip on religious practices. While the Turkish-Islamic synthesis was implemented within the parameters designated by the military and military-supported bureaucrats, historically it has been a concept that has shaped different policies and discourses of cultural identification in Turkey.

Demographically, for instance, the Turkish-Islamic synthesis has long been an official policy. As discussed earlier, the 1923 exchange was an important step toward generating a Muslim majority that would then be Turkified—a process called "integration" in the 1950s. Discursively, novelist Peyami Safa's work—along with the work of others such as Turkist sociologist Ziya Gökalp—contributed to further developing the notion of a Turkish-Islamic synthesis. After the 1980 military coup, this cultural framing rearticulated historicist humanism as a synthesis of Turkishness and Sunni Islam, and forged an assimilation policy accompanied by an aggressive discipline-and-punish campaign launched against alterity and dissidence. Reinforced by military authoritarianism, assimilation, demographic policies, and brutal oppression were widespread.

The cumulative efforts of NGOs, publishers, and music producers punctured the post-1980 military coup climate of oppression, and gradually opened modest public spaces for the articulation of difference. Concomitantly, music, food, memories, and personal stories of historical events surfaced in the public domain—configured as evidence of what survives obstructive state policies. In the 1980s and 1990s, state officials did show varying degrees of hostility against such initiatives.[5] These officials included but were not confined to members of the judiciary, law enforcement, the military, as well as some politicians. It is important to remember that after the coup, bureaucracy was reorganized and people representing undesirable ideologies—mostly from the spectrum of what is generically called the left—were largely purged. It is against this backdrop that music albums, film, cookbooks, memoirs, and novels contributed to the "memoir boom" in Turkey. The boom popularized the positioning of individuals as ethnohistorical informants whose stories were valued as personal accounts of rights violations and segregative biopolitics.

By the end of the Cold War era, the field of culture was mobilized to circulate personal and familial accounts of hardships suffered because of state policies. These stories and memories have been popularized as personified accounts of historical events.[6] Since then, audiences have often been invited to read and engage them as an expression of a collective experience related to one's background or designated origins—as was the case with the 1923 exchange. Such emphasis on individualized accounts—as representative of the experiences of a larger group who share a similar background—is congruous with the emphasis on individual rights. The growth of a culture industry around these issues has arguably contributed to the dynamic of engaging policies implemented against a particular group—as categorized bodies—through individual cases.

By the mid-2000s, (re)collecting family narratives, objects, and documents would become a common practice for self-identification.[7] Engagements with the 1923 exchange constitute a good example for this trend in Turkey. Tracing family histories, genealogies, and designated origins has therefore been configured as cultural recognition—promoted as a liberal value. It is in this context that the family history of Raşit Kemali Bonneval was made public, alongside others, as a testament of past events such as the 1923 exchange. My interlocutor Fuat's home museum ought to be considered against this backdrop. He prepared a room in his house for visitors as complementary to his stories about Crete and Cunda, their remains, and ancient ruins. His home museum can be construed as a materialization of these broader dynamics: within the space of his home, he reclaimed his family's dispossession through displaying the objects from a past life in Crete—the remains—reconfigured as family history and heritage. In the contemporary Turkish context, legacies of the 1923 appear to be rendered legible mostly through the lens of memory and cultural heritage. This is the topic of the first essay in this part, which examines the implications of tracing genealogy and designated origins.

Heritage Trips and Ruins from the Past

For some of the exchangees and their family members, recollection included heritage trips to designated maps of family origin. In the early 2000s, one of my interlocutors—whom I shall call Ayten—took a symbolic heritage trip to Hania (also transliterated as Chania in the Latin alphabet), a town located on the Greek island of Crete. The elders of her family had died before she developed an interest in family history and could ask them the details about her family's past. When I asked why she did not ask the elders when they were still alive, she said that she was "ignorant then, and not curious about such things." Whether this lack of previous interest is really "ignorance," or simply an outcome of the fact that family history did not have the same significance when Ayten was growing up, is open to question. Deprived thus of an "ethnohistorical informant" in her family, the family's history was not legible to Ayten. A few family photos that remained did not give her any clues, and so, finally she decided to take a trip to Hania, where she knew her family came from. Upon her arrival in Hania, she asked around in a desperate attempt to find people who knew her family, but in vain. All she knew was her family's nickname, and that they were from Hania.

In the absence of a family elder, she thus turned to the residents of Hania as possible informants. Her hope was to locate a former neighbor of her family or at least someone who knew of them. Speaking to some residents, she found herself in Splantzia, an abandoned neighborhood where, she was told, Muslims used to live. Splantzia is very close to the highly manicured touristic areas. Going around the buildings and houses, mostly in ruins, Ayten told me she felt deeply moved to find what she called her "roots"—even though it had become clear she would not find what she had come to look for: her family home, or at least people who knew her family. What she found, instead, were the traces of a community long gone, and ruins attesting to their past lives in Hania.

Some other exchangees took organized trips. For instance, the late Fuat was taken on a heritage trip to Crete by a documentary filmmaker. The filmmaker was planning on filming Fuat's journey to the island where he was born. But things did not go as planned. Upon their arrival in Crete, a Greek resident of the island who heard Fuat's family tale decided to help him. Together, they located Fuat's family home left behind decades earlier, which actually was the whole point of the trip for Fuat. But the filmmaker was not present to film these reportedly moving scenes and was therefore frustrated. The filmmaker was hoping that capturing the moment of Fuat finding his family home would give viewers an opportunity to relate to the pain and suffering of displacement, as a message against forced migration.

Resonating with UNESCO's and, to a certain extent, AER's earlier efforts, documentary films can be powerful visual tools for calling attention to the human consequences of segregative biopolitics. Depending on how it is done, centerstaging the human can be helpful in terms of putting human faces on events. Translating statistics—like the ones shared at the AER—into human stories is key to humanizing the outcomes of dehumanizing policies—such as moving people around as if they were pieces on a chessboard. The stories of what remains, however, are not necessarily considered as ties that connect the past and the present beyond the human element. In such engagements, it is therefore important not to insulate biopolitics like the 1923 exchange and anchor pain in a past event. In Turkey and beyond, often the only connection made with present biopolitical policies is the now-sloganized abstract statement, "Never again." Yet again, and again, it happens.

The legibility of remains is yet another matter. For instance, in the early 2000s, the son of a deceased woman—originally from Greece but deported by the Greek government and sent to Turkey for resettlement because she was Muslim and therefore subject to the 1923 Greco-Turkish population exchange—went to Hania to find his mother's house. I shall call him Kerim. Kerim was in his sixties and the time had come to revisit his mother's past, or as he put it during our interview, his roots.[8] He had all the right directions his authoritarian aunt—his mother's sister—had minutely described. And early one morning, he went to the shore, turned his back to the still-standing mosque, and started walking, following his aunt's directions.

Before long, he found his mother's house. Deeply moved, he knocked on the door and an elderly Greek woman opened it. Before he could say anything, Kerim burst into tears in front of the astounded woman. He explained that this used to be his mother's house and the reason why she had to leave. The Greek woman, who herself was originally from Turkey and had been deported during the exchange, was deeply moved; she welcomed him inside her home. Things followed one another, and before they knew it, they were both drunk with ouzo and it was not until late afternoon that he left. Grateful to the Greek woman who opened her house, her heart, and a big bottle of ouzo, Kerim told me he felt he was finally in touch with his roots. With great joy, he rushed to call his aunt in Turkey to tell her the story. However, as soon as the word Hania came out of his mouth his aunt interrupted him, yelling and asking him what on earth he thought he was doing in Hania? She had told him very clearly, she said, Kandiye, that's where they were from: Kandiye. Not Hania. What was he doing there?

"Imagine," he told me during our interview, "had my aunt also died, I would have never known where I went was not where my roots grew [*köklerimin büyüdüğü yer*]." It appears that not only was he in the wrong house, but also in the wrong town. Yet, does this make his experience in that house less real? Kerim told me that after this, he did not want to go and find the real home of his mother, because he thought "it would not be the same." When I asked about why he chose to go to Crete then and not before, Kerim responded that Crete had always been present in the family but that lately he felt the island was calling him. Crete might have always been present in Kerim's family, because he did indeed speak Greek with the Cretan dialect that he had learned from his family. The fact that he didn't know his mother's hometown, however, suggests that the details of his family history might have been a rather recent interest.

This anecdote illustrates broader tensions between the position of "ethnohistorical informant"—in this case the aunt—and attempts at rebuilding a personal past from ruins, from what remains. These attempts in turn get attached to broader narratives of cultural background and heritage, turning the question of legibility into a matter of cultural identification. In recent years, the Emigrants' Foundation has organized such heritage trips for exchangees. Many younger-generation exchangees who joined these and other heritage trips relied on the narratives of their family members as ethnohistorical informants who provided a narrative compass to find their way to lost homes, homesteads, and neighborhoods and villages.

Overall, tracing genealogies and origins can be powerful tools to address cultural identification. Genealogy—identification through tracing designated origins and filiation—enables self-identification articulated in terms of cultural heritage. In that regard, addressing cultural identification through tracing one's genealogy and origins might offer a bottom-up "democratization" of history writing and self-identification, posited against assimilationist policies and identifications. In that respect, self-identification is often configured as self-determination on a personal level. On the other hand, the very same concepts can become tools used to achieve opposite ends—that is, nationalist gatekeeping and policing origins with racialized implications, often informed by popularized discourses of historicist humanism. One should bear in mind, therefore, that these notions can be mobilized for entirely different, and in fact contradictory, purposes.

Given the dynamics explored so far, how does one address the legacies of the 1923 exchange, an important case of segregative biopolitics? What are the broader implications of pursuing remains and ruins as a means of reconsidering segregative biopolitics?

Ruins and Ruination

For the purposes of this book, I consider ruins a palimpsest of fragments that have survived time both metaphorically and literally. Within the context of the 1923 exchange, the most revisited fragments include, but are not confined to, testimonies, family objects, artifacts, music, buildings, architecture, memories, and food. Whether these remains are people who get reconfigured as ethnohistorical informants via oral history, objects that get collected, recollected, and displayed—such as in Fuat's home museum—or buildings and remains of family homes, they have contributed to tracing family histories via genealogy and designated maps of origin. It appears that in the contemporary context, segregative biopolitics is predominantly legible in cultural and personal terms, but the logics and histories that informed such policies in the first place, as well as the tools deployed in that process, are not necessarily parsed.

Of course, these excavations—collecting family histories or making cultural heritage claims—are very important and meaningful endeavors toward cultural recognition. Unfortunately, their efficacy in unearthing the underlying logics of segregative biopolitics is limited. To accompany such narratives, what is needed are additional projects to unearth these entangled logics and rewriting the particular case into the broader picture, thus treating it as more than just an instance of forced migration. In other words, a comprehensive and interconnected archaeology of knowledge of the paradigms, practices, experiences, and policies embedded in segregative biopolitics is imperative. Meanwhile, the categorization and hierarchization of bodies informed by racialized thinking continue to spawn biopolitical policies.[9] Historicist humanism is an important part of this process; it has long offered a cultural history paradigm to justify the indexing and redistribution of peoples. The sites of excavations and the narrativization of the excavated thus matter; it is important to relate past and present policies as well as the discourses and tools that inform them.

The works of critical theorist Walter Benjamin and anthropologists Ann Stoler and Yael Navaro are helpful in considering these dynamics.[10] Benjamin argues that allegories and ruins are comparable in that what a ruin represents in the realm of things is similar to what an allegory represents in the realm of thought.[11] In their co-edited book, *Ruins of Modernity*, critics Julia Hell and Andreas Schönle consider ruins in terms of the disruption between form and content, because, according to them, a ruin has lost its past meaning or function in the present. Navaro takes ruination as a metaphor and explores spatial and material melancholia through the remains of the partition of Cyprus. Their work is helpful when considering the changes ascribed to the notion of ruins and the affect associated with ruination in the postwar era.

According to Benjamin, in the ruin history has physically merged into the setting. He argues that when history becomes part of the setting as in a tragic drama, it does so as a script. Ruins, then, I propose, embody history and setting at once, but also a promise for the possibility of uncovering more if excavated. The very act of excavation, as well as the motivation behind it, attributes new meanings to ruins and remains. Whether it is a literal or metaphoric archaeology—such as recollection—excavating ruins has a symbolic and historical significance.

In an attempt to explore the ongoing relationship between colonial pasts and presents, anthropologist Ann Stoler suggests a consideration of the residues that persist and that are reproduced, as well as the processes that enable this.[12] She proposes to study the sites and circumstances of dispossession and how they are addressed in other terms, and as dissociated from imperial histories. Accordingly, ruins are primarily what people are left with—even though material ruins are also considered—and ruination is an ongoing process of imperial formation that operates via "racialized relations of allocations and appropriations."[13] Ruination, then, continues under different guises.

Given the scope of this book, unraveling these relations helps us pursue the popular modes of addressing ruins in cultural terms, and raise questions about processes of ruination in relation to different case histories of segregative biopolitics. In that respect, historicization and the social, cultural, and political analyses of particular cases, including the 1923 exchange, are extremely important. They allow us to see how each particular case operates and why. It is equally important, however, to *also* address their interconnections and relations to segregative biopolitics over time and space. Biopolitics has long informed different policies with regard to alterity, mobilized in the name of social order and stability—or as these notions are often articulated today, in the name of national security.

With this in mind, I now turn to the local dynamics in post-coup era Turkey, a time that coincides with the end of the Cold War, to consider the contexts in which what remains becomes valued, personalized, and inscribed in terms of family history, which in turn configures these remains as witnesses, stories, practices, or objects that evince cultural heritage.

The History Foundation: Democratization of History Writing and Plurality

In the 1990s and early 2000s, at the intersections of neoliberal policies, corruption scandals, on-going armed conflicts with the PKK, forcible disappearances, torture, internal forced migration, and the Kurdish claims for recognition and autonomy, the very concept of history took center stage in Turkey.[14] Widely circulated,[15] numerous documentary novels and films, memoirs, and family histories have invited their audiences to raise questions about nationalist historiography and to consider eyewitness accounts as alternative stories to reconsider the past. Perhaps one of the most revisited pasts in that context was the population exchange. The seeming symmetry between Greece and Turkey—in that there were at least two states accountable for the exchange instead of one—might have made the 1923 exchange a relatively easy topic for addressing alterity and exclusion.

The Turkish context might have its own local idiosyncrasies, but generally speaking, it was in synchrony with what was happening internationally. With the rise of the neoliberal world order, social and economic rights symptomatically and gradually received lesser attention in public, while individual rights were more and more accentuated.[16] In this period, cultural and political rights increasingly became synonymous with human rights. In addition, the emphasis on the individual resonates with the UN's adoption of individual rights, the liberal endorsement of individualism, and the more recent dissemination of the neoliberal logic that similarly favors individualism. Unsurprisingly, personal memories, stories, and accounts received considerable publicization as a means of addressing rights violations. They were largely configured as a way to promote plurality.[17]

Yet, plurality was not necessarily observed in other venues, such as economic policies or citizenship rights. This entailed, for example, ending government subsidization of small businesses and farmers, which de facto went against maintaining a plurality of business owners, in order to strengthen existing larger companies so that they could become stronger and internationally competitive. To enable their growth, what followed was the crippling of the rights of labor organizations, such as unions, which in turn contributed to the elimination of the power of dissidence, hence plurality.[18] Moreover, the accumulation of capital also entailed dispossession—for the most part of minorities.[19] Overall, the configuration of plurality did not necessarily extend to other fields—the political or economic—and remained a vastly culturally articulated phenomenon, with little restitution of other rights or demands.

A symbolic struggle for restitution occurred within the field of history. One of the key institutions in that regard is the History Foundation—an NGO founded in 1991 and initially funded by EU-related organizations and the Rockefeller Foundation. In 2006, the History Foundation's website declared that it aims to involve "ordinary people" in history writing and "endeavors to help the Turkish people form a direct, truly comprehensive and non-instrumentalist relationship with their own history and to make the subject of their own history a field for civic action."[20] Involving ordinary people in the process of history writing also enhances the "democratization value" of these endeavors, as history written from the bottom up. The efforts of the foundation are symptomatic of the reconfiguration of the relationship between individuals and history. This reconfiguration is very important in that it seeks to go beyond the previously uniformly identified national body and its genealogy.

To that aim, one of the initiatives was the Oral History Collection Project launched by the History Foundation in 2002, entitled "A Thousand Live Witnesses to History." This project calls on people in Turkey to join in the initiative of telling their life stories with the slogan "We don't lose [the stories embodied in a person], because we record [them]!" Every Sunday one oral history account was published in the popular national newspaper *Milliyet*. These accounts also incorporated stories of the Greek-Turkish population exchange, including an oral history interview with Fuat. This oral history initiative speaks to rebuilding the past from its remains. The remains here are the individuals cast as informants whose stories need to be recorded before they are lost.

The visual presentation of the poster that invited participation in the oral history project embodies the configuration of each person as informant: it is composed of black and white photos of anonymous faces placed side by side. In the poster, there are no bodies, only faces and most importantly eyes, catching the viewer's attention as they seemingly stare at him or her—reemphasizing their eyewitness value. These individuals are not presented to the audience as a whole, for who they are, but for what they can tell us about what they saw, while the black-and-white presentation of the photos invites the spectator to think about the past, which these witnesses presumably can reveal. In other words, each person is presented as a historical informant. Of course, valuing personal narratives as eyewitness accounts doesn't mean that individual narratives didn't exist before; travel literature, for one, has historically cast the author as an informant of the traveled geographies.[21] What appears to be different in this case is the reach and accessibility of ordinary people's personal histories, and the value attributed to them as informants because of the political context.

For the most part, in a concerted effort, the History Foundation sought to render the past legible at a personal level, gradually puncturing the state-sponsored national history narratives reemphasized after the 1980 coup. The foundation's earlier initiatives should thus be considered against the backdrop of the aggressive military junta campaign to establish "national unity" at the expense of rights, plurality, and democratic values, and its aftermath. The History Foundation's efforts can be construed as an attempt to address the ruination of national formations—largely informed by biopolitics—in order to rebuild a bottom-up history from the remains, and to render it legible from a more personalized perspective. The efforts of the foundation have been of great value in trying to change the status quo after the coup.

Concomitantly, an observable boom in Ottoman script and language courses marked the late 1990s and early 2000s. After the Republican reform movement toward the Latinization of the alphabet and Turkification of the language, it is not a secret that most individuals in contemporary Turkey are not equipped to read or understand documents written before the modification of the alphabet in 1928. Being able to read Ottoman—a sort of a creole of Arabic, Persian, and Turkish written with Arabic script—thus constituted another step toward personal literacy of the past, only this time it was literally a question of literacy.

National newspapers advertised different courses on this topic. One Ottoman language course was organized by the History Foundation and publicized with the personalized slogan "Dedemin mektuplarını, anılarını okumak istiyorum" (I want to read my grandfather's letters and memoirs).[22] This course advertisement thus reminds us of the significance of access to family history. The public was invited to join the campaign and learn how to read and understand Ottoman—that is, to gain literacy in the Ottoman past, with a personal slogan, reminding individuals in Turkey that they do not have access to their family documents, such as letters, notebooks, and diaries.

This invitation was a call to claim family history through unlocking the remains with the necessary linguistic skills. The History Foundation's call thus emphasized the value of family documents, and simultaneously reconfigured the relationship with the past—as a site to be reclaimed—and personalized history. In turn, gaining access to these documents—if there are any in the family's possession—would facilitate the tracing of family origins and histories. In many ways, having the necessary language skills and the configuration of the familial objects and documents as valuable remains were important steps in the process of articulating family histories and thus different family backgrounds.

Expanding its scope, the History Foundation also organized a series of family-history-writing competitions at the high school level. For example, on July 12, 2003, *Radikal*, a popular newspaper of the time, announced the foundation's high school history-writing competition with the title "History Begins with the Family" and called attention to the difficulty in tracing family background with the phrase "Anything beyond grandfathers is a myth." The newspaper dedicated a large space to the competition and displayed photos of the three student winners of the contest. One of the winners, Gizem Koşanoğlu, a sixteen-year-old high school student in Izmir/Smyrna, won the third prize, which meant about 60 USD and a book:

> When I first heard about the [family history] competition, I thought it was very interesting. Up until then, I had never been curious about my family. Even though we know all about . . . big wars, dynasties, and military battles, very few of us know where our grandmothers and grandfathers actually come from. So, one weekend, my grandfather and I sat down together, and found many old photographs, marriage certificates, and documents. He took out his old record player and cameras. I didn't know my grandfather's mother was Jewish, and that my grandfather loved singing. Getting to know my grandfather changed my perspective on my family. At least, I now have gained a grandfather.

That Koşanoğlu did not know her great-grandmother was Jewish raises questions about the scale of assimilation and visibility of the remarkable diversity of Turkey's peoples. Koşanoğlu's statement manifests the potential impact of family history on self-identification. She claims to have gained a grandfather after she got to know his background, history, and the things he enjoys. In that light, the family history competition marked a particular historical moment in the Turkish context which privileged family history as a means of cultural identification.

The historian who led the family-history competition campaign of the History Foundation in collaboration with Istanbul Bilgi University was Mete Tunçay. His statement was also published in the newspaper. According to Tunçay, during the family-history-writing competition, students from minority backgrounds had come forward and appeared less reluctant to publicly articulate their differences. He considered this to be a visible change in the ability to articulate alterity publicly, especially in comparison to before. To emphasize the change he perceived, he noted that "there are some who even write that there are crypto-Jews [Dönme] in their families."[23] As mentioned, a large group of Dönme had arrived to Turkey as part of the Greek-Turkish population exchange. "Secrecy" is a trait that is often associated with the members of this group.[24] Following the arrival of the Dönme in Turkey, members of this community have often been targets of suspicion, as historian Marc Baer asserts. This might be the reason Tunçay expressed a surprise element—"even"—when he mentioned how new generations of high school students are willing to discuss their family's background.

Newspapers promoted the family history competition on their pages, but also targeted readers beyond high school students. On March 3, 2003, *Akşam Canteen* asked its readers to consider sitting in front of their family photo album and tracing their "roots" (*kökler*) through these pictures. Accompanying the call for the competition, a small text box in the corner of the page gave brief, instruction-manual-like directions on how to write a family history. This suggests an attempt to popularize family history beyond high school students.

The History Foundation was perhaps the most visible but not the only institution that encouraged unearthing family histories and tracing origins. An escalating number of books, movies, and music albums communicated and sought to "reintroduce" Turkey's people to one another, bringing the stories of past and present peoples of Turkey into the public domain and simultaneously raising retrospective questions in an attempt to retrieve oppressed stories and draw lessons for the future. Overall, initiatives to unearth personal pasts and backgrounds through family histories have contributed to the growth of a culture of memory and to the articulation of alterity in Turkey. These efforts also sought to unearth stories and remains publicly buried under state policies of segregative biopolitics, violence, and forced assimilation.

Personal Excavations: Unearthing Family Histories and Origins

In addition to the projects of the History Foundation and the Emigrants' Foundation, various personal stories published or made into film contributed to the articulation of cultural identification. These stories often trace family origins and address different aspects of alterity, policies, and violence that targeted different groups via family histories. Some well-known examples include Yorgo Andreadis's *Tamama: The Lost Daughter of Pontus*, which tells the story of a young Muslimized Pontic-Greek girl, Tamama, rescued and adopted by a Muslim family. Tamama's identity was kept secret for decades. Later, following the discovery of her true background, Turkish filmmaker Yeşim Ustaoğlu made a film inspired by this book called *Waiting for the Clouds*. Another example is Fethiye Çetin's memoir *My Grandmother*, recounting the hidden story of the author's grandmother, whom she discovered to be Armenian. More recently Çetin collaborated with anthropologist Ayşe Gül Altınay and published *Grandchildren: The Hidden Legacy of "Lost" Armenians in Turkey*. While these stories narrate the discovery of suppressed family origins because of the political situation, they also raise crucial questions about what family heritage entails in situations of muted violence.[25] Tracing genealogies might help in addressing thorny matters, precisely because such family histories attest to state-sponsored violence and biopolitics.[26] They can be powerful tools to address massacres, genocide, or forcible disappearances from a personal point of view.

Public acknowledgment of such family stories is often framed in terms of the recognition of pain. Such limited recognition enables the bracketing of different communities—framing them in ways that do not generate a conflict with the state agenda. Further, narratives of family histories reveal the diversity of the so-called Muslim majorities of Turkey today. The popularization of tracing family origins narrativized as family history in the contemporary Turkish public domain, then, enables a personalized cultural identification. The question here, of course, is how far one is willing to go back in tracing genealogies to designate an origin to anchor one's cultural identification.

For example, a private family book traces the family background to a Venetian noble in Crete who converted to Islam when the Ottomans took over the island.[27] Later, the members of the family were deported during the population exchange. A large and elaborate family tree decorates the back of the book, with clear attempts to render the family genealogy traced back to Crete legible for the younger generations. In addition, the book includes recipes, oral traditions, and photographs of family members, objects, maps, as well as herbs from Crete to introduce the island into the repertoire of future generations. The book's layout is very similar to a museum like the one in Fuat's home, only in the form of print.

Historian Molly Greene argues that after Venice surrendered the island of Crete to the Ottomans in 1669, many Christians—among whom were numerous Venetians—converted to Islam and remained mostly Greek speakers. Because there was no large-scale resettlement of Muslims from the mainland, Greene believes that most of the Cretan Muslims were in fact those who converted to Islam from Christianity, apparently motivated by the desire to obtain a more beneficial status vis-à-vis the Ottoman rulers.[28] Following the 1923 Greco-Turkish population exchange, when the Cretan Muslims were "repatriated" to Turkey, not all of them spoke Turkish. One of my interlocutors from a different family, for example, told me during our interview that upon her arrival in Turkey after the exchange, because of her Greek accent, people in the marketplace and the street used to call her "Madam"—a term she associated with non-Muslims and therefore objected to on the grounds that she was "Muslim and not a Madam." Like religious or linguistic attributes, cultural identification is not always a straightforward or easy matter.

There are other family histories in print that circulate in the public domain. One such example revolves around recipe notebooks: *Salonika: A Family Cookbook*.[29] The book traces actress and translator Esin Eden's great-aunt's story to Salonika, Greece. The introduction, written by the late Nicholas Stavroulakis—author, artist, art historian, and cofounder and former director of the Jewish Museum in Athens—frames the family recipe notebooks as documents of cultural identification pertaining to the Dönme. During our interview, Stavroulakis told me about the difficulties of deciphering the Ottoman Salonika dialect, and how in order to unlock a text written in this dialect a specialist is needed.[30] The discussion on the difficulty of decoding the Ottoman Salonika dialect points to the significance of the History Foundation's initiative to teach Ottoman in order to gain access family documents. Only in this case, the gender emphasis is on female subjectivity—that is, recipes as opposed to a grandfather's letters, as was advertised in the History Foundation's Ottoman language courses. The historical introductions to the recipes, written by Avi Sharon and Nicholas Stavroulakis, configure the recipes as denominators of cultural identification via family heritage—the heritage in question here being culinary culture. Because little is known about the circumstances under which these recipes were inscribed, it is hard to guess whether the recipes were noted solely to preserve Salonika Dönme or family-cooking practices.

In short, family objects, photographs, and history narratives—whether displayed in a book format or in the physical space of a museum—reconfigure the relationship between individuals and history, with family members designated as informants of cultural identification. Hence, ethnohistorical informants. As population transfers, displacement, and forced migration de facto render the past less legible, museums display "what remains" in an attempt to inform their visitors. The scale of such displays differ widely, of course, ranging from home museums like Fuat's to the Population Exchange Museum (to be explored in Part Three). With their often handsomely decorated pages, family history books also contribute to the display of culture as heritage.

Family histories have thus circulated in different forms, including exhibitions. For example, for the ninetieth anniversary of the population exchange, the Emigrants' Foundation circulated a call for family photographs and objects to be displayed in an exhibition of family stories from both shores of the Aegean. The exhibition was planned to be itinerant, traveling in Greece and Turkey. In addition, as part of the commemoration of the population exchange in 2013, the exhibition catalog was printed in a coffee-table book format. The catalog includes family histories and photographs. When one opens this handsome volume, on the left-hand side, family stories from both sides of the Aegean are printed in both Greek and Turkish, and on the right, small family albums with a few photographs visually complement the family narratives. Under the photos on each page is a statement in both Greek and Turkish: "May the same suffering never be lived again!" With this exhibition, the laudable attempt of the Emigrants' Foundation to recollect the legacy of the population exchange extended its reach to the other side of the Aegean both in form and in content, and inscribed the stories of those who left within its commemorative exhibition. These efforts culminated in the personal rewritings of history through family connections, a step conducive to unearthing cultural heritage.

Archaeology, Origins, and the Bodily Implications of Genealogy

Over the last two decades, then, a symbolic and literal archaeology of knowledge has taken place in Turkey's public domain, and for the most part, it remains an incomplete project on both counts. Family histories have been an integral part of it, yes, but depending on their context, they have had different implications. For example, some of the recently publicized, painful family histories illustrate how official policies broke up families—an instance of ruination—helping unearth the remains of state-sponsored violence and atrocities including genocide, forced migration, and forced disappearances.

On the other hand, excavation of some mass graves has constituted an important aspect of the archaeology of knowledge in the most gruesome, physical sense.[31] For instance, in 2013, the Diyarbakır branch of the Human Rights Association (İnsan Hakları Derneği) launched a project entitled the Losses Are Our Past, Let's Face Our Past (*Kayıplar Geçmişimizdir, Geçmişimizle Yüzleşelim*) to document the exhuming of bodies in mass graves. The project highlights a continuing practice of mass inhumation, including the bodies of the forcibly disappeared—Kurds—left to oblivion in anonymous graves particularly since the 1980 military coup.[32] In this process, while some graves have been exhumed, this project too remains far from complete. In fact, at the time of writing this essay, not only was the process of excavation interrupted but also urban warfare and violence had erupted in the region.

All things considered, if cultural identity recognition entails "democratization"—as UNESCO's 1982 Mexico City Declaration on Cultural Policies asserted[33]—then yes, there was a relative democratization over the last two decades. Yet, it is also important to identify the parameters of acceptability in which such democratization is situated. These parameters simultaneously hierarchize the terms of articulating different aspects of alterity and related histories.[34] In addition, as discussed, from the onset of the Cold War, UNESCO has played a key role in configuring the field of culture as a site to promote peace and coexistence, with an emphasis on unity in diversity—identified as liberal humanism in this book.

What lies beneath the surface of this configuration, however, are policies of biopolitics that have continued to inform approaches to alterity. Upon ruins of biopolitics arise liberal discourses of culture; meanwhile, ruination continues. Cultural identification is construed as democratization and liberty—a correlation asserted in the 1982 UNESCO Declaration on Cultural Policies, and which has since been disseminated and developed into the UNESCO Universal Declaration on Cultural Diversity in 2001 and then the Convention on the Protection and Promotion of the Diversity of Cultural Expressions in 2005.[35]

In that context, genealogy and origins have been instrumental in making claims about one's self-identification, not only in Turkey but also elsewhere, with of course differing implications depending on the context and the community in question. Family histories in Turkey help us see beyond the singular nationalist genealogy ascribed to the Turkish national body politic. Altogether, they amount to efforts to write a bottom-up history of the peoples in Turkey, thus democratizing history.

However, precisely the same tools have been mobilized to counter such efforts with competing genealogizations. These include policing Turkish genealogy and ancestry or attempts at discrediting an individual, especially public figures or political dissidents, through public statements on "origins"—attributing to them Armenianness, Jewishness, or being Greek. Such racist approaches also highlight the "bloodline" as a means of explicating an act or figure deemed to be unpopular. In that respect, they demonstrate the resilience of racialized thinking.

For instance, headlines in various newspapers on December 18, 2008, asked whether Abdullah Gül, Turkey's president, was Armenian. Canan Arıkman, a deputy from the opposition party CHP, had claimed that Gül's mother was Armenian. A few days later, on December 21, Gül denied these claims and sought to establish his identification through his family's genealogy. Unfortunately, in a press release, instead of seizing the opportunity to engage the real problem of this issue—that is, essentialism and hate speech—he declared that his family has been Muslim and Turkish for centuries. In addition, in an impressive thirty-four-page-long PDF file, his family genealogy was made publicly available on a family-related website, which was to be construed as evidence that his family tree was free of Armenian origins.[36]

While the History Foundation and other organizations continued their efforts to render personalized histories legible within the context of Turkey via campaigns of family history that encouraged new generations to declare their backgrounds, the very same tools were thus being used to police genealogy and origins. Such approaches carry the traces of the eugenicist thought, scientific racialism, and historicist humanism embedded in modern Western European and North American intellectual histories and archives of knowledge. The eugenicist notion that one's blood determines one's character and that inherited character cannot be escaped—an approach that is reminiscent of German sociologist Karl Valentin Müller's—has thus prevailed. Similar campaigns have become commonplace, during which eugenicist approaches to genealogy and origins resurface in both discriminatory attacks and responses against those attacks.

When remains from the past are rendered legible through personal histories, they can be powerful tools to rethink the past. But when these personal histories are not coupled with a conscious attempt to reconsider violence and policies informed by the biopolitical logic, rethinking the past as such risks remaining at a very micro level and firmly anchored in the past. (This doesn't take away from the importance of the personal history, but does mark the necessity of connecting the past to the present-day concerns and dynamics in more explicit ways.) Such engagement might contribute to the bracketing of communities in matters that do not pose a threat to state agendas.[37] We can then observe state officials deploy conflicting discourses simultaneously.

For instance, when he was still prime minister, Recep Tayyip Erdoğan was similarly subjected to an "exposé" of his family origins. In response, right before the general elections of June 12, 2011, Erdoğan complained on the TV channel NTV: "We have been [called] Armenian, Jewish, and, forgive my language, Greek Orthodox. Can you imagine?" (ne Ermeniliğimiz, ne Yahudiliğimiz, ne affedersiniz Rumluğumuz, hiç bir şeyimiz kalmadı. Düşünebiliyor musunuz?).[38] On yet another occasion, during a visit to the United States in December 2009, he replied to a question about whether the anti-Armenian violence in 1915 was genocide with the following statement: "My ancestors did not commit genocide, they would do no such a thing" (Benim ecdadım soykırım yapmamıştır, yapmaz).[39] The ancestors here are Ottoman leaders, and rather than addressing the question within a historical, ethical, and legal framework, Erdoğan turns the question into one of denialism through heredity.[40] The notion of bloodline simultaneously implicates the moral character of the Turks today as well as their designated ancestors.

In short, eugenicist discourses of the body have direct implications for the policing of origins, reinforced by epistemes of historicist humanism that offer these discourses a historical and cultural framework. Concomitant with these racialized approaches are efforts to democratize history and generate an environment favorable for cultural recognition via genealogies and designated origins. This turns tracing filiation and genesis into a tool vulnerable to problematic use since it can be wielded in opposite and concurrent discourses that coexist: namely to make claims of different backgrounds and cultural identification, *and* to control and police articulated diversity.

One of the reasons for this vulnerability is because aside from its implications for familial and cultural heritage, genealogy can also have implications for lineage—bloodline, pedigree, and racialized origins. In fact, it is very much intertwined with the trope of the family of man—the racialized genealogical tree of humankind, the very image-concept and site of intervention of Edward Steichen's *The Family of Man*. Be that as it may, these dynamics do not reduce the significance of being able to address and articulate one's background and self-identification in public.

The ability to claim one's background through the family comes with intertwined histories and complicated experiences. In Turkey, NGOs and independent actors have worked for decades to make these claims public, especially after the 1980 coup. As for the vulnerability of genealogy and origins to racism, this is precisely a case in the point that I have argued in this book: these very valuable attempts to make backgrounds public was a crucial step, but beyond the individuals who traced their familial genesis, there is a necessity to develop additional frameworks that directly focus on the underlying segregative biopolitics and its logics to demonstrate the relatedness between different events, policies, and categorizations informed by these very logics. It is the biopolitical infrastructure, and its continuing relation to liberal cultural discourses, that have the potential to turn even the most laudable efforts into a racist policing of origins. This is a valid concern for Turkey and beyond.

The notions of genealogy and origins have historically had a direct impact on the categorization and hierarchization of different groups, which in turn have informed policies of regulating alterity—such as segregative biopolitics, violence, citizenship rights, and dispossession. The logic of racialized genealogies to designate someone as an undesirable subject has therefore not disappeared. Demographic concerns in terms of the regulation of categorized bodies and their numbers have also not disappeared. If not evident in state-sponsored policies, then they inform xenophobic discourses that resort to the demographic concern that white Europe, for instance, will disappear under a "floodtide" of immigrants. In that respect, concerns with numbers articulated in the AER circles in the 1950s are still relevant today.

In the second essay in this part, I turn my attention to addressing why origins and genealogy have completely different historical implications in terms of the relation of historicist humanism to segregative biopolitics. Clearly, different paradigms affect different communities in different ways, and the means of democratization for one group does not have the same implications for another, because they have been subjected to different biopolitical policies or violence at different moments in time. Addressing past experiences is important, but without the ability to weave them into present biopolitical campaigns, as well as violence and killings, the connections between the underlying logics remain missing, and "the past in the present" appears in terms of memory—construed as emancipation—and not in connection to ongoing policies and violence.

In order to demonstrate the value of the efforts described in the first essay, above, but also to show how it still remains an incomplete project in engaging legacies of segregative biopolitics and violence and the archives that inform them, I offer a relational reading between the two essays in this part. In that light, in the second essay, below, I explore multiple facets of historicist humanism and its pivotal role in human categorizations. For more than a century, historicist humanism has offered a cultural framework for biological categorization and hierarchization of race. As critic Anne McClintock has shown, the tree of the family of man was the visual trope that embodied the amalgam of the two paradigms—the cultural historical and the biological.[41] Tracing their residues diachronically, I revisit these paradigms and their broader implications. In addition to exploring how ruins of segregative biopolitics are thematically addressed through genealogies, designated origins, and heritage trips in the contemporary context, I therefore turn to excavation via genealogies and origins, and consider these forms in terms of historicist humanism.

Both family histories (the subject of the first essay) and historicist humanism (the subject of the second) have informed genealogized notions of cultural heritage with completely different political implications. Cultural policies and institutional interventions have sought to democratize the notion of heritage on a personal level (as discussed in the first essay), which implies cultural recognition. Considering the implications of these interventions meant to be positive in their own context enables us to question the scope of efficacy of institutional interventions, such as UNESCO's, in bringing recognition. This consideration also raises questions as to whether racialized thinking has truly disappeared from these paradigms of identification. Keeping this in mind, I now turn to the second essay in this part, to explore the historical implications of genealogies and origins in the archaeology of knowledge.

Origins, Biopolitics, and Historicist Humanism

IN THE 1980s, cultural identification received increasing attention and arguably contributed to the memoir boom. In this last decade of the Cold War, which also coincided with the rise of a neoliberal version of capitalism, UNESCO symptomatically underlined the importance of culture for development. This was another version of the organization's earlier interventions that sought to establish peace and coexistence via culture. UNESCO advocated the incorporation of cultural identification into cultural policy. This was because "in a world torn by dissensions," "cultural values of different civilizations" were considered to be in danger.[42]

The 1982 UNESCO Declaration on Cultural Policies defines "culture" both as the art and literature, *and* as the lifestyle, values, beliefs, and so on of a group, in addition to the fundamental rights of the human being. In that respect, this definition underscores the importance of "cultural identity" and anticipates the 2001 Universal Declaration on Cultural Diversity. The 1982 declaration highlights cultural identification claims as a form of emancipation and a sign of self-determination—all of which embody liberal values:

> The assertion of cultural identity therefore contributes to the liberation of peoples. Conversely, any form of domination constitutes a denial or an impairment of that identity.
>
> Cultural identity is a treasure that vitalizes mankind's possibilities of self-fulfillment by moving every people and every group to seek nurture in its past, to welcome contributions from outside that are compatible with its own characteristics, and so to continue the process of its own creation.
>
> All cultures form part of the common heritage of mankind. The cultural identity of a people is renewed and enriched through contact with the traditions and values of others. Culture is dialogue, the exchange of ideas and experience and the appreciation of other values and traditions; it withers and dies in isolation.

> The universal cannot be postulated in the abstract by any single culture: it emerges from the experience of all the world's peoples as each affirms it own identity. Cultural identity and cultural diversity are inseparable.
>
> ... The aim, above all, should be to open up new channels for democracy through equality of opportunity in education and culture.... The participation of all individuals in cultural life requires the elimination of inequalities based, inter alia, on social background and status, education, nationality, age, language, sex, religious beliefs, health or the fact of belonging to ethnic, minority or fringe groups.[43]

Here we see an early articulation of how asserting cultural identification is promoted as a contribution to "liberation" and "democratization." The statement foregrounds an agenda of liberal multiculturalism—a topic addressed in the Part Three. Resorting to those notions, the 1982 UNESCO declaration calls on state officials to introduce this cultural identity into their cultural policies. The 1982 declaration also correlates cultural identification with cultural heritage and liberalization as democratic values and underlines how every human being is entitled to cultural identity. In short, cultural identification and heritage are emphasized as a right.

This intervention might come across as paradoxical given how in the 1950s, UNESCO, like the AER and others, advocated the integration of emigrant and refugee communities in terms of cultural assimilation. After decades of efforts to align various groups with different nation-states—the alignment of so-called national refugees with their "proper" countries as a humane solution to conflicts—an effort that was pioneered by the 1923 Greek-Turkish population exchange in international law—the 1980s conversely opened a new trend of excavating, documenting, tracing, and claiming cultural identification as a sign of liberalization and democratization.

When considered from the point of view of emigrants and refugees, and not just minorities, the implications of UNESCO's call for cultural identity recognition as cultural policy become more evident. The very same institutions that previously embraced the logic of biopolitics that informed the spatial redistribution of peoples and considered their integration as a matter of cultural assimilation were now turning around to push nation-states to recognize alterity. It could be argued that at some point UNESCO officials recognized the brutal outcomes of nationalization and integration with the goal of assimilation. This doesn't mean local concerns with assimilation ended there. In fact, assimilation was one of the concerns of the Turkish-Islamic synthesis and the 1983 Turkish *National Cultural Policy Report*. (I analyze this report in the second essay of Part Three.)

UNESCO's call for the recognition of cultural identity is congruent with its previous support of liberal humanism. The 1982 Declaration on Cultural Policies calls for the acknowledgment of the particular, the culturally different. Some scholars appear to perceive this more recent call for cultural recognition as contradictory to UNESCO's previous approaches as well as the notion of unity in diversity. The universal appeal of liberal humanism is often cast as opposed to the recognition of the particular. Considering all the dynamics discussed so far, however, these discourses are not contradictory but complementary. What is universal is that all human beings have a cultural identity and a heritage. These particulars unify them in that regard. This approach is captured in a phrase from the 1982 declaration: "All cultures form part of the common heritage of mankind."

What we see here, however, is a blend of liberal humanism and historicist humanism, an amalgam of former modes of categorization in a manner that informs the liberal discourse of cultural identification and recognition. As mentioned, historicist humanism has long deployed genealogy and origins to categorize and hierarchize human groups in national, racial, and civilizational terms. Only this time, these modes of identification were supposed to be democratized, involving people themselves. This democratization is consistent with the family history and cultural heritage recollections of the exchangees in Turkey. As for UNESCO's 1982 declaration, it embodies a palimpsest of liberal and historicist humanisms, reinterpreted in a way that fits the then contemporary context. The structural paradigms of historicist humanism therefore resurfaces in contemporary cultural policy and racialist and racist discourses.

Today, cultural identification and recognition—explored in the essay above—contribute to a corrective of historicist humanism, such as essentialized national identities and hierarchized national cultures configured as monolithic entities, linearly traceable to a particular civilization. It is the very methods of identification built in historicist humanism—tracing origins and genealogies—that are being reproduced but with an emphasis on the particular, and therefore with different connotations.

Historicist Humanism, Civilization, and Heritage

> Greece has been the most spectacular [*éclatant*] theater in the development of humanity; coming out of the mysterious depths of the Orient [in this context, Asia Minor/Anatolia], it is a pleasure to address the ingenious land of Greece, and to salute the dawn of liberty in its manners and laws.
>
> Jean-Jacques Ampère, *La Grèce, Rome et Dante:*
> *études littéraires d'après nature*, 1850

Throughout the nineteenth and twentieth centuries, intellectuals, philologists, and scholars sought to trace the origins of different national cultures. The common heritage of humankind was construed as that of "civilization." National cultures, in turn, were configured in constellations, hierarchized in terms of their contributions to humanity via civilization. It is therefore important to note that this mode of humanism actually never disappeared, and continued to exist in different circles—including UNESCO and national cultural policies.

Humanism, of course, is a very rich term used by historians, philologists, archaeologists, and poets, among others, to refer to a wide range of practices in history.[44] In terms of the scope of this book, however, my focus here will be limited to modern cultural history. A closer look at sources from the nineteenth and twentieth centuries crystallizes a shared understanding that humanism is simultaneously universal and particular: while there appears to have been an understanding that there is a universally shared humanity, there was also an intellectual debate over which "national culture" contributed to the growth of a universal configuration of Humanity—in art, literature, but also in science—as well as the terms of that contribution.[45] This debate preoccupied intellectuals for at least two hundred years.

In addition, there appears to have been a consensus that there are designated golden ages of Humanity, such as ancient times. A glance at different sources reveals how the notion of a golden age was configured as the peak of Humanity—construed mostly as an achievement of Western Europe. These approaches situated nations in the racialized family tree of humankind and simultaneously hierarchized them. In this context, nation was a racialized term—aligned with civilization. Tracing a nation to its supposedly ancient origins—such as ancient Greece, Rome, or Persia—and making identification claims in terms of racial and civilizational belonging—primordialism—was a common practice. Overall, tracing civilizational genesis and filiation was an important tool for national culture identification in the European imaginary. These notions and methods were exported beyond Western Europe and disseminated worldwide.

Various philologists and intellectuals such as Heinrich Schliemann and Erich Auerbach embarked upon a similar project to historicize European identification anchored in ancient origins. To that end, Schliemann went digging in the Ottoman Aegean shores in 1871 and discovered the site of Homeric Troy.[46] And Auerbach, who studied realism as an attribute of so-called Western civilization, sought to trace its origins in literature during his exile in Turkey from Nazi Germany.[47] They revisited the figure whom they deemed to have greatly contributed to humanity: Homer. A centerpiece in the work of both Auerbach and Schliemann, Homer was configured as a genius in the Western European cultural memory in the nineteenth and, for the most part, the twentieth centuries.[48] Auerbach sought to show that realism was an attribute of Western civilization, traceable to the Homeric epics and Dante. As for Schliemann, his objective was to discover the city of Troy as depicted in the Homeric epics—in a location not so far from Cunda, where my interlocutor the late Fuat once lived and made his own amateur archaeological observations and expeditions to ancient ruins.

Historicist humanism has thus enabled cultural spaces—whether in narratives such as the Homeric epics or in material sites such as the ruins of Troy—to trace civilizational origins and hence to establish a shared heritage. Heritage included ancient ruins, the figure of an artistic or literary "genius" as representative of national culture, and by proxy, the nation's contribution to humanity.[49] These approaches configured humanity and civilization as Humanity and Civilization, as indicators of endorsement of a Eurocentric historicist humanism and an understanding of progress as linear. This approach prevailed in various forms throughout the twentieth century, during which many intellectuals and scholars sought to establish national "classics." Classics were configured as the best illustrations of a national culture and civilization and as a national contribution to the archive of humanity. Without naming it so, this was a concerted effort to recollect and identify the pillars of civilization, including literature, as relics of that heritage. It is therefore not only anthropologists, eugenicists, and race theorists who contributed to the configuration of civilizations—which informed racialized approaches to nations—but also philologists, archaeologists, and historians, including amateurs.

Concomitantly, in an attempt to culturally and historically situate a national culture within the hierarchized family tree of humankind, a soul searching was initiated in many countries, including Turkey. For instance, in Egypt in 1938, intellectual historian Taha Hussein wrote *The Future of the Culture of Egypt*, where he promoted the ancient Egyptian heritage.[50] In the late Ottoman and later Turkish context, a very comparable figure, historian Mehmet Fuat Köprülü, wrote about the origins of Turkish culture via literature.[51] Incidentally, Köprülü, as noted in Part One, was also the minister of foreign affairs who signed and approved Corrado Gini's work permit to teach in Turkey.

In Turkey, the search for national character thus mobilized historians, anthropologists, critics, sociologists, philosophers, artists and writers, as well as state officials. The founding of the government-sponsored Translation Bureau in 1940 epitomized the official support for such initiatives at the state level.[52] It was a cultural policy to translate world classics to make them widely accessible to Turkish-language readers. Some local intellectuals, like Hilmi Ziya Ülken, considered this move to be helpful for the local production of new classics. Later, the same cultural policy to translate classics would be adopted by UNESCO.[53] Indeed, in 1948, the inaugural issue of the *UNESCO Courier* announced that UNESCO was launching an initiative to translate the classics, and that it would establish an International Council of Philosophy and Humanistic Studies, because according to the *Courier*, "philosophers and humanists are not organized on an international scale, or at least not effectively."[54]

In Turkey, Hilmi Ziya Ülken and Peyami Safa—the president and vice president, respectively, of the Turkish Sociological Society—also contributed to the historical humanist project. In 1933, Ülken was appointed as the Associate Professor (*Doçent*) of Turkish Civilization (*Türk Medeniyeti*) at Istanbul University before he left for Berlin to continue his research on the subject.[55]

Later, adopting the idea that translation plays an important role in what he called national awakening periods, Ülken published a book in 1935 on translation and civilization entitled *Uyanış Devirlerinde Tercümenin Rolü: İslam Medeniyetinde Tercümeler ve Tesirleri* (The role of translation in the period of awakening: Translation and its impact on Islamic civilization).[56] In this book, one of Ülken's major concerns was to rethink Islamic heritage and exchanges with Europe. His endeavor was not unlike Peyami Safa's in the *East-West Synthesis (Doğu-Batı Sentezi)*. In fact, Safa's notion of synthesis was more creative in rethinking how exchanges are processed.

In that vein, Ülken published a magazine entitled *İnsan* (Human) between 1938 and 1943. One of the primary goals of the journal was to rethink the origins of the Turks, to establish their identity, and to locate a path for them to join world civilization. Indeed, in the first issue of the journal, published on April 15, 1938, Ülken explains the goal of the journal:

> What is the goal of the journal *İnsan*?
> The Turkish nation has been indecisively waiting between two worlds. It could see the technical superiority of the civilization it encountered; but it also did not abandon the values [*kıymetlerini*] of the old world. It was necessary to break out of the shell that obstructed it and to go deeper into the reasons why the West was superior, and the roots of that civilization.[57]

To that end, he proposed unearthing the contributions of Turks to history, opening the scope of the nation to the world. It is clear that in Ülken's mind, civilizations are hierarchized. It is also clear that the reasons for the progress that led to the superiority of the so-called West needed to be understood in civilizational terms. According to Ülken, it is also important to get to know one's own civilization and to bring about a Turkish renaissance—perceived as a natural outcome of awakening or soul searching. The idea is that each civilization had a golden age and that these needed to be closely studied to bring about one's own. Translation was instrumental in this process.

Ülken claims that in the process of finding themselves again, methods of the so-called West would guide the Turks ("Bu yolda kendimizi tekrar bulmak için garb metodları bize rehberlik edecektir").[58] He thus construed this as a search for an authentic self, a biologized core, that needs to be reactivated. As for the process of finding one's self, it is clear that the methods—tracing genealogy and origins, finding works of genius, studying the golden age—will be drawn from Europe. If we remember, this was precisely what Frantz Fanon had criticized.

Ülken's approach encapsulates how historicist humanism is intertwined with Eurocentric identifications. In 1938, in a later issue of *İnsan*, Ülken further elaborates on the issue of method:

> The only tool [*yegane vasıta*] to look at ourselves is to adjust our eye [*gözümüzü*] according to the advanced level of the world. Getting to know the West in depth, to accomplish our own Renaissance in the fields of thought and art, to translate [ancient] Greek [*Yunan*] and Roman [sources] in addition to the new Western [*yeni garb*] into our language are among the preparations for achieving that point of view [*bakış zaviyesini kazanma*]. In order to be creative in the civilization that we have just entered, we need to accept being the apprentice [*çıraklığını*] of that civilization first.[59]

Here, the Western European configuration of civilization appears to be dominant. This means collapsing European civilization with "universal" civilization—Civilization—and taking the "West" as the paradigm. Further, there is a temporality attributed to the notion of civilization itself, one that renders Western European civilization a universally recognized ideal and a promised future yet to be attained. Indeed, it is an evolutionary linearity of progress that is implicated here. Drawing from ancient Greek and Roman origins and the Renaissance as embodiments of the golden age of Humanity, Western Europe is configured as the master of humanity, with Turks being an apprentice of civilization. To some race theorists, the so-called Western ideal was only attainable if one had the right racial background.[60]

In addition to the ongoing translation of the classics and university-led translations of scientific and philosophical works in the 1930s, Ülken also proposed a qualitative study of the social formations informed by human exchanges with nature.[61] For Ülken, statistics alone were not enough to gain insight into social life. He therefore promoted qualitative research to supplement the quantitative in an attempt to capture the socialization of people in Turkey in relation to nature. He informed his readers that artists also joined the effort, and had started to study Turkey and the countryside, and that they would portray their findings.[62]

In addition to artists, critics, and scholars, novelists such as Peyami Safa were also important in the process of getting to know the national culture. Safa contributed to this endeavor with his novels, such as the 1931 novel *Fatih-Harbiye*, as well as nonfiction work such as *East-West Synthesis*. In 1940, the literary journal *Yücel* declared that it would dedicate its forthcoming issues to pieces that would serve the search for "finding one's self" in a humanistic manner ("humanism arayıcılığı ile kendimizi bulmak şeklinde hülasa edebileceğimiz gayeye uygun yazılar"). In response, critic Celaleddin Ezine argued that the humanistic endeavor was not new in Turkey.[63] (In terms of his own family history, Ezine was poet Nazım Hikmet's cousin and his family appears to have been the former owners of the mansion-turned-into-pension where Corrado Gini stayed when he came to teach at Istanbul University.) Some examples Ezine cited include an article by Hilmi Ziya Ülken in *İnsan* and Safa's novel *Fatih-Harbiye*; Ezine considered these texts as digging through national culture in search for one's identity.[64]

In many ways, these endeavors amounted to a yet another symbolic act of archaeology. As humanists were conducting acts of unearthing the past, Ezine considered their endeavor doomed to failure, because if one cannot achieve nationalization of the classical heritage by giving it a touch of "national genius," then all one does, he asserted, is imitate Roman and ancient Greek works.[65] Ezine argued that just like the individual is a "microcosmos" of society, society is a representation of the individual, and that the "national genius" embodies this connection. These ideas had long informed and, in turn, were informed by eugenicist thought, which configured the national as a human body.[66] Ezine proceeds to ask where the Turkish renaissance will take its inspiration from: its own origins or from the origins of Europe?[67] According to Ezine, there is no national literature that has not taken old literary works as the ideal.[68]

Indeed, Mehmet Fuat Köprülü's work on the early mystics of Turkish literature had accomplished just that: digging into the past and uncovering a national genius. Poet Yunus Emre, a thirteenth-century dervish, was duly canonized as a towering literary figure of the Turkish nation. On May 12, 1949, right around the time UNESCO was drafting its Statement on Race, the Turkish daily newspaper *Cumhuriyet* updated its readership with regard to news on "the great Turkish poet and thinker" (*büyük Türk şairi ve mütefekkiri*) Yunus Emre. Following the discovery of his tomb in the village of Sarıköy, his remains were exhumed, his skeleton reconstructed and transferred to the new Yunus Emre monument on May 6, 1949.[69] The newspaper reported that the Ankara Yunus Emre Society organized a press conference at the Ankara Palas Hotel on May 12. The president of the society explained that Yunus Emre's tomb was in ruins (*harab olmuş*) when it was found. According to the president there was no doubt they had indeed found the tomb of the genius:

> Up until now, there were fifteen or sixteen areas [*mıntıka*] where Yunus Emre's tomb was reportedly located. That notwithstanding, when the old tomb in Sarıköy was opened and the exhumed skeleton was compared to anthropological procedures, it was found that the historical knowledge on Yunus Emre completely coincided with anthropological findings. According to these findings, the [exhumed] skeleton belongs to a human being [*insan*] who was much superior to the normal [measurements] and [therefore] a genius, and thus [we can now conclusively say that] the real tomb and skeleton [of Yunus Emre] have been found.[70]

Clearly, the discursive and the biological are not mutually exclusive, and have been intertwined in many of the narratives of historicist humanism. On the biological side, there is a literature beyond Karl Valentin Müller's works—and those of his contemporaries who shared his vision—on the relationship between heredity and social achievement. For instance, Sir Francis Galton—the English eugenicist who studied the relationship between human intelligence and selective breeding—wrote a book on hereditary genius.[71] There, in addition to addressing scientists and statesmen, he also speaks of the notion of literary genius in relation to pedigree and family genealogy.

As for the notion of the national genius like Yunus Emre, a nation's grandeur in its bloodline is configured as evident in its ability to produce a grand figure: a genius. The Ankara Yunus Emre Society's statement on the poet's skeleton and tomb constitutes a popular culture interpretation of this notion. In that context, the national genius becomes *the* ancestor to anchor one's identification via establishing a national genealogy as per the methods of historicist humanism. This statement reveals an explicit tracing of origins to establish an ancestral tie with a figure of choice—configured as national identification.

Ezine's proposal to dig into one's own past or into the European past to find an ideal cultural form, however, has broader implications than just discovering the genius. In many ways, his intervention—like that of others, such as Hilmi Ziya Ülken—is a question of alignment, which implicates both civilization and methodology. And in terms of alignment, Peyami Safa has been a very important figure. Critics such as Ezine have often referred to his novel *Fatih-Harbiye* as a literary exploration of Turkish identity. As mentioned, also very important is his work *Doğu-Batı Sentezi* (East-West synthesis), posthumously published in 1963. Here, he suggests that the East and West can only be first thought through a thesis-antithesis dynamic, to be then configured as a synthesis for Turks. This dialectical thinking of Turkish culture proposed by Safa would later inform the notion of a Turkish-Islamic synthesis promoted by the Aydınlar Ocağı (Organization of Intellectuals), a group of nationalist and conservative intellectuals and businessmen.[72] Eventually, this synthesis would be integrated into the 1983 national culture report as the Turkish-Islamic synthesis, dropping the "West" from the equation. Thus, in many ways, in addition to biopolitical measures, the Turkish-Islamic synthesis developed during the military regime in the 1980s is a product of decades of historicist humanist pondering that embodied yet another palimpsest. As for Safa himself, despite reports on his Nazi sympathies, his impact on historicist humanism might be among the reasons he was selected as an alternate member of the UNESCO Turkish national committee in 1949.[73]

Overall, historicist humanism contained a series of debates within it, but in general, there were some shared notions and methods in the configuration of national culture, race, and civilization. In that regard, philologists, such as Edward Browne, E. J. W. Gibb, Jean-Jacques Ampère, and Erich Auerbach, as well as historians and archaeologists, including the amateurs—such as Schliemann and Halikarnas Balıkçısı—are among those who contributed to the development of the historicist humanist approach.[74] This doesn't mean that these figures or their approaches were the same, but that their work amounted to a humanist corpus that reinforced certain methods of inquiry and tools of identification. These included tracing origins to designated geographies and cultural settings, and taking narratives as geographic guides for heritage travels, and thus locating designated genealogies in making heritage claims. In short, this corpus contributed to the configuration of heritage and origins as methods of identification with broader racialized and civilizational implications for genealogies.[75]

In that respect, Homer and Dante were configured to be genius ancestors of "Western civilization," and duly, the site of Homeric Troy became a site of civilizational heritage in European cultural memory. It is well known that German businessman and amateur archaeological excavator Schliemann took Homer's epic poetry as a literary guidebook to locate and travel to the city of Troy in Asia Minor, Turkey's heartland today. Obviously, he was not the only one. The numerous figures who made similar literary expeditions to trace the footsteps of ancient heritage include two prominent French intellectuals: scholar Jean-Jacques Ampère and writer Prosper Mérimée. Indeed, about two decades before Schliemann, Ampère and Mérimée traveled to the then Ottoman Aegean shores to compare Homer's texts and the actual geographical locations depicted in those texts.[76] In other words, with a narrative as their guidebook, they sought to recognize the geographies in question, simultaneously attributing a realism to the text.

It must be noted that they were no ordinary travelers. Son of the famous physicist André-Marie Ampère and a close correspondent of Alexis de Tocqueville,[77] Jean-Jacques Ampère, together with Claude Fauriel, was one of the leading figures and founders of the discipline of comparative literature in France.[78] He had a keen interest in learning different literatures and languages and studying them comparatively. In his *La Science et les lettres en Orient* (Science and letters in the Orient),[79] Ampère engaged Chinese, Persian, and Buddhist traditions and revisited the classics of these "civilizations": these included what he called "Chinese theater," Firdawsi's *Shahnameh* (The book of princes), the Bhagavata-Purana, and the Ramayana. He had no problem with recognition. In fact, in this paradigm, as long as an ancient cultural heritage can be located and its canons can be traced, there is no problem with the recognition of "other civilizations." The Ottomans, for instance, never enjoyed such a recognition by philologists, even though there were works on Ottoman literature. Rather, Persian was perceived as the Latin or Greek of the "Eastern" or "Islamic civilization." This recognition, however, also had its limits, and it is coupled with a predictable Orientalism.[80]

It is this very historicist humanism paradigm that, in part, informed the philhellenic support Greece received when it sought independence from the Ottoman Empire in the early nineteenth century, and when British poet Lord Byron famously joined the war against the Ottomans. It is also in part this same paradigm—as well as demographics that configured the Greek Orthodox in Anatolia as relics of the Hellenic heritage—that informed the Greek invasion of what remained of the Ottoman state in 1919 in order to recapture those Hellenic geographies.[81] The war that ensued led to the rise of modern Turkey and the subsequent 1923 Lausanne Treaty on a Greek and Turkish compulsory exchange of religiously defined groups, namely Muslims with Greek Orthodox. In short, origins and filiation informed a claim to territory via heritage. And as anthropologist Nadia Abu El Haj's works on Israel point out, these dynamics are relevant beyond Greek-Turkish contexts.[82]

It is therefore important to remember that eugenics is not alone in informing the categorization of peoples. It is combined with a rich repertoire of cultural history archives refracted through the prism of historicist humanism that reinforce and support presumably scientific findings. How did this paradigm become so dominant? In addition to the European colonial expansion concomitant with the accumulation of European wealth in the nineteenth century, technological developments that improved the means to travel, to build, and to communicate quite possibly contributed to sealing the image of so-called Western civilization as superior—despite the racialized concerns with its "degeneration" at the time. The expansion of world exhibitions that combined cultural images with marketing goods and technology also contributed to this dynamic. The heritage attributed to "Western civilization" was then configured as a "universally acclaimed" model to follow—as *the* Civilization.[83]

But this exceptionalism attributed to so-called Western civilization does not always mean all approaches were homogenous. Historically, many debates were intertwined with such modern configurations, including those over the classics and the earlier debates discussed in terms of the "ancients" and the "moderns." In the mid-twentieth century, however, it became clear that UNESCO felt the necessity to also intervene in the terrain of historicist humanism to enable more inclusive spaces in order to develop a dialogue between the so-called Occident and Orient and their respective "civilizations." And as I will discuss below, on that front too, Ülken was an important historical actor.

For example, in 1949—the year the UNESCO-sponsored Oslo meeting to found ISA took place—a brief article appeared in the *UNESCO Courier* advocating the study of classical heritage while being more inclusive:

> The term "classical studies" has not that world compass for which Unesco strives, being confined to studies of ancient Greece and Rome. . . .
>
> Europeans of earlier days learnt from the Greek school to look upon all people of non-European civilization as barbarians and the Romans invented the notion of Pax Romana, which sanctions the rule of a single people destined, by its superior civilization, to play the part of protector of all nations wishing to live in peace. . . .
>
> . . . There is no denying that Unesco must approach the great periods of civilization with the most complete objectivity. . . .
>
> . . . Unesco has the right and the duty to give entire encouragement to efforts aimed at preserving the supra-nationalist and peaceful essence, the life and strength, of the civilization which was born in Greece, grew up under the name of European civilization and conquered half the world. . . .
>
> Nothing, in fact, can better serve the aims of Unesco than a re-awakening among Europeans, and among those of kindred civilization, of a general interest in their common past. . . .
>
> Philologists, archaeologists and classical historians are aware of their responsibility. . . . They seek to provide the public with a better knowledge and understanding of classical civilization and of its relations with the civilizations of today.[84]

A call for cultural recognition via expanding classical studies to include other "civilizations," this UNESCO statement can be read as an early institutional intervention in the fields of the production of knowledge. This suggests that the idea that the origins of European civilization lie in ancient Greece, which implies a linear identification, was embraced by UNESCO. Resorting to ancient Greek and Roman models, the statement calls for a critical engagement with the xenophobic paradigm attributed to ancient Greeks. We know from historian Nancy Bisaha's work that "barbarian" was at first a linguistic term referring to those who did not speak Greek, and that one of the earliest uses of the term can be found in Homer.[85]

Studying the classics of other "civilizations," however, was already done by such important figures as Ampère. UNESCO's call can therefore be construed as the institutionalization of such works—arguably contributing to the institutionalized curriculum of what we call humanities today. That is, humanity in the plural, through the inclusion of the humans from other geographic contexts and their histories, cultures, literatures, and arts—and by extension, historicist humanism. On the other hand, the hegemony of Western European paradigms was largely accomplished via European colonialism and imperialism. European civilizational exceptionalism generated a cultural framework that reinforced racialized superiority. Would engaging other cultural histories and literatures using the same Eurocentric paradigms of historicist humanism be effective without questioning the logics and the archive of knowledge that lie in the background? It should come as no surprise that the Martinique-born psychiatrist Frantz Fanon would condemn humanism a few years later, during the then-ongoing Algerian war of decolonization.[86] Historicist humanism, indeed, developed together with racial theories in the modern era that traced the genealogies of racialized civilizations.

Race, Origins, and Civilization: Turkey, Turks, and the Greek-Turkish Population Exchange

One of the best-known examples of such a genealogy is the nineteenth-century race theorist Arthur de Gobineau's *Essay on the Inequality of Human Races* (1853–1855).[87] Gobineau claimed that like the human body, civilizations are born, develop, reach their peak, and then decline and die. He explained decline with what he called degeneration. To him, degeneration came with the "mixing" of blood, that is, of races. Gobineau's concern with the mixing of superior and inferior races had a strong impact on German composer Richard Wagner. Wagner and Gobineau met in the 1870s, and it appears that Wagner read Gobineau's work afterward. It is not a secret that Wagner himself had an impact on Nazi ideology. Wagner's son-in-law Houston Stewart Chamberlain contributed to the dissemination of these ideas with his own interpretations of the legacy of the ancient world, which in this context was configured as heritage.[88] In his work entitled *The Foundations of the Nineteenth Century*, Chamberlain predictably refers to ancient origins and the notion of the genius that supposedly embodied a "universally" accepted brilliance that represented a civilization.[89] In that respect, we see a racialized notion of civilization in Chamberlain's work.

Overall, Gobineau's work had broader implications for the racialized configuration of nations and widely informed the notion of "civilization."[90] Deterministically, Gobineau emphasized the importance of finding ancestral origins of different groups—such as Hungarians, Chinese, and Turks—to explain their "true national" character, through creating a racialized family tree—the genealogy—of humanity, in which Turks were not placed high:

> Even if we suppose the ancestors of the Turkish nation to belong to the yellow race [like the Finns], it is easy to show why their descendants have so widely departed from that type.... We see clearly that the arguments for or against the permanence of racial type find no support whatsoever in the history of such a mixed people as the Turks. This is so self-evident, that when we notice, as we often do, some characteristic features of the yellow race in an Osmanli, we cannot attribute this directly to his Finnish origin; it is simply the effect of Slav or Tatar blood, exhibiting at second hand, the foreign elements it had itself absorbed....
>
> ... [Following the reign of Mehmet IV], there were in four centuries at least 5000 heads of families who infused European blood into the veins of the Turkish nation.[91]

Gobineau indicates that such heterogeneity is nothing to be desired. The embodied notion of race through references to blood is evident. And because of being so mixed, Turks do not figure favorably in Gobineau's scheme.

Gobineau considered the mixing of peoples as degeneration, implying that Turks are degenerate because of the lack of a pure racial filiation and genesis:

> The word *degenerate*, when applied to a people, means (as it ought to mean) that the people has no longer the same intrinsic value it had before, because it has no longer the same blood—in its veins, continual adulterations having gradually affected the quality of that blood. In other words, though the nation nears the name given by its founders, the name no longer connotes the same race; in fact, the man of a decadent time, the *degenerate* man properly so called, is a different being, from the racial point of view, from the heroes of

the great ages. I agree that he still keeps something of their essence; but the more he degenerates the more attenuated does this "something" become. The heterogeneous elements that henceforth prevail in him give him quite a different nationality—a very original one, no doubt. But such originality is not to be envied. He is only a very distant kinsman of those he calls his ancestors. He and his *civilization* with him will certainly die on the day when the *primordial race-unit* is so broken up and swamped by the influx of foreign elements, that its effective qualities have no longer a sufficient freedom of action.[92]

Emphasizing the importance of straightforward kinship to ancestors, Gobineau thus establishes genealogy as the centerpiece of national identification in his racialized family tree of humankind divided into nations. Each nation belongs to a racialized civilizational branch. "Mixing" thins the quality of the blood and therefore degenerates. As a result, to Gobineau the relationship between the signifier and the signified is broken: the name of the nation might remain the same, but what that name signifies is no longer the same. Also, it is important to note that according to this paradigm—also espoused by eugenicists to come—degeneration brings the "decline" of empires, nations, and entire races.

Almost fifteen years after the publication of *Essay on the Inequality of Human Races*, a Polish convert to Islam, Mustafa Celaleddin Paşa (Moustapha Djelaleddin Pasha) would seek to trace the genealogy of Turks and locate them on a better branch of the family tree of humankind. Historian Selim Deringil describes Mustafa Celaleddin Paşa, Count Constantine Borzecki, as a pioneer in Turcology.[93] As for Mustafa Celaleddin Paşa's own family history, Deringil states that he was the great-grandfather of Turkey's acclaimed poet Nazım Hikmet and thus indirectly related to Ezine. (I only include these references here to gesture back to the statement that there are as many diverse backgrounds in Turkey as there are families wishing to discover them.) According to Deringil, Mustafa Celaleddin Paşa's book, *Les Turcs anciens et modernes* (Ancient and modern Turks), is acknowledged to be a pioneer work that undertook the systematic analysis of the origin of Turkic peoples.[94] Historical sociologist Aslı Gür addresses Celaleddin Paşa as a key figure in the development of a particular humanist thought in Turkey, which appropriates civilizations in Anatolia as its own.[95] Furthermore, as the title of the book suggests, Mustafa Celaleddin Paşa sought to connect the then modern and ancient Turks, in a manner that is commensurable with historicist humanism.

Les Turcs anciens et modernes traces the genealogy and racial origins of Turks. In a chapter entitled "Europe and Turo-Aryanism" ("L'Europe et le touro-aryanisme"), Mustafa Celaleddin Paşa states:

> While writing the preceding chapters on the Turkish nation, I wanted to confine myself within certain limits. Yet, the recent statement made by M. Casimir Delamarre in his petition to the Senate of the French Empire, prompts me to add a few more words. [In this petition, Delamarre] requests a history teaching program [designed] to relegate Turks and Muscovites, the rejected of the family of the Aryans of Europe, to the race that represents the barbarianism [*la barbarie*] of Asia.[96]

Thus the notion of barbarianism was related to racial origins. Mustafa Celaleddin Paşa's reaction is against the French curriculum that would exclude Turks and Muscovites from the Aryan family of Europe and consider them as part of the Asian races, configured as barbarians. And as he does in the rest of his book, Mustafa Celaleddin Paşa seeks to prove the importance of the Turks by tracing their racial origins to the Caucasian Turks, by comparing the Turkish language to Latin and Greek, and by arguing that the "decline" of the Ottoman Empire was not due to its racial degeneration but because of other, political reasons.[97]

He also argues that apart from a few exceptions, all Muslim and Christian populations under the Ottoman Empire belong to the Aryan family (*même famille arienne*) and are related via origins or blood. Mustafa Celaleddin Paşa considers this dynamic to be a "great humanitarian fusion." To him, "the tolerance, equality, fraternity, solidarity," as well as their geographic position and liberties alone should have been enough to fuse "all Ottomans, Muslim and Christian, in one prosperous body, compact and powerful."[98] He concludes his book with the universal importance of humanity and its rights (*l'humanité et de ses droits*) and places "Turkey" (meaning the Ottoman state at the time) together with France, England, Austria, Italy, and Scandinavia, and hopes that the "grand nationality of Poland" will also be restored.[99] Mustafa Celaleddin Paşa's work was not a direct reply to

Gobineau per se, but the book itself crystallizes concerns with such claims as Gobineau's and with finding the right racial branch for Turks within the hierarchized family tree of humankind. In this book, originally published in 1869 and then again in 1870 in the late Ottoman era, the paradigms and methods of historicist humanism are thus evident, including tracing the racial genesis and filiation of Turks.

As for the young Turkish republic of the 1930s, Gobineau's ideas arguably marked the beginnings of institutionalized anthropological inquiry; to debunk his ideas on Turks was a priority.[100] But anthropologists were not the only ones interested in engaging the purist ideas of Gobineau. In 1941, it was none other than Hilmi Ziya Ülken who addressed Gobineau's ideas at length in his *İçtimai Doktrinler Tarihi* (History of social thought).[101] A collection of his lectures at Istanbul University between 1935–1937 and 1939–1940, Ülken's book offers an intellectual history of what he calls doctrines that had an impact on the "social philosophical system." In a chapter dedicated to anthropological theories of society ("Antropolojik Cemiyet Nazariyesi"), Ülken introduces his students to Gobineau's work.

From Ülken, Istanbul University's students learned about Gobineau's theories; his knowledge of literature and history; his impact on Chamberlain and Wagner; and how in Germany, poets supported the notion of the superiority of the German race, just as did philosophers like Fichte. In his lectures, Ülken traced Gobineau's ideas on racial genealogy back to philologists and eugenicists, including Francis Galton—who wrote about heredity and genius, among other subjects.[102] In his published lectures, Ülken explains how according to Gobineau, "many observers saw that human families have essential differences in terms of pedigree, related to the roots" (Ona göre birçok müşahitler beşeri ailelerin soy bakımından aralarında esaslı, cezri farklar olduğunu görmüşlerdir).[103]

After explaining how Mérimée, Tocqueville, and others criticized Gobineau, Ülken seeks to show his students that Gobineau's work is unscientific, philosophically flawed, and historically and philologically unsubstantiated. Still, Ülken admits, Gobineau's ideas were influential in establishing certain notions of race and the grandeur of Roman civilization via racial attributes, but adds that both Chamberlain and Hitler had to update Gobineau's ideas in order to make them applicable to their cause.[104] Ülken further asserts that if Gobineau's work had any followers, it was not for academic but rather political and personal reasons.[105] In a separate article published in 1946, Ülken also refers to Mustafa Celaleddin Paşa's *Les Turcs anciens et modernes* as a pioneering work on Turkism, and explains Celaleddin Paşa's thoughts about Turo-Aryanism and his claim that Turo-Aryans—which supposedly includes the Turks—are the race that founded Western civilization.[106]

Ülken certainly is not the only person who engaged questions of race, Gobineau, and the mixed background of Turks. But considering his connections and networks beyond Turkey, his role in the European Association for the Study of Refugee Problems (AER), his work on emigration and the Greek-Turkish population exchange, as well as his deep interest in historicist humanism and active role in UNESCO in that regard, he is an important figure for the purposes of this study.

In 1957, two years after the anti-Greek pogroms in Istanbul and the grand opening of *The Family of Man* in New York, Ülken published a book entitled *Veraset ve Cemiyet* (Heredity and society).[107] In the preface, he explains the book was written thirty-three years before the publication date, which means 1924, the year after the Greek-Turkish population exchange agreement. According to Ülken, the goal of the book was to rethink racialist heredity notions together with culturalist (*kültürcü*) approaches to discussing national culture and character. Claiming to have found a middle ground between the two paradigms—the biologist and culturalist, as discussed in Part One—he develops the notion of "social race" (*içtimai ırk*). In a separate section on heredity, he compares the notion of heritage in the field of law, as the transmission of the material possessions of a family from one generation to another, and the notion of heredity, as the biological and social transmission of family traits from one's forefathers (*dedelerimiz*) to other generations.[108] Heredity and heritage are intertwined in Ülken's thought.

In the book, Ülken wields the notions of race and social interaction to develop a concept he calls "social heredity." Using this concept, he addresses the "types" on the family tree of mankind.[109] These types he configures as part of a social race. While he refutes notions of purity of race on the grounds that such purity does not exist, except perhaps in remote places—where there supposedly is inbreeding—he still believes there are national types. A national type embodies the racialized elements of a given group. In a footnote at the end of *Veraset ve Cemiyet*, he asserts that the notion of social race has nothing to do with the biological notion of race promoted by what he calls physical anthropology (*anthropologie zoologique*).[110] According to Ülken, a social race is formed as a hybrid (*métis*)—generated when various origins or roots (*muhtelif kök*) get combined and mixed because of such factors as economic disposition (*iktisadi bünye*) and language, as well as the intangible unity of life (*manevi hayatın birliği*). A social race, then, forms an entirely different sociobiological type that constitutes the core of the nation, Ülken asserts.

With social race, Ülken seeks to explain three interconnected issues: being mixed is not degeneration and civilizations must be thought in that light; reconsidering the origins and mixedness of the Turks; and rethinking how emigration such as the Greek-Turkish population exchange can be addressed in that context. The way he engages these phenomena is thus through an attempt to synthesize the biological and the cultural embodied in his notion of social race.

> It is completely wrong to describe the [notion of] nation by pointing to similarities in anatomy and anthropology as [was the case] with the old anthropological theories and to look for signs [*tezahür*] of "racial purity": indeed, those who share these views are so careless as to state that many of the big nations are the result of mixed composites and therefore are degenerate [*soysuzlaşmış*]. On the other hand, it is also wrong to consider a nation . . . as the sum of individuals' psychology and opinions. Every national formation [*milli teşekkül*] is based on such a cultural unity that, the major types, molded by the vehicles of language and technique, begin to develop completely new psychological qualities [*vasıf*]. These attributes become more or less stable [*sarsılmaz*] with mutations caused by organic social relations.[111]

Ülken's approach here is quite parallel to Corrado Gini's; it similarly considers society to be a living organism. Even though he avoids the word "race" (*ırk*), the notion he uses here—*soysuzlaşmış* (literally, having lost one's pedigree or lineage)—has similar implications: degeneration. He may reject purist and biological configurations of race, but the biologized paradigms that inform racialized thinking are nonetheless evident in his work. Scholars like Ülken might reject biological notions of race or racial purity, but a close reading of their work and an analysis of the paradigms that inform their thought show that their work is not divorced from racialized paradigms. This might be why racialized thinking has been so resilient: although outspoken rejection of race appears to be taken for granted, the tools, methods, and discourses that inform racial paradigms have continued to be used for identification and categorization. These categories have long been deployed in the conceptualization of entire groups and nations and the configuration of civilizations.

In terms of civilizations, Ülken proposes a similar outlook:

> This is why the old civilizations which collapsed [*yıkılmış eski medeniyetlerin*] can form new social races via languages that have a rich literature and culture and absorb new ethnic groups that join their world. On its ruins [*kendi harabeleri üzerinde*], Rome formed the French social race; on its debris [*enkaz*], the old civilization of Iran generated a new social race of Iran composed of Turks, Arabs, and Farsis.[112]

According to Ülken, different groups were consolidated into national types through the influence of the language of holy books, such as Arabic and Latin. Among the examples he cites is the social type of Syria, composed of an amalgamation of what he calls "Jewish, Nasturi, Assyrian, Yakubi, Kurdish, Arab, Turkish, and even Circassian groups."[113] If indeed Ülken recognizes this to be the case for Syria, he surely would have the same view about the demographic fabric of Turkey. Indeed, he proceeds to argue that in order to identify Turks, one must consider them to be a group that "mutated" as a result of social mingling and interactions for ten centuries, which he calls the type of the "Turk of the West" (*garp türkü*).[114] He appears to posit the "Western Turks" as a mixed group different from groups in Central Asia. Accordingly, Turks are a social race that draws from the civilization of Iran; every social race carries the traces and residues of ruins of civilizations. And with this, he configures Iran as an ancient site of origin comparable to Rome.

The blueprint of eugenicist thought is also visible in the anthropomorphized configuration of civilizations with their trajectory of birth, rise, and decline. While Gobineau attributes the decline to degeneration, Ülken considers this a natural process of genealogical transmission. As a civilization crumbles, a "mutation" takes place, and different social types are formed. This in turn reinforces the idea of origins.

In Ülken's work, however, as important as these origins are, equally important is the modern-era assimilation of different groups that are part of a nation. He asserts that if a "life regime" (*hayat rejimi*) in a country is not sufficiently strong to melt away differences, and if a (national) language is unable to penetrate some communities and ethnic groups or families, then assimilation and unification cannot occur. Ülken argues that in such cases, the formation of a social type cannot be completed.[115] To rethink the implications of assimilation, it might be helpful to recall how, in the immediate aftermath of the Second World War, integration was understood to be cultural assimilation, and how Fındıkoğlu emphasized assimilation via the mosque and schools.

For Ülken, integration is vital to the development of a social type and "essential character" (*temel şahsiyet*). The social type embodies Ülken's notion of social race, and without it, a nation cannot be formed. This means, through assimilation and absorption of differences, a distinct type that would be representative of the nation should be formed. And when this doesn't happen, a nation lingers behind others in civilization. What is sought here is not racial purity, but assimilation; unification comes as an end point and not necessarily as a point of departure. In many ways, Ülken's thought is representative of the debates taking place in UNESCO and the AER at the time, where the importance of cultural assimilation and integration was emphasized in the exchanges, studies, and policies on refugees and emigrants. At the time of the publication of this book, the notion of "national refugees" continues to be prominent in terms of racialized alignment within a given country.

Ülken appears to be clear on the identification of what he calls the "family of Turks" (*Türk ailesi*), as well as its location on the branches of the family tree of humankind.[116] He also recognizes geographically informed affinities. In both his 1957 book, *Veraset ve Cemiyet*, and its updated 1971 version, *Toplum Yapısı ve Soyaçekim* (The structure of society and heredity), Ülken's social types are informed by biological and racialized elements of categorization. He configures his notion of social race as a synthesis, as it were, of the sociocultural and the biological. Yet again, it is striking how the rejection of the notion of racial purity does not exclude its essentialized biological implications. After all, not many race theorists would argue for purity but still use racialized thinking and related concepts to address peoples.

Ülken's identification of the Jews and his discussion of the partition of Palestine and the foundation of Israel exemplify this approach:

> Jews are a social type with a strong mindset for [business] economy with a highly evolved practical mind. Even if they lose their language, community, or even their religion, they do not lose these attributes. The unification of the Jews who left Hitler's Germany to the territory given to them [Israel] is a very recent phenomenon [*günün hadisesidir*]. [This unification could happen even though those Jews] converted to Protestantism, spoke German, and had no longer had any relations with to their religious community, only because they belong to the same social type.... They managed to turn Hebrew into their native language in only three years, and they could work together as part of the same social whole, despite their religious and denominational differences, because the characteristics that took root in them over [the last] 25–30 centuries have formed the essential character that we can call the Jewish type.[117]

Here, Ülken's notion of social race reveals an essentialized approach to the Jewish "social type" and character. It implies that there is a biological essence to be transmitted via the bloodline across centuries. Accordingly, despite social circumstances and attempts to assimilate Jewish communities via language and religion, their essence—configured as transmitted from generation to generation for about three thousand years—has been reactivated and has helped form the Jewish type. One attribute of such an essence is having a mind for business, and another is a biologically evolved mind identified as practical. Configuring a social type as a representative embodiment of millions of people in these terms implicates biologized notions of race.

Indeed, the 1971 edition of the book displays photos of what Ülken calls social types. The cover features photographs of males labeled as Turkish, American, English, and French. In addition, other pictures of men—including Japanese, Russians, and Chinese—are displayed as representative specimens. The photographs are presented with the following sentence: "Samples of persons [*kişi*, denoting "type" here] from different pedigrees [*soy*]." *Soy* in this case involves racial pedigree, and the "types" Ülken presents here are very much along the lines of ethnological types. And, of course, the gendered representation of the social types in general, with the Turk appearing as a male with a moustache as a particular case, adds to this problem of representability.

Overall, Ülken attempts to rethink biological race and cultural approaches that clashed on multiple scholarly fronts, which also included UNESCO, in the 1950s and 1960s. This is how he develops the notion of social race. Yet, were the notions of degeneration and racial purity the only problems in the biological paradigms of race? In this context, the problem with racialist theories appears to be reduced to those issues. This reductive approach thus enables the continuation of essentialist and racialist ideas. Like some of his contemporaries, while rejecting the notion of purity, Ülken nonetheless believed that race has a biological foundation, even though as the above examples illustrate, a racialized essentialism prevails in his model.

In his *Veraset ve Cemiyet*, following racialized statements informed by biological disposition, Ülken then turns to a discussion of culture and environment. He focuses on the Greek Orthodox who left Turkey and settled in Greece as part of the 1923 Greek-Turkish population exchange:

> [Likewise] Belgians speak various languages (French, Flemish, German) . . . but they have common attributes. These attributes differentiate them from the French and the Dutch. Even if those who speak French are born in France, their foreignness is noticeable. The same examples can be given for the Balkan Muslim tribes [*kavim*] like Albanians and Bosnians, in terms of what differentiates them from the Christian communities in the Balkans or from the Turks. Today, it is not hard to identify the essential character and social types of these people who live among us and contribute greatly to our culture and with whom we share our religion. On the other hand, even though the Anatolian Christian community has left, we can see that they show great similarities to the Anatolian Turks, thanks to the rootedness of the same life regime, same automatisms, and habits. We hear that after their emigration to Greece, some of these people act with ideological and religious animosity against us, but at the same time, they are a source of discomfort for the country where they are located because they cannot mesh with the social type of that country. When and how these communities will integrate into the places where they have been newly relocated as a result of mass migrations and regimes of new life, that is a different question.[118]

Ülken's statement on the Greek Orthodox who left Turkey for Greece acknowledges the impact of one's living environment on culture and how in cases of forced migration there can be issues with integration. The predictable outcome of this statement would be to consider the Muslims who arrived from Greece in a similar manner. But just as he does not follow up his point on the diversity of the people in Syria and connect these ideas to the local social fabric in Turkey, here too he does not fill in the blanks for the Turkish context.

In a 1951 newspaper column dedicated to the issue of emigration, Ülken highlighted the importance of assimilation.[119] His approach here echoes the dominant views expressed in AER meetings by various scholars and political figures as well as representatives of different institutions. In short, he too saw forced migration as a humane solution to promote peace:

> One must differentiate between the consequences of voluntary and forced migrations, especially in terms international law. There might be intricate legal consequences in terms of the limitation of liberties [*hürriyet*] and the forced removal [*zorla uzaklaştırılma*] of people from their centuries-long settings. It is possible to propound political reasons to justify such situations. These mainly include providing a) peace, and b) national one-kindedness [*tecanüs*].[120] For example, the Greek-Turkish population exchange, which followed incessant war between Turkey and Greece, has enabled the two countries to enter a peace process. Demographic one-kindedness [*nüfus tecanüsü*] is no less [important].... The provision of such ethnographic one-kindedness is one of the most important issues from both a national and political point of view ...
>
> In order to understand the emigrants' economic productivity [*iktisadi verimliliği*] and assimilation [*temessül*] to the local culture, it is necessary to conduct comparative research on them with regard to the years 1875–1914 [and] 1934–1951 and to prepare monographs on villages, towns, and cities.[121] A monograph should look into issues such as types of settlement, relationships between the neighbors inside and among villages and towns, differences of character, the case of learning Turkish, mutual influences, the proportion of those who find jobs, to what extent these jobs correspond to the emigrants' jobs and abilities in the countries where they came from,

the proportion of those who could not settle or cannot adapt, the issues of unemployment and instability, and overall the issue of assimilation [*temessül*].[122]

In that respect, Ülken is well aware of matters of integration and issues that might arise in the process. And the fact that he promotes the study of "character" hints at his wish to get to know what he calls the "social types" of emigrant communities. Given the dynamics addressed here and the scope of his work, there is a reasonable basis for thinking that this information will be used to promote assimilation.

Further, Ülken correlates peace with national "one-kindness," which implies the spatial redistribution of categorized bodies in a manner that aligns them genealogically with the recipient country. In other words, Ülken here views segregative biopolitics under a positive light. And within the context of Turkey, this segregative biopolitics is conducive to a Turkish-Islamic synthesis—as evinced by the Greek-Turkish population exchange. Additionally, Ülken's concern with the economic productivity of emigrants completely resonates with the biopolitical dynamics addressed in Part One.

The kinds of monographs that Ülken promotes here are qualitative social studies of different locales. The papers presented at meetings of the AER, the AWR, and international sociology congresses, in particular the works of Ülken and Fındıkoğlu, demonstrate that the authors had taken such preliminary steps and conducted some qualitative research themselves. However, it took time for such qualitative and historical studies to become prevalent in Turkey. Meanwhile, social and biological notions continued to inform the identification of different groups, including emigrants and refugees. Ülken's *Veraset ve Cemiyet* attests to this dynamic.

At the very end of his book, Ülken published the genealogical trees (*şecereler*) of several emigrants. Only there, instead of names, he marks the gender and the occupation of different generations in an attempt to understand the impact of emigration and what he calls "family mutation" on the choice of occupation. He particularly focuses on the role of education and heredity in emigrant families' choice of occupations. Heredity, then, is not only about race but is also a variable in emigrants' essential disposition for different vocations. Ülken's list of occupations includes teachers, civil servants, officers, farmers, and merchants. This vocational genealogization speaks to Ülken's concern with the economic productivity of emigrants.

As mentioned, Ülken's *Veraset ve Cemiyet* is an attempt to bridge the two paradigms of culture and biology in the figure of the "social race." Part One has addressed how these paradigms clashed in the aftermath of the Second World War, and how deeply UNESCO and the AER were entangled in these clashes. Yet, as we have also seen in Part One, trying to remove race from culture, à la Franz Boas, does not quite divorce cultural identifications from the broader implications of biological race. Ülken's work constitutes a good example of this.

At the time when Ülken published his book, UNESCO had already intervened in many fields. In anthropology, UNESCO published the Statement on Race, which promoted racial equality on the grounds that all humans belong to the same species, *Homo sapiens*. In sociology, UNESCO stepped in to establish an international sociological association in order to promote the study of human relations; it was assumed that this would be a contribution to peace. As we have seen, all these interventions generated epistemological and institutional conflict. Likewise, the fields of art, the media, and visual culture were mobilized to promote coexistence and peace. The shape this campaign took is addressed in terms of liberal humanism in this book: an emphasis on unity in diversity as a message of peace and coexistence. Overall, these interventions coexisted with biopolitical policies that informed the spatialized redistribution of populations as well as racialized configurations of identification. In that context, one other terrain in which UNESCO intervened was the field of study of historicist humanism itself.

UNESCO's Intervention in Historicist Humanism

> UNESCO believes ... that if you understand the varying cultures of the world, you won't want to fight them.
>
> Mrs. Henry P. Russell of San Francisco, on the first UNESCO Regional Conference on the West Coast in the United States;
> *UNESCO Courier*, May 1948

In May 1948, the *UNESCO Courier* declared that Civilization was in danger. It published a call for a new humanism by Dr. Pere Bosch-Gimpera, the newly appointed head of UNESCO's Philosophy and Humanities Section.

An archaeologist and anthropologist from Catalonia in Spain—who became an exile in Mexico after the Spanish Civil War—Bosch-Gimpera called for recognition of other civilizations as a move toward building world peace in the postwar era. This move was configured as a mode of inclusion, to remedy the crisis in humanism:

> With the immediate danger removed, we find ourselves faced by new and terrifying enigmas. New wars must indeed be avoided: This means that the new generations must be brought up in a true humanism, wider than the former conception which was often no more than an aesthetic and classic ideal. Technology and sciences, States and international organizations, must be placed truly at the service of mankind. New paths are therefore opened up for philosophers and humanists, who must prepare to formulate new ideals for the spirit and to institute a universal education to enable all to share in the benefits of civilization, bring the cultures of the east and the west into contact and raise to their own level backward peoples who still occupy large areas of the world's surface. No single type of civilization must dominate, nor must there be privileged master races.[123]

To build peace and to ensure development, UNESCO sought to go beyond the idealization of ancient times. New ideals were necessary to support "all men" and to "bring all peoples together in one great community without destroying their individuality or stifling their initiative by way of free and sincere co-operation."[124] In order to prevent one master race representing one civilization from dominating the world, Bosch-Gimpera advocated bringing "backward peoples" to the level of universal civilization. In the name of challenging a dominant discourse, he mobilized the very same paradigms that inform that discourse: being backward is a temporal translation of the linear identification of peoples measured against the metric of progress. Education and school curriculum are among the sites for such intervention. Bosch-Gimpera implied that a democratized historicist humanism will enable different cultures to get to know one another, which in turn will contribute to world peace. In other sections of his call, Bosch-Gimpera also asserted that UNESCO was founded to achieve this task.

A few years later, in 1951, following Bosch-Gimpera's call for a new humanism, UNESCO invited twelve international figures to attend a roundtable discussion entitled "Humanism and Education in the East and the West."[125] Among the invited, the scholar delegate representing Turkey was Hilmi Ziya Ülken. Representing the United States was Clarence Faust, the dean of humanities at Stanford University and the president of the Fund for the Advancement of Education established by the Ford Foundation.[126]

The conference took place in New Delhi on December 12–20, 1951, four short years after the partition of India. In the officially partitioned India, the unofficially partitioned world was to be addressed: the objective was to bring the "Orient" and the "Occident" into contact, to lay out the civilizational contributions of different national cultures, and to propose educational policies that were more inclusive and cognizant of these contributions. The conference was meant to be a direct intervention in the Eurocentric aspects of historicist humanism, which traced the genealogy of the "West" to ancient Greek and Roman origins. Preserving the same tools and methods of knowledge production, the idea was to open the door to other national cultures, which would have their own representation. This was a call for cultural recognition via the school curriculum—arguably configuring the study of humanity as humanities.

In New Delhi, during the first two days of the conference, there were presentations on "the concept of man in East and West," and in the last two days, the main principles of education were discussed. The presentations were followed by comments and general discussions. We learn from reports on the conference written by Ülken and the rapporteur of the conference, John Traill Christie, the principal of the Jesus College, Oxford University, that there was a consensus on a number of issues, but also points of contention.

Consensus was reached on a number of issues that were geared toward breaking away from binarisms. For example, the binarism of the "active West" and the "contemplative East" was declared to be inaccurate.[127] In addition, the positing of man against nature was raised as a problem. In terms of education, the UNESCO representatives discussed how education cannot be reduced to the "mere communication of a scientific technique" because this could damage the "soul," and therefore it was important to learn about the "cultivation of the whole man." According to the delegates, proper humanist education would integrate the individual, and "without integration of the individual there could be no integration of a society."[128] This meant "specialists and non-specialists alike should study the Humanities as part of their full education as men."[129] Humanities education was thus configured as important even if it was not a student's primary field of study. It was assumed that studying the humanities would help the individual—the student—to better integrate socially and adopt the social norms of inclusion and duly, of tolerance.

In New Delhi, Christie's paper, titled "Humanist Education in the West" ("L'Éducation humaniste en Occident"), reviewed how classical concepts had an impact on the humanist formation in Europe since the Renaissance, but most notably in the nineteenth century.[130] Christie followed the same historicist humanist tropes discussed above, and firmly grounded the humanist ideal in the literary and artistic formations of Europe—the origins of which the paper traced to Greek antiquity.[131] He then called for humanists and scientists to develop strong ties between the "Orient" and the "Occident." He proposed that educational institutions in the East and the West play an important role in this matter, and that the "East might supply the new 'Classics' that were required for the new humanism."[132] The inclusion of the so-called East is configured in historicist humanist terms; generating canons—the classics—is a demand for such cultural recognition. To be recognized, "the Orient" needed to provide comparable classics. As noted earlier, this was already a concern in Turkey, and the Translation Bureau strove to translate the classics into Turkish and Ülken himself had written about translation as a catalyst of a renaissance—a reawakening of the national culture and a vectoring factor in generating a golden age, both of which are tropes of historicist humanism. UNESCO's Translation Bureau endeavored to render classics written in other languages visible in French and English, for example, in an attempt to generate a symbolic space for inclusion of other cultures. Visibility was configured as the recognition of other civilizations. These ideas were later articulated by UNESCO in terms of liberalization—such as the 1982 Universal Declaration on Cultural Policies, which endorsed the recognition of minority cultures and configured such cultural recognition as emancipation.[133]

The scope of humanism was to be democratized via Eurocentric tools and tropes of historicist humanism. For example, at the 1951 New Delhi meeting, the very same tools for identification—such as origins and genealogy—that were used to generate Eurocentric supremacy were now being used to recognize the particular. Different countries were duly encouraged to trace their "origins" and thus genealogize their national heritage, a step with broader civilizational and racial implications.

The delegates at the New Delhi conference also promoted the idea of education as a tool for disseminating the notion of equality:

> From the earliest stages education should emphasize the dignity of the individual whatever his social status: the Gandhian conception of basic education should be developed. Nationalist tendencies in education, especially in the teaching of history, which assumed the superiority of one race over another, were to be universally discouraged. One speaker, with a measure of agreement from others, asserted that even so, it would inevitably be a long time before the mass of men could be linked to an old tradition of aristocratic culture.[134]

In other words, the UNESCO delegates, including Ülken, opposed the nationalist type of history education.

UNESCO might have genuinely sought to target narratives of superiority informed by notions of racialized purity and genealogies, but these efforts concurrently coexisted with: (1) the spatialized redistribution of bodies through forced migration, which relies on similar categorizations based on origins and racialized attributes with civilizational implications; (2) the development of ideas such as "social race" and "social type" and liberal humanism, which appears to be an attempt to move away from "race" via concepts like the social or the cultural, but in fact is not divorced from the broader implications of the biologized notions of race; (3) the spread of historicist humanism, which continued to endorse the idea of "Western heritage" or Islamic heritage, because such ideas relied on the same categorizations of origins and civilizational genealogies while simultaneously emphasizing "essential identities"; (4) the historicist humanist efforts to win recognition of the "non-Western" as the Other. It is also important to question what these (re)configurations entailed for minorities at a national level. This dynamic especially becomes poignant since these conversations took place in the recently partitioned India. Another point of consensus reached in New Delhi was the necessity to generate a new humanism based on tolerance, a notion that would eventually become more prominent in cultural policy, especially in the aftermath of the Cold War.[135] In UNESCO's report on the conference,

Christie underlines that to be effective, "tolerance" should be engaged with conviction, but without condescension.[136] Accordingly, "wars and world conflicts had not arisen from differences of civilization such as are represented by East and West, but between the uncivilized and fanatical minorities within a single civilization. It was to eliminate such uncivilized minorities by means of education that East and West might co-operate."[137]

The message is clear: more tolerance, more inclusion, more education in the classics and important works—from around the world—that contribute to humanity is necessary. Meanwhile, it is important to put less emphasis on nationalism and to monitor education in history more closely. What was missing in this picture was a direct problematization of colonialism—and its accompanying archives of knowledge—and partitions, and a more direct engagement with biopolitics. And for the case of Turkey, it was not until the 1990s and early 2000s that committees would be mobilized to monitor nationalism in history textbooks. One of the most salient institutional actors in that regard was again the History Foundation, and the family-history-writing competition can be construed as part of the endeavor to break the hegemony of nationalist historical narratives.[138]

As for the 1950s, whereas we learn from the UNESCO report that the delegates in New Delhi were wary of nationalism, we also learn from Ülken's own account that there was disagreement on the subject of what Ülken calls "patriotism."[139] In his account, Ülken underlines how the conference attendees were cautious of aggressive nationalism (*mütecaviz milliyetçilik*). That notwithstanding, Ülken reminds his readers, as he apparently also did in New Delhi, that patriotism is important. To him, all humanism must first be patriotic, a notion that resonates with his very own 1933 work *İnsani Vatanperverlik* (Humanist patriotism).[140] Ülken argued that the primary goal of humanism should remain the fostering of patriotism and educating youth in their own culture; there is nothing wrong, he asserted, with being proud of one's national culture as long as there is no contempt for others.[141]

In the Turkish report, Ülken explains that Christie indirectly referred to him (*telmih ederek*) and criticized his "patriotic humanism." According to Ülken, Christie thought that patriotic humanism can only be a pedagogical tool but not the objective of education. Ülken, however, viewed patriotic humanism as a crucial objective; to him, the ultimate goal is not to erase the notion of nations but to establish harmony among them. He claims that humanism can only be established through the participation of all nations in the "patrimony of humanity"—that is, the shared heritage of humanity (*insanlığın müşterek patrimoine'ı*). With his interjection, Ülken anticipates the institutionalization of cultural heritage under the patronage of UNESCO.

How is this goal to be accomplished? Ülken proposes to trace the heritage of humanity via an analysis of time-honored epics—including *Shahnameh*, and *Mahabharata*, among others—focusing on their similarities.[142] Yet, as we have seen with earlier philological studies, including the works of Jean-Jacques Ampère—one of the founders of the discipline of comparative literature in France—such studies had already been undertaken with the understanding that these works were important contributions to humanity. But, as we also now know, this did not stop earlier philologists from being Orientalist. This is particularly important, because in the post-1945 era, German Jewish émigrés and humanists such as Auerbach would arrive in the United States from Istanbul and contribute to the founding of comparative literature as a discipline. In the United States, comparative literature would assume a humanist role—reminiscent of UNESCO's call—as an academic platform to bring different cultural works into dialogue with one another. But for the most part, the discipline would remain Eurocentric at its core for years. The major challenge would come from the decolonization movements and thinkers.

As for Ülken's notion of "patriotic humanism," it in fact gives a name to what was actually happening on the ground. The idea that classics produced by national geniuses contribute to humanity is de facto imbued with patriotic pride. To think that a call for the excavation of origins and national genealogies in historicist humanism terms, so that "backward" people can catch up with "universal" values would not involve patriotism and national pride, as Christie appears to believe, reveals a lack of understanding of the broader implications of such articulations in those very same "backward" settings. This in turn raises questions about the actual terms of such recognition.

Ülken defines patriotic humanism as a contribution to "unity in diversity" (*çoklukta birlik*) in the international arena, and claims that in humanism, differences between nations should be maintained and not erased.[143] According to Ülken, what unifies nations is that they all have their own authentic culture and civilization, and it is this that they share universally. In some ways, the Turkish-Islamic synthesis described in the 1983 *National Cultural Policy Report* embodies Ülken's approach with the exception of excluding the ancient Greek and Roman heritage in the geographies that belong to Turkey today. On the one hand, the 1983 Turkish-Islamic synthesis tries to realign cultural policy with the Turkish-Islamic demographic core of the republic, consolidated with the 1923 Greco-Turkish population exchange. The 1983 national culture report emphasized this alignment and assimilation, as well as a reinscription of the Muslim majority in the sense of the "Turkish-Islamic origins" of the nation via culture and history.

As for Ülken's configuration of the notion of patriotic humanism, we understand from both his and Christie's accounts that his notion generated some reaction. Yet, it is also true that UNESCO's interventions in humanism ended up generating an approach that is very similar. UNESCO's cultural heritage programs that recognize differences by nationally labeling them exemplify this dynamic.

UNESCO's postwar intervention to "democratize" culture, as it were, did not mean historicist humanism disappeared. In fact, liberal and historicist humanism were intertwined at times. The emphasis in liberal humanism on the notion of "unity in diversity" meant underscoring the unity of humanity by showing the universal traits that make us all human, such as birth, death, love, hate, laughter, pain, and so on. At times, to reveal the diversity in "unity in diversity," historicist humanism was mobilized.

It should then come as no surprise that the tenets of historicist humanism resurfaced in UNESCO platforms in other ways than the call for cultural recognition. For example, in the 1950 UNESCO conference in Florence, while a democratized humanism was among the things discussed, historicist humanism's classic ideals of "national genius" were also present:

> Meeting in surroundings which proclaim the creative genius of the Florentine masters, delegates will study *Unesco's plan for the preparation of a scientific and cultural history of mankind*. And, it is fitting that in the city of men like Leonardo da Vinci, Michelangelo, Botticelli, Masaccio and Donatello, they should be called on to consider ways of improving the material and moral freedom of creative artists.[144]

UNESCO's intervention, therefore, did not mean the ideals of historicist humanism disappeared. For instance, national genius still represented the national body and demonstrated what national culture—informed by racialized thinking—is capable of producing in terms of a superior specimen. Rather, UNESCO's intervention was to encourage the inclusion of not just Western European geniuses. In short, the genius continued to be perceived as a cherished national heritage and an important figure of the "cultural history of mankind."

In a radio broadcast in Italy, UNESCO's director-general, Jaime Torres Bodet, addressed UNESCO's ideals:

> A power cannot attain its full stature in any single man or group, it is necessary that the human species should consist of many units. Given, then, that humanity is designed by nature to develop its total power of the intellect . . . a first requirement is that mankind should live in the tranquility of peace that it may the more freely and easily devote itself to its appointed work.
>
> . . . Never . . . has the connection between peace and culture of the mind been stressed more strongly than in Dante Alighieri's noble words. And so we find that in the very dawn of Italian poetry and political thought, Unesco's path is mapped. . . . We should, however, add that, though peace is necessary for the development of the mind, a humanistic training of the mind is today just as necessary for the strengthening of international peace.[145]

Following thus the historicist humanist ideal, Torres Bodet refers to Dante Alighieri, another Florentine, a famous humanist canonical figure, who had placed the Prophet Muhammad and Ali in hell in his *Inferno*, which treated Islam not as a separate religion but a schism within Christianity.[146] Torres Bodet emphasizes the importance of diversity and culture in relation to peace and humanism. He configures building tolerance as important in that regard.

The new humanism promoted by UNESCO in the late 1940s and early 1950s then, was not a substitute for historicist humanism, nor was it entirely divorced from its broader implications. Historicist humanist identifications certainly entailed a strong relationship between origins, national cultures, and civilization in terms of a shared heritage: belonging to the same genealogy and civilization, which in turn configures national culture and identification with racialized implications. Today, UNESCO-sponsored cultural heritage sites embody these dynamics with all their contradictions and loaded histories. Where does this leave us?

Nation-states have long relied on tracing genealogies and origins to configure the relationship between individuals and history—a framework where nationals are part of a larger and unified history with a standardized narrative. For the most part, the nationally configured relationship between the individual and history is anchored in particular geographies articulated through narratives of origin—simultaneously territorializing them. Anthropologist Liisa Malkki argues that such a national genealogy, in turn, enables territorial and cultural claims in terms of botanical metaphors and kinship vocabulary—such as roots and motherland or fatherland.[147] The configuration of the nation via genealogical trees has thus permeated descriptions of the relationship between individuals and the land.

The sources from the 1950s analyzed in this book commonly refer to displaced communities in terms of "uprootedness." Indeed, political figures and researchers—those clustered around the AER, the AWR, UNESCO, international circles of sociology, the Council of Europe, and others—widely configured forced migration as a necessary and corrective alignment of categorized bodies with the proper nation. One justification offered for this segregated biopolitics was of course so-called unmixing. The different sites analyzed in these first two parts can help us put into perspective the notion of unmixing and how it is imbued with racialized thinking—both biologically and culturally.

On the other hand, in contemporary Turkey, especially in the aftermath of the Cold War, there has been an intervention to rethink national culture, origins, and genealogy on a personal level. The History Foundation, for example, made significant efforts to bring personal stories to the forefront in a way that mirrors UNESCO's call for monitoring history writing in terms of human rights—a call addressed earlier in the humanism conference in New Delhi. Thanks to nongovernmental organizations like the History Foundation, making family histories, objects, memories, and cultural identification public was encouraged in what can be described as a concerted effort to democratize history and cultural identification.

Following the temporary success of these valuable endeavors, which have faded in recent years, we can now take a step back and ask how *else* ruins and ruination should be addressed. We can also ask which stories get inscribed as diversity, and which others get absorbed into national culture. We ought to address what bringing family history and heritage to the forefront entails for different communities, as their hierarchies and implicit histories of violence still bleed into the political landscape. Not all groups are the same, nor can the politics of discrimination, segregation, forced migration, violence, and massacres that targeted each group be leveled. For some, family histories are not just accounts of dispossession, but through killings and violence, loss of family members are part of that dispossession. Their stories are difficult to exhume and bring into the public domain. If anything, reading the two essays in this part in relation to each other raises the issue of one's ethical obligation to ask whether ruination has been adequately addressed.

Mobilization of the field of culture to demand recognition is important but incomplete. The emphasis on liberal values in the terrains of culture tends to generate illusions of recognition. As for the humanist tools mobilized to address history and alterity, they can be vulnerable to misuse as the same tools can be wielded for entirely different purposes: "democratization" or "discrimination" in the articulations of identifications. How much room is there to avoid the essentializing gatekeeping informed by genealogies and origins at a national level, by resorting to the same methods of identification, only at a smaller scale, the familial? This is a key question for thinking the past in the present from a broader perspective. Without accompanying efforts to raise questions about the legacies of segregative biopolitics and connecting the elements of ruins as discussed here, to what extent can the historical, political, economic, and cultural factors behind ruination be addressed? This is why it is important to consider the limits of recognition, and the limited spaces of culture in which inclusion occurs while exclusionary logics remain intact.

In order to address the broader implications of engaging the ruins of segregative biopolitics and violence through genealogy and origins as an identification practice in the contemporary context, in this essay I have also sought to trace diachronically some of the intellectual histories intertwined with these identification practices. Combining the synchronic exploration of contemporary cultural identification practices with a brief diachronic analysis of the notions of genealogy and origins in relation to historicist humanism, I have also sought to engage in a multi-sited archaeology of knowledge.

Considering some of the remains of segregative biopolitics and how they were pieced together in the aftermath of the Cold War era in Turkey, I have sought to further excavate those remains to uncover their entangled intellectual histories within the context of historicist humanism. It is apparent that UNESCO, as part of this entangled intellectual history, in addition to endorsing liberal humanism, also intervened in the field of historicist humanism to open new paths for recognition—in this case, the curriculum.

With regard to UNESCO's interventions in liberal cultural policy, the world might very well be a better place with such interventions than without, but one wonders whether justice can be attained without addressing the very ruins upon which humanism towers today. A more thoroughgoing historical and political contextualization of the biopolitical infrastructures of liberal cultural politics is therefore imperative so as not to generate an illusion of emancipation through liberal discourses, while segregative biopolitics and policing of origins remain intact. I hope a relational reading of the two essays in this part will contribute to rethinking the issues embedded in addressing the legacies of biopolitics through liberal cultural discourses. Legacies of segregative biopolitics are not merely a matter of the past, but also a paradigm and pattern that continues to shape the present.

Put differently, one must ask what kinds of histories have merged into the remains of biopolitics, à la Walter Benjamin, simultaneously inscribing micro-histories into ruins labeled as "cultural memory," and rendering them each as unconnected and particular incidents, while leaving out one of the most important aspects shared by millions of human beings throughout the twentieth and twenty-first centuries: the continuing legacy and ongoing practices of segregative biopolitics. That's one *heritage* of humankind that needs to be more adequately discussed and addressed in terms of restitution, with all its entangled histories and violence embedded in its ruins. For it is important to remember that segregative biopolitics doesn't mean physical violence and necropolitics have disappeared from the picture. With these dynamics in mind, I now turn to Part Three, to look more closely at the cultural policies of liberal multiculturalism in the contemporary context.

· PART III ·
UNITY IN DIVERSITY
Culture, Social Cohesion, and Liberal Multiculturalism

Colonialism ... means the land- and sea- appropriations of the age of great discoveries of the four hundred years of Eurocentric international law. The odium of colonialism today concerns the European nations. At its core, it is nothing other than the odium of appropriation....

Allegedly, no longer is anything taken, but only divided and developed.

... Has humanity today actually "appropriated" the earth as a unity, so that there is nothing more to be appropriated? Has appropriation really ceased?

Carl Schmitt, *The* Nomos *of the Earth in the International Law of the* Jus Publicum Europaeum, 1950

The tradition of the oppressed teaches us that the "state of emergency" in which we live is not the exception but the rule. We must attain to a conception of history that is in keeping with this insight. Then we shall clearly realize that it is our task to bring about a real state of emergency, and this will improve our position in the struggle against Fascism. One reason why Fascism has a chance is that in the name of progress its opponents treat it as a historical norm. The current amazement that the things we are experiencing are "still" possible in the twentieth century is not philosophical. This amazement is not the beginning of knowledge—unless it is the knowledge that the view of history which gives rise to it is untenable.

Walter Benjamin, "Theses on the Philosophy of History," 1940

The Museumization of Culture and the Recognition of Alterity

ON DECEMBER 20, 2010, the Population Exchange Museum (Mübadele Müzesi) opened its doors in Çatalca, a district of Istanbul on the European side, as part of Istanbul's 2010 European Capital of Culture (ECoC) celebration. Presented as the first migration-themed museum in Turkey, the museum displays objects, photographs, and stories related to the Greek-Turkish population exchange, the first internationally ratified and executed forced exchange of populations.[1] Built to preserve the memory of the exchangees in Turkey, the museum is housed in a recently renovated Greek tavern, a remnant of the deported Greek Orthodox Christian community. Inside, the permanent exhibition on the main floor opens personalized windows into the experiences and memory of the Muslims deported from Greece and settled in Turkey as part of the population exchange. In handsomely organized glass partitions, family histories and narratives of the exchange accompanied by family photos and objects welcome visitors. This exhibition therefore emphasizes family experiences and backgrounds, and materializes the family history recollection trend in Turkey. Within the space of the Population Exchange Museum history is merged into the setting in its physical form—à la Walter Benjamin—inscribing personal histories into the 1923 exchange.

The story of the museum's founding reveals it to be a palimpsest of multiple institutional motivations, discourses, and practices. This palimpsest crystallizes broader dynamics of cultural identification, cultural policy, and humanist endorsements of diversity. The ECoC, for example, is a prime locus of pan-European cultural policy. It promotes European unity and, more recently, city projects that celebrate diversity and coexistence. Istanbul 2010 shows how the ECoC has been interpreted, deployed, and advertised in the Turkish context as celebrating Istanbul's diversity and multiculturalism.[2] The founding of the museum was a historical projection of the first decade of the 2000s. It captured earlier cultural politics in Turkey, before a more decisive turn toward authoritarianism. Supported by the Turkish Ministry of Culture and Istanbul Municipality, Istanbul 2010 was configured as a site to publicize the city's culture of coexistence and tolerance.[3] Yet the object of the museum, the 1923 compulsory exchange of religious minorities with Greece, embodies opposite values: separation and segregation. The stories displayed at the museum embody the human outcome of what can happen when coexistence fails.

At the turn of the new millennium and about seventy-seven years after the exchange, the descendants of the Muslims deported from Greece mobilized and formed the Foundation of Lausanne Treaty Emigrants in Turkey. They thereby institutionalized a cultural identification as exchangees (*mübadil*), anchoring their identification to the shared experience of the compulsory exchange. The Emigrants' Foundation is one of the driving forces that contributed to the oral history collections of the exchangees. As I was told numerous times during my interviews with some of the founding members in 2004–2006, establishing a museum was one of their goals since the very inception of the foundation. Funding was a problem, however, as the foundation is a nongovernmental organization and building a museum is costly. Still, the foundation accomplished a great deal in a decade: its members established an archive of documents, recipes, and songs; collected oral histories of the exchange; administered a mailing list on the exchange with hundreds of subscribers; sponsored and assisted many documentaries and publications on the subject; formed a population exchange choir; and organized heritage trips to various locations in Greece. In many ways, their work materialized Ziyaeddin Fahri Fındıkoğlu's vision presented in his publications in *Integration*, the official journal of the AWR, in the early 1960s. Finally, after a decade, the foundation secured the necessary funding from the Istanbul 2010 ECoC Agency to establish a museum. The organizers put tremendous effort into building, assembling, and curating the museum.

This museum, however, should not be considered a "mere site of memory" in Turkey nor solely an assemblage of artifacts of the population exchange; like any other museum, it should be viewed as part of larger dynamics and cultural policy. Granted, materializing memories of the exchange is the foundation's main concern. Yet this is only part of the picture. In fact, situating valuable efforts of a nongovernmental organization like the foundation within the larger framework of transnational state policies, including the cultural policies of the European Union (EU) and the ECoC, reveals the actual terms of official endorsement of diversity. Cultural policies developed in the aftermath of the Cold War era bear the imprint of liberalization via cultural recognition, resonating with UNESCO statements on the subject. It seems that today state-sponsored discourses attempt to co-opt the efforts of NGOs in order to promote their own official agenda. This museum offers an excellent opportunity to view this dynamic through the lens of diversity. In the two essays in this part I address cultural policies with regard to alterity and cultural identification in Turkey since the 1980 military coup.

Palimpsests:
Multiculturalism and the Museumization of Culture

In this essay I wish to go beyond a close reading of the museum itself and focus on the palimpsest of motivations, discourses, and cultural policy that surround its founding. By the mid-2000s, independent efforts to escape the oppressive climate of the 1980s and 1990s via culture were institutionalized and, in fact, incorporated into official discourses in Turkey. This palimpsest reveals how official cultural policies appropriate the notion of cultural heritage and transform—and rewrite—it into a liberal mode of multiculturalism informed by a blend of humanist discourses such as unity in diversity, brotherhood, and clearly demarcated genealogies and origins for those included within that diversity. I call this process the *museumization of culture* to denote a mode of official appropriation of personal and NGO efforts. This dynamic is independent from the original motivation of founding the museum, which in itself was a laudable attempt of recollection launched by the Emigrants' Foundation. Museumization—as an official cultural policy—entails the configuration of cultural backgrounds as material for display in mediated sites and offers a metaphor to gauge official approaches to diversity as a mere matter of cultural representation. It denotes a visual culture of recognition that reductively configures visibility as recognition. Here I juxtapose cultural policies and discourses on diversity in Turkey and in the EU as crystallized around the ECoC projects of 2006–2010—both of which draw on UNESCO's statements on diversity.

The years between 2006 and 2010 are important because Istanbul was elected in 2006 to become the European Capital of Culture in 2010, when the ECoC application regulations were changed to include negotiating states in the applicant pool. In a way, the selection of Istanbul as a European Capital of Culture can be construed as underscoring diversity within the EU. After all, the EU has long been criticized for being a Christian club, and the treatment of Turkey's earlier application has often been accused of being different from the way some other states, which later joined the EU, were treated. Selecting Istanbul as the 2010 European Capital of Culture, without necessarily admitting Turkey to the EU, was thus a visible and symbolic recognition without serious consequences for the EU. Indeed, this very dynamic mimics the logic of liberal multiculturalism: a celebration of diversity without historicity and political contextualization. In addition, this period also marks the worldwide financial crisis and the bursting of the EU economic bubble, with crises hitting one member state after another. Focusing on these years of the new millennium illuminates how the notion of culture can be engaged in a relatively positive period of economic prosperity just as the economy begins to take a turn for the worse. In Turkey, these years also marked a turning point before the country's seemingly liberal policies crumbled.[4]

The contemporary cultural policies analyzed in the first section of this essay promote the values of liberal multiculturalism, that is, a tamed version of cultural recognition in which alterity, cultural rights, and representation receive some limited official endorsement. These rights are often marketed as freedom or liberty—resonating with the 1982 UNESCO statement on diversity—without really addressing underlying power discrepancies, socioeconomic disparities, segregative biopolitics, and historical patterns of violence and discrimination.

Obviously, a palimpsest approach here is not meant to equate these institutional practices: different ethics and aspirations are involved in the museumization of culture. In this case, if we take museumization literally, it is, in the case of the Population Exchange Museum, an act of recollecting family history by means of family memory narratives, photos, objects, and so on, as addressed in Part Two. But if we take it metaphorically, the museumization of culture implies a limited official endorsement of cultural difference via liberal multiculturalism and the ECoC. Despite their differences, in both cases, the act of museumization recasts objects for purposes of cultural representation and divorces them from their history and context. For instance, when an object like a padlock that belonged to family elders is museumized, it loses its initial function—keeping something locked and safe. Such an object is then reconfigured as a sign of cultural heritage through the family, and the object gets detached from its actual history—for example, we do not know how and why a family member acquired this object or put it to use.

This process takes on a different significance when transnational cultural programs such as the ECoC contribute to the museumization of culture as a way of endorsing alterity. In Turkey, when communities such as the Greeks, Armenians, Jews, and Roma are "celebrated" in these projects through exhibitions, music, or food, they are configured for display, which divorces them from history and depoliticizes and objectifies them. The celebration of diversity is itself a mode of recognition informed by liberal humanism—unity in diversity as a message of peace and coexistence—but what the terms of that coexistence entail remains an open question. Museumization of culture, then, disconnects the "object" on display from history literally or metaphorically and transforms its meaning. Therefore, considering a public act of recollection, however commendable, as yet another isolated case or site of memory without addressing palimpsests of institutional narratives and practices that surround it, obscures its broader context and power implications.

In this context, studying this palimpsest offers a framework for juxtaposing texts to flesh out their overt or concealed relations as a rewriting, so to speak. It helps clarify how different discourses of diversity get interpreted, rewritten, and transformed—especially when traveling from the EU to Turkey. The museumization of culture thus is both a site for recollection *and* a mode of state-sponsored multiculturalism. An analysis of the aforementioned palimpsest offers insight into the limits of liberal multiculturalism as materialized in the EU and Turkey in late 2000s. In this context, UNESCO's push for diversity as cultural policy is notable. In addition to the transnational dimension of this cultural policy, there was also a local discourse that shaped it in Turkey: neo-Ottomanism. "Neo-Ottomanism" as I use it here can be narrowly defined as a discourse on the past intended to legitimize contemporary neoliberal and cultural policies by drawing on anachronistic reinterpretations and the glorification of the Ottoman past in Turkey.[5] An excavation of the local context in Turkey during the first two terms of AKP rule shows how local discourses draw as much from transnational cultural policies and discourses as they do from local past cultural policies and discourses. In Turkey, this entails the Turkish-Islamic synthesis.

As for the museum itself, it is an honorable attempt at consolidating cultural heritage and identification, which also includes the incorporation of family objects and histories. It institutionalizes what the late Fuat had sought to do with his home museum. With these dynamics in mind, I now turn to the Population Exchange Museum in order to first address the museumization of culture as a mode of cultural identification through the example of the 1923 Greek-Turkish exchange of populations.

The 1923 Population Exchange Museum and Cultural Identification

During his appearance at the museum's grand opening on the Turkish TV channel TGRT, the late Atila Karaelmas, a member of the executive board of the Emigrants' Foundation and project coordinator of the museum at the time, appeared exhausted from the hard work of renovation, preparation, curation, and opening of the museum:

> First of all, one out of every three people living in Turkey is a member of a family with a migration story. And the exchange is a unique example in the world where about two million people were forcibly displaced as part of a mutual agreement between two states [as part of the 1923 Treaty of Lausanne]. This had a serious cultural impact on both countries. This impact remained locked [away from public view], but now, with the population exchange museum, we are unearthing [*açığa çıkarmak*, literally "bringing out in the open"] this culture.

Karaelmas's televised statement points at the general assumption that the 1923 exchange was silenced in Turkey up until recently.[6] Yet, as the sources analyzed in this book demonstrate, this is not exactly true. Studies were conducted on the subject and presented at the AER/AWR in the 1950s and 1960s. Cultural identification on a personal basis, on the other hand, might not have had the same kind connotation of recognition, which became especially visible during the last decade of the Cold War and which has gained momentum ever since. Moreover, Karaelmas's statement demonstrates a prominent trend in the 1990s and early 2000s whereby many citizens undertook excavations of the past to trace personal histories and genealogies. Such practices have often been construed as rescuing various cultural backgrounds from state-sponsored national identifications, as Karaelmas's statement also implies.

In their opening remarks, representatives of the Istanbul 2010 European Capital of Culture Agency emphasized how in Turkey, unlike in Greece, there was a delay in the institutionalized organization of the population exchangees. Their comments were translated into English and published in the museum's catalog: "Although in Greece, a number of museums related to the population exchange have been founded, Turkey, regrettably, was lacking such a museum—although it was on the agenda [of the Emigrants' Foundation]. We—the 2010 European Capital of Culture Agency—are proud of having supported the Foundation of Lausanne Treaty Emigrants and enabled the establishment of this museum."[7] During my research, I had heard of different versions of this comparison with Greece. Indeed, one of the board members of the Emigrants' Foundation told me that after reading Kemal Yalçın's book *The Entrusted Trousseau*, he realized how remarkably neglected the exchange was in Turkey, when Greece had museums, archives, and organizations to preserve the heritage of the Greek Orthodox refugees.[8] Here, the museum is presented as a decisive move to change this dynamic.

Indeed, institutional attempts at preserving the memory, stories, and experiences of the exchange had begun much earlier in Greece. As anthropologist Penelope Papailias's work demonstrates, this was in part because the Greek Orthodox arriving from Turkey were perceived as relics of the past Hellenic presence in Anatolia and therefore their story was believed to have national value.[9] The Greek Orthodox exchangees now settled in Greece were thus themselves considered cultural heritage, in part because their existence spoke directly to the notion of Hellenism in Anatolia and its preservation. This preservation can be construed as loosely related to the logic of historicist humanism—a genealogical narrative that can be traced back to a land, Anatolia. The remains of the Hellenic presence in that location—whether it is people, their homesteads, or ancient ruins—have been configured as relics to be recollected.

As for the Population Exchange Museum in Istanbul, a representative of the 2010 ECoC Agency touched on the need for such a museum in Turkey:

> The children and grandchildren of immigrants constitute a majority of the population in Turkey, which for the last 200 years has been target to a continuous flow of migration from territories breaking away from Ottoman rule. The European Capital of Culture Population Exchange Museum is the first Turkish museum based on the theme "migration," where these works and products that had been preserved [by the exchanged families themselves], are now being exhibited [publicly].[10]

The population exchange, of course, was not just another migration as the statement above suggests: it was a forced migration. The 1923 exchange is not addressed here for what it was, but as a regular migration, neatly aligned with other migrations. With the reference to this point, the demographic fabric in Turkey is also addressed.

As Part One has discussed, integration via assimilation was a general trend in the 1950s. Turkey at the time welcomed new Muslim emigrants, mostly coming from Bulgaria. Meanwhile, others, such as the Kurds, continued to be brutally oppressed or killed. In fact, in 1953, Remzi Bucak, the Demokrat Party deputy from Diyarbakir/Amed, asked in the Turkish parliament whether the "Eastern provinces" (*doğu vilayetleri*) in Turkey were actually a colony (*müstemleke*).[11] He also invited members of the Republican Party of Mustafa Kemal Atatürk—the former general who is often referred to as the founding figure of the Republic of Turkey—to critically reflect on their decades-long policies in the region. The early decades of the Turkish republic constitute a period of nationalization, with state violence on the one hand, and Turkification policies on the other.[12] Forced internal migration—a form of segregative biopolitics— was also part of this process. The 1934 Settlement Law was among the policies Deputy Bucak brought up in parliament.[13] This law reflects the suggestions of Rıza Nur as addressed in his memoirs. It provided a legal platform for the spatial redistribution of those who were considered to be from a non-Turkish race (*ırk*), culture (*kültür*), or lineage (*soy*). And although the law uses different words for race, lineage, and pedigree, they all have racialized implications of bloodlines, genealogical family trees—those from the same lineage configured as belonging to the same branch—and origins.

In the Turkish context, in addition to the diverse backgrounds of the residents of Anatolia, remarkable diversity also marked the Muslim communities that came to Turkey. After the military takeover in the 1980s, once again this diversity came under scrutiny. These dynamics might be one of the reasons why a migration-themed museum had never before been erected in Turkey—as the late Karaelmas also expressed during the opening ceremony of the Population Exchange Museum. Another reason could be the reluctance to remind people of their differences.

The hard work of the Emigrants' Foundation can be added to the efforts of the History Foundation to democratize history in the 1990s and 2000s—both were conducive to embracing family history in the form of personal and cultural heritage as a mode of self-identification. The remarks at the opening of the Population Exchange Museum attest to this, and the backgrounds of the exchangees were articulated as heritage to be preserved. At the turn of the millennium, the Emigrants' Foundation was brought together against the backdrop of the aforementioned dynamics in Turkey and beyond.[14] Dedicated members of the foundation thus mobilized cultural identification and heritage recollection.

Various forms of engagement with diversity articulated as multiculturalism have marked Turkey's public domain over the last two decades. In this context, food, music, space, and daily lives shared with the Greek Orthodox in the Ottoman Empire and Turkey were arguably among the most commonly revisited memory tropes of coexistence among different groups.[15] Whether it is the nostalgic undertones of *rembetika* music, celebrated tales of shared recipes such as the eggplant dish *imam bayıldı*, or romanticized narratives of peaceful coexistence, the Greek Orthodox citizens of Turkey constituted a predominant point of departure to engage issues revolving around multiculturalism in the 1990s. It is important to note that these tropes of coexistence had liberal humanist undertones, configuring food and music as signs of shared human elements but this time, rather than universal, regional and geographical aspects were emphasized. What unifies people is the shared humanity brought closer via cultural similarities. In this discourse, the commonality of geographic culture is emphasized via sensory memory—music, food, sight and smells—as shared human elements.[16] Pain is also part of it. These in turn are configured as a message of peace and coexistence; the implication is that since we are all humans belonging to the same geography, enjoying the same food and the same music, among other things, we are all brothers and sisters.

The Population Exchange Museum opened its doors at the intersections of these dynamics and as part of the Istanbul 2010 program. Family history, trousseaus, and cultural heritage are all visually and verbally addressed in the permanent collection. As mentioned, a large segment of the museum space is organized in terms of family histories. In each glass window section, a family and its history in relation to the population exchange is introduced to visitors in a picture frame. The framed text includes how the family was exchanged and where they were from in Greece. Family photos circle these narratives, and a display of family objects accompanies each framed narrative. Displayed objects include a wide variety of things such as prayer rugs, needlework, medals, perfume bottles, furniture, sheet music and instruments, copper pitchers, door locks and animal bells, millstones, wooden suitcases, chests, documents, maps and—one of the most important pieces of the exhibit—the trousseaus.

Just as the book *The Entrusted Trousseau* used the image of the trousseau to unravel personal histories of various exchangees, the trousseaus on display at the museum are central to the exhibit. The museum's catalog states that trousseaus have a special place in the exhibition: prepared for the bride-to-be, a trousseau consists of garments, embroideries, lace, and needlework, among other things. Because of its value, not all families actually used the trousseau but rather kept it as a part of the family's heritage.

This claim cannot be made for all the objects on display, such as animal bells or door padlocks. These objects initially had different functions, but they have gained a new value as signs of family heritage. In turn, the function of these objects has shifted from material to symbolic: animal bells for herding and padlocks for securing things have become dissociated from their original function/meaning and now signify the family itself. As Jean Baudrillard argues, the act of collecting objects such as antiques does not render them afunctional but gives a new meaning to them, "namely the signifying of time"—and hence, history.[17] And yet, unlike antiques, which signify time more abstractly, when these everyday objects are engaged as family objects, they invite a personalized conceptualization of time, which speaks very much to the sort of family history that the History Foundation advocated. These objects, then, have gained the meaning of family heritage: as something to be collected, preserved, and displayed; in short, to be museumized. Once collected and displayed by the Emigrants' Foundation, they gained value as *cultural heritage*—this time symbolizing a shared experience in time: the population exchange and its aftermath. The museum both museumizes culture and seeks to historicize it.

The location of the museum adds to this matrix of interwoven narratives and practices. It is, as noted earlier, in Çatalca, a district of Istanbul demographically affected by the population exchange. An important segment of the town is composed of descendants of exchangees who settled there after the Greek Orthodox inhabitants were expelled. The former Greek tavern that now houses the museum had multiple owners before it was donated to the Emigrants' Foundation for the museum project. Notably, in his opening remarks, the mayor of Çatalca addressed how well the exchangees were integrated into the fabric of Turkish society and that they were true followers of Atatürk.[18] Here, successful integration and unification—not diversity—was emphasized.

As mentioned, considering mass population movements, exiles, and conversions in the Ottoman Empire, the backgrounds of the exchangees reveal remarkable differences. Consider the families of Raşit Kemali Bonneval, Fuat, and all the others brought to Turkey because they were Muslims. They attest to the rich diversity blanketed under the category of "Islam": Christian converts, such as those from France and Venice; Jewish-convert followers of the messianic rabbi Shabbatai Zvi, often referred to as the Dönme or crypto-Jews; members of different Sufi orders, such as the Bektashis and Mevlevis; monolingual Greek speakers; bilingual Turkish speakers with a Greek accent; and so on. During the exchange, it had become clear that religion did not necessarily translate into personal allegiances, self-identification, or wishes to stay or leave. In view of this landscape of people, the exchangees embodied diversity par excellence.

This is further exemplified in the museum's catalog, published as a coffee-table book. The book also addresses the diverse backgrounds of the inhabitants of Çatalca who are descendants of the exchangees, and traces their regional culinary habits and food specialties to Greece as an extension of the museumization. In fact, the heterogeneity of the exchangees and their descendants actually demonstrates the hidden diversity of the majority often referred to as Muslim Turks. Yet, interestingly, this was not a site that Istanbul 2010 officials chose to address in terms of diversity, as they did with other communities such as the Roma, Jews, Armenians, and Greeks. This raises questions about what informs official categorizations of diversity.

Furthermore, aside from this particular case, in general, the museumization of culture structures a space of exhibition as an encounter: people visit and get "introduced" to the personal histories of the people that they have been living with side by side for decades. There are numerous other examples of this, such as Roma exhibitions in the EU. The field of culture, on the other hand, has a long, interconnected history with humanist modes of promoting diversity. With this in mind, I now turn to the palimpsest of discourses, cultural policies, and related institutional motivations that surrounded the founding of the museum.

Endorsing Diversity: UNESCO, the UN Alliance of Civilizations, and Turkey

In 2006, the same year the Istanbul European Capital of Culture application was submitted to the EU, the notion of diversity entered a cultural policy report issued by the AKP-led government. The report delineated a state-designated commission's cultural policy recommendations to the government. It promoted tolerance and emphasized the importance of establishing a consciousness that diversity is part of Turkey's rich cultural fabric.[19] It highlighted the importance of diversity in unity (*birlik içinde çokluk*) and urged the AKP leadership to sign the 2005 UNESCO Convention on the Protection and Promotion of the Diversity of Cultural Expressions.[20] The phrase "diversity in unity" reverses UNESCO's call for "unity in diversity" in the early years of the Cold War, which emphasized unity despite racialized diversity. Diversity was a given—and actually a concern—in the late 1940s and 1950s. In the catchphrase "unity in diversity," the emphasis was therefore on unity. In the 2006 cultural policy report, on the other hand, it is diversity that was emphasized.

The UNESCO Convention on the Protection and Promotion of the Diversity of Cultural Expressions represents the implementation of the principles laid out in the 2001 UNESCO Universal Declaration on

Cultural Diversity.[21] The 2001 Universal Declaration emphasizes the importance of culture in building awareness of tolerance and recognition of both cultural differences and the unity of humankind, all of which would supposedly promote peace:

> **Recalling** that the Preamble of the Constitution of UNESCO affirms that "the wide diffusion of culture, and the education of humanity for justice and liberty and peace are indispensable to the dignity of man and constitute a sacred duty which all the nations must fulfill in a spirit of mutual assistance and concern," . . .
>
> **Reaffirming** that culture should be regarded as the set of distinctive spiritual, material, intellectual and emotional features of society or a social group, and that it encompasses, in addition to art and literature, lifestyles, ways of living together, value systems traditions and beliefs, . . .
>
> **Noting** that culture is at the heart of contemporary debates about identity, social cohesion, and the development of a knowledge-based economy,
>
> **Affirming** that respect for the diversity of cultures, tolerance, dialogue and cooperation, in a climate of mutual trust and understanding are among the best guarantees of international peace and security,
>
> **Aspiring** to greater solidarity on the basis of recognition of cultural diversity, of awareness of the unity of humankind, and of the development of intercultural exchanges.[22]

The UNESCO definition of culture is rearticulated here. Reminiscent of UNESCO's earlier interventions in historicist humanism in school curricula at the 1951 conference in New Delhi, the Declaration on Cultural Diversity rearticulates the importance of the education of humanity. The declaration promotes culture to help educate humanity with regard to diversity, which in turn might generate tolerance and contribute to justice, liberty, and peace. Social cohesion and peace reappear here as important goals, in addition to a "knowledge-based economy."

In a 1996 report entitled *The Knowledge-Based Economy*, the Organisation for Economic Co-operation and Development (OECD) defines this notion as the recognition of knowledge as an important factor in economic growth and productivity.[23] Accordingly, the OECD considers knowledge-based economies to be based on the production, distribution, and use of knowledge and information—deemed essential to maximize economic performance. And because the dissemination of knowledge is facilitated by digital sources and communications networks, the notion of an *information society* gains importance. The OECD also describes knowledge as embodied in human beings—identified as human capital—and as embedded in technology. The increasing recognition of these factors in economic growth is underlined in the report. The report also points out that "knowledge-intensive service sectors, such as education, communications and information" are growing, and estimates that "more than 50 per cent of Gross Domestic Product" in major OECD economies at the time was knowledge-based.[24]

UNESCO's 2001 Universal Declaration on Cultural Diversity emphasizes a knowledge-based economy in terms of culture. It encourages the facilitation of intercultural exchanges and proclaims that diversity and tolerance are imperative for international peace and security. And it puts the education of humanity at the forefront as a possible venue to accomplish these goals. Zooming out of the 2001 Universal Declaration on Cultural Diversity for a moment to reconsider the larger picture laid out thus far, it can be said that much of this discourse on diversity towers over the dynamics, discourses, and ruins addressed in this book. As for the implications of human capital in a knowledge-based economy, this time it is not just turning the human into capital through already trained, work-ready bodies à la Corrado Gini, but also via the knowledge every human embodies and the skill sets one has acquired. In the context of UNESCO's 2001 declaration, that knowledge is culture.

UNESCO's 2001 Universal Declaration on Cultural Diversity asks member states to develop proper cultural policies:

> In our *increasingly diverse societies*, it is essential to ensure harmonious interaction among people and groups with plural, varied and dynamic cultural identities as well as their willingness to live together. Policies for the inclusion and participation of all citizens are guarantees of social cohesion, the vitality of civil society and peace. Thus defined, cultural pluralism gives policy expression to the reality of cultural diversity. Indissociable from a democratic framework, cultural pluralism is conducive to cultural exchange and to the flourishing of creative capacities that sustain public life.[25]

Reading this statement in light of the 1996 OECD report on knowledge-based economy adds to the palimpsest of cultural policies pertaining to alterity and diversity explored in this essay; cultural exchange facilitates economic growth. To that end, UNESCO calls for cultural policy that will enhance the dissemination of knowledge about diverse cultures with an emphasis on their unity. Again, such recognition of diversity is configured as democratic.

Also, consider the statement that we live in *"increasingly* diverse societies." Juxtaposed against all the dynamics addressed in this book, including segregative biopolitics, this statement suggests diversity has increasingly become a fact that needs to be addressed. Such a statement undercuts the entangled histories and ruins of segregative biopolitics. As discussed, the spatial redistribution of bodies according to their "kind" was commonplace in the aftermath of the Second World War—a process for which the 1923 Greek-Turkish exchange was an important milestone. Segregative biopolitics on the one hand and assimilation on the other have long informed the regulation of alterity. Further, this statement supposes that nation-states were not diverse to begin with. Yet, the realities of different countries, such as Spain—with Catalans, Galicians, Basques, and others—indicate otherwise.

The fact that diversity rather than assimilation is emphasized today is, of course, positive. Yet, this emphasis as a rather recent phenomenon obfuscates the historical and political contexts that this books addresses in its diachronic and synchronic analyses of palimpsests. In addition, it appears that diversity here again encompasses racialized thinking: it is implied that those who are not the same *kind* are arriving as part of immigration flows and increased mobility, and that this is why we are living in *increasingly* diverse societies— as if diversity is a new phenomenon indexed to contemporary migration. To turn around and implicate mobility as a cause of diversity today reconfigures unity in diversity as a notion looming over the ruins of segregative biopolitics and assimilation, and hence tends to depoliticize and dehistoricize it, even if that was not the intention.

UNESCO's 2005 Convention opened the principles of the 2001 Declaration to the signature of member states, with the understanding that cultural diversity, rights, and expressions were key elements of human dignity. The emphasis on human dignity here resonates with the human rights discourse, casting cultural identity as a question of rights. Acceding to the 2005 Convention, in return, would entail developing cultural policies to match the principles set forth in the Universal Declaration and the convention that followed.

The Turkish government never signed this document, as anthropologist Banu Karaca points out.[26] On the other hand, this doesn't mean UNESCO constitutes a model against which to measure the status of human rights in any country. UNESCO has its own history and at its inception, its own terms of endorsing diversity. As for the 2005 Convention, it appears to have informed the EU's cultural policy—which also requires critical scrutiny. My goal, therefore, is not to make a Euro-American-centric argument by bringing these institutional factors into the picture and cast Turkey's case during the first decade of the 2000s as a case of exceptionalism. Rather, I aim to point out the limits and pitfalls of palimpsests of institutionalized endorsements of diversity in the broader contemporary context, and to pick up on those threads to rethink the cultural and intellectual histories entangled around such institutions, especially UNESCO—one of the most powerful driving forces of cultural policy in the twentieth century.

Following the 2001 Universal Declaration on Cultural Diversity, the 2005 UNESCO Convention identified cultural diversity as a "defining characteristic of humanity" and asserted that cultural diversity "forms a common heritage of humanity."[27] The discourse of racialized diversity of the late 1940s and 1950s is reconfigured here as cultural diversity. Whether racialized thinking has disappeared, however, is questionable. Accordingly, everything belonging to humanity is to be valued as something shared. These tenets of liberal humanism are additionally articulated as a heritage of humanity. What is universal is that everyone has a cultural identity, hence, we are surrounded by diversity. The tenets of historicist humanism—culture as the heritage of humanity—thus merge into aspects of liberal humanism at yet another level. This in turn encourages practices of tracing genealogies, origins, and heritage, but at a more individual and micro level, in an attempt to reinscribe the particular into the universal.

Like the 2001 Declaration, the 2005 Convention also included articles to ensure the recognition of linguistic and cultural rights and to protect cultural pluralism. It too highlighted the importance of "democracy, tolerance, social justice and mutual respect between peoples and cultures" for local and international peace and security.[28] "Celebrating the importance of cultural diversity" for human rights is among the premises articulated in the convention.[29] The EU signed the 2005 Convention with pending reservations, and celebrated diversity in its cultural policies. In 2010, Turkish officials did the same, as was evident in the display and marketing of multiculturalism during Istanbul 2010. On the whole, Turkish and EU cultural policies intersected in the Istanbul 2010 European Capital of Culture project, where Ottoman tolerance of alterity—largely understood as religion at the time—was an important underlying theme. It was implied that Ottoman tolerance was evidence of Turkey's "liberal" stance on diversity at the time.

In the years leading to Istanbul 2010, neo-Ottomanism was configured as a discourse of liberal multiculturalism under the AKP, but this discourse did not emerge overnight and cannot be reduced to a reformulation of the EU's cultural policy or UNESCO's declarations and convention on diversity. Its threads can be traced synchronically to another initiative Turkey undertook at the time, the United Nations Alliance of Civilizations, as well as diachronically to an earlier local discourse and cultural policy, the Turkish-Islamic synthesis. A reconsideration of this palimpsest helps us rethink what informs the discourse of tolerance in the field of culture in Turkey.

The Istanbul 2010 application dossier, official EU reports on the subject, and the programs implemented as part of the event all indicate that Turkish officials and some cultural actors undertook a similar approach to culture and reconfigured it for the local Turkish context with a neo-Ottomanist touch. Among the factors that enabled this was surely the financing of the project: Istanbul received the largest funding of any ECoC projects up until that point. In part this was because Turkey cast the project as part of the UN's Alliance of Civilizations.

The Alliance of Civilizations initiative was sponsored by the prime ministers of Turkey and Spain in 2005—Recep Tayyip Erdoğan and José Luis Rodríguez Zapatero—and was institutionalized by the United Nations. The objective of the alliance is to promote dialogue and tolerance as a remedy to the so-called clash of civilizations—a notion that grained strength in the aftermath of 9/11 in association with political scientist Samuel Huntington, who had previously predicted that conflicts after the Cold War would be cultural and civilizational. Huntington—reproducing historicist humanism paradigms informed by racialized thinking—also viewed multiculturalism in the United States under a negative light, believing it diluted white American civilizational ties to white Europe.

The UN Alliance of Civilizations initiative explicitly focuses on "civilization" and promotes recognition of difference or alterity from that perspective.[30] The discourse of civilization, as discussed in Part One, has long informed racism and notions of colonial superiority, and was used as a rationale for imperial domination.[31] Unfortunately, instead of engaging the political and historical reasons as to why certain conflicts or acts of violence are addressed along the lines of civilizational rifts—as is the case with the discourse of the clash of civilizations—or questioning the very economic, political, and historical foundations of what informs the notion of civilization in the first place, the UN Alliance actually embraces civilization as an identificatory paradigm.

Taking a position—no matter how well-intended it may be—within the same discourse without questioning its historical and political implications thus reproduces the same paradigms, rather than debunking them. In the first decade of the 2000s, the AKP's approach to liberal multiculturalism was intertwined with the paradigms of the UN Alliance of Civilizations.[32] This approach configures diversity as the coexistence of Muslims—predominantly Sunnis—Armenian and Greek Christians, and Jews. Incidentally, this construction also speaks to the Kemalist interpretation of the Lausanne Treaty that sealed the 1923 Greek-Turkish population exchange.[33] In the early years of the Turkish republic, Lausanne was reductively interpreted to recognize only Greeks, Armenians, and Jews as minorities. Rıza Nur's memoirs, discussed in the Introduction, offer important insights into the approaches to the notion of minorities at the time. In general, Turkey's commitment to the Alliance of Civilizations—especially with the support of former prime minister Ahmet Davutoğlu—has arguably further contributed to the development of neo-Ottomanism as a cultural policy.

As part of this initiative, Turkey launched numerous projects and two national action plans with the objective of promoting dialogue and tolerance among civilizations. On April 12, 2008, the UN Alliance of Civilizations Turkish national action plan was published in the Turkish *Official Gazette* (*Resmi Gazete*); it included Istanbul 2010 as part of the effort to publicize Istanbul's culture of tolerance and coexistence.[34] The national plan, accompanied by a memorandum signed by the prime minister of the time—Recep Tayyip Erdoğan—adopted the civilizational discourse.[35] This approach positions Turkey, and by extension the Ottoman Empire, as representatives of Islamic civilization. In that regard, it configures the Ottoman Empire as an exemplar state in which different religious groups appear to be taken as emblematic of different civilizations—Christian, Muslim, and Jewish—and wherein these groups coexisted peacefully.[36] Istanbul 2010 European Capital of Culture was one of the projects sponsored as part of the 2008 Alliance of Civilizations Turkish national action plan.[37] This might be one of the reasons for the very large budget allocated to Istanbul 2010, as it was not only the EU but also the UN Alliance of Civilizations that was involved. In addition, both of them provided platforms to attract more tourists.

The official ex-post evaluation report prepared for the European Commission Directorate-General for Education and Culture states that the Turkish Ministry of Finance provided 95.04 percent of the entire budget for Istanbul 2010 using taxpayers' money, with only 0.56 percent coming from the EU.[38] It also noted how the government's corporate—read: neoliberal—mentality dominated some of the activities: "[The] international campaign primarily consisted of a broad effort to attract tourists to Istanbul based on the 'brand value' of Istanbul (using the slogan 'Istanbul, the most inspiring city in the world') rather than to promote the cultural programme itself to potential audiences."[39] According to this evaluation, Istanbul 2010 marketed diversity, coexistence, and tolerance, rather than promoting the content. This marketing can be construed as a move in terms of a knowledge-based economy, turning alterity into human capital for display. Independent of the worthy efforts of different organizations and artists who were funded by this project, state officials appear to have co-opted such efforts to advertise and market their own limited version of diversity.

In line with the corporate approach, about 14.5 percent of the entire budget—nearly 42 million euros—was spent on Istanbul 2010 promotional campaigns. There was an 11 percent increase in tourism in Istanbul during 2010. Sixty percent of total expenditures in 2009 and 70 percent in 2010 were allocated to the restoration and renovation of existing heritage sites. The Population Exchange Museum was built at the intersections of these dynamics and was one of the heritage sites supported by the Istanbul 2010 funds. As for the museum site itself, with a budget of 1,200,000 Turkish liras, it received only 0.2 percent of the entire funding allocated to the Istanbul 2010 project.

European Capital of Culture as a Transnational Diversity Project

The 2006 report of the selection meeting to determine the 2010 European Capitals of Culture clearly states the objective of the ECoC initiative: "to highlight the richness and diversity of European cultures and the features they share, as well as to promote greater mutual knowledge and understanding among Europe's citizens."[40] The initiative was thus cast as a project to introduce European Union citizens to one another's cultures. Since the mid-2000s, the EU's cultural policies have increasingly focused on projects that promote diversity and peaceful coexistence among different parties. For example, the European Commission, in a 2007 document entitled *European Agenda for Culture*, states that "to simultaneously bring our common heritage to the fore and recognise the contribution of all cultures present in our societies, cultural diversity needs to be nurtured in a context of openness and exchanges between different cultures. As we live in increasingly multicultural societies, we need therefore to promote intercultural dialogue and intercultural competences."[41]

This carefully formulated statement emphasizes two things: recognition of cultural differences in the mode of celebrating diversity, *and* promotion of European heritage as a shared cultural identification marker. Further, the earlier UNESCO statement that "we live in *increasingly* multicultural societies" resurfaces here, as if Europe's nation-states were monocultural prior to recent migrations to and within Europe. This assumption is evident in the EU's cultural policies from 2006 to 2010.

Within this cultural-policy agenda, the ECoC is a pan-European initiative that seeks to foster both difference—casting diversity as richness—and common ties that bring people together, that is, Europeanness. In fact, another EU intercultural cities project launched after 2006—when Istanbul was selected as the 2010 European Capital of Culture—states that it aims to stimulate "inclusive debate and policy making in pilot cities, taking an intercultural approach to migration, integration and social cohesion"; "to encourage pilot cities to develop comprehensive intercultural strategies to manage urban diversity"; and "to act as an inspiration for other cities in Europe."[42] The goal is to urge cities to "develop an intercultural strategy to transform their policies, public spaces, institutions and the relationships between communities" in order to establish diversity as the norm and as a source of dynamism to affirm the heritage and identity of all people.[43] The terms of this affirmation are not made clear, as the relationship between visibility via cultural representation and affirmation is not unambiguous.[44] Taking cities as a micro project, this EU cultural policy seeks to foster a cultural identification within the broader context of the EU.[45] The claimed objective is to develop an intercultural approach to migration, which appears to be different from the context of the 1950s. Cities are thus configured as sites of mediated diversity as applicant city agencies are asked to rethink relationships between communities in spatial terms.

In a recent edited volume that engages the cultural politics of Europe since the 1980s, historian Kiran Klaus Patel describes the ECoC as the most prominent European cultural policy and argues that it constitutes a site for negotiating Europeanness—especially "as part of and in reaction to European integration."[46] Patel further calls attention to the dynamics of "Europeanization" and how negotiations of European identity, as well as the aspirations and challenges of European cultural policy, are crystallized through the ECoC.[47] For him, it is important to explore how such cultural policies localize Europeanization and how, in return, they Europeanize the local.[48] Local actors are important in this process, as they interpret policy and bring it to life in a locale; indeed one of the criteria for being selected a European Capital of Culture is that citizens are integrated into the process and take an active part in the activities organized as part of the ECoC year.[49]

The European Capital of Culture is not only a pan–European Union project but one in which local actors bring their own interpretations and versions of the project into the picture. A palimpsest-based approach reveals the dynamics of the local rewriting of the broader ECoC project. Therefore, it is not "Europeanness" per se that I address in connection with Istanbul 2010, but rather one of the main values attributed to "Europeanness" and endorsed by all these aforementioned institutionalized cultural policies: diversity—and by extension, discourses of integration and coexistence.

Of course, launching a cultural policy with an emphasis on diversity does not necessarily mean a similar emphasis will be adopted in other policies. A good example for this is the case of the Roma in the late 2000s: even though they are EU citizens, thousands of Roma, puzzlingly cast as the "biggest minority in Europe" in the European Union's cultural policy,[50] were deported by the French president at the time, Nicolas Sarkozy, in the middle of an EU Roma cultural integration project and Roma exhibitions in Brussels. Sarkozy's deportation is a prime example of segregative biopolitics: the spatial redistribution of categorized bodies to regulate numbers—in this case, via deportation.

That this happened during the EU's Roma integration efforts and Roma exhibitions is yet another dimension of these dynamics. This example of the museumization of a cultural background shows how, in mediated sites like exhibitions, a large community such as the Roma is not only configured as curiously homogeneous—as the biggest minority of Europe—but also as a foreign element with whom other citizens need to be made better acquainted through such initiatives. Indeed, such an approach engages the Roma as if they were historically separate from the rest of Europe and seeks to "reintroduce" members of this community by mediating encounters with their culture. Such an approach to cultural representation resonates with the dynamics of the photography exhibition *The Family of Man* in that it appears to engage the politics of visibility as a matter of recognition. If there is an EU-wide recognition, then why were they deported from France?

Similarly, in the Turkish context, the gentrification of the Sulukule neighborhood, which the Roma of Istanbul had inhabited for centuries, was expedited as part of Istanbul 2010.[51] In Istanbul, then, buildings—not actual people themselves, the Roma—stood for the city's multicultural heritage, along with music; as they and their relatives were being evicted by the government, Roma musicians appeared in the 2010 festivals organized to celebrate the diversity of Istanbul.[52]

In her analysis of the cultural policies of the Istanbul 2010 ECoC project, Banu Karaca notes how the diverse backgrounds of the population in Turkey are introduced in cultural policy statements, which configure the peoples of Turkey as a mosaic.[53] She states that as in the European Union, cultural policy statements of this sort have become normative in Turkey. Diversity is discursively affirmed via cultural policies, in harmony with the EU's cultural policies.[54] Karaca further argues that "the Ministry of Culture and Tourism as well as the Istanbul municipal departments generally prefer a tamed version of diversity, one that is clearly divorced from political claims," and that in this context, "art has become a preferred platform to address issues of diversity."[55] According to Karaca, such an approach simultaneously aestheticizes multiculturalism with apolitical references to the past and thus configures most minorities as nostalgic remnants of a "multi-ethnic empire"—the Ottoman Empire.[56]

Karaca's argument that both the EU's cultural policies and the ECoC endorse artistic activities that aestheticize diversity is very important. Building upon her contribution, I would like to add that it is in fact not only art but cultural frameworks—broadly defined—that are part of such approaches to diversity. Culture, as the UNESCO 2001 Universal Declaration on Cultural Diversity suggests, consists not only of art and literature, but also ways of living, lifestyles, value systems, and people's beliefs. What we see in the ECoC, as well as in other EU and Turkish cultural policies, is therefore a blend of these sites in the configuration of a heritage of diversity.

Demands for rights and recognition are channeled to the fields of culture, and art is only part of this general picture. I therefore propose viewing these dynamics as significant examples of a larger framework, a whole approach to culture itself in Turkey and beyond: art, music, dance and the performative (as anthropologists Banu Karaca and Öykü Potuoğlu-Cook show), and buildings and architecture (as political scientist Bilgin Ayata points out), but also food and family objects, among other things, all fall into this category.[57] All in all, what comes across is a configuration of culture as a site for regulating the recognition of alterity. It is clearly a particular mode of multiculturalism that is being promoted in these cultural policies and discourses of diversity that cross over time and space, carrying the traces of previous discourses.

National Family Frames:
The Politics of Visibility and Terms of Recognition

The politics of visibility reveals that silences woven around ruins and ruination are not homogeneous. When an aspect of a community becomes visible, or a commodity, recognition does not necessarily follow, nor does this visibility necessarily have an impact on other fields. This is why pinpointing the limits of recognition is important. For example, in a 2007 editorial published in the now-defunct Turkish daily *Radikal*, columnist Yıldırım Türker criticizes those who consume Roma culture represented as festive and entertaining in TV serials, but who turn a blind eye to the gentrification of Roma neighborhoods.[58] Similarly, the fact that Greek music was very popular and "Greek winehouses" flourished and mushroomed in Istanbul in the early 2000s,[59] catering mostly to middle- and -upper-class citizens, illustrated the great demand for one aspect associated with Greek culture. This apparent rapprochement, however, was not translated into other domains; the Greek Orthodox seminary in Heybeliada (or, Halki), for instance, where the Greek Orthodox patriarchs in Istanbul were educated, has remained closed.

These two examples demonstrate how interest and demand for one cultural aspect associated with a community do not necessarily lead to an affirmation of identification but might simply be a matter of window dressing or marketing.[60] Such instrumentalization of different communities as material for consumption operates at different levels: it publicly disconnects these communities from the legacy of state discrimination and biopolitical policies (depoliticization) and simultaneously objectifies them for a neoliberal window display. Recognition cannot be reduced to visibility, and commodification and popularity rarely point toward social justice.

This dynamic is an instance of what anthropologist Elizabeth Povinelli calls bracketing communities. In her work on recognition, Povinelli identifies how liberal multiculturalism configures this notion.[61] She argues that in liberal approaches to multiculturalism, alterity is not necessarily considered a threat to national coherence, but as something to be incorporated and absorbed.[62] Accordingly, following recognition, it is expected that now-recognized groups will forget about their traumas, histories, and experiences of hardship and violence, incoherences, and apprehension, and not remain live testaments of these policies and their inflicted wounds. The family histories addressed in this book have the great potential to bring these testimonies to the forefront, but whether this potential is fully mobilized in all cases remains an open question.

Unless ruination is also addressed, liberal discourses of multiculturalism tend to domesticate demands related to alterity, obfuscate matters of appropriation, and thus divorce recognition from political context and history. Once domesticated, Povinelli asserts, alterity can be absorbed in the national framework without breaking social cohesion—a keyword for integration, biopolitics, and cultural policies addressed in this book. This raises questions about the terms of unity in diversity in relation to what Povinelli calls "absorption."

This means that once alterity makes it into the metaphoric family picture of the nation à la *Family of Man*, this framing is expected by the privileged to be enough to move on. Or, as Povinelli puts it, "normative citizens would be freed to pursue their profits and enjoy their families without guilty glances over their shoulders into history or at the slum across the block."[63] Povinelli also argues that this modality of cultural recognition of difference brackets different groups and that this bracketed recognition informs the regulation of difference by delaying the confrontation with social injustice and violent history.[64] It is perhaps not assimilation that is in place here, but absorption via recognition.

Alterity therefore has continued to be a threat depending on whom, where, and when, and the liberal discursive mode appears to provide a picture frame for the national family in which the subject position of alterity is predetermined: curbed, absorbable, and happy to be part of the unity in diversity celebrations. Just because a group's music, food, or way of life gains visibility or even becomes popular at a given time, does not necessarily mean recognition follows. Such modes facilitate the most sterilized manner of endorsing alterity, conveniently veiling power and ignoring injustices and disparities. The implications of *unity* in diversity in such cases need therefore to be elaborated and carefully unpacked. It is also important to remember that segregative biopolitics often accompanies these dynamics, and of course, depending on the background and the issue involved, recognition itself is also hierarchized.

Some scholars have considered hierarchization among communities as a reason for such sterilized endorsements. In her analysis of the Roma in the context of the Istanbul 2010 ECoC, Potuoğlu-Cook asserts that in comparison to the Armenians and the Kurds, the Roma offered what she calls a "pleasant, 'safe face' of cultural pluralism" in the Istanbul 2010 project.[65] Potuoğlu-Cook highlights how the ECoC did not address politics of stratification, and that, as far as state officials were concerned, the Roma came with less "threatening" baggage than did Kurds or Armenians, indicating a hierarchy of preference among groups. Yet it is my sense that it is in fact the adopted model of liberal multiculturalism that stratifies diversity and generates hierarchies of depoliticized cultural representability in the process of bracketing different groups for recognition.

For instance, addressing Kurds in the Istanbul 2010 application dossier would have necessitated a discussion of state violence and internal forced migrations in Turkey before and during the conflicts with the PKK, or neoliberal policies that killed local economies and generated demographic accumulation in urban arenas,[66] among other things. In short, this would have entailed explicitly addressing social injustice and dispossession. It is indeed notable that the Istanbul 2010 ECoC application dossier mentions Kurds only once: in the "Istanbul, a Refuge of All Times" project, which bypasses the Kurds of Turkey and mentions only Iraqi Kurds who sought refuge in Turkey as they fled Saddam Hussein.[67] This narrative is juxtaposed with the story of German Jews who escaped from the Nazis—including the historicist humanist Auerbach—and found refuge in Istanbul during World War II. These examples and the dismissal of local Kurds from the application dossier indicate a conscious choice of subject matters favorable to a positive and marketable window display; a display of what political theorist Wendy Brown would call "tolerance" and one that simultaneously depoliticizes its subject.[68]

Aside from the application dossier, however, the grand opening of Istanbul 2010 did include Kurdish singer Rojin, who sang in Kurdish, along with others, including an Armenian opera singer, Kevork Tavityan.[69] This limited inclusion resonates with the local dynamics of the time in conjunction with the 2009 Oslo peace negotiations between state officials and the PKK, publicized as a democratic opening (*demokratik açılım*) at the time. A democratic opening therefore implied inclusion and a liberalization of cultural identification.

Recognition of different communities was limited mostly to cultural identification. For example, an Istanbul 2010 project, "Harmony of Diversity: A Lyrical History Project," turned history into a celebration of coexistence.[70] Designed by the late Turkish actor and director Ali Taygun, a Robert College and Yale University alumnus, this project proposed that Armenians,

Greeks, and Jews enriched the Ottoman social fabric and contributed to Ottoman cultural identification with their music. Integrating Armenians or Roma into such narratives did not appear to pose a problem. As long as public engagement with diversity is regulated through the museumization culture—and filtered through the brotherhood mode of liberal humanism—it remains possible for government officials to market the illusion of egalitarian inclusion as multiculturalism. This understanding appears to inform the politics of bracketing different groups. In this process, even though independent actors or NGOs might have differing intentions and ideals, state officials can co-opt creative work and instrumentalize it for official agendas, such as neoliberalism or governmentality.

Overall, during its first two terms (2002–2011) in office, the AKP developed a discourse of liberal multiculturalism in the form of neo-Ottomanism and absorbed independent personal and institutional attempts to address alterity in visible terms. During that time, AKP's leaders extended symbolic acts of recognition and adopted linguistic rights to a certain degree, without actually committing themselves to adjusting policy to improve uneven citizenship rights or account for state violence, segregative biopolitics, and dispossession. With this in mind, I now turn to the notion of neo-Ottomanism, which informed a local discourse of diversity in Turkey under the first two terms of the AKP regime.

Neo-Ottomanism:
A Dehistoricizing Discourse of History, Diversity, and Tolerance

AKP officials "rediscovered" multiculturalism in the Ottoman past as a history of tolerance. They thus configured the Ottoman era as a model of coexistence. Neo-Ottomanism, as endorsed by state officials, operates in different ways. First, it anachronistically anchors multiculturalism as a historical phenomenon, rather than a contemporary issue. Second, it seemingly historicizes alterity, but does so through a manipulated and anachronistic vision of history. Third, as pointed out earlier, it problematically reproduces the earlier Republican interpretations of the Lausanne Convention that conveniently recognized Greeks, Armenians, and Jews as minorities and undermines many others. Fourth, it enables the circumvention of political demands as well as problems such as current social, economic, or legal acts and policies as well as histories of appropriation—that is, ruination, to use Ann Stoler's term.[71] Fifth, while doing so, it also undermines its own historical genealogy: the Turkish-Islamic synthesis. In many ways, neo-Ottomanism draws from that reinterpretation and its configuration of the "Turkish majority" as a synthesis of Sunni Islam with a Turkish identification.[72]

Neo-Ottomanists, just like the military and some intellectuals after the 1980 coup, appear to consider different Muslim groups within the Sunni Islamic "melting pot." However, the histories, politics, and violence embedded in that melting are not addressed. The alignment of Islam with Turkish national identity has racialized implications and is in fact the backbone of segregative policies, as exemplified by the 1923 Greek-Turkish population exchange. It should come as no surprise, then, that the exchangees are not included in this diversity, despite their remarkably different backgrounds, but are instead presented as migrants who became aligned with their proper country and who make up part of the Muslim Turkish majority—an "integration" success story.

The AKP's added twist here is to build this configuration into an emphasis on Sunni Islam civilizational discourse, to promote the Ottoman Empire as its embodiment and as the cultural heritage of Turkey, and to then export it as a model of coexistence to platforms such as the UN Alliance of Civilizations and the ECoC. This model, posited as a sign of "Islamic [read: Sunni] Civilization," casts the recognized Greeks, Armenians, and Jews as symbols of other civilizations. For state officials, this arguably facilitates their recognition. Yet, as mentioned, civilization is a category with a highly racialized history, charged with eugenicist racism. The neo-Ottoman model thus undermines history at multiple levels.

For the most part, the discriminatory policies informed by biopolitics that have marked the twentieth and twenty-first centuries are conveniently swept under the carpet. This does not mean that state officials do not gauge different groups according to a hierarchy of preference; on the contrary, it means there are patterns of addressing alterity beyond community-specific governmentalities. These patterns favor visibility and demonstrate how neo-Ottoman tolerance is deployed as a historical discourse that in fact dehistoricizes alterity. It is clear that some Turkish officials conceptualize multiculturalism as a historical legacy—with all its anachronisms—rather than a contemporary phenomenon. This is evident in the configurations of multiculturalism in the Istanbul 2010 ECoC project; Ottoman plurality was advertised as a model of multiculturalism and evidence of the empire's tolerance of differences.

In a 1996 interview on tolerance and difference in the Ottoman Empire, historian Aron Rodrigue articulates how notions of tolerance and difference today are very different from what they actually meant in the Ottoman Empire.[73] According to Rodrigue, rather than a celebration of diversity as a virtue to be promoted, plurality was simply a matter of fact for the Ottoman polity. Equally problematic, Rodrigue states, is addressing Ottoman tolerance as if this concept carried the same implications as it does today; in the Ottoman context, tolerance simply meant not having a policy of erasing differences or changing the composition of communities. This was carried out as a mode of governmentality, not celebration.

Attributing to Ottoman plurality an anachronistically idealized context of multiculturalism and peaceful coexistence speaks directly to the notion of the museumization of culture, that is, divorcing communities from their historical and political contexts to bracket them and then turn them into a display of cultural difference. Ottoman diversity as cultural heritage has been appropriated by state officials to market Turkey as a brand.

Though it is often associated with the rhetoric of the neoliberal AKP, the neo-Ottomanist mosaic approach to Ottoman identities is not an AKP invention. Rather, it is a vast terrain developed by multiple actors.[74] The AKP simply consolidated it as a neoliberal cultural policy and marketed it as diversity. Ottomanism had been a subject of political debate as early as the nineteenth century, pioneered by such important intellectuals as Namık Kemal.[75] And, as mentioned, today's neo-Ottomanism also draws from the discourse of the Turkish-Islamic synthesis.

An emphasis on tolerance in relation to diversity is of course not unique to the Turkish context. "Tolerance" is a loaded word that also needs a careful reconsideration. Mustafa Celaleddin Paşa's use of the term in the world of empire-states of the nineteenth century is not the same as its use in marketing neo-Ottomanism as a model for coexistence in twenty-first century nation-states. As Wendy Brown has shown, today tolerance is a widespread liberal discourse that depoliticizes and regulates aversion rather than addressing it with an emphasis on power and justice.[76]

"Tolerance," according to Brown, is a "strand of depoliticization" that "tends to cast instances of inequality or social injury as matters of individual or group prejudice." This depoliticization "involves removing a political phenomenon from comprehension of its *historical* emergence and from a recognition of the *powers* that produce and contour it. No matter its particular form and mechanics, depoliticization always eschews power and history in the representation of its subject."[77] In that regard, instead of taking aversion as an isolated issue of cultural or personal lack of tolerance, it is important to recognize the deployment of power that actually informs it. It is equally important to address the terms of endorsing the notion of tolerance.

As discussed in Parts One and Two, liberal discourses of tolerance in the postwar era configured tolerance as a step toward building social harmony and world peace. Studying different classics in translation as world literature and emphasizing shared aspects of humanity such as *The Family of Man*, were cast as building tolerance among different nations and hence as conducive peace. But in those cases, tolerance was not a notion for minorities. And despite the ample presence of diverse groups and emigrants as addressed in Part One, liberal discourses produced internationally were rarely translated into domestic politics in the 1950s. Segregation, apartheid, forced population transfers, and partition on the one hand, and resettlement to dilute demographic cohesion and assimilation on the other—all such domestic policies configured alterity as a site to be managed. Liberal discourses of multiculturalism, on the other hand, domesticate demands and in the context of Turkey, also became an official discourse that seeks to draw its political legitimacy from an imperial model. In all cases, dehistoricization remains intact.

In the second half of the first decade of the 2000s, official discourses of Ottoman tolerance in Turkey presented it as an ideal model of coexistence without mention of aversion or power issues. This was therefore a historical representation that actually dehistoricized alterity. It also promoted an imperial model of regulating alterity and ignored what that entails for Turkey today.

Both Brown's critique of depoliticization and Povinelli's exegesis of bracketed recognition emphasize the importance of historicization. This emphasis is closely linked to unraveling the politics of discrimination and state-sponsored violence, as well as the legacies of segregative biopolitics and processes of ruination. Povinelli's work offers a critique of liberal multiculturalism as a domesticated recognition of difference that brackets communities; Brown's work considers liberal modes of regulating aversion to alterity as depoliticization. Both call attention to the fact that such approaches to differences depoliticize and dehistoricize the subject and operate as tools of governmentality. It is not entirely clear how best to address social justice in that context. What is clear is that the liberal mode of multiculturalism also helps circumvent "difficult" issues for states. Historicization, in that respect, is not an abstract matter but a concrete demand to trace such issues as the confiscation of properties, the politics of violence and mass murder, the realities of forcible disappearances, and the consequences of segregative biopolitics, among other things. Furthermore, the process of bracketing in itself needs to be historically contextualized and called into question. Both Brown and Povinelli criticize this mode as flattening the subject and emphasize the importance of addressing history not as a privileged mode but as a tool to explore multiple facets of injustice. It should be borne in mind, though, that historicization in itself does not automatically question power.

Multiculturalism on Display and Istanbul 2010

References to Turkey's Ottoman heritage can be found throughout the Istanbul 2010 application dossier:

> [In Istanbul] an accumulation of minorities were virtually in the majority; under the Ottomans this harmonious social structure flourished uninterrupted for six hundred years.... Yet this "beautiful harmony," which is embedded in the city's foundations and entwined in the branches of its family tree, is not just a pleasant memento from a bygone era. Istanbul retains still its rich cosmopolitan character, sometimes concealing and sometimes revealing the evidence of its unrivalled physical and cultural legacy.[78]

"Minority" is a modern term as Aron Rodrigue warns us,[79] and therefore it is anachronistic to resort to such a term to refer to Ottoman plurality and to define hierarchies that existed among different groups over the six hundred years of Ottoman rule across different provinces. Additionally, such an approach configures Ottoman plurality as an idealized remedy for "affirming" plurality and different identities. Social coherence is also emphasized here via a timeless, frozen "beautiful harmony" among groups.

As for the contemporary packaging of the Ottoman past as an accumulation of multiple minority identities, Rodrigue cautions us that it is wrong to conceptualize different peoples before the modern era in terms of majorities and minorities in the Ottoman and the Middle Eastern contexts because they did not carry the same implications as minority/majority have today.[80] Such an interpretation of Ottoman identities, moreover, is problematic because it assumes Ottoman identities were divided into neat categories of people often simplistically termed Muslims, Jews, Armenians, and Greek Orthodox. This sort of conceptualization eclipses the diversity within these groups themselves and thus treats them as static, timeless, and homogenous entities, like a mosaic,[81] unchanging throughout time. It locks different groups into cultures or other identifications as if they were monolithic, stemming from a single root and genealogy.[82] This kind of anachronistic interpretation of Ottoman identifications also excludes groups like the Assyrians and the Alevis from the "Ottoman heritage." Such engagement with diversity as a mosaic implies that each tile represents one community, and that each is frozen in time and appears homogenized on display in the museumization of culture. The anxiety to celebrate difference and the mosaic approach thus detach alterity from politics and history and simultaneously bracket them.

A poignant example is the case of the Assyrians. Several years ago, Turkish president Abdullah Gül visited Sweden accompanied by Yusuf Çetin, the deputy patriarch of the Assyrian Orthodox Christians of Turkey. During this visit, a Swedish parliamentarian of Assyrian background asked Gül why the Assyrians in Turkey cannot benefit from the rights granted to minorities such as the Armenians and Jews. In response, Gül reportedly expressed his sorrow and claimed that this is because the Lausanne Treaty of 1923 does not recognize Assyrians as a minority. This Kemalist interpretation of Lausanne has informed multiple policies, including those of today, when Assyrians are subjected to yet another dispossession. At the time of completing this book, the AKP-appointed governor of the province of Mardin appropriated Assyrian churches and other properties, and put them under the jurisdiction of the state Directorate of Religious Affairs (Diyanet).[83] Meanwhile, one of the four items of "documentary heritage" Turkey has with UNESCO's Memory of the World—the same platform that canonized *The Family of Man*—is the Old Assyrian Merchant Archives of Kültepe, which was registered with

UNESCO in 2015. This example crystallizes the dynamics embedded in the museumization of culture at yet another level.[84]

The cases of the Roma in Turkey and in France—and, by extension, the EU—are important reminders that the anxiety to celebrate difference does not necessarily translate into social and economic policies. For example, the evaluation report of the 2010 ECoC states that, although the original application dossier for Istanbul had committed Turkey to defining a new narrative of citizenship, there were no clear visions in the cultural activities themselves, which reportedly was in part because of how the arrangements were put in place.[85] The report concludes that the publications and promotional literature of the Istanbul 2010 ECoC Agency as well as its cultural projects shared an ethos that "emphasised values of tolerance and celebrated the diversity of cultures and ethnic groups present in the city"—especially "the cultures of Istanbul's Jewish, Greek and Armenian communities amongst others."[86] The emphasis on Jewish, Greek, and Armenian communities is not a coincidence; as mentioned, they are the most commonly acknowledged minorities in Turkey. Nevertheless, the reconceptualization of the inclusive citizenship addressed in the Istanbul 2010 application dossier and mentioned in the evaluation report seems to have been superficial: while these communities were celebrated as a showcase of diversity, their members are still discouraged from becoming army officers, diplomats, or police officers in Turkey. The evaluation report concludes that the Istanbul 2010 activities were informed by a desire to emphasize tolerance and celebrate diversity.

As mentioned, the Kurdish presence in the city was largely ignored, and the Roma culture was reduced to music and buildings. The only immigration-related project proposed in the application dossier was a film project mostly geared to immigrants in the EU in general. Only one out of the four immigration-themed film projects was planned for Turkey. This project also ignored issues that linger in Istanbul's communities to this day:

> This project aims to create a common ground for communication through the universal language of cinema, throwing light on various aspects of the immigration issue as it is experienced in different countries and in different cultures. The hope is that the different approaches of creative minds will produce a fresh and humane vision for this shared problem; and that this project

will constitute the first step towards a comprehensive solution that considers and respects the principle of co-existence. Istanbul is significant in this context as it has received many immigrants throughout history, including the Jews and Muslims after their expulsion from Spain, Poles after the Crimean War, White Russians after the Russian Revolution, German dissidents and Jews before and during World War II, Bosnian Muslims during the Balkan War, and ethnic Turks as a result of the population exchange between Greece and Turkey in 1922.

Istanbul's prosperity has meant that the city has also attracted a remarkable number of migrants from inside Turkey. Moreover, starting from the 1960s, Turkey has sent millions of emigrants to European countries. Today the Turkish population living abroad has grown to a significant size and the project can also serve as a platform for the second or third generation of immigrants to voice their expectations.[87]

The immigration project configured Turkey as a historical haven for refugees. It referred to the exchangees as "ethnic Turks"—again a blanket term to indicate that all the diverse family histories and trajectories mentioned here (and many others that did not find their place in the pages of this book) had been successfully integrated. And here they were referred to as just an emigrant group among others, as if they were not subjected to segregative biopolitics. The exchangees were therefore written into this story that configures Turkey as a pillar of tolerance that admits all sorts of "undesirables," as if Turkey did not have undesirables of its own.

In addition to all these groups cited, there are multiple forms of diversity in Istanbul that seem to be lost within the very discourse of diversity itself. Istanbul remains a city of migration: there are many Africans who have come to work or study, a sex labor market that brings in mostly Ukrainian and Russian women, a flow of Moldovan women as domestic workers, Armenian immigrants from Armenia, and refugee camps set up for Chechens in Fenerbahçe, an upper-middle-class neighborhood. At the time of writing this essay—after Istanbul 2010—Syrian refugees are also now part of the picture. Furthermore, because of forced internal migration—yet another instance of biopolitics, only this time internally—many Kurds expelled from their hometowns also reside in the city.[88] Alevis and their neighborhoods were also not part of this celebration proposed in the application dossier.[89] These forms of settlement were excluded from the repertoire of celebration, resulting in a manicured version of diversity. And whenever a group did not seem to fit into the postcard picture of "beautiful harmony and peaceful coexistence"—the national family photograph—that aspect of the group was simply written out. This is how the bracketing of what was displayed appears to have operated. Vast class differences, moreover, were excluded from the notion of diversity.

One of the dominant engagements with diversity in Turkey at the time, then, was historically anchored rather than considered to be a present-day matter. This exclusion is in direct contrast with the following statement: "Istanbul is a melting point where many languages are spoken, a multitude of Traditions followed and various ethnicities expressed.... The rich legacy that Istanbul has inherited is inclusive, not exclusive. Like the philosophy underlying today's expansion of Europe, it is an indication of great wealth."[90] The spirit of Istanbul here is likened to Europeanness—as part of the EU—in that diversity is considered to be an asset.

A similar de/historicization is manifested in the following statement by Egemen Bağış, former chairman of the ECoC application advisory board and former minister of EU affairs and Turkey's chief negotiator in accession talks with the EU: "In history," he writes, "different cultures in Istanbul existed in total peace and harmony, people of different cultures saw Istanbul as a refuge heaven [sic]."[91] Here again, diversity is referred to in the past tense and is configured as a historical phenomenon. As the image of a refugee haven is reproduced here, it becomes a key concept to emphasize tolerance.

The application dossier concludes, "Istanbul will use this opportunity to evaluate and draw lessons from its own imperial past, looking at how the amazingly rich ethnic mix of Istanbul managed to live together and to function as a society of many 'nations' [*millet* in Turkish; alluding here again to the Ottoman *millet* system and using it in the sense of "nation"]."[92] In the AKP model of liberal multiculturalism, *millet* is used to refer to different groups living under the Ottoman Empire as "nations" even though the *millet* was consolidated as a legal status only in the nineteenth century and only recognized Jews, Armenians, and Greek Orthodox as minorities. Contemporary neo-Ottomanist approaches appear to configure the "Muslim majority" of Turkey in terms of the Ottoman Turkish *millet*. This anachronism is in part informed by the Turkish-Islamic synthesis, but also by the repertoires of historicist humanism that divide civilizations according to racialized origins—and depending on the thinker, that also have religious implications.

In the neo-Ottomanist approach to diversity, then, state officials view Sunni Islam as a melting pot, not as a site of diversity. Although during the Ottoman era, cultural identifications did not have the same implications as diversity or multiculturalism do today, there was a wide variety of backgrounds, differences, and forms of intra-communal interactions, as historians Aron Rodrigue, Christine Philliou, and Leslie Peirce remind us.[93]

This selective approach to who qualifies for recognition of their cultural differences is evident in the lack of endorsement of the Population Exchange Museum as a site of heterogeneity and in the anxiety to emphasize the integration of the emigrants. Conceptualizing Sunni Islam as a melting pot has long informed policies in Turkey—including the 1923 exchange—and the previous emphasis in the Turkish-Islamic synthesis appears to have shifted to neo-Ottomanism.[94] By the time Istanbul 2010 was organized, alterity—which obviously considered a select group only and excluded all others—had become a commodity. The museumization of cultural backgrounds very much fits into this paradigm, as, when appropriated by state officials, it reduces alterity to cultural display—with all its anachronisms, exclusions, and inaccuracies—and depoliticizes it. Museumization thus becomes a tool for governmentality.

In the second essay of this part, I turn to trace the broader implications of the Turkish-Islamic synthesis promoted as a cultural policy in the aftermath of the 1980 military coup, during which the military authored, sponsored, and brutally enforced a reinterpretation of Kemalism. My goal here is to historically and politically contextualize this aspect of the palimpsests of cultural policy that informed the Istanbul 2010 ECoC project. Through an interrelated reading of the two essays in this part, I seek to synchronically and diachronically trace the implications of liberal cultural policies by attending to both the transnational and the local contexts. Reading the two essays in relation to one another reveals the shift from the post-1980 coup era to the first decade of the 2000s. It also allows us to trace both liberal multiculturalism transnationally and the neo-Ottomanist shape it has taken in Turkey and the implications of the Turkish-Islamic synthesis of neo-Ottomanism locally.

The Turkish-Islamic Synthesis and Coexistence after the 1980 Military Coup

If, therefore, conclusions can be drawn from military violence, as being primordial and paradigmatic of all violence used for natural ends, there is inherent in all such violence a lawmaking character.

                        Walter Benjamin, "Critique of Violence," 1921

THE TURKISH-ISLAMIC SYNTHESIS is a political paradigm that has marked modern Turkey's history. Demographically and discursively, it has informed a variety of policies such as segregative biopolitics, assimilation, absorption, and dispossession. As a discourse, it draws from paradigms of historicist humanism in an attempt to trace the origins and genealogies of peoples in Turkey, with differing emphases on Islam and Turkishness depending on the context. For example, the First Turkish National History Congress, organized in 1932, is commonly referred to as an important platform where Turkish national history was propounded.[95] The conference presentations also included papers on the contributions of the Turks to Islamic civilization—a move that is very much on par with the dominant paradigms of historicist humanism—in which Léon Cahun, the nineteenth-century French Orientalist who wrote on the subject, was also cited.[96]

The efforts to generate a Muslim majority and then Turkify—i.e., assimilate—them and secularize them were very salient. Those who could not be assimilated were killed or subjected to a discipline-and-punish campaign of violence on the one hand and segregative biopolitics on the other. The 1923 exchange embodied such policies par excellence. Further, as sociologist Ayhan Aktar has demonstrated, the Turkification of the economy was closely related to the 1923 population exchange.[97] The interpretations of the Turkish-Islamic synthesis differed depending on the context, and the paradigm itself took different forms across time and space. Today, however, it is commonly associated with the 1980 military coup.

The Turkish-Islamic synthesis was officially included in the 1983 *National Cultural Policy Report* prepared in the aftermath of the 1980 military coup[98]—

an era which also marks the last decade of the Cold War. The coup d'état mainly targeted what the military called "degenerate" or "deviant" ideologies—which implied Marxism or any faction associated with it.[99] The 1983 report opens with a message by the minister of state and deputy prime minister of the military junta government, Turgut Özal.[100] A former World Bank employee (1971–1973), Özal implemented the IMF's policies in Turkey; he would later become the first elected civilian prime minister after the coup and, in 1989, the president of Turkey.[101] In his June 9, 1982, message to the Special Committee of Experts who prepared the report, Özal states that development must proceed through a consideration not only of the economy but also of the human (*beşerî mülahazalar*).[102] This is why, he states, culture is important and needs to be incorporated into education: to ensure development. In referring to what he calls UNESCO's definition of culture, Özal also identifies culture as the consciousness of the historical development of a group. This identification is embedded the 1983 Turkish *National Cultural Policy Report*.[103]

The emphasis on culture as integral to economic development was not Özal's invention. It was previously articulated in a UNESCO document entitled *Cultural Policy: A Preliminary Study*. This 1969 study is based on a roundtable organized in Monaco on December 18–22, 1967. French sociologist Pierre Bourdieu, who wrote about the field of culture, was a participant, and Richard Hoggart at the University of Birmingham, a key figure in the founding of the field of cultural studies, was among the observers.[104] The report does not highlight culture as a state-centered project, but argues that cultural policy should target the means of disseminating culture instead. It appears to make an exception, however, for "developing countries," where an awareness of nationhood is not yet established and state intervention might be necessary, but concludes that in such cases, state intervention must be carefully navigated.[105]

In the World Bank's annual *World Development Report* prepared between 1980 and 1983, Turkey is classified as a middle-income developing country.[106] The case of Turkey in 1983 thus seems to fit the bill described by UNESCO in 1969: Turkey was a developing country. In that regard, it appears that the state officials and experts involved in the preparation of the 1983 *National Cultural Policy Report* considered state intervention in the field of culture to be justified. The committee identified the key issue of Turkey to be a lack of national consciousness. Working in subcommittees, the group of academics who contributed to this report commissioned under the military junta government included renowned figures such as the late Şerif Mardin, Ahmet Yaşar Ocak, Bahattin Ögel, Avni Akyol, Muharrem Ergin, and Mehmet Kaplan. The report was produced in an environment where state officials advocated national awareness as a means to establish social peace, overcome political rifts, and ensure balanced development. All of these objectives can be critically analyzed and compared to what was actually happening on the ground, but on paper, the role of cultural policy was to establish national unity.

The 1983 Turkish *National Cultural Policy Report* openly cites previous UNESCO cultural policy reports, and declares culture to be key for national unity, which in turn is deemed crucial for successful development. UNESCO's 1969 *Cultural Policy: A Preliminary Study*, for example, asserts that to boost development, it is not enough to consider quantitative data such as statistics. Culture should also be taken into consideration and developed in conjunction with the historical, social, and cultural contexts of a setting. The emphasis on culture as integral to development is a recurring rationale in UNESCO's statements.

Social cohesion presumably brings stability, and stability is closely associated with development. In the opening pages of the 1983 *National Cultural Policy Report*, Özal addresses this issue:

> At the base of our country's recent crisis [*buhran*] lies the fact that a very seriously erratic and volatile [*istikrarsız ve tutarsız*] structure of social and cultural values has been engraved in the minds of our youth. Only this way could the efforts to divide the country have been elaborated, and the groups who attack their own state and people have come to existence. It is also in this same way that efforts to work and produce have been hindered, and economic and social stability damaged. All efforts to strengthen society today have to deal with both material and human elements.
>
> Development can only become an attainable goal if it targets not only capital but also the human element and builds a whole [i.e., achieves integration].[107]

Özal's suggestion to mobilize culture as a means to promote stability and development configures it as a site of governmentality. The crisis Özal refers to is the civil war of the 1970s—a conflict that was never called by its proper name in Turkey. The civil war took place between various groups across a wide spectrum of the left and the right, and carried "sectarian" undertones. According to Özal, the civil war was caused by "seriously erratic and volatile" social and cultural values. With this, he appears to refer to Marxism and its varied versions and interpretive communities. The broader cultural project here is to eliminate class struggle and Marxist ideologies from the schools, cultural institutions, and labor organizations, and to replace them with a Turkish-Islamic synthesis that would cement national unity.

What Özal calls erratic and volatile sets of values that turn people "against their own people and state" is articulated as "degenerate" and "deviant" by Kenan Evren—the leading general behind the 1980 coup d'état and the head of the junta's National Security Council.[108] The unity of the nation as a body—reemphasized in nationalist categorical terms—and the concern with the nation in terms of numbers (biopolitics) are abundant throughout the records of the National Security Council's Advisory Parliament. To the equation of ideologies that "degenerate" the national body, Kenan Evren added the PKK. These degenerate ideologies, according the Evren, not only dissolve family values—because, he says, a PKK adherent murdered a family member—but also aim at destroying the "free and secular democratic system." In his speeches delivered before and after the coup, Evren often referred to "degenerate ideologies" as "deviant."[109] In these speeches, he called for cleansing deviant ideologies from schools, because according to Evren, they alienate youth from the unity of the nation.[110]

Youth were often articulated in state discourses of the time and were clearly viewed as a site of social engineering. Like Özal, Evren also argued that "divisive" ideologies had penetrated Turkish society

> through the youth by degenerating their understanding of the basic principles of our republic and our national unity, such as loyalty to one's nation, the flag, the national anthem, norms, traditions, ancestors, national history, respect for the state, and civic duties. Turkish people lived in the full bond of *brotherhood for centuries* and struggled against the enemy and all hardships as one body and soul during and after the War of Independence [the war fought between 1919 and 1922 that led to the 1923 exchange]. In order to attain this

aim [to divide the country], the religious beliefs, professions, political opinions, and regional particularities of the people were merely used as a tool to make Turkey vulnerable by dividing Turkish society into enemy groups and classes.[111]

Evren's speech reproduces the discourses of brotherhood and social harmony without being inclusive. In addition to his insinuation of the manipulation of religious belief, Evren also addresses regional particularities—which probably is a covert reference to the Kurds. His reference to the division of Turkish society into enemy groups and classes does not seem to take histories of exploitation, exclusion, violence, biopolitics, and dispossession into consideration. Rather he concentrates on the outcome—conflict—and seeks to address this outcome from the perspective of national security rather than social justice. Evren's reference to the Turkish people as a unified national body resonates with biologized approaches to the nation as a living organism (that is, eugenics).

To protect the health of the national body, Evren's solution is to eradicate the spheres of influence of so-called degeneration. For instance, thousands of teachers, whom he claimed to have "deviated from Atatürk's path" and to have collaborated with criminals, were prosecuted, terminated, incarcerated.[112] In speech after speech, Evren called on Turkey's youth to "serve the country and the nation in full integrity and unity" and to take Atatürk's principles as their guiding light, and not be deceived by "deviant ideologies."[113] Unity in this context entailed adopting the military-imposed Turkist nationalist ideology and a controlled version of Sunni Islam. Marxism was the main target of these policies.

As for the official emphasis on brotherhood, just as today, it rerouted political demands to another platform. Likewise, today, what is discussed is not citizenship or democratic self-determination, for example, but a narrative of brotherhood informed by racialized thinking and religion. In this paradigm, brotherhood is configured as the natural outcome of sharing the same genealogy or branch in the family tree of humankind.

A 1981 speech Evren delivered in the city of Maraş encapsulates this dynamic. Evren reminded his audience that they share the same race and religion: "People coming from the same race, believing in the same religion, possessing the same traditions and norms, forms this nation."[114] With this definition, all non-Muslims were automatically excluded from the "people" of Turkey. According to Evren, "Turks" should not kill their "brother Turks" on the grounds of religious and sectarian differences. This is because, he asserts, Sunnis and Alevis believe in the same Koran. This was the core of his speech in Maraş, most likely because almost two years before he spoke there, a brutal massacre of Alevis had taken place in the city. Evren claimed that the Maraş massacre was one of the reasons for the military intervention in 1980.[115] Considering what happened on the ground, beyond the façade of Evren's words, is helpful in considering this issue.

On December 19–26, 1978, more than a hundred people, including infants and children, died in a massacre in Maraş.[116] This crime reveals the killers' brutal extermination logic. Martial law was declared, but the leading 68 suspects were never caught. The prime suspect, Ökkeş Kenger, was apprehended and put on trial before a military court, but was found not guilty.[117] As for those who were convicted, they were released in 1991. Although right after the massacre Kenger confessed to playing a role in the brutal violence, he later retracted his testimony, claiming that it was given under duress. Kenger changed his last name to Şendiller and in 1991 became a deputy in the Turkish parliament. In parliament, he was elected to the Human Rights Commission.[118] In 2009, as part of the liberal multiculturalism discourse campaign, AKP officials decided to launch an initiative to address the case of the Alevis and wanted to organize a workshop on the subject.[119] To the public's consternation, AKP officials declared Ökkeş Kenger/Şendiller to be an "expert" on Alevis and invited him to this event.[120] In addition, to this day, the military establishment in Turkey refuses to make the court records of the Maraş massacre public. Various attempts by lawyers and deputies to obtain the records over the past few years have been unsuccessful.[121] The trajectory of this case across different regimes shows the limits of the rhetoric of brotherhood and how the logic of the Turkish-Islamic synthesis actually operates on the ground at yet another level.

The Maraş massacre was not the only case—there were other pogroms that also targeted Alevis. In addition to the groups loosely defined as the right and the left, sectarianism also added to the civil war climate of the 1970s. The PKK was also founded at that time, and eventually became more active toward the end of the decade. In short, the country was the site of a civil war—which the military used as a rationale for pursuing its own bloody campaign in the name of bringing peace, social cohesion, stability, and democracy to the country. The civil war was always referred to as a future threat and never a present-day reality. The impunity of the culprits of Maraş and the secrecy that surrounds the court records strongly suggest that the military has not wanted to solve this crime.

On the other hand, not admitting there was a civil war was a strategic move: it was easier to generate public consent for the military's actions when civil war was cast as a future threat and not as a present reality. To do otherwise might have generated other demands. On September 27, 1980—about two weeks after the coup—the junta gathered in parliament, identified Turkey as being on the "brink" of a civil war and fratricide, and pledged to remove the undesirable elements that inhibited the "functioning of democracy."[122] In his opening speech, the appointed prime minister and former general Bülend Ulusu addressed these elements that he believed were caused by the constitution of 1961 adopted after the 1960 coup d'état—the coup that overthrew Adnan Menderes.

According to Ulusu, it is clear that the 1961 constitution was not compatible with "Turkey's natural disposition" (*Türkiye'nin bünyesi*).[123] The constitution might have been written with the "best of intentions," Ulusu says, but grants too much "liberty without any limits" (sınırları belirsiz bir özgürlük anlayışı).[124] He argues that the constitutional rights established in 1961 also generated an unfavorable climate for the state whereby a claim of neutrality and autonomy could be used "even" against the state, and the government could be seriously impeded "under the pretext of law." It appears that it was democracy itself that bothered the military and was perceived as unsuitable for Turkey's citizens in view of their "natural disposition." Again, the topic was not treated as a social and political issue, but rather as a biologized one.

Ulusu further claims that this climate enables politics under the guise of science—by which, without a doubt, he means academia. First, then, undesirable elements would be removed with surgical precision. Next, a military-sponsored antidote, a blend of a Turkish-Islamic synthesis to promote integration and unity, would be forcefully administered to cure the body of the Turkish nation. The terms of the synthesis were strongly centralized and controlled, and one of the key domains to bring about these changes was the schools.

It is in this climate that the *National Cultural Policy Report* was commissioned. Education was an important component of the report. On the ground, the junta had already taken steps toward bringing education under its control. For example, in 1981, to forge national unity via higher education, the military government, working hand in glove with Deputy Prime Minister Özal, established the Turkish Higher Education Council (Yükseköğretim Kurulu, YÖK), which ended the autonomy of universities and centralized the government's control over them. Article 4 of the law regulating higher education states that the purpose of higher education is to educate students who, among other things, are honored and happy to be Turkish; embody the values of the Turkish nation; are conscious of their duty and responsibility to the state; think scientifically and freely; have a balanced and healthy mind, body, soul, morality, and emotions; will contribute to the development of the country; and who can sustain themselves financially.[125] In addition, the law expects students to contribute to the happiness and welfare of "the country and nation of the Turkish state as an indivisible whole" via "programs to serve economic, social and cultural growth, and to help Turkey become a constructive, creative and elite member of contemporary civilization."[126]

The law states that the main principle guiding higher education is that students should gain an awareness of their duty to the nation in full compliance with Kemalist nationalism. This puts the emphasis on history as a implement for sowing the seeds of national consciousness—a notion that Özal had addressed as important in his message to the Special Committee of Experts who drew up the 1983 *National Cultural Policy Report*. To that end, culture must be mobilized. The second most important principle, according to the law on higher education, is the notion of national culture. Accordingly, higher education is in the service of national culture to preserve its "Turkish traditions" and to develop it within "universal culture" (*evrensel kültür*) without losing its essence. The blueprint of a national culture configuration informed by historicist humanism is notable here: to contribute to universality, national culture needs to be developed and its essence needs to be preserved via higher education. Article 5b of the law asserts that higher education must be at the disposal of national culture so that "students develop a strong sense of national unity and solidarity [*milli birlik ve beraberlik*]." As far as the junta was concerned, Turkey's students were not being educated in full compliance with the "country's realities."[127]

Just as the military deemed the checks and balances of a democratic system that holds the state accountable as well as civic liberties that guarantee pluralism inappropriate for Turkey, it also cast higher education in such a way as to fit the junta's vision of the country's realities—that is, education must be controlled. Higher education, then, was not about critical thinking but about becoming good nationals whose goal in pursuing education should be to become productive citizens who can contribute to the national economy. Hence, the objective was to forge a Turkish-Islamic synthesis to unite, develop, and raise economically productive citizens—reminiscent of Francisco Franco's fascist policies and his national Catholicism, a policy that critic Eduardo Matos-Martín considers biopolitical.[128] Unsurprisingly, Evren and the military did not view their methods and tools as fascistic. In fact, they saw their own intervention as anti-fascist, while condemning Marxist solidarity against fascism as "strange," "ideological," and "an abuse of freedom."[129] The Cold War era configuration of fascism as an isolated case rather than as a complex logic that has continued under different guises resurfaces in such assumptions.

In 1979, on the first anniversary of the Maraş massacre, Evren and other generals warned the elected government and Turkey's political parties that "our nation can no longer tolerate those who sing the communist international instead of our national anthem, those who try to establish every kind of fascism in our country instead of the democratic system and those instigators of Islamic law, anarchy, destructionism and secessionism."[130] Capitalizing on the memory of the Maraş massacre, this warning was a threat of the coup d'état that would come. Since the military has not released the Maraş court case records to the public, and when the relatives of the massacred ask for access to the documents, they are reportedly asked a very large sum of money, which they cannot afford, the military is still implicated today. Even if the particular bureaucrats running the military have changed over the years, it appears that institutional allegiances have not.

When General Evren and his junta came to power a year later, they arrested Marxists and Kurds and tortured them in the infamous Prison No. 5 and Metris Prison, among others; imposed a state of emergency law that became a daily reality for the Kurds for years; crippled unions, especially those deemed to be leftist; implemented policies in line with the IMF's recommendations; imposed a tight grip on practitioners of Islam; launched a misogynistic attack against pious women whose rights to education and faith were brutally violated—because they were not allowed to wear a veil in school, they were forced to choose between the two rights; made the Sunni interpretation of Islam the basis of a compulsory "religious culture and morality" course in primary and secondary schools; and promoted a Turkish-Islamic synthesis that favored the Sunni interpretation of Islam.[131] The idea was to fight communism with Islam, but it had to be with the military's own version of the religion.[132]

With new laws and regulations, the military curtailed plurality in the parliament and unions, and thus made sure that liberties were clearly limited in the 1982 constitution—which was approved with a 91.4 percent "yes" vote in a referendum held in November 1982.[133] All this the generals did while "defending democracy" with the enthusiastic support of the international community—not unlike the case of General Augusto Pinochet of Chile, whose bloody fascist regime was praised for bringing democracy and freedom to Chile by politicians such as British prime minister Margaret Thatcher. These dynamics yet again raise questions about what democracy and liberal discourses emphasizing freedom and liberty entail.

This context is key to understanding the implications of the military-era Turkish-Islamic synthesis for contemporary discourses of liberal multiculturalism in Turkey, the environment that gave rise to an anachronistic and reductive neo-Ottomanism adopted as a national culture, as well what the History Foundation, among others, was up against when it launched its projects from the early 1990s onwards. It also clarifies how diversity could be promoted as a liberal value in the 2000s, while a crippled plurality—for example, problems with the electoral system, suppression of unionization, and the regulation of higher education—and unequal access to rights remained intact. I now turn to analyze the Turkish-Islamic synthesis as proposed in the 1983 *National Cultural Policy Report* against this backdrop.

The Turkish-Islamic Synthesis, Historicist Humanism, and the 1983 National Cultural Policy Report

The 1983 Turkish *National Cultural Policy Report* consists of thirteen reports prepared by thirteen different subcommittees. The members of the subcommittees appear to have been assigned, because there were some whose names were included but who did not send their evaluation of the questions at hand, such as composer Nevzat Atlığ, who didn't attend the meetings, or critic Metin And, who didn't send his opinion for the report. In addition, there were cases in which the subcommittee could not convene because of a lack of attendance and only one person took over writing the entire report. There was an uneven distribution of pages allocated to each subcommittee report, but at sixty-five pages, the longest of them all is the report on culture, religion, and morality. This subheading captures the military's demands regarding higher education.

The opening pages of the 1983 cultural policy report consist of borrowed, reinterpreted, and at times translated segments of UNESCO cultural policy publications from 1969 to 1976. Yet, the report's definition of culture— claimed to be borrowed from UNESCO—remains selective and skewed at best. As mentioned, it defines culture reductively as a tool to configure national consciousness and history. After a generic opening with references to UNESCO, the report quickly switches its tone and repeats the concerns with national unity, the indivisibility of the nation-state, and the importance to reestablish national unity as expressed in the National Security Council as well as in Kenan Evren's speeches.[134] The report begins by stating that the objective is to provide equal citizenship rights, with social justice and democracy. In order to ensure these, new generations need to be healthy both in body and in mind, committed to democracy, the nation, and to Atatürk's principles. The report also extensively addresses the importance of the family in generating desirable Turkish nationals.

Although each subcommittee report offers somewhat differing interpretations of the synthesis, all were based on an argument that was originally developed by historian İbrahim Kafesoğlu in the 1970s before being included in the 1983 *National Cultural Policy Report*.[135] There were also others who contributed to the development of this notion, each emphasizing one or another aspect of Turkishness and Islam, depending on the agenda. For example, in his *East-West Synthesis*, novelist Peyami Safa discusses this notion in several essays.[136] In one, a 1961 piece entitled "The Changing Meaning of the Human," Safa resorts to the paradigms of historicist humanism. He configures the notions of origins and genealogy as a dialectic between ancient Greek-Roman-Christian heritage, which he claims forged "Western civilization." He rethinks Turkey in that light, as a Turkish-Islamic synthesis with the "West." That is to say, in Safa's thought, a triadic Turkish-Islamic-Western synthesis forms the foundation of Turkey's culture.[137] The synthesis here implies an amalgam of different components of culture, and addresses their crossing over time and space as an exchange, but still in linear terms. Safa's synthesis can be thought of as complimentary to Hilmi Ziya Ülken's notion of social race, which supposedly is the result of an embodied aggregation of the biological and the sociocultural.

A palimpsest of its own, the Turkish-Islamic synthesis was further construed in the 1970s as a determining factor in Turkey's national culture. At first, like Safa, other intellectuals also contended that the synthesis was one between European, Turkish, and Islamic cultures, but in the aftermath of the 1980 coup, Kafesoğlu and his entourage dropped the European component and focused on the Turkish-Islamic aspects instead.[138] In his synthesis, Kafesoğlu extols the Ottoman Empire for its religious tolerance (*dini tolerans*), philanthropy (*insaniyetperverlik*), approach to dominance (*hakimiyet anlayışı*), and position as the pinnacle of civilization.[139] Kafesoğlu's configuration thus has important implications for neo-Ottomanist approaches to culture and the discourses that developed as a result.

As for the 1983 report, it reads much like a medical diagnosis. It examines the condition of the Turkish body and the causes of that condition through the lens of national culture. The subcommittees differed about when the crisis emerged: in the nineteenth century, in the 1950s, in the 1960s and 1970s, and so on. Their shared objective, however, was to rebuild national unity through culture. Some subcommittee reports described the country's culture as Islamic and Turkish and condemned "adulation of Europe." Others recommended a Safa-like synthesis of European, Islamic, and Turkish cultures. Overall, while there are some differences in the interpretations of the synthesis in the report, the logic of historicist humanism is evident in the efforts to restore the origins, genealogy, and civilization of Turkish national culture.

The diagnosis of Turkey's predicament was configured as a symptom of a larger crisis, presumably caused by deviation from the so-called national essence. Rather than considering the civil war of the 1970s as the outcome of a series of social, economic, bureaucratic, and political problems, there was a tendency to conceptualize it as a cultural problem. Kenan Evren's speeches, along with the 1983 report itself, also endorsed this diagnosis.

The Subcommittee on History argued that the so-called crisis had developed historically; accordingly, it was the result of the ongoing spiritual problem that marked the last one or two centuries. Here the subcommittee is implicitly referring to the Tanzimat reforms, a movement that is widely associated with the notion of Europeanization. Another cited historical landmark is the 1950s—that is, the Menderes era—during which, the report asserts, industrialization and urbanization developed too fast, and yet, because of the neglect of the social sciences and studies on Turkish history and culture, younger generations had been plunged into a spiritual crisis. The report claims that this caused Turkey's youth to turn away from their national essence and hence rendered them vulnerable to foreign ideologies.[140] The term "foreign ideologies" implies Marxism and its variations. This deviation again suggests a linear trajectory, a hypothetical straight line that connects today's youth to their origins and "authentic" culture. Overall, the history subcommittee report, like others, highly culturalizes the civil war and turns the whole matter into a civilizational crisis caused by the neglect of the Islamic origins of Turks:

> The human element can use technical knowledge and skills for or against the nation to which one belongs [in particular], and more generally, humanity. The for or against efforts of the human element are caused by humans' national or cosmopolitan character [yapı]. This character is secured by the [Ministry of] National Education.... The administrative strata do not have a true consciousness of national history. This leads to activities that harm Turkish culture. These activities, instead of focusing on the Turkish-Islamic heritage [focus on other things]: including the emphasis on the archaeology of states that have long disappeared, such as the Hittite Empire, Byzantium, and Rome; the declaration of Ephesus and [Demre, the site of the sarcophagus of] St. Nicholas as holy places where Christians hawk their religious beliefs

[Hıristiyanların dini inançlarını kamçılayacak şekilde buraların kutsal yer ilan edilmesi], in particular the festivals of Western Anatolia, in places like Fethiye, Ephesus, and Side, which try to revive the life of Rome-Byzantium.[141]

The subcommittee thus called for the Turkish-Islamic canon alone be incorporated into national education, and rejected everything else in the rich and diverse history of Anatolia. It viewed other traces and ruins under a xenophobic light, quite comparable to Rıza Nur's views in the aftermath of a war decades earlier. The advice of this committee's members to the government, then, was to build a national character as a bulwark against cosmopolitanism, to purge foreign elements so that "humans" realize their national character and do not work against their own nation. As mentioned, historicist humanism consists of a rich archive of knowledge, and not all members of the subcommittee agreed with one another. In that respect, the Turkish-Islamic synthesis interpretation of historicist humanism by this particular subcommittee is also critical of other humanists of Turkey such as Halikarnas Balıkçısı, who, as historical sociologist Aslı Gür shows, had embraced all the ancient Greek and Roman heritage in Anatolia as Turkey's own.[142]

In addition, the report asserts that because the Turkish republic is already well established, there is no longer a need to distance Turkish nationals from Ottoman history. The report deems a reconsideration of the production of knowledge on the subject to be imperative. Accordingly, taking "scientific methods as the basis for viewing national history" and analyzing problems from the perspective of "national history" is essential.[143] According to the report, then, the past should be read from the perspective of national history. This implies that only then can the Turkish nation continue to develop economically without becoming estranged from its own culture, origins, and essence. This is striking, because the report, just like Evren's speeches and discussions in the National Security Council, repeatedly asserts that foreign ideologies have "brainwashed" Turkey's youth. But the proposed remedy that highlights configurations of national culture is not considered an ideology, nor is the notion of nation—a major export of Enlightenment philosophy—deemed "foreign."

The 1983 *National Cultural Policy Report* also points out the necessity of conducting research on external and internal problems. It includes in this category the Armenians and Greeks, sectarianism, as well as those who have not been assimilated via Islam. The report asserts the importance of history and the production of knowledge in this field to deal with these supposedly internal and external problems.[144] Hence, it advocates a "scientific" investigation of various groups in Turkey:

> There are some groups that come from different ethnic origins [*menşe'*] and have integrated into Turkish culture thanks to Islam, or unfortunately have not become sufficiently integrated because of wrong attitudes. Anthropological, sociological, religious, folkloric, etc., research on these groups must be conducted as soon as possible. Studies produced in the West with regrettably bad intentions can be thus neutralized.
>
> Studies on religious communities living in Turkey should be conducted in the same vein [*aynı mahiyette*] and within the framework of Turkish history.
>
> If studies are conducted on these two matters, it will be easier to achieve integration internally and to find remedies for external interventions.[145]

Studying alterity in order to better manage these kinds of differences is reminiscent of the logic of the colonial production of knowledge: to study the Others in order to domesticate and better govern the unruly crowd. Moreover, as discussed in the preceding essays, the members of the 1983 report's History Subcommittee were inaccurate in contending that social sciences were neglected in Turkey or that integration was not studied. What we do see here, on the other hand, is a concern with assimilation and a weaponization of historiography. Overall, assimilation is interpreted as an urgent necessity and academic fields are to be mobilized to achieve this goal. Yet another instance of the politics of expertise is notable here.

In response, the military established a new research institute: the High Council of Atatürk Culture, Language, and History (Atatürk Kültür, Dil ve Tarih Yüksek Kurumu).[146] Included under the broader umbrella of the council was the Turkish Historical Society (Türk Tarih Kurumu), well known for fostering scholarship in the 1990s and 2000s to deny the Armenian genocide. The website of the council states its vision as "restoring Turkish culture as a civilization, from which all humanity can benefit" (Türk kültürünün, yeniden bütün insanlığın yararlanabileceği bir medeniyet hâline gelmesini sağlamaktır).[147] This neo-Ottomanist notion of Turkey's national culture was embodied in Turkey's Alliance of Civilizations initiatives. The narrative that reconfigures Turkey's culture as an Islamic civilization via a particular interpretation of Ottoman heritage is the very backbone of neo-Ottomanism.

The 1983 cultural policy report thus has broader implications for contemporary discourses of neo-Ottomanism, encompassing both Turkey and the Middle East. For example, the section on history articulates the necessity of an official policy on religion, emphasizing that secularism does not mean religious policy should be neglected.[148] In addition, the scholars who authored this section call attention to the importance of the study of Middle Eastern Muslim countries. Here they imply that developing a policy vis-à-vis the Islamic countries in the Middle East would highlight Turkey's cultural, religious, and historical ties to the region,[149] and especially considering that these countries were formerly part of the Ottoman Empire, it would reinstate Turkey's aura of leadership. With neo-Ottomanism, the Turkish government has indeed sought to restore that aura, a step that initially enjoyed remarkable success but then suffered a dramatic setback after tensions with Syria started to build up again.

As for neo-Ottomanism, in former prime minister Davutoğlu's vision of the Ottoman heritage, we do not encounter a discourse of xenophobia, but rather of tolerance, with its own limited recognition of alterity. There are other subcommittee reports that also support this vision. The report of the Subcommittee on Social Structure and Cultural Change,[150] for example, emphasizes how deeply rooted the notions of tolerance and equality are in Turkey's "traditional culture" and argues that given that state officials intend to develop a cultural policy, incorporating these notions in that policy would be desirable. This suggestion materialized with the Istanbul 2010 ECoC project and in the neo-Ottomanist discourse that revolved around it.

As discussed earlier, tolerance as a liberal value was incorporated into cultural policy. The question begs to be asked: Would it not be more effective to bring an end to the impunity of those who commit violence against communities that are different—defined not just in terms of background but also in terms of gender and sexuality? The list of such questions is long. Would it not make more sense to allow an exemption for Alevis or any others who do not wish their children to take the mainstream Sunni version of Islamic culture course in school, rather than forcing them to take the course against their will?[151] Or for the court cases of the Maraş massacre to be released to the public and the prime suspect—whose acquittal was controversial at the time—not to have been invited to an Alevi workshop as an expert on the subject? Or for any dissidence not to be automatically associated with broad and vague interpretations of terrorism? Or for democratically elected Kurdish politicians not to be imprisoned on the basis of vague allegations, and for forcible disappearances to be brought under legal scrutiny? The result of the absence of acts like these is an environment that fosters destruction and dispossession, and makes the promotion of tolerance as a national essence that needs to be reactivated no more than empty words. Finally, tolerance is a notion that operates on the plane of alterity, but not in terms of class. It casts alterity as something to be tolerated and as not a right.

On the other hand, the emphasis on Islam and the study of different groups to better integrate (read: assimilate) them in Turkey reveals the importance attributed to demography in the 1983 cultural policy report. The report of the Subcommittee on Social Structure and Cultural Change exemplifies this:

> Culture no doubt has a big impact on structural differences caused by rapid population growth. It is quite possible to use culture as a lever [*manivela*] if there is a desire to change this structure in one way or another. This is because demographic change is in a way a question of attitude, no matter what the economic and social factors might be. It is possible to change the attitude of culture toward human beings. Here we do not want to declare a particular view on population planning, because such a decision depends on what our target is.[152]

The report discusses demographic regulation, population growth, and the ratio of youth to older generations. It alludes to population engineering and configures culture as a site for the regulation of rapid population growth, which in turn raises questions about *which* population's growth is to be regulated.

Likewise, the report of the Subcommittee on Culture, Religion, and Morality is also concerned with demography and statistics. According to the authors, Islam has been adopted by the entire Turkish nation (*milletimizin tamamının benimsediği İslamiyet*). They offer this as a rationale for addressing religion in the report.¹⁵³ As evidence, they present the figure of 99.8 percent, and thereby dismiss the diversity of the groups categorized under Islam and then propose to study those that are different in order to better integrate and assimilate them. The scholars who authored this subcommittee report also argue that Turks who have adopted Christianity cannot be tolerated because, according to them, what enables the continuity of the Turks is Islam.¹⁵⁴ Having established the "fact" that Islam is the essence necessary for the continuity of Turks, the report resorts to statistics to address criminalization: "According to state statistics from 1965–1969, the number of literate people sent to prison is higher than the number of illiterate people. This is certainly proof that our education system has no spiritual support."¹⁵⁵ Criminalization is problematically associated with lack of Islam in education, rather than other variables that inform the incarceration of targeted, literate/more educated communities. That is, criminalization of certain groups is not perceived as a consequence of state policy, but very problematically as a sign of cultural deviation via education. For the authors of the report, deviation from Islam implies a rise in crime. They suggest that education must therefore be reformed. And it was. Tolerance and Islamic education were proposed to resolve these issues respectively, without a consideration of the problems with the legal system and power—in other words, without considering justice.

Additionally, according to the members of Subcommittee on Culture, Religion, and Morality, economic prosperity or social justice are of little relevance; they do not bring happiness. The "evidence" they adduce is the cases of Japan and Sweden, which, they claim, suffer from crises such as crime, drugs, and suicide.¹⁵⁶ The subcommittee concludes that Islam is crucial for integration of the population, which in turn will generate a national unity within the diversity, and that the activities of Christians and missionaries must be closely monitored and students need to be warned against "their propaganda."¹⁵⁷ Similarly, the subcommittee asserts that any admiration for Byzantium and the Hellenes must be prevented. Instead, everything needs to be reconfigured according to the Islamic tradition, by which is again meant mainstream Sunnism.

Overall, this section of the report reflects a Turkish-Islamic synthesis par excellence, one that proposes several interventions via culture. First, to establish Sunni Islam as the norm and to integrate all the diverse groups that fall within the broader spectrum of Muslims, Islam must become a policy for population regulation. Not only schools, but also the *family*—as a primary unit of governmentality—must be targeted for regulation. Second, any diversity beyond Islam is not to be trusted and necessitates surveillance. Christians and the tenets of historicist humanism in Western Europe, namely the ancient Greek heritage and anything related to Greeks, for that matter, are to be excluded from the Turkish-Islamic cultural configuration. Instead, Sunni Muslim origins and essence must be emphasized. In the 1983 cultural policy report's Turkish-Islamic synthesis, a state-controlled logic of historicist humanism, anchored in Turkish and Muslim origins—understood as a timeless essence—resurfaces.

What further emerges from this report is the notion that "synthesis" implies assimilation. Hence, the diverse elements of Turkey's social fabric are to be subjected to a series of state-centered regulations so that they can be molded according to the version of Islam that the state controls and standardizes. Non-Muslim citizens of Turkey are directly configured as foreign, a step that reproduces racialized thinking paradigms. In all this, an essentialist idea of culture and body is evident.

Beyond origins and embodied essence, the historicist humanism promoted here also depicts the ideal human. According to the report of the Subcommittee on Culture, Religion, and Morality, the most important thing is the development of the "model human" (*model insan*).[158] The report asserts that this must be the qualitative objective of the Turkish educational system:

> We need to increase the number of the "model humans," who will be the ones to carry out [economic] development. . . . The preparation of the model human will be made possible by the prevention of harmful philosophies and ideologies that obstruct [economic] development.
>
> What type of human will enable development? This type. . . . is the "modern *veli* [saint, a mystic patron]," as Mehmet Kaplan also expresses in his *Dream of a Grand Turkey*. The growth and social hegemony of this type is a necessity.[159]

The model or the ideal human is a notion that has a counterpart in historicist humanism. In race, depending on the context, it is the biologically unmixed or those who might be mixed in blood but who can still contribute to humanity. In Italian and Nazi fascism, it was antiquity and ancient Greek and Roman configurations of beauty and strength—entwined with the racialized superiority they represented—that were considered to be the model, the ideal human. On the other hand, this also meant producing model citizens who would follow the ideal human model, and with their labor contribute to development.

It is a particular assimilative national culture that is configured here, to protect development from struggles for rights and from ideologies and philosophies deemed harmful. Marxism and the right to unionize are clearly targeted here. Indeed, the report suggests that in order to achieve labor peace, workers should be subject to religious education in factories, workplaces, and big industrial centers.[160] The report goes on to offer Islam as a tool for intervention against labor organizations and circumventing class struggle, while the politics of expertise is mobilized to take over the fields of history, demography, school curricula, and labor organization, among others. Diversity in this context is discouraged and alterity is underscored as a threat.

While not all scholars and authors of the subcommittee reports appear to have agreed on everything, many ideas articulated in the general report found their way into official policies, such as amplified research on Armenians, Kurds, and Greeks from a Turkist nationalist perspective. The production of knowledge hostile to alterity and to critical engagement with history and state policies became common ground. Gatekeeping the nation's genealogy, origins, and heritage via a reemphasis on the mainstream Sunni interpretation of Islam—disregarding Alevi interpretations, among others—was a priority. With this restored nationalism, the idea was to unify a deeply divided country. Unity was stressed, not just against diversity in terms of background, but also at the expense of political plurality.

There are other issues raised in the 1983 *National Cultural Policy Report* that found their way into later policies, whether intentionally or not, which are important to note here. For instance, some of the recommendations of the report by the Subcommittee on International Cultural Relations—whose members included Ekmeleddin Ihsanoğlu, a well-known academic and a former candidate for president—were put into motion by the mid-2000s, when officials took an active role in cultural collaborations that displayed their vision of the country's cultural assets.[161] The Alliance of Civilizations and the Istanbul 2010 ECoC project are examples of this. This subcommittee also called for determining Turkey's position in greater civilization and developing policies accordingly. In many ways, Turkey's approach to the UN Alliance of Civilizations project fits with this recommendation. And finally, the subcommittee's push to change Turkey's image abroad, through organization and education, have been undertaken by both government officials and others—in particular the cleric Fethullah Gülen and his followers, who built schools abroad and later had a fallout with the government.

The Turkish-Islamic Synthesis, Brotherhood, and Liberal Multiculturalism

Wielding Islam to fight communism was a well-known Cold War policy that had a significant impact on the political landscape of the Middle East and beyond. In Turkey too, this idea had been entertained before. For example, in 1955, members of Adnan Menderes's Demokrat Party were already proclaiming in parliament that the greatest threat in the world was communism, and that if communism is lightning, Islam is a lightning rod; if communism is poison, Islam is the antidote; if communism is a plague, Islam is the vaccine.[162] The Turkish-Islamic synthesis, as proposed in the 1983 *National Cultural Policy Report*, therefore, embodies all these palimpsests. If one of the outcomes of the Turkish-Islamic synthesis and its dissemination in the 1980s onwards—the end of the Cold War and its aftermath—has been the transformation of neo-Ottomanism into an official state discourse, another has been the reactions against it, such as the History Foundation's endeavor to rescue history from its officially endorsed narratives.

Recollection of the 1923 population exchange is involved at multiple levels here. First, as a case of segregative biopolitics, it was a demographic move toward generating a majority population based on a Turkish-Islamic synthesis. Depending on the context, the emphasis on the elements of this synthesis would change, but for the most part the *synthesis* implied *assimilation*—a broader concern of the so-called free world in the aftermath of the Second World War. Let us recall that in the early 1960s Fındıkoğlu described (Sunni) mosques and (Turkish language) schools as effective sources of assimilation.[163]

Second, in the oppressive social, political, and cultural environment generated after the 1980 coup, the synthesis was reconfigured as an imposed norm for national culture, particularly in the school curricula. Any sign of diversity was seen as a threat to national security. In this climate, the 1923 exchange of populations resurfaced in the public domain at first as a means of emphasizing Greek-Turkish brotherhood. But this was not received without resistance. In 1982, a novel by Dido Sotiriou, *Farewell Anatolia* (entitled *Earth Drenched in Blood* in the original Greek, and *Say Hi to Anatolia* in Turkish), on the deported Greek Orthodox from Turkey to Greece was banned by the junta. The book had already been published in Turkish translation earlier, but it was not until it was republished in the same year that the junta sought to censor it. The ending of the novel in the Turkish translation conveyed a message of Greek-Turkish brotherhood that actually did not exist in the original Greek version. This rewriting via translation was probably done to soften the reaction against the book. Still, the novel could not escape the national security logic and was forbidden. Eventually, some publishers and music producers in Turkey's culture industry combined efforts with institutions like the History Foundation, and a more favorable climate for addressing alterity and diversity was gradually opened. The Emigrants' Foundation was institutionalized against this backdrop.

The third way in which the 1923 exchange is implicated in the Turkish-Islamic synthesis entails the representation of the exchangees by the Istanbul 2010 ECoC Agency. In statements issued for the opening of the Population Exchange Museum, the emphasis was on the successful integration of the exchangees. Yet, their diverse backgrounds—despite the presence of multiple family histories on display in the museum that attest to this—were not integrated into the diversity narrative that dominated Istanbul 2010. The exchangees were thus consolidated as successful examples of the Turkish-Islamic blend—the core idea of the synthesis.

Remembering the presentations at the AER and AWR in the 1950s and 1960s, assimilation appears to have continued to be a concern decades after the 1923 exchange, but it would take the 1980 coup d'état for the recollection of the Greek-Turkish population exchange to be considered a national security issue. Given the atmosphere of intimidation that reigned during the years of military dictatorship, it is not surprising that a novel was perceived as a threat to Turkey's "indivisibility" and unity. It is also not surprising that discourses of brotherhood and liberal humanist values were deployed as a way of overcoming censorship and oppression. In such a context, emphasizing the pain and suffering of peoples, or the similarity of the music or the food that they enjoy, and the proximity of their lifestyles, can be powerful tools to make a statement. In cases such as these, liberal humanism may not have the same implications as *The Family of Man*.

That notwithstanding, messages of brotherhood can also be complicated. A good example is the case of the late politician, journalist, and poet Bülent Ecevit. On June 18, 1974, Ecevit—the prime minister at the time—was accused in the Turkish parliament of not being fit to defend the interests of Turkey against Greece in Cyprus.[164] Mehmet Altınsoy, a deputy from the opposition Demokratik Party, based this claim on a poem Ecevit had written in the 1940s, pertaining to Turkish-Greek brotherhood. According to Altınsoy, Ecevit had written the poem to his "brother(s)" from Athens and therefore was not to be trusted.[165] For those familiar with Turkish, Greek, and Cypriot histories, this accusation against Ecevit might come as a surprise, as he was the prime minister who sent Turkish troops to Cyprus on July 19, 1974, against Greece and the Greek Cypriots, on the grounds of putting an end to the bloodshed on the island, which eventually led to the partition of the island. One wonders whether the accusation of being a humanist traitor only a month before might have put extra pressure on Ecevit, other than what was happening on the island.

After the 1980 coup, at time when an aggressive campaign of assimilation was launched, puncturing the climate of oppression was not easy. Personal and communal stories were suppressed in the name of forging a unified national body. When they could not be suppressed, the bodies themselves were removed: internal forced migration, forcible disappearances, and incarceration were the order of the day. In all cases, a logic of biopolitics is evident. In terms of knowledge production, a systematically defensive and denialist knowledge production after the coup was institutionalized. We might have—among other things—the 1983 *National Cultural Policy Report* to thank for it. Liberal humanism and discourses of brotherhood were mobilized by independent actors to make depoliticized political statements in the post-1980 era. During that time, even claiming brotherhood could be found problematic.

There has been a shift from that climate to the liberal multiculturalism that emerged during the first two terms of the AKP. As discussed, multiple actors took part in this process. There has, however, also been a crossing of discourses and concepts that have been integrated into different frameworks. The notions of brotherhood, heritage, and culture have been reconfigured within frameworks that range from oppression to limited recognition, from assimilation to a limited acknowledgment of diversity, from a Turkish-Islamic synthesis to neo-Ottomanism. The same is also true of the discourse of unity in diversity, whose meaning has also shifted depending on the context.

That the Population Exchange Museum could finally find funding and open its doors was welcomed by many family members of the exchangees. Rescuing the remains of cultural heritage and recollecting family memories constitute a very meaningful act for people who trace their histories to the lost maps of designated geographic origins. And even though the ECoC Agency did not promote the Population Exchange Museum as part of the liberal multiculturalism project ingrained in the Istanbul 2010 project, exchangees have attested to the remarkable diversity of Turkey's so-called Muslim majority—the very diversity that had once preoccupied racial purists.

Given the global turn toward a preoccupation with national security and attacks on multiculturalism in recent years, liberal multiculturalism might appear to be preferable to what is happening today. The visual culture popularized by *The Family of Man* has become so successful that visibility is often conflated with recognition—as was the case with *The Family of Man* itself. Depending on the context, one might consider even such limited recognition to be an important step. Meanwhile, discourses of brotherhood are abundant. When solidarity is defined via a shared human essence, bloodline, and belonging to the same racialized branches of humankind, rather than via notion of social justice, how far can that recognition and sense of solidarity go? Those limits are what I have sought to expose here. Yet, without accompanying policies and historical and political contextualization the picture remains largely incomplete. It is also not certain what exactly is meant by recognition nor what is expected.

For instance, as sociologist Loïc Wacquant demonstrates, in the United States, poverty is racialized, criminalized, and gentrified—reproducing previous dynamics of segregation but under a more democratic disguise, because sadly, alterity and class are often addressed separately.[166] Important works on this subject in Turkey have appeared in recent years, including by Deniz

Yonucu and Zeynep Gönen. As for the case of the United States, while the dynamics described by Wacquant were happening on the ground, the Academy Awards brought visibility to African American actors Halle Berry, Denzel Washington, and Sidney Poitier in 2002. Meanwhile, the privileged appear to expect those who receive limited recognition to be content with their visibility and accept it as recognition. Although symbolic, such visibility—as was also the case with the ECoC projects—is of course better than none, and the liberty of self-identification is naturally an important step. But it is only one step.

Unless social, economic, and political rights are also addressed, and cultural recognition goes beyond visibility, diversity remains little more than something that is capitalized, commodified, and put on display. As the examples addressed throughout this essay have shown, state officials do not necessarily engage actual demands unless these demands come with public support. The museumization of culture not only depoliticizes and dehistoricizes its objects on display as a way of regulating alterity, but also capitalizes on them. In the face of social disparities that can be informed by racialized thinking or the redistribution of resources, cultural policy should perhaps be more geared toward social justice. Government officials will probably not do this on their own, but as addressed, changes do not come overnight and without public support. Visibility is important as a step in that direction, but it should not be considered the end of the journey.

Similar questions with regard to the notion of liberal multiculturalism and the importance of recognition have preoccupied political theorists as well as UNESCO itself. For example, Canadian philosopher Charles Taylor addressed the importance of recognition in humanist education in his essay "The Politics of Recognition."[167] One of the issues he discussed was the importance of recognition for one's coherent identification of the self, and in that light, the significance of a more inclusive humanities curriculum. In many ways, he was advocating an inclusive humanism that bridges both liberal and historicist humanism within the context of school curricula: by creating inclusive curricula, it was possible, he asserted, to bring recognition of cultural difference as well as the contribution of different groups to humanity. His argument can be seen as a logical outcome of UNESCO's interventions in liberal but also historicist humanism. His intervention can be construed as bringing visibility by including alterity within the space of education and the curriculum.

Political theorist Nancy Fraser quickly replied that recognition alone is not enough, and underlined the importance of the social and economic redistribution of resources. UNESCO appears to have heard her call. UNESCO's *World Culture Report 2000: Cultural Diversity, Conflict and Pluralism* was dedicated to cultural recognition and social issues, including sustainability and poverty, and incorporated Fraser's essay "Redistribution, Recognition, and Participation: Towards and Integrated Concept of Justice."[168] Some of the topics in the report include cultural heritage sites, as well as "Museum Strategy in the Information Society," which laid out effective digital tools and technologies for museumization and archiving. Many facets of liberal multiculturalism are addressed in this report, embodying the merging of humanism, recognition, museumization, and heritage and cultural identification. The importance of social and economic rights aside, this document openly articulated concerns with justice. To what extent these concerns have been successfully integrated into policies remains questionable.

For example, at the time of writing this book, the attitude of the AKP government with regard to Kurds has changed once again. Urban warfare, cities in complete ruins, and large numbers of civilian causalities at the hands of the state security forces have again become part of the daily news. The situation might make the reader wonder: Surely liberal multiculturalism discourses are better than the current situation? Eyal Weizman argues that in many human rights and humanitarian cases, rather than finding solutions to problems, one is forced to make a choice between two bad options, and the choice is usually the less-worse-case scenario.[169] Yet, why is the public, not just in Turkey but in general, forced to choose between discipline-and-punish campaigns *or* policies that aim at pacification via limited recognition? And if indeed there can be such an easy switch in policy—the pendulum swinging from liberal multiculturalism à la neo-Ottomanism to securitarianism in which civilian lives do not seem to count for much—then how representative, and in fact, effective have been the changes in recent years?

The object of criticism here, then, is not diversity but the limits of liberal multiculturalism, not cultural recollection but political co-option of such recollection by state officials in order to market their neoliberal agenda. In the 1950s, international liberal cultural policies emphasized peace and social cohesion because they enabled economic development. But in the postwar period, such discourses accompanied an aggressive segregative biopolitics in domestic affairs, also in the name of stability and peace. These policies continued after the Cold War and in the 2000s, during which economic demand and peaceful coexistence in local contexts have become sources of capital accumulation.

One must remember, however, that only about a month and a half after the Istanbul 2010 Population Exchange Museum opened, British prime minister David Cameron announced the failure of state multiculturalism, which eventually led to the Brexit. Visible and invisible walls separate the privileged from the poor and the underprivileged, and often these categories are racialized. Syrian refugees lose their lives in the name of maintaining the separation between worlds. A so-called Muslim ban marked the early months of the Trump administration in the United States. Racism resurfaces in multiple ways. And only seven months after the museum opened its doors, Norwegian mass killer Anders Breivik took seventy-seven lives to blood-cement the white supremacy and xenophobia of his 1,518-page-long "European Declaration of Independence." To nurture hope for social justice, these are important reminders of the need to continuously reconsider the implications of aversion and tolerance in relation to alterity and to continuously identify and push the limits of governmentality disguised as multiculturalism and popularized via humanist discourses.

IN LIEU OF A CONCLUSION
Cultural Analysis in an Age of Securitarianism

IN AN ARTICLE in the first issue of Corrado Gini's revived *Revue Internationale de Sociologie* in 1954, Carl Schmitt reminds his readers that what at the time was called "world history in the West and the East is the history of development in the objects, means, and forms of appropriation interpreted as progress."[1] For the purposes of this book, these are important reminders: eugenics, humanism, segregative biopolitics, and cultural policy were mobilized as tools to secure economic growth and promote capitalist interests. As the essays in this book indicate, they each were interpreted as progress within their context. Progress, of course, is a linear notion of development in itself; it is very much informed by the European archives of cultural history, evolution, and eugenics. This configuration has long informed approaches to change in a linear manner. If we were to rethink the broader implications of these notions, they can also be interpreted as a means of regulating the processes of appropriation—past and present.

By the time his article appeared, Schmitt had been transferred to Nuremberg to be interrogated as a potential defendant for war crimes in the military trials,[2] where he rejected the accusations that his work might have had an influence on Nazi war crimes. He also refused to repent and claimed he had done nothing wrong. Eventually he was released. But he became an academic outcast, permanently stripped of his professorship in Germany, and he never expressed remorse for his support of the Nazi regime. His writings clearly indicate his position. He was critical of liberal democracy, because he believed taking plurality into consideration within a country weakened the strength and authority of the state. He probably underestimated how state officials would become creative in taming demands in the years to come.

According to Schmitt, the primary function of the state is to secure order and national unity, and he did believe liberal democracy was incompatible with this endeavor. The legal regulations of the 1980 military coup era in Turkey resonate with this approach. The military junta established the legal and institutional structures of an illiberal democracy in Turkey, all in the name of defending democracy and stability, and with the support of the international community. The notions of democracy and liberal values need to be reconsidered in that regard, and juxtaposed with social, cultural, economic, and legal regulations in order to unravel their broader implications.

Every essay in this book demonstrates an instance of liberal intervention—liberal humanism, liberalization of cultural identification and recognition, and liberal multiculturalism. Each intervention was considered to be a change for the better in its own context and interpreted as expanding recognition from subhuman to human, from a single vision of civilization to multiple civilizations, from national assimilation to cultural diversity. These discourses and the cultural policies they informed recognized alterity to varying degrees. As the palimpsests of cultural politics and segregative biopolitics analyzed in the book show, recognition means different things in each case. They also come with their own limitations and inconsistencies. As discourses, concepts, and categories cross over space and time, their implications change, but all in all, they have culminated in today's liberal terms of recognition. The palimpsests analyzed here demonstrate once again how nothing happens in a vacuum.

In recent decades, the liberal outlook has increasingly become public with regard to alterity, while biopolitical management of alterity has continued under different guises, such as gentrification and unequal access to social and economic rights. The result has been racialized poverty, criminalization and incarceration, and explicit segregation and building of walls. Whether physical or social, mobility has been confined to spaces of designated liberty. As architect Léopold Lambert's work *Weaponized Architecture* demonstrates, architecture and infrastructure are also used to generate segregative lines, when highways, bridges, or dams (as is the case in Turkey) are built in such a way that they act as barriers and create spatial frontiers between communities. The logic of segregative biopolitics continues to spatially redistribute peoples, including through incarceration that removes "undesirables" from sight and the living spaces of the privileged, as sociologist Loïc Wacquant's work shows. To this, I would add that such removal also enables neoliberal branding of urban spaces as "clean and marketable."[3] Race and racialized thinking have not disappeared and continue to inform segregative biopolitics. Indeed the tools, means, and objects mobilized to address racism, alterity, and recognition have been co-opted or pushed only to a certain limit, without engaging with their logics and concrete outcomes, including appropriation—that is, dispossession.

Schmitt was very clear about how the field of the political, as a site where lines are drawn between friends and enemies, should operate. He was therefore also critical of US foreign policy and liberal humanitarianism; he found them hypocritical in trying to expand patterns of intervention justified through such notions as humanity.[4] Schmitt believed the language of "space-disregarding universalizations such as humanity" blurred the lines between war and peace, warring parties and neutral states.[5] After all, military intervention in the name of humanitarianism would enable processes of appropriation without officially calling them colonization or even without an official declaration of war. History has proven him right in that regard.

The foreign interventions in Iraq and Syria, along with Afghanistan, are among the more recent cases that demonstrate this. Anthropologist Lila Abu Lughod points out in her work how Laura Bush—the US first lady at the time—mentioned Afghan women's rejoicing after being "liberated" by the Americans.[6] Liberating Muslim women from Muslim men, Abu Lughod shows, was a rationale for the US intervention in Afghanistan. Abu Lughod is critical of the deployment of Islam in that respect, as well as the lengthy explanations about Islam and women that widely circulated in the public domain after the horrible attack on the World Trade Center on September 11, 2001, as if information about Islam would help understand the reason for the attack. Abu Lughod calls into question such culturalization of violence, as if the reason for the attack was essentially about Islam and as if there were no dubious patterns of historical support for various conservative groups in order to protect capitalist interests against the communists during the Cold War. As Abu Lughod puts it, the reason "why the caves and bunkers out of which Bin Laden was to be smoked dead or alive, as President Bush announced on television, were paid for and built by the CIA" is not given any consideration.[7]

Rather than addressing the structures of power and histories of strange bedfellows, culturalization of violence or any undesirable attribute comes in handy for generating public consent for humanitarian interventions, but also for mobilizing segregative biopolitics in the name of securitarianism. As noted earlier, securitarian logic takes the probability of a crime or perceived threat as its basis. This logic has continued to inform segregative biopolitics, with highly racialized undertones. In that respect, the culturalization of violence is of course a euphemism, as racialized thinking and claims of civilizational incommensurabilities inform such discourses. As Laleh Khalili shows, such cultural representations have justified asymmetric warfare—beginning with the early colonial wars during which colonists did not think their opponents were civilized equals, and therefore did not think it was necessary to fight as they would with their equals.[8] Today, in instances such as these, paradigms of historicist humanism resurface in generating consent for securitarian and militaristic action. Laura Bush's statement therefore mirrors earlier discourses of the "civilizing mission" embedded in French and British colonialisms, among others.

Granted, the phrase "civilizing mission" is rarely used so explicitly today, but until recently, one only had to visit the Royal Central African Museum in Brussels—the very capital of the European Union and the place where the EU's cultural policies are consolidated—to encounter that phrase as well as a gigantic plaque that welcomed visitors at the entrance of the museum for decades: "Belgium Brings Civilization to Congo." In 2013, the museum was closed for renovation, and reportedly, it will be under restoration until June 2018. It is therefore not clear what will happen after the renovation. Some newspapers discussed this as "Belgium is facing its colonial past." What does it take, one might ask, to *face* such a past exactly? Does making the colonized visible—by way of including pictures of workers from the Belgian Congo as was the case with *The Family of Man*—suffice to bring recognition? This very criticism that Roland Barthes articulated decades ago remains valid to this day. Furthermore, such bold statements might be disappearing from the public domain, but are the racialized logics that inform such thought patterns also disappearing? The less implicit, and in fact disguised under liberal values, such statements become, the more pervasive they can be in informing segregative biopolitics and military interventions with imperialist or neocolonial aspirations to protect racialized capitalist interests with the consent of the masses.

The culturalization of violence is an extension of such thinking. Today, in the context of Islam, it entails attributing violence to cultural and religious traits with heavily racialized undertones, as if there are no concrete economic and political reasons as to why the Middle East offers the political landscape it does today. Cold War era policies offer important clues in that regard. The enthusiastic support for the bloody juntas of Augusto Pinochet and Kenan Evren attests to this. Washing their hands of this history of violence and intervention, Euro-North-American powers have measured countries or even entire regions—such as the Middle East—against the metric of liberal values. Meanwhile, not all countries are held equally accountable for their abuse of rights, and when they are, not all rights abuses count as human rights violations. Economic precarity with crippled labor and unionization rights is rarely condemned as a violation of human rights, as is the case in Turkey, the United States, and Spain. Several years ago, when Turkish Airlines barred female flight attendants from wearing red lipstick, it received much wider European press coverage than the repeated violations of workers' rights by the Turkish company that fired hundreds of employees for exercising their then legal right to strike.[9] Such a climate reproduces an Orientalist dynamic.

Unsurprisingly, human rights discourses deployed by state authorities circumvent the racialization of poverty—dispossession—and prefer to focus on liberal rights. Laura Bush's statement about how Muslim women are oppressed exemplifies this trend, and interventions disguised as humanitarianism are discursively configured as lessons of civilization. President George Bush claimed invading Iraq would bring democracy and freedom to the country. Liberal humanitarian discourses have indeed been used for different military expeditions. In such a context, even though Carl Schmitt is a highly controversial figure, his work has been reincarnated since it is relevant when considering political dynamics today—without supporting his political position and project.[10]

Indeed, Schmitt remarked that just because colonialism is condemned does not mean that appropriation has disappeared:

> Colonialism here means the land- and sea- appropriations of the age of great discoveries of the four hundred years of Eurocentric international law. The odium of colonialism today concerns the European nations. At its core, it is nothing other than the odium of appropriation. In this repudiation, progressive liberalism and Marxist communism agree completely. Allegedly, no longer is anything taken, but only divided and developed. An important rep-

resentative of political science at a leading university in the United States recently wrote to me: "Land appropriation is over and done with." I replied that it has become even more serious with the appropriation of space.... Has humanity today actually "appropriated" the earth as a unity, so that there is nothing more to be appropriated? Has appropriation really ceased?[11]

According to Schmitt, those with different political positions might have condemned colonialism as an explicit form of appropriation, but he views deterritorialized notions like humanity as a danger because to him they open a path for different spaces to continue to be appropriated. This is in part because Schmitt's work operates on clear paradigms such as friends or enemies. In an earlier work, *The Concept of the Political*, Schmitt argues that politics revolves around regulating and distinguishing between friends and enemies. This distinction determines who is to be included or excluded, and is de facto spatialized.[12] "Humanity" is a term that eclipses these categories, and he is suspicious of it, because to his mind, in it one loses sight of who is included and who is excluded in the universal space encompassed by all humanity, even though this lack of visibility does not mean the divisions and related paradigms disappear. To him, they just become easier to manipulate. Segregative biopolitics relies on such categorizations of inclusion and exclusion too. It spatializes the distinction between insiders and outsiders. And as the cases addressed in this book demonstrate, these distinctions are informed by racialized thinking.

In Schmittian terms, managing conflict is the task of the state and to that end, establishing order is crucial. To ensure this process, people are indexed, codified, and ordered according to their background. Eugenicist thought and biological approaches reinforced by cultural histories of historicist humanism have long informed the racialized thinking deployed to justify such categorization and redistribution of peoples. Today, the logics of segregative biopolitics have not disappeared and continue to inform policies often mobilized under the guise of securitarianism—a term heavily informed by the culturalization and racialization of violence.

Schmitt's work is also relevant in another respect when considering today's dynamics. As mentioned, he argues that at the core of all social, legal, and economic order lies appropriation, distribution, and production. In an environment where appropriation is a reality but is creatively obfuscated to avoid demands for restitution and justice, production is overemphasized to the extent of exploitation, with an absence of social security and rights, and the distribution of wealth is disproportionate, with a large portion accumulated in the hands of very few and a large portion of the remaining resources allocated to securitarianism, as is the case in the United States. In this environment, distribution does indeed become an issue since the remaining resources to be redistributed are relatively scarce. Rather than asking why it is that public resources are so scarce to begin with, or questioning the policies that have contributed to this outcome, the racialization of distribution becomes a common political strategy to generate public support for segregative biopolitics. This can be observed in the discourses of present-day politicians like President Donald Trump or France's fascist National Front Party leader, Marine Le Pen. When the scarcity of public resources is not questioned, and money is poured into the security industry—which in itself is justified through the culturalization and racialization of violence or "liberal humanitarian interventions"—not only are the disgruntled pacified, but also fascist discourses resurface. The outcome is yet another rationale for segregative biopolitics.

Further, the notion of land appropriation via demographics and mixing is still salient today. In addition to statements by many politicians, Norwegian mass killer Anders Breivik's 1,518-page-long "European Declaration of Independence" is an ominous testament to this. Possibly a reference to the dystopia of *1984*, his is titled *2083* and "predicts" the year when Europe will disappear under a floodtide of immigrants and Muslims. This means, in a eugenicist statistical approach, Breivik took the lives of white Norwegians—most of whom were at a summer camp organized by the youth division of the ruling Norwegian Labor Party—to stop the "degeneration" of Europe via the overpopulation of bodies from what he clearly considered the "wrong" category. Over a hundred pages of this troubled text are dedicated to Ottoman history and Turkey—which he calls the Islamic Ottoman Turkish Empire—and seasoned with racist statements against Islam and Muslims. In the disturbing pages of his "manifesto" the acts of violence committed in Middle Eastern contexts are attributed to Middle Easterners' inherent, biological disposition. Once again, the notions of essence, biologized character, and race are intertwined in his prose. He views the case of Muslims in Europe as a demographic takeover of the land in terms of numbers: "Multiculturalism (cultural Marxism/political correctness), as you might know, is the root cause of the ongoing Islamisation of Europe which has resulted in the ongoing Islamic colonisation of Europe through demographic warfare (facilitated by our own leaders)."[13] This argument represents an appropriation of Corrado Gini's and others' interpretations of demographics and equates multiculturalism with cultural Marxism and political correctness. In this discrepant logic, political correctness implies that essential differences between peoples do exist—the signified—but rather than calling these essential differences for what they are, euphemisms—the signifier—are used. Breivik therefore taps into the already widely circulating racist discourses and reproduces already existing paradigms. And the youth he killed in the summer camp were quite possibly targeted because he associated them with "cultural Marxists" whom he held responsible for multiculturalism.

To fight Muslims—which it condemns for their "inherent" violence—the manifesto calls for mass assassinations, attacks on nuclear sites in Europe, and other forms of despicable violence in an organized manner. As a justification, it asks how many "sisters" will be raped by Muslims—"Europeans will be ravaged, robbed, beaten, terrorized or killed by Muslims"—and speculates on the numbers as well as predicts a Muslim-Christian war. As examples of Muslim threats, the text cites India and Anatolia, and posits linear genealogies between past and present peoples. And unsurprisingly, it also references the 1923 population exchange along with the partition of India and Pakistan as well as of Palestine, and praises this type of segregative biopolitics. In fact, it calls these cases "apartheids" implemented by erecting a security fence, presumably necessary for keeping Muslim terrorists out.

It is unclear how much following these disturbing accounts have. But even for non-followers, there is a broader connection to racism, as the very first reactions against Breivik's crime revealed. When he single-handedly murdered seventy-seven people, news agencies at first speculated that because the controversial Danish *Jyllands-Posten* Muhammad cartoons were reprinted in Norway, terrorists associated with Islam might be the culprits.[14] This racist assumption proved to be wrong, as the murderer was revealed to be a white male supremacist. Upon this revelation, the press turned around and started speculating that he must be unstable. This was before Breivik passed a psychiatric evaluation.[15] He was thus cast as an aberrant case, without taking into consideration that his despicable act was just a violent and deeply disturbing symptom of the broader racism that made the press immediately jump to the conclusion that the culprits were "Muslim terrorists" in the first place. Liberal distaste for violence led to condemnation of the attack even though the broader implications of the logic that this white supremacist acted upon appear to have been shared. Today, parts of Breivik's arguments resonate among the white supremacists in the United States who seek to highlight their European ties.

The attacks claimed by the Islamic State (ISIS) and fascism appear to feed off each other. And the culturalization and racialization of violence contribute to the marginalization of Muslims and configure them as an unchanging, static, monolithic entity—connecting a group that adopted violence with everybody else. Such approaches feed into securitarianism and are reminiscent of eugenicist approaches to crime, where one's background determines whether one poses a threat and, accordingly, becomes a target of the security apparatus. This in turn raises questions about the implications of such marginalization in terms of the recruitment rates for ISIS. The securitarian logic capitalizes on such conflicts, not only at the level of states but also of peoples. In-depth studies that take into account both the diachronic and the synchronic elements of these dynamics are needed. And if cultural and social policies are to be developed, they clearly need to be reconsidered with these dynamics in mind and reconfigured to raise questions about logics of categorization and their historical and political implications, instead of reproducing them uncritically in the name of recognition. And if they are to be reproduced, they should not be politically shallow. And, finally, the contextualization of cultural heritage needs to be addressed.

If Schmitt was right in arguing that at the core of the social, legal, and economic order lie processes of land appropriation, distribution, and production, then I would propose to add the notion of *cultural order* to this equation. In the light of the material analyzed in this book, my use of the term "cultural order" is threefold. First, to denote cultural policy launched to establish stability, coexistence, and peace, with the goal of generating an environment conducive to economic growth. While in the 1950s liberal discourses of culture entailed international peace, in the aftermath of the Cold War they entailed turning alterity into an object for display cast as a systematized site for the accumulation of capital. Second, to point to the categorization of peoples according to their cultural background and to use this categorization to sort and order people, in an attempt to bring a cultural order to a given space. This is the core of segregative biopolitics, and while the term "culture" is used as an umbrella rubric today, racialized thinking is very much embedded in its identification paradigms. Third, cultural order also implies the regime of cultural recognition in place today that discursively structures recognition in liberal terms. Spatialized inclusion and exclusion à la Schmitt organize recognition in terms of visibility: when one can be visible via cultural fields, the visibility in that space is configured as inclusion. In neoliberal contexts, we witness a state-level appropriation of cultural sites that were previously used for making demands for recognition. Liberal cultural politics has thus changed since the 1950s, but its relation to segregative biopolitics remains intact.

Culminatively, the cultural order ensures that conflict is avoided—or if we rethink the issue in critic Eyal Weizman's terms—it holds the promise that the option of "the least of all possible evils" will be chosen; that is, rather than seeking to resolve a problem, it will be managed.[16] Consider the contemporary context: the rise of securitarian logic, racialized accounts of violence, support for fascism, and enthusiasm for segregative biopolitics in the broader world context—particularly in the global north—and a recently rekindled war in Turkey that has generated new ruins in cities where the population is predominantly Kurdish, a high rate of civilian casualties and tragic deaths, disturbing images of abuse taken by some men who wear balaclavas and identify themselves as security officials, devastating destruction of Kurdish heritage sites, such as Sur, among other things. The case of the UNESCO World Heritage Committee being hosted in Istanbul in July 2016, and the committee's not allowing space to raise voices critical of the destruction of Kurdish sites previously included in UNESCO's World Heritage list, is a sobering example of the limitations of the cultural order.[17]

As noted, if the pendulum can swing so rapidly, to what extent can we speak of the effectiveness of these policies, beyond cosmetic visibility? Does rendering alterity visible in hegemonic public spaces dissolve the divisions between the excluded and the included? The laudable efforts of independent actors aside, recognition cannot be granted in the field of culture alone, but needs to be expanded to consider social justice and restitution in social, economic, and political terrains as well. Choosing liberal cultural policies over securitarian logic may very well be an instance of selecting the lesser evil, but it does not resolve conflicts, injustice, racism, and inequalities; rather, it manages them.

And today, when management is the goal, neither fascism and racialized thinking, nor the rise of securitarian logic and the popularization of segregative biopolitics, should come as a surprise. Reminiscent of Adam Smith's assertion that peace is imperative for economic growth, UNESCO's cultural policy has long emphasized the importance of social cohesion and peace for the economy. In that regard, UNESCO has been a powerful platform for promoting international peace and coexistence—as was the case in the 1940s and 1950s—but also for managing potential international conflicts with liberal cultural politics. At the time, this entailed liberal humanism—that we are all *Homo sapiens*, despite our racialized differences. Toward the end of the Cold War, the organization gradually turned its attention to diversity and coexistence within national borders. In addition to the efforts of independent actors, UNESCO provided an important impetus for the liberalization of cultural identification. Genealogies and family histories are part of this trend, as was also the case in Turkey. Abroad, one of the best-known and earliest examples is African-American author Alex Haley's *Roots: The Saga of an American Family*, which had an impact in popularizing oral history, family history, and heritage in the 1970s.[18] The book was turned into a TV series and was widely disseminated, including in Turkey, with a record number of viewers.

By the 1990s and early 2000s, tracing the legacies of biopolitics via cultural heritage had become common. The attention paid to the 1923 Greek-Turkish population exchange exemplifies this. Recognition became increasingly emphasized via culture, which was clearly a very important but incomplete step. In the absence of social, economic, and political factors that rendered alterity and recognition a problem to begin with, recognition rarely restructures the social, economic, and political order and rights. This depoliticization and dehistoricization might be among the reasons why expressions of alterity and cultural heritage were so easily co-opted by the state at a time when it was convenient to do so: without discussing appropriation, limiting distribution to the discursive fields of recognition, and stressing production, displaying alterity can easily be turned into a lucrative business. It is therefore important to examine the limits of these cultural policies, practices, and discourses informed by liberal values, and to unpack what that entails in each setting. As I have sought to show in this book, no text, no policy, and no work of art is scripted in isolation.

This fact also includes segregative biopolitics, since as its underlying logics cross over time and space they inform different policies that take different forms depending on the context. In that respect, modern-day policies of segregative biopolitics tower over the ruins of human categorizations generated by the twin archives of culture and biology, or, namely, the paradigms of historicist humanism and eugenics. Settlement policies have historically been part of imperial rule, and the Ottomans also practiced it. But with the advent of the modern era, these "scientific" tools structured the categorization of bodies and systematized segregative biopolitics. And the legal precedent set in the international arena with the 1923 Greek-Turkish population exchange generated a legal framework for it. In that respect, these modern developments resonate with Schmitt's notion of progress and reveal how the tools and means developed to ensure appropriation can be interpreted as progress.

The references to the 1923 exchange to implement new segregative biopolitics, such as the Potsdam Agreement and the partitions of India and Palestine, also reveal themselves in a palimpsest. This book has sought to reconsider this palimpsest in the aftermath of the Second World War, where, given the atrocities of the Holocaust and fascism, one might have logically expected their logics to be put more effectively into question with the rise of powerful institutions like the UN and UNESCO.

Like segregative biopolitics, notions of liberal humanism, liberalization via cultural identification, and liberal multiculturalism can also change as they become incorporated into different policies and initiatives, and cross over time and space. The different time periods and contexts addressed in the diachronic and synchronic analyses of the palimpsests of discourses and policies covered in this book encapsulate how, despite their differences, they also share similarities and trends. Liberal discourses have a broader appeal, and tend to be interpreted as a move for the better, even though facts on the ground might indicate otherwise. What each essay also shows is that the radical historical contextualization of liberal cultural politics and policies is important, but that historicization on its own does not necessarily mean questioning power. Exposing logics that inform policies is also an important step toward that goal, but more work needs to be done on the ground.

One thing is certain though, governments usually do not make changes unless there is a dynamic social momentum and strong public opinion in favor of change. The American civil rights movement is a case in point. As examined in the case of the entangled legacies of the 1923 exchange and beyond, with each public move for change, there was a countermove—an attempt to resort to different policies to manage the demands for diversity and plurality. Here, cultural politics was formed in a dialectic move between public demands and acts of governmentality. And even if economic interests constitute the major force that shapes policies, public consent is usually generated through the mobilization of repertoires of culture. Schmitt's call to remember that the tools and means developed to appropriate are interpreted as progress is an important reminder. If recognition takes place in visual space, it is also important to keep that visibility without surrendering it to state appropriation. For this is how the cultural order manages those sites. And this management also allows for the state to step in during times of conflict—also launched to promote certain political interests—and claim sites of demand for recognition as its own.

Cultural analysis in an age of rising securitarianism has its own challenges, no doubt. Meanwhile, an abundance of discourses of Orientalist and scientific racialist archives of knowledge are in circulation, and with the Human Genome Project, DNA testing to trace family origins, the implications of being human are reconfigured. Or as Turkish author Peyami Safa wrote more than half a century ago, the implications of being human are once again changing. Securitarian culture comes with its structures of power. In addition to the military, the militarized police take centerstage to protect capitalist interests. The development of nonlethal technologies to disperse disgruntled crowds aside, urbanization—a spatial growth model supported by the IMF and the World Bank—is also under the scrutiny of security forces, as a recently leaked Pentagon video demonstrates.[19] The video, labeled dystopian by the press, predicts a chaotic future for urban centers and raises concerns about population growth, scarcity of resources, and lack of stability, all of which threaten security. All things considered, including ongoing ruination, there is a reasonable basis for anticipating that segregative biopolitics, in the name of security, will continue to shape the spatial distribution of categorized bodies.

In light of these dynamics, to some, liberal cultural politics might come across as progress even if racialized and spatialized bases of political order have not disappeared. And there are also reasonable grounds for doubting that fascism was ever truly faced, beyond case-by-case treatments. For how does one face fascism or racism? Or colonialism? This is also a question for the Turkish contexts analyzed in this book. Does condemning a term make its logics disappear or stop informing policies? As discussed in Part Three, the question Remzi Bucak, a deputy from the Demokrat Party, posed in 1953 in the Turkish parliament with regard to the status of the "Eastern provinces" (*doğu vilayetleri*) and whether they were a colony (*müstemleke*) raised the same issues. There is a whole Republican history to consider in that regard; historian Zeynep Türkyılmaz offers an important historical background to this question.[20]

Facing the past on a personal level is important since it is among the factors that generate momentum for change in the status quo as was the case in post-1980 era Turkey. But facing the past is also a problem of bureaucracy and of the wealthy, since questioning a past era might also call into question the legitimacy of the position of people in power today. As critic Luis Martín-Cabrera has pointed out, the Spanish judge who caused General Pinochet's arrest was applauded in Spain for championing human rights, but when the same judge, Baltasar Garzón Real, started to investigate the crimes of Spain's own fascist dictator General Franco, unrelated charges were brought against him and he was stripped of his post.[21] Mobilizing fields of culture to call for change and recognition can therefore be very important, but this in itself is not enough. Regimes might change, discourses and cultural rhetorics might shift, but power alignments, as well spatialized patterns of inclusion and exclusion, are persistent.

Cultural policies build on one another, and rethinking categories and repertoires that they tap into might be useful for excavating their recurring paradigms. In an attempt to revisit its humanist paradigms, in 2011 the *UNESCO Courier* dedicated an entire issue, titled "Humanism, A New Idea," to humanism. Prepared for the fiftieth anniversary of UNESCO's first humanism congress, convened in New Delhi in 1951—where Hilmi Ziya Ülken proposed a patriotic humanism—the *Courier* sought answers for the future of humanism, with mixed opinions presented on both historicist and liberal humanism as well as calls for uniting all "mankind."

The special issue opens with a piece that introduces "new humanism":

> In 1951, during a "Discussion on the Cultural and Philosophical Relations Between East and West" held in the capital of India, New Delhi, from 13 to 20 December, UNESCO endorsed the idea of a new holistic humanism. The world was recovering from a terrible war that had sullied the myth of technological progress dominating Western culture. In a discussion document entitled "Towards a New Humanism," the participants at the meeting spoke of "confused intelligence that has lost its soul" and a "crisis of humanism." They advocated a "spiritual revolution" and "common spiritual progress" calling for greater exchange between East and West....
>
> Six decades later, the challenges facing the world have moved on, as has our understanding of the meaning of humanism....
>
> "In the context of globalization," says the final report on the meeting, "this concept has to concentrate on cultural diversity, dialogue in the age of the Internet, and reconciliation between the North and the South."...
>
> According to a section of the report entitled "Towards a new humanism and reconciled globalization," the purpose of the new humanism is to create a climate of empathy, belonging and understanding, along with the idea that progress with respect to human rights is never definitive and requires a constant effort of adaptation to the challenges of modernity.[22]

The crisis of humanism in question is of course the Second World War, which caused the crumbling of the illusion of technological progress. From the ashes and the ruins of this war UNESCO attempted to build a new humanism. Liberal humanism on the one hand and historicist humanism on the other, the notion of human became a site to develop cultural and educational policies in an attempt to be more inclusive and establish peace.

In *Humanism in Ruins* I have attempted to address the limits and paradigms of these interventions, including the case of the 1951 UNESCO conference on humanism. That UNESCO has officially recognized the gap between the global North and the global South and that its "new humanism" emphasizes human rights may be a positive step, but what these terms entail on the ground is also important. As anthropologist Lynn Meskell's work shows, UNESCO is also at the intersection of political and economic decisions that need to be taken into consideration.[23] Given all the dynamics addressed in this book, have we really moved away from the ruins of modern-era appropriation? To what extent does UNESCO adhere to its own postulates if in other sites it officially remains silent about ongoing destruction and ruination?

The palimpsests analyzed here demonstrate how segregative biopolitics constitutes the infrastructure of liberal cultural policies of alterity.[24] The implications of these terms and the terms of their relation might change, but the structural relationality remains intact. Combining a diachronic with a synchronic analysis, I have sought to trace these relations and interconnections in order to raise questions about the limits of recognition and the resilience of racialized thinking.

It is easy to be blind to these structural relations, and critical theorist Walter Benjamin's approach to these dynamics offers a sobering account in that respect. In 1930, the German Jewish thinker sent a copy of his book *The Origin of German Tragic Drama*—in which he discusses how in ruins history merges into a setting in the form of a script—to Carl Schmitt.[25] The correspondence between the two has been a subject of controversy, given that Benjamin took his own life fleeing from the Nazis and that Schmitt, the crown jurist of the Third Reich, was a supporter of the Nazi regime. Although the controversy falls outside the scope of this book, bringing Benjamin's perspective back into the picture as a critique of the power structures described by Schmitt is important as it offers a critical perspective on the world depicted by Schmitt. I shall therefore turn back to the epigraph by Walter Benjamin that opens this book.

In his "Theses on the Philosophy of History," Benjamin presents his approach to culture and power:

> Whoever has emerged victorious participates to this day in the triumphal procession in which current rulers step over those who are lying prostrate. According to traditional practice, the spoils are carried in the procession.

They are called "cultural treasures," and a historical materialist views them with cautious detachment. For in every case, these treasures have a lineage which he cannot contemplate without horror. They owe their existence not only to the efforts of the great geniuses who created them, but also to the anonymous toil of others who lived in the same time period. There is no document of culture which is not at the same time a document of barbarism. And just as such a document is never free of barbarism, so barbarism taints the manner in which it was transmitted from one hand to another.[26]

Benjamin's account might rearticulate some historicist humanism paradigms, but he posits the problems with these paradigms from a critical perspective. He reminds his readers that one needs to distance oneself from the transmission and dissemination of humanist values of culture—such as the work of geniuses—and how in the name of civilization and progress many horrors have been committed. History, he concludes, needs to be brushed against the grain. According to Benjamin, if history is not addressed against its officially accepted versions and against the grain of so-called progress, then only new wars and novel forms of violence and repression—foreshadowing ruination—will follow. Benjamin's work, together with Frantz Fanon's call for a reconsideration of equality and humanism, offers an important critique of the notion of progress.

Following Benjamin's line of thought, then, without critical contextualization, the transmission of any "cultural treasure" and its dissemination will carry the taint of the brutality embedded in its production. And in the absence of such criticism, the celebration of these documents in the name of liberal inclusion will likely be interpreted as progress—in the sense that Schmitt defined it: as yet another tool or means to facilitate the process of appropriation. It is therefore not only the interrelations of concepts, discourses, works of art and culture, and cultural policy that reveal themselves as palimpsests, but also the very ruins of segregative biopolitics over which they tower. This is the task I have sought to undertake by excavating the ruins of the 1923 Greek-Turkish population exchange and its entangled legacies, to address how these legacies were engaged in the aftermath of the Second War, and to raise questions about the logics of segregative biopolitics and the historicist humanist and eugenicist repertoires that informed them.

According to Benjamin, a document of culture, which signifies a glorious moment in so-called civilization, simultaneously attests to the ruins of violence and exploitation of peoples over which its humanist value system looms. When that second segment is dismissed or ignored, it becomes easier for such an object to be appropriated by state officials or others to promote their agenda or maintain the status quo. Or when what is appropriated is culture itself, it is in the form of museumization—a modern tool of objectification and display. Schmitt's notion of appropriation interpreted as progress becomes more significant in such a context.

It is in these palimpsests that I have sought to reconsider the interrelatedness of liberal cultural politics and segregative biopolitics, and to address their broader implications via the case of the 1923 exchange of populations. And it is within these palimpsests that I have unearthed *explicit* crossing of policies, peoples, and objects. But I have also encountered a more *implicit* crossing of notions, tools, and methods such as racialized thinking, fascist eugenicist approaches, humanism, and segregative biopolitics. In them I have discovered structural ties between liberal cultural politics and biopolitics, but also between historicist and liberal humanism and eugenics.

And now as this journey of exploration, with all its categorization, classification, capitalist exploitation, dispossession, and reconfigurations of the "human," draws to an end, we see before us the terminus: the ruins of modernity.[27]

NOTES

Introduction

1. İskender Özsoy, *İki Vatan Yorgunları: Mübadele Acısını Yaşayanlar Anlatıyor* [The exhausted of two motherlands: Those who suffered the pain of the population exchange tell their story] (Ankara: Bağlam, 2005), 38–42.

2. Marquis de Condorcet, *Éloges, et autres pièces* [Praise, and other pieces] (Paris: Chez Le E.A. Lequien, 1820), 297, 401, 468, 490–91. See a personal letter from Bonneval to Montesquieu dated October 2, 1728 (in the Municipal Library of Bordeaux); and Giovanni Giacomo Casanova, *Mémoires de J. Casanova de Seingalt écrits par lui-même* [Memoirs of J. Casanova de Seingalt written by himself] (Paris: Garnier Frères, 1880), 387–429. While the authenticity of the memoirs has been questioned, the Bibilothèque Nationale de France has recently purchased the manuscript of Casanova's memoirs and Pléiade has published an unabridged version. Casanova's account of his encounter with Bonneval in Istanbul, however, necessitated separate research on its own as Bonneval's conversion to Islam was very controversial and the Western European accounts of this conversion were contentious.

3. Claude-Alexandre de Bonneval, *Anecdotes vénitiennes et turques, ou Nouveaux mémoires du comte de Bonneval* [Venetian and Turkish anecdotes, or new memoirs of Count Bonneval] (London: Aux Dépens de la Compagnie, 1740).

4. Charles-Augustin Sainte Beuve, "Le Comte-Pacha Bonneval" [The Count-Pasha Bonneval], in *Causeries du Lundi* [Monday chats], 2nd ed. (Paris: Garnier Frères, 1853), 5:499–523. For instance, Lady Georgiana Fullerton published a novel entitled *The Countess of Bonneval*—a romance imagining how Bonneval's wife of ten days must have felt when he left her behind in France. Georgiana Fullerton, *La Comtesse de Bonneval: histoire du temps de Louis XIV* [The Countess of Bonneval: The history of the time of Louis XIV] (Paris: Librairie d'Auguste Vaton et Charles Douniol, 1857). There were other novels that took Bonneval's life as a basis, such as Octave Féré and D.-A.-D Saint-Yves, *Les Amours du comte de Bonneval* [The loves of Count Bonneval] (Paris: Dentu, 1866). For a biography of Bonneval, see Albert Vandal, *Le Pacha Bonneval* [Bonneval Pasha] (Paris: Au Cercle Saint Simon, 1885).

5. Bonneval's family residence in France, Château de Bonneval, is open to tourists for visits and to others for special events such as weddings. Parts of the residence are museumized and one of the highlights is Comte de Bonneval's room on display: La Chambre du Pacha (the chamber of the Pasha).

6. Harold Bowen, "Aḥmad Pasha Bonneval," *Encyclopaedia of Islam*, 2nd ed.,

P. Bearman, Th. Bianquis, C. E. Bosworth, E. van Donzel, and W. P. Heinrichs, eds. http://dx.doi.org/10.1163/1573-3912_islam_SIM_0416.

7. These claims can be found in the sources cited above, for example.

8. Ayhan Aktar, "Homogenizing the Nation, Turkifying the Economy," in *Crossing the Aegean: An Appraisal of the 1923 Compulsory Population Exchange Between Greece and Turkey*, Renée Hirschon, ed. (New York: Berghahn Books, 2004), 89. Aktar quotes Mahmut Celal (Bayar), Turkey's minister of exchange, addressing this issue as a problem.

9. See Penelope Papailias, *Genres of Recollection: Archival Poetics in Modern Greece* (New York: Palgrave Macmillan, 2005); Kemal Arı, *Büyük Mübadele: Türkiye'ye Zorunlu Göç, 1923–1925* [The Great exchange: Forced migration to Turkey, 1923–1925] (Istanbul: Tarih Vakfı Yurt Yayınları, 1995). Elsewhere, I have engaged such locutions in terms of geographic identification. See "Documenting the Past and Publicizing Personal Stories: Sensescapes and the 1923 Greco-Turkish Population Exchange in Contemporary Turkey," *Journal of Modern Greek Studies* 26 (2008): 451–87.

10. For more on the connected histories of Greece and Turkey, see Umut Özkırımlı and Spyros Sofos, *Tormented by History: Nationalism in Greece and Turkey* (London: Hurst, 2008).

11. See Artemis Leontis, *Topographies of Hellenism: Mapping the Homeland* (Ithaca, NY: Cornell University Press, 1995).

12. This was applicable for Greek Orthodox settled in Istanbul before 1918. For more, see Alexis Alexandris, "Religion or Ethnicity: The Identity Issue of the Minorities in Greece and Turkey," in *Crossing the Aegean*, 117–32. The Muslims in the Greek Dodecanese Islands (Rhodes, Kos, and others) were not included in the Lausanne Treaty because the islands were an Italian colony at the time.

13. Michael Barutciski, "Lausanne Revisited: Population Exchanges in International Law and Policy," in *Crossing the Aegean*, 23–37. For a detailed analysis of the preceding population transfers in relation to the Ottoman context and international law, see Umut Özsu, *Formalizing Displacements: International Law and Population Transfers* (Oxford: Oxford University Press, 2013).

14. Renée Hirschon, "'Unmixing Peoples' in the Aegean Region," in *Crossing the Aegean*, 3–12, 25.

15. Ibid., 25.

16. Ibid., 26–27.

17. Approaching this question from the point of view of humanitarianism, historian Keith Watenpaugh demonstrates how "ending suffering" and colonialism, paternalism, and notions of superiority have concurrently informed the humanitarianism of the first decades of the twentieth century in particular. He also shows how acknowledging suffering was also hierarchized depending on whose suffering it was. In addition, he traces the changes from ending suffering to welfare during that time. See Keith Watenpaugh, *Bread from Stones: The Middle East and the Making of Modern Humanitarianism*

(Oakland: University of California Press, 2015), 4, 12, 180, 189. That being said, as I seek to show in the following parts, suffering has remained a dominant discourse in the aftermath of 1945 and has continued to this day.

18. For an astute analysis of war ruins and elegiac humanism in the case of Lebanon, see Ken Seigneurie, *Standing by the Ruins: Elegiac Humanism in Wartime and Postwar Lebanon* (New York: Fordham University Press, 2011).

19. Weizman traces the notion of "lesser evil" to the philosophical works of Leibniz, who wrote about the "best of all possible worlds." It was Voltaire who picked up on Leibniz's notion and wrote the satire *Candide* to mock such approaches. See Eyal Weizman, *The Least of All Possible Evils: Humanitarian Violence from Arendt to Gaza* (London: Verso, 2011).

20. Weizman argues this in *The Least of All Possible Evils*. For an elaborate discussion of the history of the international human rights regime and how the 1970s were decisive in the shaping of this field, see Sam Moyn, *The Last Utopia: Human Rights in History* (Cambridge, MA: Belknap Press, 2010).

21. Matthew Frank, "Fantasies of Ethnic Unmixing: 'Population Transfer' and the End of Empire in Europe," in *Refugees and the End of Empire: Imperial Collapse and Forced Migration in the Twentieth Century*, Panikos Panayi and Pippa Virdee, eds. (New York: Palgrave Macmillan, 2011), 89–96.

22. Mark Mazower, *No Enchanted Palace: The End of Empire and the Ideological Origins of the United Nations* (Princeton, NJ: Princeton University Press, 2009), 134, 140–41.

23. On population exchanges in the partition of India, Palestine, and Cyprus, see Mazower, *No Enchanted Palace*, 134, 140–41; Hirschon, "'Unmixing Peoples' in the Aegean Region," xiv–xvii, 11, 23, 28.

On the Potsdam agreement, see Martin Kornrumpf, "Enforced Mass Migration in Europe 1912–1954," *Integration* 1:1 (July 1954): 5. Kornrumpf argues that the 1923 exchange agreement had elements that were integrated into the Potsdam agreement. Potsdam generated another population transfer, in this case sixteen million Germans during 1945–1949. Kornrumpf himself was one of the key figures "responsible for the administration of the expellee affairs in Bavaria" Germany. He was working for the Bavarian Ministry for Labor and Social Welfare as the deputy to the first commissioner, Dr. Wolfgang Jaenicke. See Stephen Kenneth Lane, "The Integration of the German Expellees: A Case Study of Bavaria, 1945–1969," PhD diss. (Columbia University, 1972), 31, 44, 151. For more on Potsdam in relation to the Greco-Turkish exchange, see Barutciski, "Lausanne Revisited," 26.

24. "About the UN," http://www.un.org/en/about-un/index.html.

25. Mazower, *No Enchanted Palace*.

26. Marc Baer, "The Double Bind of Race and Religion: The Conversion of the Dönme to Turkish Secular Nationalism," *Comparative Study of Society and History* 46:4 (2004): 682–708. Baer was the first scholar to bring up the importance of race as a critical category in considering the Dönme during the 1923 population exchange.

27. Ibid., 694.

28. As quoted in ibid. Also, as cited in Baer, see Rıza Nur, *Hayat ve Hatıratım* [My life and memories] (Istanbul: Altındağ Yayınevi, 1967–1968), 3:1081.

29. Nur, *Hayat ve Hatıratım*, 3:1051.

30. Ibid.

31. Ibid.

32. I am grateful to Sam Dolbee for reminding me of this point. For more on Nur, see Seçil Yılmaz's doctoral dissertation, "Love in the Time of Syphilis: Medicine and Sex in the Ottoman Empire, 1860–1922" (2016), *CUNY Academic Works*, http://academicworks.cuny.edu/gc_etds/1426. I also thank Seçil Yılmaz for her generous feedback on the subject.

33. Nur, *Hayat ve Hatıratım*, 3:1018.

34. For an analysis of this dynamic through the population exchange, see Aktar, "Homogenizing the Nation, Turkifying the Economy."

35. Nur, *Hayat ve Hatıratım*, 3:1044–45.

36. Ibid., 1045.

37. Ibid.

38. "İskân Kanunu" [Settlement law], *Resmi Gazete* [Official Gazette], June 21, 1934, no. 2733. The minister of defense who signed this law was Aziz Zekâi Apaydın, the same person whom Rıza Nur reports to have raped a chambermaid during the Lausanne conference.

39. Rogers Brubaker, "Aftermaths of Empire and the Unmixing of Peoples: Historical and Comparative Perspectives," *Ethnic and Racial Studies* 18:2 (April 1995): 189–218. Also see Hirschon, "'Unmixing Peoples' in the Aegean Region," 3–12. Greece, Bulgaria, and the Ottoman state (before it crumbled) had already made agreements to exchange their minorities, but the Ottoman part of the agreement could not be implemented when war broke out. It was not until 1923, when the Lausanne Treaty was signed, that Greece and Turkey officially agreed to exchange their populations, under the sponsorship of the League of Nations.

40. Hirschon, "'Unmixing Peoples' in the Aegean Region," 4.

41. See Hirschon's edited volume *Crossing the Aegean*. For a historicizing account, see Frank, "Fantasies of Ethnic Unmixing."

42. Robert J. C. Young, *Colonial Desire: Hybridity in Theory, Culture and Race* (London: Routledge 1995).

43. Nur, *Hayat ve Hatıratım*, 2:320.

44. Young, *Colonial Desire*; Warwick Anderson, "Racial Hybridity, Physical Anthropology, and Human Biology in the Colonial Laboratories of the United States," *Current Anthropology* 53: Supplement 5 (April 2012): 95–107. For an early theorization of the subject, see Arthur de Gobineau, "The Meaning of the Word 'Degeneration'; The Mixture of Racial Elements; How Societies Are Formed and Broken Up," in *The Inequality of Human Races* (New York: Howard Fertig, 1967 [1915]), 23–36. For eugenics in Europe in general, see Richard Soloway, *Demography and Degeneration: Eugenics and the Declining*

Birthrate in Twentieth Century Britain (Chapel Hill: University of North Carolina Press, 1995). Also see Frank Dikötter, "Race Culture: Recent Perspectives on the History of Eugenics," *American Historical Review* 103:2 (April 1998): 467–78; John P. Jackson Jr., *Science for Segregation: Race, Law, and the Case Against Brown v. Board of Education* (New York: New York University Press, 2005), 20–21; Ayça Alemdaroğlu, "Politics of the Body and Eugenic Discourse in Early Republican Turkey," *Body & Society* 11:3 (2005): 62.

45. I am grateful to Sara Pursley for her feedback, which helped me articulate this category.

46. Anne McClintock, *Imperial Leather: Race, Gender and Sexuality in the Colonial Context* (New York: Routledge, 1995), 37–39, 50–51. As quoted in McClintock, also see Johannes Fabian, *Time and the Other: How Anthropology Makes Its Object* (New York: Columbia University Press, 1983), 13–15.

47. This, in part, is also how anthropology developed in Turkey in the 1930s. See Büşra Ersanlı, *İktidar ve Tarih: Türkiye'de Resmi Tarih Tezinin Oluşumu* [Power and history: The development of the official history thesis in Turkey] (Istanbul: İletişim: 2003).

48. Rogers Brubaker and Frederick Cooper, "Beyond 'Identity,'" *Theory and Society* 29 (2000): 1–47.

49. Michel Foucault, "Lecture 17 March 1976," in *"Society Must Be Defended": Lectures at the Collège de France, 1975–1976* (New York: Picador, 2003), 239–64.

50. For an early and important discussion of race and Foucault's thought, see Ann Laura Stoler, *Race and the Education of Desire: Foucault's History of Sexuality and the Colonial Order of Things* (Durham, NC: Duke University Press, 1995).

51. Ann Laura Stoler, "Colonial Aphasia: Race and Disabled Histories in France," *Public Culture* 23:1 (2011): 121–56.

52. "Germany: Staff Concluding Statement of the 2016 Article IV Mission," International Monetary Fund, May 9, 2016, http://www.imf.org/external/np/ms/2016/050916.htm.

53. *Zabıt Ceridesi* [Turkish parliamentary records], 3rd Assembly (November 6, 1924): 72–88. Regarding the term *Kıpti*, I thank historian Zeynep Türkyılmaz for her feedback on its translation and confirming that this term denotes "gypsy" in Ottoman Turkish contexts during that time.

54. Elizabeth Povinelli, "The Cunning of Recognition: A Reply to John Frow and Meaghan Morris," *Critical Inquiry* 25:3 (Spring 1999): 634. See also her book-length study, *The Cunning of Recognition: Indigenous Alterities and the Making of Australian Multiculturalism* (Durham, NC: Duke University Press, 2002).

55. And when implemented internally, spatial redistribution and mobility restrictions consolidate and seal the alterity of the targeted group. Segregation in the United States, apartheid in South Africa, and the internally forced migration of Kurds in Turkey exemplify this. On internal displacement in the case of Turkey, see Bilgin Ayata and Deniz Yükseker, "A Belated Awakening: National and International Responses to the Internal Displacement of Kurds in Turkey," *New Perspectives on Turkey* 32 (2005): 5–42.

56. Ella Shohat and Robert Stam, *Unthinking Eurocentrism: Multiculturalism and the Media* (London: Routledge, 1994). Shohat and Stam situate these debates in a broader context and rethink Eurocentrism through a critical analysis informed by postcolonial critiques. They also address ancient Greece as a trope of origins in this Eurocentric framework of linear identification.

57. Nancy Bisaha, *Creating East and West: Renaissance Humanists and the Ottoman Turks* (Philadelphia: University of Pennsylvania Press, 2004). Here, Bisaha traces the complex historical threads of intellectual responses to the Ottoman threat concretized with the "fall" or the "conquest" of Constantinople/Istanbul when the Ottomans seized the city in the fifteenth century. Following this, the Eastern Roman Empire/Byzantium crumbled, and Bisaha shows how in order to make sense of this perceived threat, Renaissance intellectual figures resorted to two main historical endeavors: to return to ancient Greece and Rome to adopt their ways of engaging alterity (i.e., barbarism, especially of the ancient Greeks), and to revisit the Crusades because they believed they offered an insight into previous wars between Muslims and Christians. Overall, what she shows is how a discursive East and West emerges from these historical endeavors in the search for "origins."

58. For an excellent analysis of Turkish humanism, see Aslı Gür, "Political Excavations of the Anatolian Past: Nationalism and Archaeology in Turkey," in *Controlling the Past, Owning the Future: The Political Uses of Archaeology in the Middle East* (Tucson: University of Arizona Press, 2010), 68–89.

59. Laleh Khalili, *Time in the Shadows: Confinement in Counterinsurgencies* (Stanford, CA: Stanford University Press, 2013), 11–43.

60. Frantz Fanon, *The Wretched of the Earth* (New York: Grove, 1963).

61. See Brian Silverstein, "Reform in Turkey: Liberalization as Government and Critique," *Anthropology Today* 26:4 (2010): 22–25.

62. As will be elaborated in the essays that follow, I borrow this definition from Roland Barthes, and the term "liberal humanism" from anthropologist Faye Ginsburg, to refer to the kinds of discourses identified by Barthes and addressed by anthropologist Liisa Malkki. Faye Ginsburg, "Producing Culture: Shifting Representations of Social Theory in the Films of Tim Asch," in *Timothy Asch and Ethnographic Film*, E. D. Lewis, ed. (New York: Routledge, 2003), 149–62. I thank Jennifer Varela for bringing this work to my attention. Also see Roland Barthes, "The Great Family of Man," in *Mythologies* (New York: Hill and Wang, 1972), 100–102; Liisa Malkki, "Speechless Emissaries: Refugees, Humanitarianism, and Dehistoricization," *Cultural Anthropology* 11:3 (August 1996): 377–404.

63. The signs that read "We are all refugees" after the death of little Aylan Kurdi, a Kurdish Syrian boy, are a symbolic variation of such "We are all humans" discourse. Variations of this phrase have marked at least the last decade. Some had problematic implications with a limited act of solidarity that did not necessarily extend beyond a humanist discourse.

64. Aslı Iğsız, "Polyphony and Geographic Kinship in Anatolia: Framing the

Turkish-Greek Population Exchange," in *The Politics of Public Memory in Turkey*, Esra Özyürek, ed. (Syracuse, NY: Syracuse University Press, 2007), 162–90.

65. In developing this framework, I have found anthropologist Miriam Ticktin's work on humanitarianism and biopolitics most inspiring. See Ticktin, "Policing and Humanitarianism in France," *American Ethnologist* 33:1 (February 2006): 33–49. Within the context of humanitarianism and the regulation of the immigrant and refugees via the body, see by Ticktin, "How Biology Travels: A Humanitarian Trip," *Body & Society* 17:2&3 (2011): 139–58. Additionally, see Ilana Feldman and Miriam Ticktin, *In the Name of Humanity: The Government of Threat and Care* (Durham: Duke University Press, 2010). See also Didier Fassin, *Humanitarian Reason: A Moral History of the Present* (Berkeley: University of California Press, 2012). For a different take on biopolitics and immigration, see Fassin, "Biopolitics of Otherness: Undocumented Foreigners and Racial Discrimination in French Public Debate," *Anthropology Today* 17:1 (February 2001): 3–7. For a powerful reconsideration of biopolitics via hunger strikes in prisons in Turkey, see Banu Bargu, *Starve and Immolate: The Politics of Human Weapons* (New York: Columbia University Press, 2016).

66. For a critique and different take on such approaches to humanism, see Paul Gilroy, *Between Camps: Nations, Culture, and the Allure of Race* (London: Penguin, 2000).

67. I am grateful to Ismail Aji Alatas for his extensive feedback on the palimpsests analyzed in this book.

68. For a different take on relationality as poetics, see Papailias, *Genres of Recollection*. Here, Papailias considers such relationality between genres of historical representation such as documentation, archiving, and historical writing in Greece addressed through archival poetics—a poetics that relates these practices.

69. Gérard Genette, *Palimpsests: Literature in the Second Degree* (Lincoln: University of Nebraska Press, 1997).

70. Ibid., 1.

71. Gérard Genette, *Paratexts: Thresholds of Interpretation* (Cambridge: Cambridge University Press, 1997).

72. I thank Mikiya Koyagi for his comments on the discussion of transnationalism in an earlier version of this work.

73. For an excellent analysis of the era, see Begüm Adalet, *Hotels and Highways: The Construction of Modernization Theory in Cold War Turkey* (Stanford, CA: Stanford University Press, 2018). For another insightful analysis, see Burçak Keskin Kozat, "Negotiating an Institutional Framework for Turkey's Marshall Plan: The Conditions and Limits of Power Inequalities," in *Turkey in the Cold War: Ideology and Culture*, Cangül Örnek and Çağdaş Üngör, eds. (London: Palgrave Macmillan, 2013), 198–218.

74. Kay Schaffer and Sidonie Smith, *Human Rights and Narrated Lives: The Ethics of Recognition* (New York: Palgrave Macmillan, 2004).

75. Ibid., 13, 15, 31.

76. David Lowenthal, *The Heritage Crusade and the Spoils of History* (Cambridge: Cambridge University Press, 1998).

77. Astrid Erll, "Cultural Memory Studies: An Introduction," in *Cultural Memory Studies: An International and Interdisciplinary Handbook*, Astrid Erll and Ansgar Nünning, eds. (Berlin: Walter de Gruyter, 2008), 1–18. For Turkey, see Esra Özyürek, ed., *The Politics of Public Memory in Turkey* (New York: Syracuse University Press, 2007). Also see Leyla Neyzi, "Oral History and Memory Studies in Turkey," in *Turkey's Engagement with Modernity: Conflict and Change in the Twentieth Century*, Celia Kerslake, Kerem Öktem, and Philip Robins, eds. (New York: Palgrave Macmillan, 2010), 443–59.

78. Anthropologists Elizabeth Povinelli, Banu Karaca, and Ceren Özgül have raised important questions in that regard.

79. Charles W. Mills, *Black Rights/White Wrongs: The Critique of Racial Liberalism* (Oxford: Oxford University Press, 2017). I thank Begüm Adalet for bringing this work to my attention.

80. Ann Stoler, "Imperial Debris: Reflections on Ruins and Ruination" *Cultural Anthropology* 23:2 (2008): 191–219. Stoler considers ruination in terms of colonial and imperial contexts to address how the effects of empire are reactivated and remain, as well as an ongoing political project to reconsider how imperial structures are reappropriated within the politics of the present. Anthropologist Yael Navaro, on the other hand, engages the notion of ruination as a metaphor to address the aftermath of violence and war and considers material remains as well as subjectivities and residual affect as ruination. Yael Navaro-Yashin, "Affective Spaces, Melancholic Objects: Ruination and the Production of Anthropological Knowledge," *Journal of the Royal Anthropological Institute* 15 (2009): 1–18.

81. Yael Navaro-Yashin, *The Make-Believe Space: Affective Geography in a Postwar Polity* (Durham, NC: Duke University Press, 2012).

82. Stoler, "Imperial Debris."

83. Léopold Lambert, *Weaponized Architecture: The Impossibility of Innocence* (Barcelona: DPR 2012).

84. Liisa Malkki, "Speechless Emissaries."

85. Ibid., 398.

86. Margaret Thatcher, "Speech on Pinochet at the Conservative Party Conference," October 6, 1999, Margaret Thatcher Foundation, http://www.margaretthatcher.org/document/108383.

87. "After the Coup in Cairo," *Wall Street Journal*, July 7, 2013.

88. Stuart Hall, "The Emergence of Cultural Studies and the Crisis of the Humanities," *October* 53 (Summer 1990): 11–23.

89. Michael Werner and Bénédicte Zimmermann, "Beyond Comparison: *Histoire Croisée* and the Challenge of Reflexivity," *History and Theory* 45:1 (February 2006): 30–50.

90. I thank Miray Çakıroğlu for her feedback, which helped me articulate this point.

91. Jo Guldi and David Armitage, *The History Manifesto* (Cambridge: Cambridge University Press, 2014).

92. Anthropologists Ceren Özgül, Çağrı Yoltar, Miriam Ticktin, Özlem Zerrin Biner, and Yael Navaro, among others, have developed important frameworks of analysis on such subjects as humanitarianism, domination and boundaries, and religion.

93. For an important philosophical treatise on the subject, see Rosi Braidotti, *The Posthuman* (Cambridge: Polity, 2013).

94. Michel Foucault, *Security, Territory, Population: Lectures at the Collège de France 1977–1978* (New York: Picador, 2007).

Part I

1. "Mülteciler Kongresi Bu Sabahtan Itibaren Çalışmalarına Başladı" [Congress on refugees commenced its work this morning], *Akşam*, September 15, 1954, 3; "Rapports de la 4e Assemblée Générale" [Reports of the Fourth General Assembly], *Integration: Bulletin International*, European Association for the Study of Refugee Problems, 1:3–4 (1954): 163–85.

2. Hilmi Ziya Ülken, "Un Aperçu bibliographique du problème de réfugiés en Turquie" [A bibliographical overview of the problem of refugees in Turkey], *İstanbul Üniversitesi Sosyoloji Dergisi* [Istanbul University Sociological Review] 10–11 (1955–1956): 106–14. Instead of publishing this work in *Integration*—the official journal of the AER and later of the AWR (Association for the Study of the World Refugee Problem)—Ülken published it in Istanbul University's journal, which he himself edited at the time.

3. For more on Fahreddin Kerim Gökay and eugenics, see Ayça Alemdaroğlu's "Politics of the Body and Eugenic Discourse in Early Republican Turkey," *Body & Society* 11:3 (2005): 61–76. Also see Yücel Yanıkdağ, *Healing the Nation: Prisoners of War, Medicine, and Nationalism in Turkey 1914–1939* (Edinburgh: University of Edinburgh Press, 2013).

4. Fahreddin Kerim Gökay, "Avant Propos" [Foreword], *Integration* 1:3–4 (1954): 4.

5. "The Study of Refugee Problems," *International Review of the Red Cross* 1:9. (December 1961): 511. The International Red Cross attended the AER and the AWR joint meetings and reported that the two associations decided to merge in their annual congress on October 15–22, 1961, convened in Salonica and Athens.

6. Mark Mazower's work on the United Nations shows how, at its inception, the UN was established not to intervene in human rights violations, but rather to preserve power relations. See Mark Mazower, *No Enchanted Palace: The End of Empire and the Ideological Origins of the United Nations* (Princeton, NJ: Princeton University Press, 2009).

7. Mükerrem Sarol, a physician and a minister at the time, writes in his memoir that he had a phone conversation with Gökay on the day of the pogrom, and asked Gökay how it was that he could sit so comfortably in his office while terrible violence occurred outside. Sarol reports that Gökay appeared unresponsive to his concerns and without answering him, passed the phone to the minister of interior next to him, who reportedly told Sarol that the scale of violence was exaggerated. The following days,

however, would prove the minister of interior wrong. *Bilinmeyen Menderes I* [The unknown Menderes] (Istanbul: Kervan Yayınları, 1983): 444–48. In addition, according to Hikmet Bil, the head of the Kıbrıs Türktür (Cyprus is Turkish) foundation, Gökay was among a group of people who plotted the September 6–7 anti-Greek pogrom. Bil claims the others included the prime minister of the time, Adnan Menderes, and the Ottoman historian/minister Mehmet Fuat Köprülü. See interview with Hikmet Bil in Can Dündar, *O Gün: 6–7 Eylül 1955* [That day: September 6–7, 1955], documentary film, 2005. Also see Dilek Güven, *Cumhuriyet Dönemi Azınlık Politikaları Bağlamında 6–7 Eylül Olayları* [The September 6–7 events in the context of republican-era minority policies] (Istanbul: Tarih Vakfı Yurt Yayınları, 2005), 72–78.

8. The pogrom was discussed in the Turkish parliament in terms of a declaration of martial law, and concerns were raised by deputies that the pogrom was so grave it could erase the Turkish presence from the world of civilized nations and hence, civilization itself. In his speech in the parliament, Fuat Köprülü declared that the "events" were launched by some *çapulcu* (marauder) and some patriots with heightened nationalistic sensitivities due to events in Cyprus, but that it was the communists who made it worse because it was they who had planned the pogrom. *TBMM Zabıt Ceridesi* [Turkish parliamentary records], period 7 (September 12, 1955): 80:668–94. Following the pogrom, communist writers and organizers were arrested in Turkey as the culprits. Later, they were released, and during the 1960 military coup both the prime minister, Adnan Menderes, and the mayor-governor of Istanbul, Fahreddin Kerim Gökay, were tried. Gökay was released and returned to politics afterward. Menderes was executed. See Güven, *6–7 Eylül Olayları*; Hasan Izzettin Dinamo, *İkinci Dünya Savaşı'ndan Edebiyat Anıları* [Literary memoirs from World War II] (Istanbul: De Yayınları, 1984). In 1961, right after Gökay was released and a month after Menderes was executed by the military, Gökay decided to step down as the president of the AER/AWR, after about ten years in that post. To recognize his "successful contributions," the AER/AWR elected him the honorary president of both refugee associations. Ironically, the location where this election took place was Greece, where the eleventh general assembly of the AER/AWR had convened on October 14–21, 1961. René Oderbolz, Secretary General, "XIth General Convention of the Aer/Awr in Greece: October 14th–21th, 1961," *Integration* 9 (1962): 7–9.

9. "Telafiye Çalışalım" [We shall try to make amends], *Cumhuriyet*, September 14, 1955, 2.

10. I thank Eduardo Matos Martín for his comments that helped me articulate this point. This of course doesn't mean they all agreed on how to engage capitalism, but that their approaches concretize a common ground in the so-called free world. For an autopsy of Corrado Gini's ideas on economy, see Francesco Cassata, "A 'Scientific Basis' for Fascism: The Neo-Organicism of Corrado Gini," *History of Economic Ideas* 16:3 (2008): 49–64.

11. The policies of the post-1980 military coup era and the 1983 *National Cultural*

Policy Report (discussed in Part Three), which endorsed a Turkish-Islamic synthesis as cultural policy, epitomize these dynamics in Turkey: social order is established to ensure economic growth at the expense of plurality, citizenship and labor rights, and academic freedom, among other things.

12. See, for example, Zeynep Gönen and Deniz Yonucu, "Legitimizing Violence and Segregation: Neoliberal Discourses on Crime and Criminalization of the Urban Poor Populations in Turkey," in *Lumpencity: Discourses of Marginality/Marginalizing Discourses*, Alan Bourke, Tia Dafnos, and Markus Kip, eds. (Ottawa: Red Quill Books, 2011), 75–98.

13. Martin Kornrumpf, "Enforced Mass Migration in Europe 1912–1954," *Integration* 1:1 (1954): 5–7 (emphasis mine).

14. Daniele Macuglia, "Corrado Gini and the Scientific Basis of Fascist Racism," *Medicina nei Secoli: Arte e Scienza* 26:3 (2014): 821–55.

15. The fact that the continent was divided by the Iron Curtain was repeatedly shown as one of the reasons for the refugee problem in Europe. Other than the proceedings of the AER and for a local example, see Professor Nurullah Kunter's "Hukuki Meseleler: Sığınma Hakkı" [Legal matters: The right to seek asylum], editorial, *Cumhuriyet*, September 21, 1955, 2.

16. Manohar Sardessai, "Le Problème des réfugiés en Inde" [The problem of refugees in India], *Integration* 2:4 (1955): 223–47.

17. Corrado Gini, "Refugees and Over-Population," *Integration* 1:3–4 (1954): 170.

18. Mazower, *No Enchanted Palace*, 24, 104–48, 195.

19. Corrado Gini, "570 000 National and International Refugees in Italy," *Integration* 1:1 (1954): 21–23.

20. Werner von Schmieden, "Le Conseil de l'Europe et le problem des réfugiés" [The Council of Europe and the problem of refugees], *Integration* 3:1–4 (1956): 9–13.

21. Ella Shohat, The Invention of the Mizrahim," *Journal of Palestine Studies* 29:1 (Autumn 1999): 5–20.

22. Jean-Jacques Berreby, "L'Intégration des réfugiés juifs des pays musulmans en Israël et ses conséquences possibles sur les caractères de la nation" [The integration of Jewish refugees from Muslim countries in Israel and its possible consequences for the character of the nation], *Integration* 2:2 (1955): 84–90.

23. Ibid., 87.

24. "AER: Association Européenne pour l'Étude de Problème des Réfugiés" [AER: European Association for the Study of the Refugee Problem], *Integration* 1:1 (1954): 9.

25. Ibid., 10–11. The fields of expert committees in the AER are telling in that regard: Statistics, Bibliography, Legal Problems, Economic Integration, Agriculture, Financial and Social Policy, Sociology, Youth, Housing, Health, Ethnography/Folklore, Internal Migration, Emigration, Cultural Problems, International Refugees. Curiously, the English version of the committees removes certain categories such as "sociology."

Since the English version appears right after the French, it is possible that this was an oversight.

26. Werner von Schmieden, "Le Conseil de l'Europe et le problème des réfugiés et des excedents de population" [The Council of Europe and the problem of refugees and surpluses of population], *Integration* 1:1 (July 1954): 40–45. In this talk, Schmieden discussed the importance of establishing the Council of Europe, as a move toward the unification of Europe—defined as outside the Iron Curtain. The transition from national to European was an important step in that respect, and has direct implications for today.

27. Gini, "Refugees and Over-Population," 169–71.

28. Ibid., 170. This "more positive" attitude toward emigration as something beneficial might have been in part due to the fact that Gini supported Italian emigrants in the United States, and argued that emigrants can physically change when adapting to their new country.

29. I am grateful to Begüm Adalet for calling my attention to the fact that while human capital was implicated in Adam Smith's work, it was promoted as an ideology during the Cold War, especially in the 1960s.

30. Walter Schätzel, "Le Problème de la nationalité des réfugiés" [The problem of the nationality of refugees], *Integration* 1:2 (1954): 118–24.

31. Ibid., 122.

32. H. V. Muhsam, "Labour Force Characteristics and Economic Absorption of Immigrants in Israel," *Integration* 8:2 (1961): 71–86. Muhsam was also a United Nations social affairs officer in 1957–1958. In 1948–1952 he was the principal statistician for the Israeli government. In 1961–1962 he was a visiting scholar in sociology and public health at the University of California, Berkeley. Among his books are *The Supply of Professional Manpower* (1959) and *The Valuation of Men and the Principles of Cost-Benefit Analysis of Family Planning Activities* (1975). For more on him, see "Guide to the Papers of the Muehsam Family 1828–1999," Leo Baeck Institute, Center for Jewish History. For a critical analysis of Muhsam, see Nadia Abu El-Haj, *The Genealogical Science: The Search for Jewish Origins and the Politics of Epistemology* (Chicago: University of Chicago Press, 2012), 99–105.

33. Ziyaeddin Fahri Fındıkoğlu, "The Hungarian Refugees in Turkey, Their Integration, and Their Standing," *Integration* 4:4 (1957): 319–25. Fındıkoğlu was a renowned Turkish sociologist. Following Corrado Gini's death in 1965, a colloquium entitled "About Professor Gini and His Thought" was organized in Rome on March 12–15, 1966. Fındıkoğlu specifically requested permission from the Istanbul University administration to attend this colloquium. This suggests that either Fındıkoğlu knew little about Gini's thought, which appears to be unlikely since they collaborated on multiple platforms, or he did not have major objections to Gini's thought.

34. "Étapes et envergure de l'intégration des réfugiés" [Stages and extent of the integration of refugees], *Integration* 1:1 (1954): 51–52.

35. According to Jerry Z. Muller, "social scientists who thrived under the Nazi regime did so not primarily because of the affinity of their theories to Nazi ideology but because those who wielded power believed in the utility of their empirical research." While Karl Valentin Müller is considered to be one of those figures, it is also clear that there was a good reason why Nazi sympathizers and power holders found Müller's empirical work informed by racial theories compelling. Jerry Z. Muller, *The Other God That Failed: Hans Freyer and the Deradicalization of German Conservatism* (Princeton, NJ: Princeton University Press, 1987), 268–75, 371–73.

36. Ibid., 274.

37. Joan Campbell, *Joy in Work, German Work: The National Debate, 1800–1945* (Princeton, NJ: Princeton University Press, 1989), 350–51.

38. Ibid.

39. Although some works sought to address the psychology of refugees, these were not really brought up to criticize eugenicist approaches. See, for instance, Émile Sicard, "De la Nécessité de ne pas considérer isolément le problème actuel des réfugiés" [On the necessity to not consider the actual problem of refugees in isolation], *Integration* 2:2 (1955): 72–77.

40. Schätzel, "Le Problème de la nationalité des réfugiés," 118–19.

41. Ibid., 122.

42. Aslı Iğsız, "Documenting the Past and Publicizing Personal Stories: Sensescapes and the 1923 Greco-Turkish Population Exchange in Contemporary Turkey," *Journal of Modern Greek Studies* 26 (2008): 451–87; Aslı Iğsız, "Polyphony and Geographic Kinship in Anatolia: Framing the Turkish-Greek Population Exchange," in *The Politics of Public Memory in Turkey*, Esra Özyürek, ed. (Syracuse, NY: Syracuse University Press, 2007), 162–90.

43. Z. F. Fındıkoğlu, "Contribution au problème de l'installation des émigrés musulmans de la Grèce en Turquie" (A contribution to the problem of settling Muslim emigrants from Greece in Turkey), *Integration* 8:5 (1961): 189.

44. Political scientist Barış Ünlü calls this process a Turkishness contract among the Muslims of Anatolia. See his article "The Kurdish Struggle and the Crisis of the Turkishness Contract," *Philosophy and Social Criticism* 42:4–5 (2016): 189–93. I thank Deniz Yonucu for bringing this piece to my attention.

45. Fındıkoğlu, "Contribution au problème de l'installation des émigrés musulmans de la Grèce en Turquie," 190.

46. Ibid., 193n10.

47. Eugenio Regazzini, "Corrado Gini," in *Leading Personalities in Statistical Sciences: From the Seventeenth Century to the Present*, Norman L. Johnson and Samuel Kots, eds. (New York: Wiley, 1997), 291–96.

48. Macuglia, "Corrado Gini and the Scientific Basis of Fascist Racism." Also see Jean-Guy Prévost, *Total Science: Statistics in Liberal and Fascist Italy* (Montreal: McGill-

Queen University's Press, 2009); John P. Jackson Jr., *Science for Segregation: Race, Law, and the Case against Brown v. Board of Education* (New York: New York University Press, 2005), 106. As quoted in Jackson, also see Paul Weindling, "Fascism and Population in Comparative European Perspective," *Population and Development Review* 14 (1988): 109; Cassata, "A 'Scientific Basis' for Fascism."

49. Emiliana P. Noether, "Italian Intellectuals under Fascism," *Journal of Modern History* 43:3 (1971): 630–48; Francesco Cassata, *Building the New Man: Eugenics, Racial Science and Genetics in Twentieth-Century Italy* (Budapest: Central European University Press, 2011).

50. Cassata, *Building the New Man*; Jackson, *Science for Segregation*.

51. Cassata, *Building the New Man*, 353–62.

52. Jackson, *Science for Segregation*, 50, 72, 88.

53. Ibid., 50.

54. Ibid., 89.

55. Carleton S. Coon, *The Story of Man* (New York: Knopf, 1954), 187–88, quoted in Jackson, *Science for Segregation*, 99.

56. John P. Jackson, "'In Ways Unacademical': The Reception of Carleton S. Coon's *The Origin of Races*," *Journal of the History of Biology* 34 (2001): 247–85.

57. Jackson, *Science for Segregation*, 17.

58. It was Ömer Celâl Sarc, a professor of statistics and the president of Istanbul University, who recommended Gini to the university's Faculty Assembly. Sarc's proposal to invite Gini in order to establish and organize the Institute of Statistics at the university was approved at the assembly meeting on March 7, 1950. See the dean's petition to the rector of the University, Istanbul University Archives.

59. For more on Gini's activities in Istanbul, see Hilmi Ziya Ülken, "1952 Milletlerarası Sosyoloji Kongresi ve Corrado Gini" [1952 International Congress of Sociology and Corrado Gini], *Yeni Sabah*, February 12, 1951, 2. Also see Ülken, "İhtisas ve Cemiyet" [Expertise and community], *Yeni Sabah*, December 18, 1950, 2.

60. For the three months he was in residence, his total gross income was designated to be 2,312 Turkish liras—roughly worth 825 USD at the time, according to the historical records of the Turkish Central Bank. (The Türkiye Merkez Bankası shows 1 USD as equivalent to 2.8 TL in November 1950.) Of this amount, Gini was allowed to take only a third with him when he left the country and was required to spend the balance in Turkey—a measure, no doubt, taken in order to ensure this large sum would remain in Turkey. For more on the terms of Gini's contract, see *Sözleşme* (Contract) dated November 28, 1950, prepared for Corrado Gini, Corrado Gini Papers, Istanbul University Archives. To put this amount into perspective, compare Hilmi Ziya Ülken's monthly salary in 1956, which was 150 Turkish liras. See the letter by Arif Müfid Mansel, the dean of humanities, written to the office of the rector asking for university funding in the amount of 1,404 USD so that Ülken could attend the UNESCO-sponsored

Sociological Association congress as well as the AER meeting in Vaduz, Lichtenstein. Hilmi Ziya Ülken Papers, Istanbul University Archives.

61. Letter of Ömer Celâl Sarc to Corrado Gini, Gini Papers, Istanbul University Archives. The cost of the hotel was 10 Turkish liras a night. The Mano, a mansion converted into a pension, was owned by a Greek of Istanbul. The mansion originally belonged to Mahmut Bey, the father of writer Celaleddin Ezine, cousin of the famous poet Nazım Hikmet. For more on the Mano, see Pervin Yanıkkaya Aydemir, *Moda Semti Arka Plan Çalışması, Akdeniz Sesleri Projesi* [Background study of the neighborhood of Moda—Mediterranean voices project], October 2003 (part of Turkey's History Foundation's collaboration with the London-based and European Union–funded Med-Voices project).

62. "Türk Sosyoloji Cemiyetinin Tanışma Çayı" [Tea party meeting of the Turkish Sociological Society], *Cumhuriyet*, February 8, 1951, 2.

63. The lecture notes were edited and summarized by economist Haydar İzzet Furgaç under the title *Démographie et Sociologie* [Demography and sociology] (Istanbul: Istanbul University Press, 1952), no. 528. Ülken's review appeared as "*Démographie et Sociologie*, Corrado Gini," *Sosyoloji Dergisi* [Journal of Sociology] 2:7 (1952): 151–52.

64. For the original, see T. C. Başbakanlık Cumhuriyet Arşivi [Archives of the Prime Ministry of the Republic], T.C. Başbakanlık Muamelât Umum Müdürlüğü Kararlar Müdürlüğü [Republic of Turkey, Prime Ministry General Directorate of Administrative Procedures, Directorate of Resolutions], Resolution (*Karar*) 3/11699. A copy of this resolution can be found in the Corrado Gini Papers, Istanbul University Archives.

65. "Yabancıların Türkiye'de Ikamet ve Seyahatleri Hakkında Kanun" [Law regarding foreigners' stay and travel in Turkey], Article 5683, July 15, 1950. This regulation was published on July 24, 1950, in *Resmi Gazete* [Official Gazette] 3:7564, 2258.

66. Corrado Gini, *İstatistik Metodolojisi* [The methodology of statistics] (Ankara: Başbakanlık İstatistik Genel Müdürlüğü, 1947), no. 259. This book was translated into Turkish by Ratip Yüceuluğ, an adviser to the Turkish Prime Ministry's Directorate General of Statistics. Later, during his correspondence with the rector of Istanbul University, Gini requested that Yüceuluğ act as his translator and assistant. Rector Sarc assured him this was not possible, so Gini settled for Haydar İzzet Furgaç, who would later become a statistics adviser to UNESCO and dean of the School of Economics, Istanbul University. See the correspondence between Ömer Celal Sarç and Corrado Gini, October 30, 1950, Gini Papers, Istanbul University Archives. Corrado Gini, *Nüfus Siyasetinin İlmi Esasları* [The scientific bases of demographic policies] (Ankara: Başbakanlık İstatistik Genel Müdürlüğü, 1950), no. 315. The original Italian of this work was a collection of Gini's course lectures at the University of Rome published in 1931, during the Mussolini dictatorship, under the title *Le basi scientifiche della politica della popolazione: corso impartito nella R. Università di Roma raccolto a cura del Dott. Giulio Rugiu* (Catania: Studio Editoriale Moderno, 1931).

67. Gini, *Nüfus Siyasetinin İlmi Esasları*, 170–83.

68. Ibid., 184–96. It is also important to note here that Gini did not really oppose migration, which in part might be because he had to address the presence of many Italian emigrants elsewhere. In his work on Italian emigrants, he argued that they could physically develop characteristics of the host population. He also supported birth control policies rather than killing like the Nazis. He was not exactly a purist when it came to race, but there is good evidence that he was a racist and that he believed in racial hierarchies.

69. *Integration* 1:1 (1954): 10.

70. Francesco Cassata, *Il fascismo razionale: Corrado Gini fra scienza e politica* (Rational fascism: Corrado Gini between science and politics) (Rome: Carocci Editore, 2006), 194–213. Also see Cassata "Un'internazionale di destra: L'Institut International de Sociologie (1950–1970)" [A right-wing international: The International Institute of Sociology], *Studi storici* 46:2 (2005): 407–35. I thank Massimiliano Tomba for his help with the translation.

71. Campbell, *Joy in Work, German Work*, 350–51.

72. Political scientist Jean-Guy Prévost uses the "politics of expertise" in discussing how statistics became a site of rivalry and dominated social studies in Italy, particularly before and during the fascist years. Corrado Gini was also part of that dynamic as analyzed by Prévost. Though used for the context of Italy specifically, I borrow this term from him, as it captures the broader dynamic I am describing here. For more, see Prévost, *Total Science*.

73. United Nations Educational, Scientific and Cultural Organization, *International Sociological Association: Draft Minutes of Constituent Congress Held in Oslo 5–10 September, 1949*, SS/ISA/10 (October 1949): 14. Note that the actual congress in Oslo itself was held on September 5–11, 1949, and did not end on the tenth of September, contrary to what the title suggests.

74. Paul Preston, *The Spanish Civil War: Reaction, Revolution and Revenge* (London: Harper Perennial, 2006), 112.

75. Hemingway authored a short story on the Greco-Turkish War: Ernest Hemingway, "On the Quai at Smyrna," in *The Complete Short Stories of Ernest Hemingway* (New York: Scribner, 1998), 63–64. The story addresses the fire set by officials to drive Armenians and Greeks out of Smyrna.

76. Robert Van Gelder, "Ernest Hemingway Talks of War and Works," *New York Times*, August 11, 1940, 2.

77. "Weighed in the Balance," *Time* 58:17 (October 22, 1951): 23.

78. UNESCO, *International Sociological Association: Draft Minutes of Constituent Congress Held in Oslo*, 6.

79. Ibid.

80. Muller, *The Other God That Failed*, 371–72. Muller bases this claim on his inter-

view with one of the sociologists present at the meeting, René König. Corrado Gini tells a different story in the *Proceedings of the 14th International Congress of Sociology (Rome 30th August–3rd September 1950)*, Corrado Gini, ed., 1:182–86. It appears that it was the director-general of UNESCO (and not the International Sociological Association Committee) who eventually invited Gini, a prominent figure of his time. See *Proceedings of the 14th International Congress of Sociology*, 1:184.

81. Hilmi Ziya Ülken, "İkinci Dünya Sosyoloji Kongresi, Liege 1953" [The Second World Sociology Congress, Liège 1953], *İstanbul Üniversitesi Sosyoloji Dergisi* 10–11 (1956): 186–91; Philippe Périer, "Actes du XIVe Congrès international de sociologie (Rome, Août–Septembre 1950)" [Proceedings of the XIVth International Congress of Sociology], *Les Études Sociales*, Organe de la Société d'Économie et de Science Sociales École de Le Play 22 (September 1953): 1–17; Muller, *The Other God That Failed*, 371–74. Also see *Proceedings of the 14th International Congress of Sociology*, 1:182–94.

82. UNESCO, *International Sociological Association: Draft Minutes of Constituent Congress Held in Oslo*, 5.

83. Following the election of the executive committee, "Professor GINI said that since he was unable to agree to the list of officers and members of the provisional Executive Committee he would have to consult with his colleagues in Italy as to whether or not Italy should remain a member of the I.S.A. The CHAIRMAN said that it was clear that this would have to be done by all the delegates present." UNESCO, *International Sociological Association: Draft Minutes of Constituent Congress Held in Oslo*, 8–9.

84. Ibid., 5, 8–9.

85. My translation. See Hilmi Ziya Ülken, "Avant-Propos" [Foreword], in *Actes du XVe Congrès International de Sociologie. Organisé à Istanbul (11–17 Septembre 1952) au nom de l'Institut International de Sociologie* [Proceedings of the 15th International Congress of Sociology. Organized in Istanbul (September, 11–17, 1952) in the name of the International Institute of Sociology], Actes Publiées par Hilmi Ziya Ülken, Président de la Société Turque de Sociologie [Published by Hilmi Ziya Ülken, President of the Turkish Sociological Society] (Istanbul: Istanbul University Press, 1954), vols. 1, 5.

86. Stephen Turner, "A Life in the First Half-Century of Sociology: Charles Ellwood and the Division of Sociology," in *Sociology in America: A History*, Craig Calhoun, ed. (Chicago: University of Chicago Press, 2007), 152–53. I thank Aslı Gür for bringing this book to my attention.

87. Ibid.

88. Ibid.

89. Muller, *The Other God That Failed*, 372.

90. *Proceedings of the 14th International Congress of Sociology*, 1:184–85.

91. Cassata, "Un'internazionale di destra."

92. On January 21, 1950, the rector of Istanbul University wrote a letter to sociologist Fahri Ziyaeddin Fındıkoğlu explaining that UNESCO had contacted the Turkish

Ministry of Foreign Affairs, asking for sociologists who could collaborate in founding the new sociological association. A copy was also sent to the president of the Turkish Sociological Society, Hilmi Ziya Ülken. Whereas Ülken attended the 1949 Sociological Association as the representative of Turkey's sociologists, in 1950, other names appear to have been suggested. On June 17, 1950, a letter from the Ministry of Education to the Rectorate of Istanbul University lists attending invitees as Fahri Ziyaeddin Fındıkoğlu, Selmin Evrim, and Dr. (Ziya?) Somar. This suggests that Ülken preferred to attend the institute's conference in Rome also organized in September 1950, and proposed these other names instead. See letter of the rector of Istanbul University to Fahri Ziyaeddin Fındıkoğlu, dated January 21, 1950, and another letter of the Ministry of Education to the Rectorate of Istanbul University on June 17, 1950, Fahri Ziyaeddin Fındıkoğlu Papers, Istanbul University Archives. Indeed, we know that Ülken attended the institute's conference as the delegate (*délégué*) of Turkey. See *Proceedings of the 14th International Congress of Sociology*, 1:3–4.

93. Ülken, "1952 Milletlerarası Sosyoloji Kongresi ve Corrado Gini," 2. Remarkably productive, Ülken wrote weekly columns for several newspapers. His column in *Yeni Sabah* appeared on Mondays and was entitled "Sosyolog Gözile"—literally, "With the eye of a sociologist."

94. Hilmi Ziya Ülken, "Milletlerarası XV. Sosyoloji Kongresi" [15th International Congress of Sociology], in *Dünyada ve Türkiye'de Sosyoloji Öğretim ve Araştırmaları* [Education and sociological research in Turkey and in the world] (Istanbul: Türk Sosyoloji Cemiyeti Yayınları, 1956), 34–37. This 1956 volume offers a collection of Ülken's newspaper columns. While I could track down many of his editorials through archives, I found many others I had not seen before in this book. Unfortunately, Ülken was not very precise and did not specify which piece was published in which newspaper. It might very well be that Ülken himself had trouble in tracking down the exact date and newspaper of each piece; he was remarkably prolific, writing for newspapers, journals, books, and conferences. He appears to have sought to inform the general public about social matters and sociology through his editorials. *Yeni Sabah* allocated weekly editorial space in a revolving manner, one day of the week to a sociologist, the next to a scholar of law, the third to a critic, and so on, each of whom would communicate his or her "expertise" and insights to the newspaper's readers. After the 1960 military coup, Ülken was suspended from his position at Istanbul University. He moved to Ankara and started teaching philosophy in the School of Theology at Ankara University. In a handwritten note addressed to the Istanbul University Rectorate in 1962, he refused to return to his previous position in Istanbul University. The rectorate had received approval from the faculty assembly to reinstate Ülken. See Hilmi Ziya Ülken's letter to the Istanbul University Rectorate, August 18, 1962, Hilmi Ziya Ülken Papers, Istanbul University Archives.

95. Ülken, "İkinci Dünya Sosyoloji Kongresi, Liege 1953."

96. Ülken, "1952 Milletlerarası Sosyoloji Kongresi ve Corrado Gini," 2.

97. Ülken, "Milletlerarası XV. Sosyoloji Kongresi."
98. Muller, *The Other God That Failed*, 372.
99. Carl Schmitt, "Nehmen-Teilen-Weiden. Ein Versuch die Grundfragen jeder Sozial-und Wirtschaftsordnung vom NOMOS her richtig zu stellen" [Appropriation/distribution/production: An attempt to determine from Nomos the basic questions of every social and economic order], *Revue Internationale de Sociologie, Organe de l'Institut International de Sociologie* [International Review of Sociology—Official Publication of the International Institute of Sociology] 1 (1954): 59–71. The *Revue Internationale de Sociologie* was a tricky project as it was no longer published after 1939, until Corrado Gini decided to revive both the institute and its official publication, the *Revue*. Because of the lack of funding, the first issue had to wait until 1954. We learn from Reinhard Mehring's biography of Schmitt that on May 26, 1953, Carl Brinkmann asked Schmitt for a contribution to an "Italian journal." The article in question turned out to be his "Nomos" paper, and on October 27, 1953, Schmitt wrote to Brinkmann to let him know he gave the text to a German journal because the Italian journal appeared to be delayed and he did not want to keep German readers waiting. He did agree, however, to have the text reprinted in the so-called Italian journal. This Italian journal was no doubt the *Revue Internationale de Sociologie*, published in Italy after its revival by Gini. Carl Brinkmann was on the editorial board of the first issue of the *Revue*, together with Corrado Gini and others. The journal only published three issues in 1954, and then came to a halt again, until it resumed, with one issue a year for the period of 1964–1966. Given the irregularity of the *Revue*, Schmitt was correct about the delay of the "Italian journal." See Reinhard Mehring, *Carl Schmitt: A Biography* (Cambridge: Polity, 2014), 669n206. For the editorial board of *Revue*, see the three issues published in 1954. I thank Guy Burak for helping me access these issues of the *Revue*.
100. Suvat Parin, "XV. Milletlerarası Sosyoloji Kongresi Üzerine Notlar" [Notes on the 15th International Congress of Sociology], *İstanbul Üniversitesi Edebiyat Fakültesi Sosyoloji Dergisi* 3:12 (2006): 151–61; Cassata, *Il fascismo razionale*, 196–98; Muller, *The Other God That Failed*, 371–72. Hilmi Ziya Ülken states that over 110 people from more than twenty countries had originally declared their intention to attend but only about half of them could make it. Still, Ülken said, the number of participants reached about eighty when Turkish attendees were added to the equation. Ülken, "Avant-Propos," *Actes du XVe Congrès International de Sociologie*, 1:220.
101. "Stratification sociale chez les émigrés en Allemagne Occidentale" (Social stratification among the émigrés in West Germany), *Actes du XVe Congrès International de Sociologie*, 1:220.
102. Ahmet Emin Yalman, a famous journalist of Dönme background in Turkey, complained about this in a court case he brought against Peyami Safa on the grounds of defamation. In a text he wrote to appeal to the cassation court (Yargıtay), Yalman also accused the judge, who found Safa not guilty, of being an ardent Nazi supporter.

There, Yalman also discusses how Peyami Safa spent the World War II years building support for Nazi Germany. For more, see "Yargıtay Ceza Dairesi Reisliğine Takdim Alınmak üzere, Istanbul Asliye İkinci Ceza Hâkimliğine: Ahmet Emin Yalman'ın Peyami Safa Aleyhine Açtığı Dâva ile Alâkalı Temyiz Istidası," Dosya 946/238, [Petition of appeal to the Second Court of First Instance to be presented to the Cassation Court on the Ahmet Emin Yalman vs. Peyami Safa court case, File 946/238] (Istanbul: Vatan Matbaası, 1946). For more on Peyami Safa's interest in Hitler, see journalist Nadir Nadi's memoir *Perde Aralığından* [From the opening in the curtain] (Istanbul: Cumhuriyet Yayınları, 1964), 39. For more on Ahmet Emin Yalman, see, for example, Marc Baer's *The Dönme: Jewish Converts, Muslim Revolutionaries, and Secular Turks* (Stanford, CA: Stanford University Press, 2009).

103. For the titles, also see the official program of the Fifteenth International Congress of Sociology. In 1952, the second issue of *Sosyoloji Dünyası* [The World of Sociology], the official journal of the Turkish Sociological Society, dedicated a special section to the program, organizing committee, and the scientific committee, and published a list of themes at the congress. See "Quinzième Congrès International de Sociologie (Fifteenth International Congress of Sociology) (Istanbul, 11–17 Septembre)," *Sosyoloji Dünyası* [World of Sociology] 1:2 (1952): 55–66.

104. Peyami Safa, *Doğu-Batı Sentezi* [East-West synthesis] (Istanbul: Çeltüt Matbaası, 1963).

105. "La Sociologie et le roman" [Sociology and the novel], *Actes du XVe Congrès International de Sociologie*, 2:213–14.

106. Ibid., 214.

107. See, for example, "Preface" and "The Significance of Sociology: Opening Address by L. Wirth," *International Bulletin of Social Science: International Congress of Sociology International Congress of Political Science*, special issue, 3:2 (Summer 1951): 189–90, 197–202.

108. *Proceedings of the 14th International Congress of Sociology*, vol. 1.

109. Ibid., 148–49.

110. Critics Ella Shohat and Robert Stam discuss how Sauvy is also the figure who coined the term the "Third World." For more on this and the notion of race as it traveled across the Atlantic, see their book *Race in Translation: Culture Wars Around the Postcolonial Atlantic* (New York: NYU Press, 2012).

111. *Proceedings of the 14th International Congress of Sociology*, 1:149.

112. Jennifer Platt, *A Brief History of ISA 1948–1997*, International Sociological Association 50th Anniversary (Québec: International Sociological Association, 1998), 27–29; *Proceedings of the 14th International Congress of Sociology*, 1:1–9. Also see *Integration 1954–1956*, as well as Cassata "Un'internazionale di destra," and Ülken, "İkinci Dünya Sosyoloji Kongresi, Liege 1953," 187.

113. Ülken, "İkinci Dünya Sosyoloji Kongresi, Liege 1953," 186–91; Périer, "Actes du

XIVe Congrès international de sociologie"; Muller, *The Other God That Failed*, 371–74. Also see *Proceedings of the 14th International Congress of Sociology*, 1:182–94.

114. Jennifer Platt, "ISA Presidents: Louis Wirth," http://www.isa.sociology.org. Wirth, born in Germany, was of Jewish background, and according to Platt, very sensitive to race matters. He was the first president of the International Sociological Association, from its founding in 1949 until his death in May 1952.

115. Hilmi Ziya Ülken, "Séance de clôture" [Closing session], *Actes du XVe Congrès International de Sociologie*, 154–55. For a discussion on this matter, see Cassata, *Il fascismo razionale*, 196–97.

116. Ülken, "Séance de clôture."

117. Parin, "XV. Milletlerarası Sosyoloji Kongresi Üzerine Notlar," 151–61; Cassata, *Il fascismo razionale*, 196–98; Muller, *The Other God That Failed*, 371–72; Ülken, "Avant-Propos," *Actes du XVe Congrès International de Sociologie*, 1:220.

118. Part of the reason for this might have been the death of Louis Wirth on May 4, 1952. Wirth, as mentioned in an earlier note, was the president of the UNESCO-supported International Sociological Association, and from Ülken's talk at the 1952 sociology congress in Istanbul, we understand that it was Wirth who had contacted the Turkish authorities in an attempt to prevent the Gini-led sociological convention from taking place there. Wirth considered sociology "as a science and as a basis for social action" and it seems he was determined to fight against the Gini-led International Institute of Sociology. See "Obituaries: Louis Wirth," *International Social Studies Bulletin* 4:4 (1952): 627–28.

119. "Statement on 'Race,'" United Nations Educational, Scientific and Cultural Organization (UNESCO): Meeting of Experts on Race Problems, Unesco House, December 12–14, 1949, UNESCO/SS/Conf.1/6, Paris, December 8, 1949. Drafted and accepted by: Ashley Montagu (United States), Morris Ginsberg (United Kingdom), Claude Lévi-Strauss (France), Ernest Beaglehole (New Zealand), Juan Comas (Mexico), Humayun Kabir (India), Franklin Frazier (United States), L.A. Costa Pinto (Brazil).

120. Jackson, *Science for Segregation*, 102; Christopher Douglas, *A Genealogy of Literary Multiculturalism* (Ithaca, NY: Cornell University Press, 2009), 2. For more, see Vernon J. Williams Jr., *Rethinking Race: Franz Boas and His Contemporaries* (Lexington: University Press of Kentucky, 1996).

121. Elazar Barkan, *The Retreat of Scientific Racism: Changing Concepts of Race in Britain and the United States between the World Wars* (Cambridge: Cambridge University Press, 1991), 341.

122. "Statement on 'Race.'" Also see Humayun Kabir, "What Is Race?," *UNESCO Courier* 2:12 (January 1, 1950): 10. A later collective volume published by UNESCO is entitled *What Is Race?* (Paris: UNESCO, 1952). For UNESCO studies of race during the 1950s in countries like Brazil, see Shohat and Stam, *Race in Translation*, 177–78. Also see

"Fallacies of Racism Exposed: UNESCO Publishes Declaration by World's Scientists," "The Scientific Basis for Human Unity," and Alfred Metraux, "Race and Civilization," *UNESCO Courier* 3:6–7 (July–August 1950): 1, 8–9; Robert J. C. Young, *Colonial Desire: Hybridity in Theory, Culture, and Race* (London: Routledge, 1995), 6; and Aldon D. Morris, "Sociology of Race and W.E.B. DuBois: The Path Not Taken," in *Sociology in America: A History*, Craig Calhoun, ed. (Chicago: University of Chicago Press, 2007), 520.

123. "Fallacies of Racism Exposed," 1.

124. See, for example, "Within the Four Seas ... All Men Are Brothers," *UNESCO Courier* 3:2 (March 1, 1950): 1.

125. "Introduction," *International Social Science Bulletin* 2:2 (Summer 1950): 157–59.

126. See, for instance, ibid.

127. For example, on March 17, 1954, the AER held a congress in Rome, and there Fahreddin Kerim Gökay gave a talk entitled "Situation des réfugiés en Turquie" [The situation of the refugees in Turkey], where he tied the case of emigrants in Turkey to humanity and human suffering. *Integration* 1:1 (1954): 20.

128. Ibid., 11.

129. *UNESCO Courier* 1:7 (August 1948): 5; *UNESCO Courier* 1:3 (April 1948): 7.

130. See for instance, "All Wars Are Fought against Children," *UNESCO Courier* (May 1, 1950): 1.

131. "Mülteciler Kongresi Bugün Sona Eriyor" [The congress on refugees ends today], *Milliyet*, September 17, 1954, 2. Despite my various attempts at locating archival material on this refugee exhibition in the archives of Istanbul University and the Turkish parliament, I have not been able find as of yet any documents on the subject.

132. "Rapports de la 4e Assemblée Générale," 164–65.

133. "Mülteciler Kongresi Bugün Sona Eriyor," 2.

134. "Edward Steichen at *The Family of Man*, 1955," MoMA, https://www.moma.org/learn/resources/archives/archives_highlights_06_1955. According to MoMA, the exhibition was numbered 569, and held between January 24 and May 8, 1955.

135. *The Family of Man: The 30th Anniversary Edition of the Classic Book of Photography Created by Edward Steichen for the Museum of Modern Art, New York* (New York: Museum of Modern Art, 1988), 184–85.

136. From Turkey, in addition to Evliya Çelebi's "Book of Travels," there are four more registered items of documentary heritage: Kandilli Observatory and Earthquake Research Institute Manuscripts (registered in 2001), the Hittite Cuneiform Tablets from Boğazköy (registered in 2001), the Works of Ibn Sina in the Süleymaniye Manuscript Library (registered in 2003), and the Old Assyrian Merchant Archives of Kültepe (registered in 2015). See "Full List of Registered Heritage," *Memory of the World*, http://www.unesco.org/new/en/communication-and-information/memory-of-the-world/register/full-list-of-registered-heritage/registered-heritage-page-1/.

137. "Safeguarding the Memory of the World—UNESCO Recommendation

concerning the Preservation of, Access to, Documentary Heritage in the Digital Era," *Memory of the World*, http://en.unesco.org/programme/mow/recommendation-documentary-heritage.

138. "The Family of Man," *UNESCO Courier* 9 (February 1956): 19.

139. "Editorial," *UNESCO Courier* 9 (February 1956): 3.

140. "The Family of Man," *UNESCO Courier* (1956): 19.

141. *The Family of Man: The 30th Anniversary Edition*, 3.

142. Fred Turner, "The Family of Man and the Politics of Attention in Cold War America," *Public Culture* 24:1 (2012): 55–84. Also see Sarah E. Young, "A Post-Fascist *Family of Man*? Cold War Humanism, Democracy and Photography in Germany," *Oxford Art Journal* 35:3 (2012): 316–35.

143. "Historical Summary," *Edward Steichen: The Family of Man*, UNESCO Memory of the World, http://www.steichencollections.lu.

144. Young, "A Post-Fascist *Family of Man*?"

145. "USIA: An Overview," Electronic Research Collections, US State Department, Federal Depository Libraries, University of Illinois at Chicago Library, http://dosfan.lib.uic.edu/usia/usiahome/oldoview.htm#overview.

146. Ibid.

147. Ibid.

148. *La Grande famille des hommes* [The great family of man], January 1, 1956, video 18 min. 48 sec., Institut national de l'audiovisuel (Bry-sur-Marne, France), http://www.ina.fr/video/VDD11021509.

149. Young, "A Post-Fascist *Family of Man*?"

150. *The Family of Man: The 30th Anniversary Edition*, 82–83. I thank the graduate students—in particular Shimrit Lee, Maysam Taher, Jennifer Varela, and Rustin Zakar—in my Forced Migration seminars at New York University for their very insightful comments on this subject in general.

151. Jay Ruby, "Out of Sync: The Cinema of Tim Asch," *Visual Anthropology Review* 11:1 (1995): 23. I thank Jennifer Varela for bringing this matter and the related articles to my attention.

152. Faye Ginsburg, "Producing Culture: Shifting Representations of Social Theory in the Films of Tim Asch," in *Timothy Asch and Ethnographic Film*, E. D. Lewis, ed. (New York: Routledge, 2003), 159.

153. Ibid.

154. For an earlier assessment that addresses the research as unethical, see Michael McCally, Christine Cassel, and Daryl G. Kimball, "U.S. Government-Sponsored Radiation Research on Humans 1945–1975," *Medicine & Global Survival* 1:1 (1994): 4–16. Also see *Human Radiation Experiments Associated with the US Department of Energy and Its Predecessors*, US Department of Energy, Assistant Secretary for Environment, Safety, and Health, July 1995. This report was published under the direction of Secretary of Energy

Hazel R. O'Leary to declassify and make public the US Department of Energy records related to human experimentation. For an earlier work that discusses health hazards before the US government officially acknowledged the experiments, see Philip L. Fradkin, *Fallout: An American Nuclear Tragedy* (Tucson: University of Arizona Press, 1989).

155. "Family of Man," *Memory of the World*, http://www.unesco.org/new/en/com munication-and-information/memory-of-the-world/register/full-list-of-registered -heritage/registered-heritage-page-3/family-of-man/.

156. Ibid.

157. Mark Mazower, *No Enchanted Palace*, and *Governing the World: The History of an Idea* (New York: Penguin, 2012).

158. Mazower, *No Enchanted Palace*, 1–27.

159. Ibid., 17.

160. Ibid., 131–35.

161. Ibid., 131–32.

162. Ibid.

163. Ibid., 132.

164. Todd Shepard, "Algeria, France, Mexico, UNESCO: A Transnational History of Anti-Racism and Decolonization, 1932–1962," *Journal of Global History* 6 (2011): 273–97. Also see Todd Shepard, *The Invention of Decolonization: The Algerian War and the Remaking of France* (Ithaca, NY: Cornell University Press, 2006). As for how counterinsurgencies were organized and interconnected since at least the Boer Wars, see Laleh Khalili, *Time in the Shadows: Confinement in Counterinsurgencies* (Stanford, CA: Stanford University Press, 2013).

165. Khalili, *Time in the Shadows*.

166. Cangül Örnek, "Türk Ceza Kanununun 141 ve 142. Maddelerine İlişkin Tartışmalarda Devlet ve Sınıflar" [State and class in debates about the Turkish Penal Code Articles 141 and 142], *Ankara Üniversitesi SBF Dergisi* [Journal of the Faculty of Political Science, Ankara University] 69:1 (2014): 124–25.

167. Shepard, "Algeria, France, Mexico, UNESCO," 286.

168. *TBMM Zabıt Ceridesi* 19:3 (May 24, 1957): 290.

169. Mazower, *No Enchanted Palace*, 141.

170. Ibid., 143. I thank Lerna Ekmekçioğlu for her generous comments that helped clarify the implications of the genocide convention.

171. Ibid., 143–44.

172. Ibid., 105–48. In particular, the work of Joseph Schechtman, addressed in Mazower's book, is important for such ideas. See Schechtman, *European Population Transfers, 1939–1945* (New York: Oxford University Press, 1946), and *Population Transfers in Asia* (New York: Hallsby Press, 1949). According to Mazower, Schechtman wanted to complete the spatialized redistribution of categorized groups in the Middle East and Asia.

173. Mazower, *No Enchanted Palace*, 135.

174. Ibid., 25.
175. Samuel Moyn, *The Last Utopia: Human Rights in History* (Cambridge, MA: Belknap Press, 2010).
176. *The Family of Man: The 30th Anniversary Edition*, 166–67.
177. Young, "A Post-Fascist *Family of Man?*," 326–27.
178. Ibid., 326. Also, as cited in Young, see in German, Viktoria Schmidt-Linsenhoff, "Denied Images: The Family of Man and the Shoa," in *The Family of Man 1955–2001, Humanismus und Postmoderne : eine Revision von Edward Steichens Fotoausstellung* [The Family of Man, 1955–2001: Humanism and postmodernism—a reappraisal of the photo exhibition by Edward Steichen], Jean Back and Viktoria Schmidt-Linsenhoff, eds. (Marburg: Jonas Verlag, 2005).
179. "La Grande famille des hommes" [The great family of man], *Le Monde*, January 20, 1956, http://www.lemonde.fr.
180. See Roland Barthes, "The Great Family of Man," *Mythologies* (New York: Hill and Wang, 1972), 100–102.
181. "History: Brown v. Board of Education Re-enactment," Supreme Court Landmarks, *United States Courts*, http://www.uscourts.gov/about-federal-courts/educational-resources/supreme-court-landmarks.
182. Barthes, "The Great Family of Man," 101–2.
183. Ibid., 102.
184. *The Family of Man: The 30th Anniversary Edition*, 72–73.
185. Some critics have objected to Barthes's reading of the exhibition, and argued that the heterogeneity of the photographs cannot be erased, and that Steichen's narrative is not the only one at the exhibit. For such a reading of the exhibition, see Ariella Azoulay, "'The Family of Man': A Visual Universal Declaration of Human Rights," in *The Human Snapshot*, Thomas Keenan and Tirdad Zolghadr, eds. (Berlin: Sternberg Press, 2013), 19–48. Here Azoulay considers *The Family of Man* to be an exhibition with the potential of raising human rights violations through the heterogeneity of the photographs, and considers it a visual universal declaration of human rights. I thank Shimrit Lee for bringing *The Human Snapshot* to my attention.
186. This—i.e., free and fair elections—was a common definition of democracy until recently. Cast against the Soviet communist bloc's system, "authoritarianism" and "democracy" were, for the most part, defined in terms of the existence or absence of a fair and competitive electoral system. In recent years, scholars have started to raise questions about whether this definition, which seemingly worked during the Cold War, is adequate for after the Cold War in general, and particularly in the post-9/11 world context. See, for example, Tom Ginsburg and Tamir Moustafa, eds., *Rule by Law: The Politics of Courts in Authoritarian Regimes* (New York: Cambridge University Press, 2008). Also see Steven Levitsky and Lucan A. Way, eds., *Competitive Authoritarianism: Hybrid Regimes after the Cold War* (New York: Cambridge University Press, 2010).

187. Herman Kreider, *First Lessons in Modern Turkish* (Istanbul: Robert College, 1945); American Board in Turkey, "Personnel records for Herman H. Kreider," in Digital Library for International Research Archive, item 13203, http://www.dlir.org/archive/items/show/13203.

188. Penelope Papailias, *Genres of Recollection: Archival Poetics in Modern Greece* (New York: Palgrave Macmillan, 2005).

189. See André Lefevere, *Translation, Rewriting, and the Manipulation of Literary Fame* (London: Routledge, 1992). I thank Anton Shammas for introducing me to this book.

190. For a different discussion of UNESCO and canonical heritage sites and human rights, see Rodney Harrison, *Heritage: Critical Approaches* (London: Routledge, 2013).

191. "The Historical Collection in a Contemporary Context," *Steichen Collections: The Family of Man*, http://www.steichencollections.lu/en/The-Family-of-Man.

192. Moyn, *The Last Utopia*, 176–211.

193. Ibid., 178.

194. Barkan, *The Retreat of Scientific Racism*. Also see Michelle Brattain, "Race, Racism, and Antiracism: UNESCO and the Politics of Presenting Science to the Postwar Public," *American Historical Review* 112:5 (December 2007): 1386–1413. For a more recent work that considers race and science, see Michael Yudell, *Race Unmasked: Biology and Race in the Twentieth Century* (New York: Columbia University Press, 2014).

195. Anne McClintock, *Imperial Leather: Race, Gender, and Sexuality in the Colonial Contest* (London: Routledge, 1995), 21–74.

196. Ibid., 39.

197. Elizabeth Hoyt, "The Family of Mankind: Some New Light?," *Mankind Quarterly* 2:1 (July 1,1961): 13–15.

198. This is evident in his own description of what he calls "progressive" humanism should be like, instead of what he sees.

199. I am grateful to Deniz Yonucu for bringing this quote to my attention. See Frantz Fanon, *The Wretched of the Earth* (New York: Grove, 2004), 163, 316. In *Imperial Leather*, Anne McClintock has historicized Fanon's conceptualization of "white bourgeois values," and shown how the family of man was historically configured white and bourgeois—unmasking the complex connections between race, class, and gender. For more on Fanon and humanism, see Anthony Alessandrini's important analysis, *Frantz Fanon and the Future of Cultural Politics: Finding Something Different* (Lanham, MD: Lexington Books, 2014). As for the notion of equality being a bourgeois value, this does not mean there should be no solidarity nor an aspiration for equal rights. Rather, the issue here is the adoption of the notion of equality following the limited, white bourgeois configuration of the term, associated with the Enlightenment and the French Revolution. In every respect, the principles of the French Revolution promoted a white configuration of such concepts as fraternity, liberty, and equality. The philosophical as-

pects of humanism fall outside the scope of this book, but there is a rich literature on the subject, including Ayten Gündoğdu's *Rightlessness in the Age of Rights: Hannah Arendt and the Contemporary Struggles of Migrants* (Oxford: Oxford University Press, 2015).

200. For those who argued the inequality of human races, UNESCO's Statement on Race was too radical. Harvard and later University of Pennsylvania professor of anthropology Carleton Coon, for example, published *The Origin of Races* in 1962. In this book, he argued that each race took a different time to evolve into *Homo sapiens*. Temporalizing evolution of the human races, he therefore sought to demonstrate that whites progressed faster than others, and sought to refute the claim that being *Homo sapiens* renders all humankind equal.

201. Schmitt, "Nehmen-Teilen-Weiden." Henceforth, my references will be to the English translation of this piece, "Appropriation/Distribution/Production: An Attempt to Determine from *Nomos* the Basic Questions of Every Social and Economic Order," *The* Nomos *of the Earth in the International Law of the* Jus Publicum Europaeum (New York: Telos Press, 2003), 324–35.

202. Ibid., 327–28.

203. Ibid., 328.

204. For instance, he describes how liberalism prioritizes production to solve the "social question," whereas socialism puts the emphasis on distribution.

205. "Unesco Acts to Free Books, Art, Films from Customs Charges," *Unesco Courier* 3:3 (April 1, 1950): 2. On copyrights, see in the same issue, "The Artist and His Freedom," 6–7.

206. Sidonie Smith and Kay Schaeffer, *Human Rights and Narrated Lives: The Ethics of Recognition* (New York: Palgrave Macmillan, 2004).

Part II

1. One of the most famous cases that exemplify this is lawyer Fethiye Çetin, who discovered her grandmother was Armenian. Çetin wrote a memoir in Turkish about this discovery, which has been translated into English. See Fethiye Çetin, *My Grandmother: An Armenian-Turkish Memoir* (London: Verso, 2012). Also see a volume Çetin published jointly with anthropologist Ayşe Gül Altınay, *The Grandchildren: The Hidden Legacy of "Lost" Armenians in Turkey* (New Brunswick, NJ: Transaction, 2014).

2. On the memoir boom in the international arena, see Astrid Erll, *Memory in Culture* (New York: Palgrave Macmillan, 2011), 2. Also see Kay Schaffer and Sidonie Smith, *Human Rights and Narrated Lives: The Ethics of Recognition* (New York: Palgrave Macmillan, 2004), 1.

3. See Victoria E. Bonnell and Lynn Hunt, eds., *Beyond The Cultural Turn: New Directions in the Study of Society and Culture* (Berkeley: University of California Press, 1999). In their preface, the editors of the book, Bonnell and Hunt, point out how in growing numbers, historians and historical sociologists started turning their attention

to the study of culture in the 1980s. In his contribution to the volume, "The Concept(s) of Culture," William H. Sewell Jr. traces the rise of cultural analysis in the 1970s. As addressed in Part One, after the Second World War, UNESCO also emphasized culture instead of race. As Sewell points out, however, this engagement with culture does not necessarily appear to have extended to the scrutiny of power discrepancies including colonialism or the ties of the field of cultural anthropology to colonialism.

4. My use of "personal" here is inspired by Penelope Papailias's use of the word in the context of personal archives, in that it "highlights the control and management of archives by individuals, families, or groups and the manner in which they knit their identities and histories into them." See Penelope Papailias, *Genres of Recollection: Archival Poetics in Modern Greece* (New York: Palgrave Macmillan, 2005), 3.

5. See Aslı Iğsız, "Polyphony and Geographic Kinship in Anatolia: Framing the Turkish-Greek Population Exchange," in *The Politics of Public Memory in Turkey*, Esra Özyürek, ed. (Syracuse, NY: Syracuse University Press, 2007), 162–87. Note that I have revised my earlier interpretation of liberal cultural discourses.

6. See Aslı Iğsız, "Documenting the Past and Publicizing Personal Stories: Sensescapes and the 1923 Greco-Turkish Population Exchange in Contemporary Turkey," *Journal of Modern Greek Studies* 26 (2008): 451–87.

7. Astrid Erll, "Cultural Memory Studies: An Introduction," in *Cultural Memory Studies: An International and Interdisciplinary Handbook*, Astrid Erll and Ansgar Nünning, eds. (Berlin: Walter de Gruyter, 2008), 1–18; Schaffer and Smith, *Human Rights and Narrated Lives*.

8. For a critical analysis of the roots narrative, see Liisa Malkki, "National Geographic: The Rooting of Peoples and the Territorialization of National Identity among Scholars and Refugees," *Cultural Anthropology* 7:1 (1992): 24–44.

9. Léopold Lambert, *Weaponized Architecture: The Impossibility of Innocence* (Barcelona: DPR 2012). Lambert's book offers good examples of this phenomenon.

10. Yael Navaro-Yashin, "Affective Spaces, Melancholic Objects: Ruination and the Production of Anthropological Knowledge," *Journal of the Royal Anthropological Institute* 15 (2009): 1–18.

11. Walter Benjamin, *The Origin of German Tragic Drama* (London: Verso, 1998), 177–78. For a different approach, see Julia Hell and Andreas Schönle, "Introduction," in *Ruins of Modernity*, Julia Hell and Andreas Schönle, eds. (Durham, NC: Duke University Press, 2010), 6–7. This book is based on a 2005 conference at the University of Michigan under the same title, "Ruins of Modernity."

12. Ann Stoler, "The Rot Remains: From Ruins to Ruination," in *Imperial Debris: On Ruins and Ruination* (Durham, NC: Duke University Press, 2013), 5.

13. Ibid., 8, 9–11.

14. National Security Council, *12 September 1980: Before and After* (Ankara: Ongun Kardeşler, 1982). This book, prepared by the General Secretariat of Turkey's National

Security Council, explains the rationale for the coup. It advocates IMF policies and considers unions a threat to stability. Stability, according to the council, is crucial for economic growth. For more, see, for example, Cihan Tuğal, "Nato's Islamists: Hegemony and Americanization in Turkey," *New Left Review* 44 (March–April 2007): 5–34. For a cultural critique of the period, see Nurdan Gürbilek, *The New Cultural Climate in Turkey: Living in a Shop Window* (New York: Zed Books, 2011).

On November 3, 1996, a traffic accident in Susurluk, Turkey, unraveled one of Turkey's biggest corruption scandals. The collision of a truck with a car exposed the passengers of the car, who included a deputy in the Turkish parliament, a police officer, and an ultranationalist counterguerilla leader, about whom there was an Interpol Red Notice for committing a massacre.

15. Pandora Bookshop in Istanbul used to categorize bestsellers according to their genres and report on sales by category. According to Pandora's *Kitap Gazetesi* [Book gazette], of the 5,705 books published in 2003, 811 were history books. During my interviews with the staff at Pandora in 2004 and 2005, they noted that amateur history books, memoirs, and historical novels were among the top sellers, and that there had been a sharp increase in such publications since the end of the 1990s. Various other publishers whom I interviewed confirmed this observation. At the time of writing, I contacted the Turkish Statistical Institute (former State Statistics Institute) for the exact numbers and to confirm these data. I was told that, unfortunately, this was not possible: since Turkey adopted the ISBN system in 2008, exact statistics before this date are not available. I am grateful to Libra Books' owner, publisher and independent researcher Rıfat Bali for his help in this process and for sharing with me his own investigation of the statistics. At this point, all I can say, then, is that professionals and amateurs working in bookstores and publishing houses at the time believed that there was indeed an increase.

16. See Wendy Brown, "'The Most We Can Hope For . . .': Human Rights and the Politics of Fatalism," *South Atlantic Quarterly* 103:2–3 (2004): 451–63. Also see Schaffer and Smith, *Human Rights and Narrated Lives*.

17. For an ethnographic study of plurality and belonging, see Kabir Tambar, *The Reckoning of Pluralism: Political Belonging and the Demands of History in Turkey* (Stanford, CA: Stanford University Press, 2014).

18. See, for instance, Feroz Ahmad, "Military Intervention and the Crisis in Turkey," *MERIP Reports* 93 (January 1981): 5–24. I am grateful to Başak Ertür and James Martel for reminding me of Ahmad's article. Also see "Turkish Test," *Wall Street Journal*, September 17, 1980, 30.

There has been a growing trend of deunionization globally. See, for example, statistics provided by the Organisation for Economic Development and Co-operation (OECD): "Trade Union Density," *OECD-Stat*, data accessed December 20, 2015. For an analysis of deunionization from the perspective of Turkey, see Aziz Çelik, "The Right to Strike Only Exists on Paper in Turkey," *Equal Times*, February 4, 2015. Also see Çelik's

"Trade Unions and Deunionization during Ten Years of AKP rule," *Perspectives* 1 (2013). For a survey of previous eras, see Çelik, "Milli Güvenlik Gerekçeli Grev Ertelemeleri" [The postponement of strikes on the grounds of national security], *Çalışma ve Toplum* 3:18 (2008): 87–132.

19. See Ceren Özgül, "From Muslim Citizen to Christian Minority: Tolerance, Secularism, and Armenian Return Conversions in Turkey" (Ph.D. diss., CUNY, 2013). Also see Ayşe Parla and Ceren Özgül, "Property, Dispossession, and Citizenship in Turkey; or, The History of the Gezi Uprising Starts in the Surp Hagop Armenian Cemetery," *Public Culture* 28:3 (2016): 617–53. For an earlier work on the subject, see Ayhan Aktar, *Varlık Vergisi ve Türkleştirme Politikaları* [The capital tax law and policies of Turkification] (Istanbul: İletişim, 2000).

20. Tarih Vakfı, http://www.tarihvakfi.org.tr/english/historyfoundationofturkey.asp (accessed August 20, 2006).

21. I am grateful to Kader Konuk for reminding me of this phenomenon.

22. "Osmanlıca Modası!" [Ottoman fashions], *Akşam Canteen*, January 27, 2003.

23. "Sararmış Fotoğrafların Gizli Tarihi" [The secret history of yellowed photographs], *Akşam Canteen*, March 3, 2003.

24. See Leyla Neyzi, "Remembering to Forget: Sabbateanism, National Identity and Subjectivity in Turkey," *Comparative Study of Society and History* 44:1 (2001): 137–58; Marc Baer, "The Double Bind of Race and Religion: The Conversion of the Dönme to Turkish Secular Nationalism," *Comparative Study of Society and History* 46:4 (2004): 682–708. Also see Baer's book *The Dönme: Jewish Converts, Muslim Revolutionaries, and Secular Turks* (Stanford, CA: Stanford University Press, 2009).

25. See Lerna Ekmekçioğlu, *Recovering Armenia: The Limits of Belonging in Post-Genocide Turkey* (Stanford, CA: Stanford University Press, 2016). Also see Fatma Müge Göçek, *Denial of Violence: Ottoman Past, Turkish Present, and Collective Violence against the Armenians, 1789–2009* (Oxford: Oxford University Press, 2014).

26. On Muslim Armenians and issues of conversion, see Ceren Özgül, "Legally Armenian: Tolerance, Conversion, and Name Change in Turkish Courts," *Comparative Studies in Society and History* 56:3 (2014): 622–49.

27. I am grateful to my interlocutor, whom, for privacy purposes, I shall name Nesrin, for her willingness to share her copy with me and for her generosity during our interviews.

28. See Molly Greene, *A Shared World: Christians and Muslims in the Early Modern Mediterranean* (Princeton, NJ: Princeton University Press, 2000). Greene reconsiders French historian Fernand Braudel's understanding of the Mediterranean in terms of religious divides and suggests considering the Mediterranean through continuities, such as the Venetian-Ottoman transition in Crete.

29. Esin Eden and Nicholas Stavroulakis, *Salonika: A Family Cookbook* (Athens: Talos, 1997).

30. Nikos Stavroulakis, personal interview, December 2003.

31. "Faili Meçhul Kemikler Önce Kayboldu, Sonra Aynı Torba İçinde Gömüldü" [Bones of unresolved death/crime first disappeared, then were buried in the same bag], *Radikal*, June 23, 2013; İsmail Saymaz, "Dersim Katliamında 78 Yıl Sonra İlk Kazma Vuruluyor" [First excavation to take place 78 years after the Dersim massacre], *Radikal*, April 14, 2015; "JİTEM Sorgu Merkezinde Toplu Mezar Bulundu" [Mass grave found at the interrogation center of the gendarmerie's intelligence and anti-terror organization], *İlkha*, January 11, 2012; "Toplu Mezardaki Kemikler Adli Tıpta" [Forensic medicine has the bones (found) in the mass grave], *Bianet*, September 23, 2013, http://bianet.org/bianet/insan-haklari/150118-toplu-mezardaki-kemikler-adli-tipta.

32. "Kayıplar Geçmişimizdir, Geçmişimizle Yüzleşelim" [The losses are our past, let's face our past], *Bianet*, April 29, 2013, http://bianet.org/bianet/insan-haklari/146230-kayiplar-gecmisimizdir-gecmisimizle-yuzleselim. The article also explains how the Diyarbakir branch of the Human Rights Association prepared a report in 2011 indicating that 253 mass graves still awaited exhumation. To see some of these reports, see the association's website: http://www.ihddiyarbakir.org. These include, for example, "Kayıplar ve Toplu Mezarlar/Geçmişle Yüzleşme Çalıştayı Sonuç Bildirgesi" [(The forcibly) disappeared and mass graves/concluding proclamation of workshop on facing the past], May 29, 2013. In this report, the association delineated the importance of tracing mass graves from 1915—marked as the year of the Armenian genocide—to today. Also see, for instance, "Türkiye'de Toplu Mezarlar Raporu" [Report on mass graves in Turkey], 2014.

33. UNESCO, "Mexico City Declaration on Cultural Policies, 1982," World Conference on Cultural Policies, Mexico City, July 26–August 6, 1982.

34. Ekmekçioğlu, *Recovering Armenia*.

35. See UNESCO's website, http://www.unesco.org.

36. Following some criticism, the genealogical tree was removed from the website: http://www.satoglu.com/gtree.html.

37. Elizabeth Povinelli, *Economies of Abandonment: Social Belonging and Endurance in Late Liberalism* (Durham, NC: Duke University Press, 2011).

38. *59 Saniye*, August 6, 2014, http://www.59saniye.com/tayyip-erdogan-afedersiniz-rum/.

39. "Ecdadımız soykırım yapmadi yapmaz da" [Our ancestors did not commit genocide and they would not do such a thing], *Haberaktüel*, December 14, 2009, http://www.haberaktuel.com.

40. It is clear from numerous nostalgic statements on the Ottomans that in the rehierarchized genealogy of the Turks, the Ottoman sultans are cherished today as powerful symbols of the golden age of the Turks. This relationship simultaneously casts Ottoman sultans and notables as "ancestors"—generating yet another genealogical tree for the nation, one that embraces the Ottoman past as heritage, but also one that resorts

to the same gatekeeping of the ancestors. "Ancestors" are powerful symbols of the Turkish-Islamic synthesis, representing the golden age of the history of Turks. This is evident in the reactions against the TV series *Muhteşem Yüzyıl—The Magnificent Century*, which portrayed Suleiman the Magnificent. The makers of the series have been targeted numerous times, and called, among other things, immoral traitors who are foreign to their own roots and their own ancestors.

41. Anne McClintock, *Imperial Leather: Race, Gender, and Sexuality in the Colonial Contest* (London: Routledge, 1995).

42. UNESCO, "Mexico City Declaration on Cultural Policies, 1982."

43. Ibid.

44. This term of course did not emerge in a vacuum in modern times. For a work that sheds light on earlier humanists, see Nancy Bisaha, *Creating East and West: Renaissance Humanists and the Ottoman Turks* (Philadelphia: University of Pennsylvania Press, 2004). Here, Bisaha shows how upon the fall of Constantinople to the Ottomans, the Renaissance humanists followed two main trajectories to understand themselves and the "enemy" that posed a threat: the Crusades and ancient Greek and Roman sources.

45. As will be discussed later in this essay, it is important to keep in mind that, particularly in the nineteenth century, the configuration of "nation" often implicated a group with a shared identity that could be traced to its origins, such as ancient heritage that simultaneously territorialized the notion of origins.

46. See Sasha Colby, *Stratified Modernism: The Poetics of Excavation from Gautier to Olson* (Bern: Peter Lang, 2009), 9–36. For racialized references to civilization and ancient "heritage," see Heinrich Schliemann, *The Site of the Homeric Troy* (London: Nichols and Sons, 1875). Also see Schliemann, *Troy and Its Remains* (London: John Murray, 1875), iii–xxiv, 57–63, 220–32, 321–57; Schliemann, *Troja* (New York: Harper and Brothers, 1884), 1–28. For more on excavations and Ottoman approaches to antiquities, see Zainab Bahrani, Zeynep Çelik, and Edhem Eldem, "Introduction: Archaeology and Empire," and Zeynep Çelik, "Defining Empire's Patrimony: Late Ottoman Perceptions of Antiquities," both in *Scramble for the Past: A Story of Archaeology in the Ottoman Empire, 1753–1914*, Zainab Bahrani, Zeynep Çelik, and Edhem Eldem, eds. (Istanbul: SALT, 2011), 13–43; 443–79.

47. Kader Konuk, *East-West Mimesis: Auerbach in Turkey* (Stanford, CA: Stanford University Press, 2010).

48. In literary studies, such an unproblematized configuration of the "genius" has been effectively rejected, particularly during the last decade of the twentieth century. A number of works interrogating the notion of the "canon" were published during that time, generating a framework for questioning national literature repertoires. See, for example, John Guillory, *Cultural Capital: The Problem of Literary Canon Formation* (Chicago: University of Chicago Press, 1993). Also see André Lefevere, *Translation, Rewriting, and the Manipulation of Literary Fame* (New York: Routledge, 1992).

49. The figure of the genius supposedly embodies the "national" and/or "racial character" through literature as representative of past glories—as exemplified in glorified epics and tales of heroism. Philologists, historians, and intellectuals who addressed "origins" in terms of cultural history include Taha Hussein in Egypt and Mehmet Fuat Köprülü in Turkey. Interestingly, they would both serve as ministers in their respective countries.

50. Taha Hussein, *The Future of Culture in Egypt* (Washington, DC: American Council of Learned Societies, 1954).

51. See, for instance, Mehmed Fuat Köprülü, *Early Mystics in Turkish Literature* (New York: Routledge, 2006.) This work was first published in Ottoman in 1918, and then revised and published again in modern Turkish. Note that his name is spelled interchangeably as Mehmed and Mehmet depending on the source.

52. For an astute study on the subject, see Şehnaz Tahir Gürçağlar, *The Politics and Poetics of Translation in Turkey (1923–1960)* (Amsterdam: Editions Rodopi, 2008).

53. "A Hundred Groups with a Common Aim," *UNESCO Courier* 3:4 (May 1, 1950): 2. Later, the same project would be articulated in terms of "East-West Appreciation: A Unesco 'Major Project,'" *UNESCO Courier* 6 (June 1957): 3–25.

54. Jean-Jacques Mayoux, "Translation of Classics to Be Promoted by UNESCO," *UNESCO Courier* 1:1 (February 1948): 7.

55. Eyyüp Sanay, *Hilmi Ziya Ülken* (Ankara: Kültür ve Turizm Bakanlığı Yayınları, Başbakanlık Basımevi 1986), 12.

56. Hilmi Ziya Ülken, *Uyanış Devirlerinde Tercümenin Rolü: İslam Medeniyetinde Tercümeler ve Tesirleri* [The role of translation in the period of awakening: Translation and its impact on Islamic civilization] (Istanbul: İş Bankası Kültür Yayınları, 2011). The book was originally published under the title *Uyanış Devirlerinde Tercümenin Rolü* [The role of translation in the period of awakening] in 1935 by Vakit Newspaper Press. The second edition of the book appeared in 1947 under the title *İslam Medeniyetinde Tercümeler ve Tesirleri* [Translation and its impact on Islamic civilization]. For an analysis of Ülken's approach to translation and humanism, see Gürçağlar, *The Politics and Poetics of Translation in Turkey*.

57. Hilmi Ziya Ülken, "Maksad" [The goal], *İnsan* [Human] 1:1 (April 15, 1938): 1–2.

58. Ibid., 2.

59. Hilmi Ziya Ülken, "Memleketi tanımak" [Getting to know the homeland], *İnsan* 1:5 (October 1, 1938): 377–79.

60. As discussed in Part One, *Mankind Quarterly* fought against racial equality.

61. Ülken, "Memleketi tanımak," 378–79.

62. Ibid., 378.

63. Celaleddin Ezine, "Türk Hümanizmasının izahı—I" [An explanation of Turkish humanism, I], *Hamle* 1:1 (August 1940): 6–10. Here Ezine refers to Peyami Safa's book within the context of humanism in Turkey. For the second part of this piece, see Celaleddin Ezine, "Türk Hümanizmasının izahı—II" [An explanation of Turkish hu-

manism, II], *Hamle* 1:3 (October 1940): 1–6. I am grateful to Kader Konuk for bringing this piece to my attention. The piece is also cited in Konuk's seminal book *East-West Mimesis*, 231n87.

64. Ezine, "Türk Hümanizmasının izahı—I," 6.
65. Ibid., 7.
66. Ibid., 8.
67. Ibid.
68. Ezine, "Türk Hümanizmasının izahı—II," 1.
69. "Yunus Emre Anıtı" [The monument of Yunus Emre], *Cumhuriyet*, May 12, 1949, 3.
70. Ibid.
71. See Francis Galton, *Hereditary Genius: An Inquiry into Its Laws and Consequences* (London: Macmillan, 1869).
72. On the impact of Peyami Safa's thought on the Aydınlar Ocağı, see Bozkurt Güvenç, Gencay Şaylan, İlhan Tekeli, and Şerafettin Turan, *Türk-İslam Sentezi* [The Turkish-Islamic synthesis] (Istanbul: Sarmal Yayınevi, 1991), 171–96.
73. "Unesco Türkiye Millî Komisyonu Yönetim Kurulu Üyeleri Seçildi" [Members of the executive board of the Unesco Turkish National Commission have been elected], *Cumhuriyet*, May 12, 1949, 3. In addition to Safa, Muhsin Ertuğrul—a key figure in Turkish theater—was elected as a substitute member. Among the main board members were author Halide Edib Adıvar and composer Adnan Saygun.
74. For philological discussions and examples, see Harry Thurston Peck, *History of Classical Philology* (New York: Macmillan, 1911), vii–ix, 1–4; H. A. R. Gibb, "Arab Poet and Arabic Philologist," *Bulletin of the School of Oriental and African Studies* 12:3/4 (1948): 574–78; Edward Browne, "Editor's Preface," in *A History of Ottoman Poetry*, E. J. W. Gibb, ed. (London: Luzac, 1907), 5:v–viii; E. J. W. Gibb, "Special Introduction" by Theodore P. Ion, and "Introduction," *Ottoman Turkish Literature* (Washington, DC: M.W. Dunne, 1901), ix–xiii and 1–32, respectively; Edmund Bosworth, "Edward Granville Browne," and Albert Hourani, "H.A.R. Gibb," in *A Century of British Orientalists*, C. Edmund Bosworth, ed. (Oxford: Oxford University Press, 2001), 74–88 and 154–85, respectively. On Halikarnas Balıkçısı, see Aslı Gür, "Political Excavations of the Anatolian Past: Nationalism and Archaeology in Turkey," in *Controlling the Past, Owning the Future: The Political Uses of Archaeology in the Middle East* (Tucson: University of Arizona Press, 2010), 68–89.
75. This doesn't mean such configurations did not exist before, but that with the professionalization of academic disciplines and the production of knowledge, they became more systematic configurations of identification with national, racial, and civilizational undertones.
76. Jean-Jacques Ampère, "Une Course dans l'Asie Mineure: Lettre à M. Sainte-Beuve" [A course in Asia Minor: Letter to Mr. Sainte-Beuve], *Revue des Deux Mondes*

29 (January 15, 1842): 161–85. Sainte-Beuve was a prominent French critic and this correspondence offers insights on the details of the trip Ampère took to trace the ancient Greek heritage on the Aegean shores. Ampère published the same letter in his book that broadly identifies a method he calls "voyage critique," or "critical travels," which seeks to compare the written work of great poets to the geographies that gave rise to such poets, who portrayed those geographies in their poetry. He thus follows the footsteps of Homer to Asia Minor and of Dante to Italy. See Ampère, *La Grèce, Rome, Dante: Études littéraires d'après nature* [Greece Rome and Dante: Literary studies following nature] (Paris: Didier, 1850), 351–89.

77. *Correspondance d'Alexis de Tocqueville avec P.-P. Royer-Collard et avec J.-J. Ampère* [Correspondence of Alexis de Tocqueville with P.-P. Royer-Collard and with J.-J. Ampère], annotated, compiled and prefaced by André Jardin as part of Alexis de Tocqueville *Oeuvres Complètes*, tome XI [Complete works of Alexis de Tocqueville, vol. 11] (Paris: Gallimard, 1970).

78. Michel Espagne, *Le Paradigme de l'etranger. Les chaires de littérature étrangère au XIXe siècle* [The paradigm of the foreign: The chairs of foreign literatures in the 19th century] (Paris: Les Éditions du Cerf, 1993), 7–40. Also see Sainte Beuve's piece on Ampère, "Jean-Jacques Ampère," *Revue des Deux Mondes* 77:2 (1868): 5–50.

79. Jean-Jacques Ampère, *La Science et les lettres en Orient* [Science and letters in the Orient] (Paris: Librairie Académique, 1865).

80. See Ampère, *La Grèce, Rome et Dante*.

81. Papailias, *Genres of Recollection*; Artemis Leontis, *Topographies of Hellenism: Mapping the Homeland* (Ithaca, NY: Cornell University Press, 1995). Also see Vassilis Lambropoulos, *The Rise of Eurocentrism: Anatomy of Interpretation* (Princeton, NJ: Princeton University Press, 1992).

82. Nadia Abu El Haj, *Facts on the Ground: Archaeological Practice and Territorial Self-Fashioning in Israeli Society* (Chicago: University of Chicago Press, 2002). Also see Nadia Abu El Haj, *The Genealogical Science: The Search for Jewish Origins and the Politics of Epistemology* (Chicago: University of Chicago Press, 2012).

83. Historian Pim Den Boer argues that "universalism" is a French Republican attribute, mostly thanks to the Universal Declaration of Human Rights. For more, see "Loci memoriae—Lieux de mémoire," *Cultural Memory Studies: An International and Interdisciplinary Handbook*, Astrid Erll and Ansgar Nünning, eds. (Berlin: Walter de Gruyter, 2008), 19–26.

84. Carsten Hoeg, "Classical Studies and UNESCO," *UNESCO Courier* 2:8 (September 1949): 5.

85. Bisaha, *Creating East and West*, 45.

86. See Frantz Fanon, *The Wretched of the Earth* (New York: Grove, 2004). Originally published in 1961, the book comes with a famous preface by Jean-Paul Sartre, who condemns humanism, which he associates with colonialism, for wanting the "natives to

be universal" but simultaneously applying racially informed practices that differentiate them. As for Fanon himself, he proposes a new humanity, one that does not treat the colonized as nonhuman, but redistributes the relations between humans. Fanon calls this a new humanity, which would lead to a new humanism beyond the European configuration of the term.

87. See Gobineau, *Essai sur l'inégalité des races humaines* (Paris: Librairie de Firmin Didot Frères, 1853). His work appeared in English translation later: *The Inequality of Human Races* (New York: G.P. Putnam's Sons, 1915). Gobineau is often described as a founding figure of racialist demography.

88. Houston Stewart Chamberlain, *The Foundations of the Nineteenth Century* (New York: John Lane, 1911), 1:1–250.

89. Ibid., lxxxix–xciv.

90. For a recent study that pays close attention to the wider implications of Gobineau's work for how today's cultural theory uses the same key concepts as nineteenth-century race theories, and thus reifies these concepts instead of debunking them, see Robert J. C. Young, *Colonial Desire: Hybridity in Theory, Culture, and Race* (London: Routledge, 1995).

91. Gobineau, *The Inequality of Human Races*, 127–31.

92. Ibid., 25 (emphasis mine).

93. Selim Deringil, *Conversion and Apostasy in the Late Ottoman Empire* (New York: Cambridge University Press, 2012), 174.

94. Ibid.

95. Gür, "Political Excavations of the Anatolian Past," 252n29.

96. Moustafa Djelaleddin, *Les Turcs anciens et modernes* (Paris: Librairie Internationale, 1870), 229.

97. Ibid., 62–63, 229–300.

98. Ibid., 40–41. It should be noted that all throughout, Mustafa Celaleddin Paşa laces the history of the Slavs through that of the Ottomans.

99. Ibid., 361–62.

100. As scholar Büşra Ersanlı demonstrates in her work, after reading texts like Gobineau's, Atatürk (often referred to as Turkey's "founding father") sent his protégée Afet İnan to Switzerland to master scientific methods of anthropometry and to study with Eugène Pittard. İnan's "mission," as Ersanlı shows, was to scientifically debunk demeaning theories about the Turks and find a better branch for the Turkish nation on Gobineau's racialized family tree of humankind. In this process, İnan applied the "science" of anthropometry in skull measurements and classification to build her theses of the history of the Turkish nation. While the goal was to substantiate that the Turks have the "right" kind of genealogy, this objective was less directly motivated by the desire to prove the superiority of the Aryan race (as implied in Speros Vryonis's work) than to locate Turks in a hierarchically "respectable" racial category. See Ersanlı, *İktidar*

ve Tarih: Türkiye'de Resmi Tarih Tezinin Oluşumu [Power and history: The development of the official history thesis in Turkey] (Istanbul: İletişim: 2003), 40, 146–51; Arı İnan, *Afet İnan* (Istanbul: Remzi Kitabevi, 2005); Afet İnan, *Atatürk Hakkında Hatıralar ve Belgeler* [Memories and documents regarding Atatürk] (Ankara: Türk Tarih Kurumu Basımevi, 1959), 227–33; Speros Vryonis Jr., *The Turkish State and History: Clio Meets the Grey Wolf* (New York: Aristide D. Caratzas, 1991), 57–78.

101. Hilmi Ziya Ülken, *İçtimai Doktrinler Tarihi* [History of social thought] (Istanbul: İstanbul Üniversitesi Neşriyatı, Yedidevir Basımevi, 1941).

102. Ibid., 247–49.

103. Ibid., 244.

104. Ibid., 248.

105. Ibid.

106. Hilmi Ziya Ülken, "Tanzimat Devrinde Türkçülük" [Turkism in the era of the Tanzimat], in *Millet ve Tarih Şuuru* [Consciousness of the nation and history] (Istanbul: Dergah Yayınları, [1948] 1976), 166–72. It should be noted that some of the essays in this book were published earlier in journals and magazines, as was this article. It was originally published in 1946, in a magazine called *İstanbul Mecmuası*. Although I have found information on this earlier edition in a compiled bibliography, I could not locate a hard (nor digital) copy of the original essay. My reference therefore is to the second edition of the book. For the original publication, see "Tanzimat Devrinde Türkçülük" [Turkism in the era of the Tanzimat], *İstanbul Mecmuası* 5:52 (February 15, 1946). This is the citation published in the Hilmi Ziya Ülken bibliography, dedicated to the corpus of his work. See Muhsin Balakbabalar, "Ord. Prof. Hilmi Ziya Ülken" [Ordinarius Professor Hilmi Ziya Ülken], *Ankara Üniversitesi İlahiyat Fakültesi Dergisi* [Journal of the Faculty of Theology, Ankara University] 31:1 (1972): iii–xxii.

107. Hilmi Ziya Ülken, *Veraset ve Cemiyet* [Heredity and society] (Istanbul: İstanbul Universitesi Edebiyat Fakültesi Yayınları, 1957).

108. Ibid., 65.

109. For example, on March 12, 1951, Ülken published a piece entitled "İptidailere Dair Sosyolojik Tetkikler" [Sociological analyses of the primitives], in his weekly column in the daily *Yeni Sabah*. In this piece, he discusses Corrado Gini's anthropological surveys in Libya, Poland, Syria, and Mexico, and invites sociologists of Turkey to conduct their own qualitative research. He also suggests studies on mobility (the exact word he uses is *göçebeler*, which can be translated as "nomads" or "migrants"), newly settled villages, sects, and so on. He also challenges Gini's contention that acquired characteristics can be inherited by questioning the biological bases of that argument—informed by biologist Lamarck's work—in light of the then new research findings on human and animal cells.

110. Ülken, *Veraset ve Cemiyet*, 271n2. In this section of the book, he claims that pathological changes are transmitted to future generations by social race and that they are heditary. Even though he claims he wrote the book thirty-three years before its

publication, it is very likely that he developed parts of these ideas during his interactions with the UNESCO-led International Sociological Association and the Corrado Gini-led Institute of Sociology, as well as with UNESCO's humanism projects and the European Association for the Study of Refugee Problems (AER).

111. Ülken, *Veraset ve Cemiyet*, 196.

112. Ibid., 196–97.

113. Ibid., 197.

114. Ibid., 198.

115. Ibid., 198–99.

116. Indeed, on December 18, 1950, Ülken would dedicate his newspaper column in the daily *Yeni Sabah* to a report on Corrado Gini's lecture at Istanbul University's Faculty of Letters the day before. The lecture was about the impact of population density on social life, and we learn from Ülken that one of the topics covered by Gini was the question of "expertise" (*ihtisas*). According to Gini, in countries where the population density is low, scientific and scholarly research lags behind because of the lack of bodily resources. Ülken grapples with this question in his column, and considers the question of scholarly expertise in Turkey through the lens of population density, and concludes that the reason for a heavy reliance on secondary sources in Turkey is not related to the lack of numbers. Because, he reasons, during the golden age of Islamic civilization, population density was not that high either. Rather, the problem is that science has not developed in Islamic civilization for the last century, he asserts, and that Near Eastern countries assiduously attempted to penetrate the Western system (*garp bünyesi*). Ülken's suggests that "the family of Turks [*Türk ailesi*] should find its stability, and its professional life should be secure, stable, and organized so that the path to expertise can be completely open." This is why, he deems it important for scholars to contribute to the order of the social life, rather than being secluded in their ivory tower and of no use to anyone (*fildişi kulesine çekilmiş ve kimseye yaramayan*). See Ülken, "İhtisas ve Cemiyet" [*Expertise and society*], *Yeni Sabah*, December 18, 1950, 2. In that light, Ülken and his circles at the AER indeed shared this disposition of the expert scholar who would contribute to the governance and regulation of emigrants. As for Ülken, he also clearly saw his work as a contribution to elevating the family of Turks within the family tree of humankind, and by proxy, Islamic civilization.

117. Ülken, *Veraset ve Cemiyet*, 205–7; Ülken, *Toplum Yapısı ve Soyaçekim* [The structure of society and heredity] (Istanbul: Doruktekin Yayınları), 205–6.

118. Ülken, *Veraset ve Cemiyet*, 206–7.

119. Hilmi Ziya Ülken, "Göçmen dâvamız II" [Our case of emigrants, II], *Yeni Sabah*, June 4, 1951, 2.

120. While today *tecanüs* is translated as "homogeneity," here the implication is being of the same kind. The corpus of Ülken's work, as well as the debates in the AER and congresses of sociology, indicates that there was an awareness of the fact that popu-

lations are not homogeneous. Rather, the concern appears to have been the alignment of those of the same "kind" (implicating racialized connotations of religion). Statements such as the "national refugee is one who belongs in his/her proper country" (discussed in Part One) followed by concerns of integration and assimilation attest to this.

121. Ülken himself translates *temessül* as "assimilation" and puts the word within parentheses in his text.

122. Ülken, "Göçmen dâvamız II," 2.

123. "Philosopher Calls for a New Humanism," *UNESCO Courier* 1:4 (May 1948): 7.

124. Ibid.

125. *Humanisme et éducation en Orient et en Occident* [Humanism and education in the East and the West] (Harlaam, Netherlands: Joh. Enschede & Zonen, 1953).

126. Ibid., 8. Also see UNESCO, "Discussion on the Cultural and Philosophical Relations between East and West," UNESCO/CUA/43, Paris, April 28, 1952, 2. This encounter is interesting as one of the main discussions at the meeting in New Delhi concerned the importance of promoting the study of science. In 1957, UNESCO and the Ford Foundation sponsored the founding of the Middle East Technical University (METU) in Ankara. On the Ford Foundation's contribution of the founding of METU, see Timothy Mitchell, "The Middle East in the Past and Future of Social Science," in *The Politics of Knowledge: Area Studies and the Disciplines*, David L. Szanton, ed. (Berkeley: University of California Press, 2004), 25–26n12.

127. UNESCO, "Discussion on the Cultural and Philosophical Relations between East and West," 3.

128. Ibid., 5.

129. Ibid., 6. Accordingly, the report reads, "in particular, Philosophy should be imparted in lectures and classes (preferably not for examination) to all students of Science. The Philosopher could learn from the Scientist, but could also show the Scientist the limits of the scientific field."

130. John Traill Christie, "L'éducation humaniste en Occident" [Humanist education in the West], in *Humanisme et éducation en Orient et en Occident*, 68–78.

131. Ibid., 68–69.

132. Ibid., 5.

133. UNESCO, "Mexico City Declaration on Cultural Policies, 1982."

134. Ibid.

135. See Hilmi Ziya Ülken's own account of the conference, *Şark ve Garp: Kültür Münasebetleri ve İnsan Telakkisi Hakkında Hindistan'da, Yeni Delhi'de Toplanan Konferans Müzakereleri (12–20 Aralık 1951)* [East and West: Proceedings of the conference on cultural connections and considerations of the human in New Delhi, India (December 12–20, 1951)] (Istanbul: Milli Eğitim Basımevi, 1953), 20–21.

136. UNESCO, "Discussion on the Cultural and Philosophical Relations between East and West," 6.

137. Ibid.

138. See for example, *Proceedings of Second International History Congress June 8–10, 1995: Tarih Eğitimi ve Tarihte "Öteki" Sorunu* [History education and the problem of the "other" in history] (Istanbul: Tarih Vakfı Yurt Yayınları, 1998). Also see Betül Çotuksöken, Ayşe Erzan, and Orhan Silier, eds., *Ders Kitaplarında İnsan Hakları Tarama Sonuçları* [Human rights in school textbooks] (Istanbul: Tarih Vakfı Yayınları, 2003). These are among the publications of the History Foundation, including proceedings of the conferences the foundation had organized on the subject. The family-history-writing competition can be considered within this context.

139. See Ülken, *Şark ve Garp*, 18–19.

140. Hilmi Ziya Ülken, *İnsani Vatanperverlik* [Humanist patriotism] (Istanbul: Remzi Kitaphanesi, 1933). He later revised this work and published it in French, *Humanisme des cultures: contribution à la recherche d'un humanisme intégral* [The humanism of cultures: A contribution to the research of an integrated humanism] (Ankara: Ankara Üniversitesi İlahiyat Fakültesi Yayınları, 1967).

141. In addition Ülken, other writers had already discussed the relationship between patriotism and culture via humanism. At the 1935 International Congress of Writers in Paris this relationship was one of the main topics. *Pour la défense de la culture: les textes du Congrès international des écrivains*, Paris, juin 1935 [For the defense of culture: Proceedings of the International Congress of Writers], prepared by Sandra Teroni and Wolfgang Klein (Dijon: Éditions universitaires de Dijon, 2005). I am grateful to Kader Konuk for bringing this congress to my attention.

142. As part of this humanist endeavor, he would also later publish a piece on humanism and the Turkish epic himself. See Hilmi Ziya Ülken, "Humanisme et littérature épique en Turquie" [Humanism and epic literature in Turkey], *Orientalia Suecana* 7 (1958): 122–33.

143. Ülken, *Şark ve Garp*, 18.

144. "Major Discussion Proposed for Florence Conference: UNESCO's Contribution to United Nations Peace Mission," *UNESCO Courier* 3:4 (May 1, 1950): 5 (emphasis mine).

145. "Italy, Host to Unesco's Conference, Welcomes M. Torres Bodet," *UNESCO Courier* 3:4 (May 1, 1950): 5.

146. See Konuk, *East-West Mimesis*.

147. Malkki, "National Geographic."

Part III

An earlier version of the first essay was published as "Palimpsests of Multiculturalism and Museumization of Culture: Greco-Turkish Compulsory Religious Minority Exchange Museum as an Istanbul 2010 European Capital of Culture Project," *Comparative Studies of South Asia, Africa, and the Middle East* 35:2 (2015): 324–45.

1. Gülen Göktürk and Onur Yıldırım have noted that there were also Greek Protestants (converts) who left for Greece. See their conference paper "The Exchange of the Unexchangeables: The Protestant Greeks of Asia Minor from Converstion to Transfer," Association for the Study of Nationalities, annual meeting, 2014. According to Göktürk, this was a mistake because the Greek Protestants didn't know they were not subject to the exchange. I would like to thank Göktürk for clarifying this point.

2. A similar approach to diversity is delineated in the cultural policy plans for 2007–2013 in Devlet Planlama Müsteşarlığı [State Planning Organization], *Kültür Özel İhtisas Raporu (2007–2013)* [Culture special expert report, 2007–2013]. This policy targeted not only Istanbul, but all of Turkey.

3. In 2005, the Turkish government co-sponsored an Alliance of Civilizations initiative with Spain; the initiative was institutionalized by the United Nations and promoted as a remedy for the "clash of civilizations" in the aftermath of 9/11. Numerous projects and two national action plans were launched in Turkey to promote dialogue and tolerance among "civilizations" as part of this initiative. One of the projects outlined in the first national action plan was the Istanbul 2010 European Capital of Culture celebration. "Türkiye Cumhuriyeti Medeniyetler İttifakı Ulusal Planı," [Alliance of civilizations national plan of the Republic of Turkey], appendix to "Genelge: Başbakanlıktan Konu: Medeniyetler İttifakı Ulusal Planı" [Memorandum: From the prime minister's office; subject: National (action) plan on the alliance of civilizations], *Resmi Gazete* [Official Gazette], April 12, 2008, 10 and 11.

4. For more on the subject, see the dissertation of anthropologist Serra Hakyemez, "Lives and Times of Militancy: Terrorism Trials, State Violence and Kurdish Political Prisoners in post-1980 Turkey" (Ph.D. diss., Johns Hopkins University, 2016).

5. Another strain of neo-Ottomanism, which falls outside the scope of this essay, is the nationalist one. Tanıl Bora, one of Turkey's leading publishers and intellectuals, notes how different nationalisms actually borrow from one another. Likewise, neo-Ottomanism borrows from Kemalist nationalism. See Bora, "Nationalist Discourses in Turkey," *South Atlantic Quarterly* 102:2–3 (Spring/Summer 2003): 433–51. For a different perspective, see Yılmaz Çolak, "Ottomanism vs. Kemalism: Collective Memory and Cultural Pluralism in the 1990s Turkey," *Middle Eastern Studies* 42:4 (July 2006): 587–602. For a different discussion of the notion of pluralism and history, see Kabir Tambar's *The Reckoning of Pluralism: Political Belonging and the Demands of History in Turkey* (Stanford, CA: Stanford University Press, 2014). Also see Jeremy Walton's "Practices of Neo-Ottomanism: Making Space and Place Virtuous in Istanbul," in *Orienting Istanbul: Cultural Capital of Europe?*, Deniz Göktürk, İpek Türeli, and Levent Soysal, eds. (London: Routledge, 2010), 88–103.

6. This was also my own assumption before I discovered literature published by the AER and the AWR. Yet another assumption shared by scholars was that the exchangees were invisible upon their arrival in Turkey in the 1920s. Historian Aytek Soner

Alpan's work shows that some were politically active. See Alpan, "But the Memory Remains: History, Memory and the 1923 Greco-Turkish Population Exchange," *Historical Review* 9 (2012): 199–232.

7. Şekib Avdagiç, chairman of the executive board of the Istanbul 2010 European Capital of Cultural Agency, quoted in *Avrupa Kültür Başkenti Mübadele Müzesi/ European Capital of Culture Population Exchange Museum* (Istanbul: Lozan Mübaddileri Vakfı, 2011), 7.

8. Lozan Mübadilleri Vakfı, interview with the author, July 2005.

9. Penelope Papailias, *Genres of Recollection: Archival Poetics in Modern Greece* (New York: Palgrave Macmillan, 2005), 93–138.

10. Avdagiç, *Avrupa Kültür Başkenti Mübadele Müzesi*, 8. The punctuation and wording are as printed in the original English translation of the museum's catalog.

11. See *T.B.M.M. Tutanak Dergisi* [Turkish parliamentary records], 78th Assembly (May 7, 1953): 104–12.

12. Umut Özkırımı and Spyros Sofos, *Tormented by History: Nationalism in Greece and Turkey* (London: Hurst, 2008).

13. "İskan Kanunu" [Settlement law], *Resmi Gazete*, June 21, 1934, Article 2510, issue 2733.

14. For more on the foundation of the Emigrants' Foundation, see Aslı Iğsız, "Palimpsests of Multiculturalism and Museumization of Culture: Greco-Turkish Population Exchange Museum as an Istanbul 2010 European Capital of Culture Project," *Comparative Studies of South Asia, Africa, and the Middle East* 35:2 (2015): 324–45.

15. Based on my interviews with numerous individuals during my fieldwork, it is my sense that because Greece and Turkey are counterpart states, engaging past ruptures through Greek and Turkish/Ottoman contexts was easier than addressing issues related to Kurds, especially in the 1990s.

16. Aslı Iğsız, "Polyphony and Geographic Kinship in Anatolia: Framing the Turkish-Greek Population Exchange," in *The Politics of Public Memory in Turkey*, Esra Özyürek, ed. (Syracuse, NY: Syracuse University Press, 2007), 162–90; and Aslı Iğsız, "Documenting the Past and Publicizing Personal Stories: Sensescapes and the 1923 Greco-Turkish Population Exchange in Contemporary Turkey," *Journal of Modern Greek Studies* 26 (2008): 451–87.

17. Jean Baudrillard, *The System of Objects* (New York: Verso, 2000), 74–75.

18. Cem Kara, mayor of Çatalca Municipality, *Avrupa Kültür Başkenti Mübadele Müzesi*, 10. The museum also has a corner dedicated to Atatürk.

19. Devlet Planlama Müsteşarlığı, *Kültür Özel İhtisas Raporu*, 22.

20. Ibid., 10, 15, 18–20. The State Planning Organization's cultural policy report includes an appendix with a Turkish translation of the UNESCO Universal Declaration on Cultural Diversity and of the action plan prepared by UNESCO, 31–36.

21. Rodney Harrison, *Heritage: Critical Approaches* (London: Routledge, 2013), 140–65.

22. UNESCO Universal Declaration on Cultural Diversity, November 2, 2001, http://www.unesco.org.

23. *The Knowledge-Based Economy* (Paris: Organisation for Economic Co-operation and Development, 1996).

24. Ibid., 9.

25. UNESCO Universal Declaration on Cultural Diversity (emphasis mine).

26. Banu Karaca, "Europeanisation from the Margins? Istanbul Cultural Capital Initiative and the Formation of European Cultural Policies," in *The Cultural Politics of Europe: European Capitals of Culture and European Union since the 1980s*, Kiran Klaus Patel, ed., (London: Routledge, 2013), 168; "Declarations and Reservations," *Convention on the Protection and Promotion of Cultural Diversity and Expressions 2005*, http://portal.unesco.org/en/ev.php-URL_ID=31038&URL_DO=DO_TOPIC&URL_SECTION=201.html. The list of the signatory states can be found on the UNESCO website. Turkey is not listed anywhere, including among those that expressed reservations.

27. UNESCO, *Basic Texts of the 2005 Convention on the Protection and Promotion of Cultural Diversity and Expressions* (Paris: UNESCO, 2011), 3.

28. Ibid., 3–5.

29. Ibid., 3.

30. Aslı Iğsız, "From Alliance of Civilizations to Branding the Nation: Turkish Studies, Image Wars, and Politics of Comparison in an Age of Neoliberalism," *Turkish Studies* (December 2014): 1–16.

31. Laleh Khalili, *Time in the Shadows: Confinement in Counterinsurgencies* (Stanford, CA: Stanford University Press, 2013).

32. For one of the earliest sobering critiques on the subject, see Bilgin Ayata, "Tolerance as a European Norm or an Ottoman Practice? An Analysis of Turkish Public Debates on the (Re)Opening of an Armenian Church in the Context of Turkey's EU Candidacy and Neo-Ottoman Revival," KFG Working Paper Series 41 (Berlin, 2012).

33. Kemalism refers to the national ideology of Mustafa Kemal Atatürk.

34. Iğsız, "From Alliance of Civilizations to Branding the Nation," 4.

35. Ibid.

36. "Medeniyetler İttifakı Ulusal Planı" [Alliance of civilizations national plan], *Resmi Gazete*, April 12, 2008, 10.

37. Ibid., 11.

38. According to the report, the entire budget allocated to Istanbul 2010 was 577,300,00 Turkish liras (288,900,000 euros), which drastically exceeded the sum initially expected. Among the reasons other potential sponsors were reluctant to donate money included the global economic situation and the issues of management within the agency, but also the "dominance of the government amongst the funders." J. Rampton et al., *Ex-Post Evaluation of 2010 European Capitals of Culture* (London: Ecorys, 2011), 70–71.

39. Ibid., 76.

40. Claude Frisoni et al., *Report of the Selection Meeting for the European Capitals of Culture 2010* (Brussels: Selection Panel for the ECoC 2010, 2006), 2. Even though the selection criteria did not explicitly mention "multiculturalism" but rather "diversity," the ex-post evaluation report on Istanbul 2010 gives us important clues on the commission's approach to diversity as multiculturalism: all cities (Pécs, Hungary; Essen, Germany; Istanbul, Turkey) selected for the year 2010 highlighted their multicultural aspects, and the evaluation report noted each city's display of and engagement with multiculturalism. Rampton et al., *Ex-Post Evaluation*, 23–95.

41. Commission of the European Communities, *Communication from the Commission to the European Parliament, the Council, the European Economic and Social Committee and the Committee of the Regions on a European Agenda for Culture in a Globalizing World* (Brussels: Commission of the European Communities, 2007).

42. European Commission, "Intercultural Cities" (Policy Development), http://ec.europa.eu.

43. Ibid.

44. On the differences between theory and practice of diversity within the context of the European Union, see Gideon Calder and Emanuela Ceva, eds., *Diversity in Europe: Dilemmas of Differential Treatment in Theory and Practice* (London: Routledge, 2011). Although the volume engages a wide range of differential treatments in theory and practice, it surprisingly eclipses cultural representation dynamics in relation to social and economic issues.

45. Following the success of the 1985 Athens European City of Culture, "a 1999 Decision of the Parliament and of the Council transformed the concept into the European Capital of Culture ... and created a more predictable, consistent and transparent rotational system for the designation of the title.... The 1999 Decision also maintained the possibility for non-Member States to nominate candidates for the ECoC title. It was amended in 2005 in order to integrate the ten Member States that acceded to the EU in 2004." It was in the same spirit that the Istanbul application dossier was processed, even though Turkey was not an EU member. Rampton et al., *European Capitals of Culture*, 2–20. See also, European Commission, *European Capitals of Culture: The Road to Success 1985–2010* (Brussels: European Commission, 2009).

46. Patel, "Introduction," in *The Cultural Politics of Europe: European Capitals of Culture and the European Union since the 1980s*, Kiran Klaus Patel, ed. (London: Routledge, 2013), 2–3.

47. Ibid., 2–4.

48. Ibid., 5–11.

49. Ibid., 4–5.

50. Describing the Roma as the "biggest minority in Europe" suggests that European identity is a project that should seek to mold different national identities into an integrated notion of Europeanness, and that those who fall outside the category of

"European" are minorities. Even though the Roma have been part of Europe for centuries, the fact that they are not included in the pan-European project as "European" but as a "minority" is a telling identificatory paradigm that raises questions about what informs the concepts of diversity and "integration" in European Union cultural policies. See European Commission, "Intercultural Dialogue and Roma Culture" (Policy Development), http://ec.europa.eu

51. See Karaca, "Europeanisation from the Margins?," 168. See also Öykü Potuoğlu-Cook, "Summer of Shame: Displaced Roma in Istanbul, Turkey," *Anthropology News* 52:3 (2011): 15.

52. Karaca, "Europeanisation from the Margins?," 168.

53. Ibid., 157–76.

54. See Commission of the European Communities, *European Agenda for Culture in a Globalizing World*; Rampton et al., *Ex-Post Evaluation*; and Frisoni et al., *Report of the Selection Meeting*.

55. Karaca, "Europeanisation from the Margins?," 167.

56. Ibid. Also, Ottoman historian Leslie Peirce cautions that such anachronistic approaches to Ottoman demography as "multiethnic" or "multi-religious" imply the "endorsement of the ultimate goal of human equality in difference." Especially in the early modern period, this was "not a view the Ottomans would have endorsed." She prefers "polyglottism" instead to denote multiple languages spoken both literally and metaphorically (as mutual understanding and common reference points) among groups that shared more than belonging to a religious community. See Peirce, "Polyglottism in the Ottoman Empire: A Reconsideration," *Braudel Revisited: The Mediterranean World, 1600–1800*, Gabriel Piterberg, Teofilo F. Ruiz, and Geoffrey Symcox, eds. (Toronto: University of Toronto Press, 2010), 76–98. Similarly, Christine Philliou also calls attention to other forms of difference beyond religious ones in the Ottoman Empire. See Philliou, "The Millet System and Its Discontents," paper presented at the Program in Hellenic Studies Seminar Series, Columbia University, October 2006.

57. For an analysis of how the performative and dance are intertwined with choreographing multiculturalism in the context of the Istanbul 2010 European Capital of Culture project, see Öykü Potuoğlu-Cook, "Uneasy Vernacular: Choreographing Multiculturalism and Dancing Difference Away in Globalised Turkey," *Anthropological Notebooks* 16:3 (2010): 93–105. In "Tolerance as a European Norm or an Ottoman Practice?," which focuses on the "restoration" project of the Armenian church Sourp Khatch/Akhtamar in 2007, explores how the restoration site became a venue to reinvent Turkish national identity through narratives of Ottoman tolerance. Ayata, "Tolerance as a European Norm or an Ottoman Practice?"

58. Yıldırım Türker, "Sulukule'den Gelen Gürültü" [Noise coming from Sulukule], *Radikal*, November 12, 2007.

59. From my field notes, May–June 2001.

60. For example, Viktor Levi—advertised as a Greek winehouse—was a popular locale in Istanbul in the early 2000s. While the walls displayed framed newspaper clips and other texts narrating that Levi was a Jewish citizen residing in Istanbul who used to own a tavern, his background was completely eclipsed and turned into a brand name for a "Greekified" winehouse by the owners, who also owned a Greek winehouse almost next door, which was also named after a minority citizen of Istanbul, Pano Papadopoulos. In fact, this approach speaks very much to the museumization of culture, with the selective display of backgrounds (at times to the extent of that identifications are inaccurate) for purposes of consumption.

61. Elizabeth Povinelli, "State of Shame: Australian Multiculturalism and the Crisis of Indigenous Citizenship," *Critical Inquiry* 24:2 (1998): 582.

62. Ibid.

63. Ibid.

64. See Elizabeth Povinelli, *Economies of Abandonment: Social Belonging and Endurance in Late Liberalism* (Durham, NC: Duke University Press, 2011).

65. Potuoğlu-Cook, "Uneasy Vernacular," 101.

66. See Zeynep Gönen and Deniz Yonucu, "Legitimizing Violence and Segregation: Neoliberal Discourses on Crime and Criminalization of the Urban Poor Populations in Turkey," in *Lumpencity: Discourses of Marginality/Marginalizing Discourses*, Alan Bourke, Tia Dafnos, and Markus Kip, eds. (Ottawa: Red Quill Books, 2011), 75–98.

67. Istanbul 2010 ECOC Agency, *Application File: City of the Four Elements* (Istanbul: Istanbul 2010 ECOC Agency, 2004), 49. I thank Connor Mendenhall for making this text available to me.

68. Wendy Brown, *Regulating Aversion: Tolerance in the Age of Identity and Empire* (Princeton, NJ: Princeton University Press, 2006).

69. "Üç Dilden Açılım Her Telden Açılış" [Opening out in three languages, a versatile opening] *T24*, January 1, 2010, http://t24.com.tr/haber/3-dilden-acilim-her-tel den-acilis,66115.

70. Istanbul 2010 ECOC Agency, *Application File*, 70–71.

71. Ann Stoler, "The Rot Remains: From Ruins to Ruination," in *Imperial Debris: On Ruins and Ruination* (Durham, NC: Duke University Press, 2013).

72. See İsmet Akça, "Hegemonic Projects in Post-1980 Turkey and the Changing Forms of Authoritarianism," and Güven Gürkan Öztan, "The Struggle for Hegemony between Turkish Nationalisms in the Neoliberal Era," both in *Turkey Reframed: Constituting Neoliberal Hegemony*, İsmet Akça, Ahmet Bekmen, and Barış Alp Özden, eds. (London: Pluto, 2014), 13–46, 75–91.

73. Nancy Reynolds, "Interview with Aron Rodrigue: Difference and Tolerance in the Ottoman Empire," *SEHR* 5:1 (1996), http://web.stanford.edu/group/SHR/5-1/text/ rodrigue.html.

74. I would like to thank Ilker Hepkaner for his comments that helped clarify this point.

75. Yılmaz Çolak points out this phenomenon in his article "Ottomanism vs. Kemalism."

76. Brown, *Regulating Aversion*.

77. Ibid., 15.

78. Istanbul 2010 ECOC Agency, *Application File*, 23.

79. Reynolds, "Interview with Aron Rodrigue."

80. Ibid.

81. As Reynolds also points out during her interview with Aron Rodrigue, the "mosaic" model was posited in the 1950s by H. A. R. Gibb and Harold Bowen in *Islamic Society and the West: A Study of the Impact of Western Civilization on Moslem Culture in the Near East* (London: Oxford University Press, 1951).

82. For a critique of the mosaic approach to diversity in Turkey, see, e.g., Ayşe Gül Altınay, "Ebru: Reflections on Water," *Ebru: Reflections of Cultural Diversity in Turkey*, Ayşe Gül Altınay, ed. (Istanbul: Metis, 2007), 19–25.

83. On former president Gül's statements about Assyrians, see Muzaffeer İris, "Süryaniler Lozan'ın Neresinde?" [Where are the Assyrians situated in terms of Lausanne?], *Radikal*, March 28, 2012. Also see Uygar Gültekin, "Diyanet Wins the Church Lottery from Mardin," *Agos*, June 23, 2017.

84. See "Full List of Registered Heritage," *Memory of the World*, UNESCO, http://www.unesco.org/new/en/communication-and-information/memory-of-the-world/register/full-list-of-registered-heritage.

85. Rampton et al., *Ex-post Evaluation*, 80–81.

86. Ibid.

87. Istanbul 2010 ECOC Agency, *Application File*, 95.

88. See Bilgin Ayata and Deniz Yükseker, "A Belated Awakening: National and International Responses to the Internal Displacement of Kurds in Turkey," *New Perspectives on Turkey* 32 (Spring 2005): 5–42.

89. On the urban regulation of Alevis, Kurds, and dissidents, see Deniz Yonucu, "The Absent Present Law: An Ethnographic Study of Legal Violence," *Social & Legal Studies* 20:10 (2017): 1–18.

90. Istanbul 2010 ECOC Agency, *Application File*, 36.

91. Ibid., 17.

92. Ibid. The *millet* system defined Britain, France, and Russia as protectors of the three groups—Armenians, Greek Orthodox Christians, and Jews—identified as minorities. This phenomenon has been preserved in anachronistically attributing to different groups a status as minorities. For more, see, for example, Benjamin Braude, "Foundation Myths of the *Millet* System," in *Christians and Jews in the Ottoman Empire: The*

Functioning of a Plural Society, Benjamin Braude and Bernard Lewis, eds. (Teaneck, NJ: Holmes & Meier, 1982), 69–88.

93. Reynolds, "Interview with Aron Rodrigue"; Philliou, "The Millet System and Its Discontents"; Peirce, "Polyglottism in the Ottoman Empire."

94. On Sunni Islam as a melting pot, see Gökhan Çetinsaya, "Rethinking Nationalism and Islam: Some Preliminary Notes on the Roots of 'Turkish-Islamic Synthesis' in Modern Turkish Thought," *Muslim World* 3–4:89 (July–October 1999): 350–76. Also see Çolak, "Ottomanism vs. Kemalism."

95. Büşra Ersanlı, *İktidar ve Tarih: Türkiye'de Resmi Tarih Tezinin Oluşumu* [Power and history: The development of the official history thesis in Turkey] (Istanbul: İletişim: 2003).

96. *Birinci Türk Tarih Kongresi* [First Turkish history congress] (Ankara: T.C. Maarif Vekaleti, 1932).

97. Ayhan Aktar, "Homogenizing the Nation, Turkifying the Economy," in *Crossing the Aegean: An Appraisal of the 1923 Compulsory Population Exchange Between Greece and Turkey*, Renée Hirschon, ed. (New York: Berghahn Books, 2004), 79–96; Ayhan Aktar, *Varlık Vergisi ve Türkleştirme Politikaları* [The capital tax law and policies of Turkification] (Istanbul: İletişim, 2000).

98. This cultural policy is outlined in Devlet Planlama Teşkilatı [State Planning Organization], *Milli Kültür Özel Ihtisas Raporu* [National culture special expert report] (Ankara: Devlet Planlama Teşkilatı, 1983).

99. *12 September in Turkey: Before and After*, prepared by the National Security Council (Ankara: Ongun Kardeşler, 1982).

100. Devlet Planlama Teşkilatı, *Milli Kültür Özel Ihtisas Raporu.*

101. "Cumhurbaşkanlarımız: Turgut Özal," [Our presidents: Turgut Özal], *Türkiye Cumhuriyeti Cumhurbaşkanlığı* [Presidency of the Republic of Turkey], http://tccb.gov.tr/cumhurbaskanlarimiz/.

102. Devlet Planlama Teşkilatı, *Milli Kültür Özel Ihtisas Raporu*, xxii.

103. One of figures active in both UNESCO and in the drafting of the 1983 *National Cultural Policy Report* was Professor Ercüment Kuran. In 1982, he attended UNESCO's World Conference on Cultural Policies in Mexico City where these ideas about development and cultural policy were reiterated.

104. *Cultural Policy: A Preliminary Study*, Studies and Documents on Cultural Policies 1 (Paris: UNESCO, 1969).

105. Ibid., 11.

106. *World Development Report 1980* (Washington DC: World Bank, 1980); *World Development Report 1981* (Washington DC: World Bank, 1981); *World Development Report 1982* (Oxford: Oxford University Press published for the World Bank, 1982); *World Development Report 1983* (Oxford: Oxford University Press published for the World Bank, 1983).

107. Devlet Planlama Teşkilatı, *Milli Kültür Özel Ihtisas Raporu*, xxii.
108. *12 September in Turkey*, 191.
109. Ibid., 108, 325–26, 329.
110. Ibid., 108.
111. Ibid., 339 (emphasis mine).
112. Ibid., 344.
113. Ibid., 326.
114. Ibid., 320–21.
115. Ibid., 56–58.
116. *Millet Meclisi Tutanak Dergisi* [Journal of Records of the National Assembly] 2 (December 28, 1978): 28.
117. Aziz Tunç, *Maraş Kıyımı: Tarihsel Arka Planı ve Anatomisi* [The Maraş massacre: Its historical background and anatomy] (Istanbul: Belge, 2011).
118. *TBMM Tutanak Dergisi* [Journal of Records of the Turkish Parliament] 14:92 (March 3, 1994): 397–400. Ironically, this was the day Kurdish deputy Leyla Zana's immunity from legal investigation as a deputy was revoked, and on that day Şendiller gave a talk on the limits of human rights.
119. I thank ethnomusicologist Ozan Aksoy for his comments on the subject.
120. "Maraş Sanığı Şendiller'e Alevi Çalıştayı Daveti!" [Invitation of Maraş suspect Şendiller to the Alevi workshop!], *Radikal*, December 12, 2009.
121. İsmail Saymaz, "Maraş Katliamı, Özel Hayatmış" [The Maraş massacre, private life], *Radikal*, January 8, 2015.
122. *Milli Güvenlik Konseyi Tutanak Dergisi* [Journal of Records of the National Security Council] 1:4 (September 27, 1980): 82–83.
123. I translate *bünye* as "natural disposition" here. *Bünye* has a bodily connotation in Turkish and implies the physique as well as the structure and functioning of the body.
124. *Milli Güvenlik Konseyi Tutanak Dergisi*, September 27 1980, 83.
125. "Yükseköğretim Kanunu" [Law on Higher education], *Resmi Gazete* 21:3 (November 6, 1981), order 5. The law can also be accessed via the Higher Education Council's website: http://www.yok.gov.tr.
126. "Higher Education Law," *Laws Turkey*, http://www.lawsturkey.com/law/the-law-of-higher-education-2547.
127. *12 September in Turkey*, 281.
128. Eduardo Matos-Martín, "Thinking Biopolitics: Reflections on Franco's Dictatorship through Contemporary Fiction and Film" (Ph.D. diss., University of Michigan, 2010).
129. *12 September in Turkey*, 7, 39, 44, 76, 160.
130. Ibid., 160.
131. Serra Hakyemez, "Margins of the Archive: Torture, Heroism, and the Ordinary in Prison No. 5, Turkey," *Anthropological Quarterly* 90:1 (2017): 107–38. On the legal re-

quirement for compulsory education in "religious culture and morals," see "1982 Türkiye Cumhuriyeti Anayasasının İlk ve Son Hali" [First and final versions of the 1982 Constitution of the Republic of Turkey], Article 24, Adalet Bakanlığı [Ministry of Justice], http://www.adalet.gov.tr.

132. No doubt to ensure gatekeeping, the military also reactivated Penal Code Articles 141 and 142. Adopted from the Italian Penal Code in Mussolini's fascist Italy in 1936, these articles targeted mostly class-based struggles. Cangül Örnek, "Türk Ceza Kanununun 141 ve 142. Maddelerine İlişkin Tartışmalarda Devlet ve Sınıflar" [State and class in debates about the Turkish Penal Code Articles 141 and 142], *Ankara Üniversitesi SBF Dergisi* [Journal of the Faculty of Political Science, Ankara University] 69:1 (2014): 109–39. According to Örnek, the 1949 and 1951 amendments to the law established that violence was necessary to change a system. Therefore, if any group, organization, or party had "changing the system" articulated as their goal, they could be tried for violence against the state. The Menderes government's 1951 amendment made defendants charged under these articles of the penal code subject to capital punishment. The 1951 amendment additionally banned racist organizations, in the name of fighting fascism. Article 163, until it was abolished by Turgut Özal in 1991—together with 141 and 142—criminalized using religion as an organizing principle of the legal, economic, and social system of the state. In practice, all these articles were meant to discipline and punish freedom of assembly and expression. In order to ensure their implementation, the military officially activated State Security Courts pursuant to Article 143 of the 1982 constitution.

133. *Halk Oylaması Sonuçları: 2007, 1988, 1987, 1982, 1961* [Results of the referendums: 2007, 1988, 1987, 1982, 1961], Türkiye İstatistik Kurumu (TÜİK) (Ankara: Türkiye İstatistik Kurumu Matbaası, May 2008), 2.

134. Devlet Planlama Teşkilatı, *Milli Kültür Özel Ihtisas Raporu*, 1–26.

135. Bozkurt Güvenç, Gencay Şaylan, İlhan Tekeli, and Şerafettin Turan, *Türk-İslam Sentezi* [The Turkish-Islamic synthesis] (Istanbul: Sarmal Yayınevı, 1991), 37–48, argue that the Turkish-Islamic synthesis is a doctrine originally developed in 1973 by Kafesoğlu in the Aydınlar Ocağı (Organization of Intellectuals, or as historian Erik Jan Zürcher calls them, Hearths of the Enlightened). According to Zürcher, the main goal of this organization was "to break the monopoly of left-wing intellectuals on the social, political and cultural debate in Turkey." *Turkey: A Modern History*, 3rd ed. (London: I.B. Tauris, 2005), 288.

136. Güvenç et al., *Türk-İslam Sentezi*, 171. Here the authors refer to Safa's earlier writings, from the 1930s.

137. Peyami Safa, "İnsanın yeni mânası" [The new meaning of the human], in *Doğu-Batı Sentezi* [East-West synthesis] (Istanbul: Çeltüt Matbaası, 1963), 36–41.

138. İbrahim Kafesoğlu, *Türk-İslam Sentezi* [The Turkish-Islamic ayntheiss] (Istanbul: Aydınlar Ocağı, 1983).

139. Devlet Planlama Teşkilatı, *Milli Kültür Özel İhtisas Raporu*, 157–58.

140. Ibid., 486–91. The history subcommittee consisted of Bahaeddin Ögel (chair), Ercümen Kuran (associate chair), Abdülhalûk Çay (rapporteur), and members Altan Köymen, Bayram Kodaman, Hayri Bolay, Rıfat Önsoy, Refet Yinanç, Reşat Genç, Bahaettin Yediyıldız, Ahmet Yaşar Ocak, Bilal Şimşir, Musa Gürgün, and three members who did not attend the meetings (Halil Cin, Mustafa Erkal, and Aydın Taneri).

141. Devlet Planlama Teşkilatı, *Milli Kültür Özel İhtisas Raporu*, 490–91.

142. Aslı Gür, "Political Excavations of the Anatolian Past: Nationalism and Archaeology in Turkey," in *Controlling the Past, Owning the Future: The Political Uses of Archaeology in the Middle East*, Ran Boytner, Lynn Swartz Dodd, and Bradley J. Parker, eds. (Tucson: University of Arizona Press, 2010), 68–89.

143. Devlet Planlama Teşkilatı, *Milli Kültür Özel İhtisas Raporu*, 492.

144. Ibid., 494–95.

145. Ibid., 495–97.

146. "Atatürk Kültür, Dil ve Tarih Yüksek Kurumu Kanunu" [Law for the High Council of Atatürk Culture, Language and History], Article 2876, date of acceptance August 11, 1983, *Resmi Gazete*, issue 18138 (August 17, 1983): 1–31.

147. *Atatürk Kültür, Dil ve Tarih Yüksek Kurumu*, http://www.ayk.gov.tr/s9-hak kmzda/misyon-ve-vizyon/.

148. Devlet Planlama Teşkilatı, *Milli Kültür Özel İhtisas Raporu*, 129.

149. Ibid., 498–99.

150. This subcommittee was chaired by Erol Güngör, the associate director was Mustafa Erkal, and the rapporteur was Mustafa Çalık. The subcommittee members included Şerif Mardin, Mehmet Eröz, Amiran Kurtkan Bilgiseven, Nihat Nirun, Turan Yazgan, and Enis Öksüz. Devlet Planlama Teşkilatı, *Milli Kültür Özel İhtisas Raporu*, 501.

151. During the time the AKP has been in office, the right of exemption of the children of Alevis or atheist families who do not wish to subject their children to Sunni Islam has been systematically denied. As a result, on February 2, 2011, fourteen citizens of Turkey filed a lawsuit with the European Court of Human Rights charging the Turkish state with discrimination against Alevis in the education system. In a press release issued by the Registrar of the Court on September 16, 2014, the court made public its unanimous decision that Turkey was guilty of violating the right to education. "Turkey Must Reform Religious Education in Schools to Ensure Respect for Parents' Convictions," European Court of Human Rights, press release issued by the Registrar of the Court, ECHR 257 (2014), September 16, 2014.

After the decision of the European Human Rights Court, former prime minister Ahmet Davutoğlu discussed the importance of "religious culture" and emphasized the necessity to centralize and disseminate the "correct version" of religion so that "discrepant" interpretations cannot find purchase. Yet, the problem here is that the course in question is not a history of religions and religious cultures, but the Sunni interpretation of religion. "Davutoğlu: Bir Ateistin Dahi Din Kültürü Bilgisi Sahibi Olması Zarurettir" [Davutoğlu: "It is imperative for even an atheist to have knowledge of religious culture"], *T24*, September 17, 2014, http://t24.com.tr/haber/davutoglu-bir-ateistin-dahi-din-kulturu-bilgisi-sahibi-olmasi-zarurettir,270997.

152. Devlet Planlama Teşkilatı, *Milli Kültür Özel Ihtisas Raporu*, 504.

153. Ibid., 511.

154. Ibid., 516.

155. Ibid.

156. Ibid., 522–25.

157. Ibid., 549–50.

158. Ibid., 542–44.

159. Ibid., 544. Mehmet Kaplan was a professor of Turkish literature and a member of the Special Committee of Experts that prepared the 1983 cultural policy report. In his book *Büyük Türkiye Rüyası* [Dream of a grand Turkey] he argues that in literature, many types emerge and constitute a model for society. According to him, literature has the power to generate desirable types, among which he counts the *gazi* (warrior) who protects borders and the revolutionary. The "modern *veli* type"—a religious erudite and mystic open to the world and attentive to social matters—is where Turkey's future lies, according to Kaplan. Mehmet Kaplan, *Büyük Türkiye Rüyası* (Istanbul: Dergah, 1962, 1992), 36–38. In many ways, both the 1983 *National Cultural Policy Report* and the "modern *veli* type" are reminiscent of the activities, self-promoted image, and profile of the Fethullah Gülen movement (see below).

160. Devlet Planlama Teşkilatı, *Milli Kültür Özel Ihtisas Raporu*, 572.

161. Ibid., 113–22.

162. *TBMM Zabıt Ceridesi* [Turkish parliamentary records], period 10, 5:1 (February 12, 1955): 433.

163. Z. F. Fındıkoğlu, "Contribution au problème de l'installation des émigrés musulmans de la Grèce en Turquie" (A contribution to the problem of settling Muslim emigrants from Greece in Turkey), *Integration* 8:5 (1961).

164. Şemsi Belli, *Çocukluğundan Liderliğine Kadar Bülent Ecevit: Belgesel İnceleme* [Bülent Ecevit from his childhood to his leadership: A documentary analysis] (Istanbul: Ak Kitab, 1965), 63–68.

165. *Millet Meclisi Tutanak Dergisi* 6:97 (June 18, 1974): 213, 220–25.

166. Loïc Wacquant, *Punishing the Poor: The Neoliberal Government of Social Insecurity* (Durham, NC, Duke University Press, 2009). As Shohat and Stam demonstrated in *Race in Translation*, however, Wacquant appeared to be comfortable with addressing race in the United States but unwilling to engage it within the context of France.

167. Charles Taylor, "The Politics of Recognition," in *Multiculturalism: Examining the Politics of Recognition*, Amy Guttmann, ed. (Princeton, NJ: Princeton University Press, 1994), 25–74.

168. *World Culture Report 2000: Cultural Diversity, Conflict and Pluralism* (Paris: UNESCO, 2000), 48–57.

169. Eyal Weizman, *The Least of All Possible Evils: Humanitarian Violence from Arendt to Gaza* (London: Verso, 2011).

Conclusion

1. Carl Schmitt, "Appropriation/Distribution/Production: An Attempt to Determine from *Nomos* the Basic Questions of Every Social and Economic Order," in *The Nomos of the Earth in the International Law of the* Jus Publicum Europaeum (New York: Telos Press, 2003), 347.

2. I thank Richard Gunde for his feedback that helped me articulate my point with precision.

3. I thank Eduardo Matos Martín for helping me articulate this point. Also for the politics of infrastructure in Turkey, see Nilay Ozok-Gündoğan, "Social Development as a Governmental Strategy in GAP," *New Perspectives on Turkey* 32 (Spring 2005): 93–110; Begüm Adalet, "It's Not Yours if You Can't Get There: Mobility and State Making in Turkey," *The Funambulist* 17 (May–June 2018): 38–41.

4. Claudio Minca and Rory Rowan, "The Question of Space in Carl Schmitt," *Progress in Human Geography* 39:3 (2015): 268–89.

5. Ibid., 275.

6. Lila Abu Lughod, "Do Muslim Women Really Need Saving? Anthropological Reflections on Cultural Relativism and Its Others," *American Anthropologist* 104:3 (2002): 783–90.

7. Ibid., 784. Also see Ella Shohat, "Area Studies, Gender Studies, and the Cartographies of Knowledge," *Social Text* 20.3 (2002): 67–78.

8. Laleh Khalili, *Time in the Shadows: Confinement in Counterinsurgencies* (Stanford, CA: Stanford University Press, 2013).

9. Aslı Iğsız, "Brand Turkey and the Gezi Protests: Authoritarianism in Flux, Law, and Neoliberalism," in *The Making of a Protest Movement in Turkey: #Occupy Gezi*, Umut Özkırımlı, ed. (London: Palgrave Macmillan, 2014), 25–49.

10. For a remarkable example that shows how this can be achieved, see anthropologist Miriam Ticktin's "Policing and Humanitarianism in France," *American Ethnologist* 33:1 (February 2006): 33–49.

11. Schmitt, "Appropriation/Distribution/Production," 346–47.

12. Minca and Rowan, "The Question of Space in Carl Schmitt."

13. Anders Breivik, "2083: A European Declaration of Independence," London, 2011. Unpublished text.

14. Charlie Brooker, "The News Coverage of the Norway Mass-Killings Was Fact-Free Conjecture," *Guardian*, July 24, 2011.

15. Ingrid Melle, "The Breivik Case and What Psychiatrists Can Learn from It," *World Psychiatry* 12:1 (February 2013): 16–21.

16. Eyal Weizman, *The Least of All Possible Evils: Humanitarian Violence from Arendt to Gaza* (London: Verso, 2011).

17. "Destruction of Kurdish Sites Continues as Turkey Hosts UNESCO," *France 24*, July 20, 2016, http://www.france24.com/en/20160714-turkey-unesco-heritage-sites-damage-kurdish-diyarbakir-sur.

18. Robert Perks and Alistair Thomson, "Critical Developments: Introduction," in *The Oral History Reader*, Perks and Thomson, eds. (London: Routledge, 1998), 1–20.

19. On nonlethal crowd control, see Iğsız, "Brand Turkey and the Gezi Protests." The policy of urbanization has a long history, but for a more recent example, see "Developing Countries Need to Harness Urbanization to Achieve the MDGs: IMF-World Bank Report," World Bank, press release, April 17, 2013; Nick Turse, "Pentagon Video Warns of 'Unavoidable' Dystopian Future for World's Biggest Cities," *Intercept*, October 13, 2016, http://theintercept.com/2016/10/13/pentagon-video-warns-of-unavoidable-dystopian-future-for-worlds-biggest-cities/. I am grateful to Jesse Brent for sharing this video with me.

20. Zeynep Türkyılmaz, "Maternal Colonialism and Turkish Woman's Burden in Dersim: Educating the 'Mountain Flowers' of Dersim," *Journal of Women's History* 28:3 (2016): 162–86.

21. Luis Martín-Cabrera, *Radical Justice: Spain and the Southern Cone beyond Market and State* (Plymouth, UK: Bucknell University Press, 2011).

22. "UNESCO in 2011: Towards a New Humanism and Globalization That Rhymes with Reconciliation," *UNESCO Courier* 64:4 (October–December 2011): 2.

23. Lynn Meskell, "UNESCO's World Heritage Convention at 40: Challenging the Economic and Political Order of International Heritage Conservation," *Current Anthropology* 54:4 (2013): 483–94. I thank Miray Çakıroğlu for reminding me of this text.

24. I would like to thank the anonymous reviewers for helping me articulate this point.

25. Marc de Wilde, "Meeting Opposites: The Political Theologies of Walter Benjamin and Carl Schmitt," *Philosophy and Rhetoric* 44:4 (2011): 363–81. I thank Isaac Hand for bringing this article to my attention.

26. Walter Benjamin, "Theses on the Philosophy of History," in *Illuminations* (New York: Schocken Books, 2007), 256.

27. Julia Hell and Andreas Schönle's co-edited *Ruins of Modernity* (Durham, NC: Duke University Press, 2010) inspired me to rethink and reinterpret this term for the purposes of my work. Modernity, as a discourse, is often associated with the categories of practice and dynamics analyzed in this book.

INDEX

Adalet ve Kalkınma Partisi (AKP): cultural attitudes in, 127, 177–78, 184, 189, 190, 199–200, 201, 204, 207–8, 214, 231–32, 234, 305n151; Erdoğan, 24–25, 127, 189, 191; neoliberalism of, 25, 201. *See also* AKP

AER/AWR, 44–54, 67, 178, 295n6; concern with numbers in, 45, 47–49, 129; convention of 1953 in Strasbourg, 49; convention of 1954 in Istanbul, 41, 43, 46, 51, 53, 62; convention of 1954 in Rome, 47; cultural assimilation promoted by, 132, 153, 156–57, 230; eugenicists in, 39, 41–42, 45, 46, 48–49, 50, 51–52, 56, 57, 61, 92; expert committees in, 265n25; and fascism, 45–46, 48, 57, 68–69, 86; and forced migration, 53, 88, 156–57, 167; founding of AER, 56–57, 61–62, 63, 69, 70, 71, 270n73; founding of AWR, 41; and Gini, 61, 62, 64, 69, 271n80; Gökay as president of, 34, 39, 43, 62, 264n8; and Greek-Turkish population exchange, 42, 178; and human suffering, 43, 76, 77, 276n127; *Integration*, 42, 44–45, 49, 54, 57, 61, 69, 71, 174, 263n2; and national refugees, 47–49; and segregative biopolitics, 34, 41, 42–43, 44, 52, 69, 71, 80, 112; and Ülken, 35, 41, 56, 60, 63, 70, 150, 156, 157, 158, 292nn110,116; vs. UNESCO, 76, 77, 132, 153. *See also* Gini; Ülken; Greek-Turkish population exchange; integration; segregative biopolitics

Afghanistan: United States intervention in, 239, 240, 241

AKP (Justice and Development Party). *See* Adalet ve Kalkınma Partisi

Alevis, 204, 206–7, 214–15, 224, 228, 305n151

Algeria: counterinsurgency of French colonizers in, 28, 44, 87, 99; decolonization of, 28, 44, 87, 91, 145, 278n164; French attempts to keep from the UN, 87; and French brutality in the Turkish parliament, 87; Turkey in relation to Algerian decolonization in the 1950s, 23, 87

Ampère, Jean-Jacques, 141, 145, 289n77; in Asia Minor/Anatolia, 134, 142, 288n76; and comparative literature in France, 142, 164; on Greece, 134; and historicist humanism, 141; *La Science et les lettres en Orient*, 142; letter to Sainte Beuve, 288n76. *See also* comparative literature; heritage trips; historicist humanism; Orientalism; ruins; Sainte Beuve; travel literature

Anadol, Kemal: *The Great Separation*, 103–4

And, Metin, 219

Andreadis, Yorgo: *Tamama: The Lost Daughter of Pontus*, 122

anthropology, 32, 149, 158, 259n47, 262n78, 263n92; physical anthropology, 14, 62, 151

apartheid, 5, 44, 76, 85, 102, 202, 244, 259n44. *See also* segregation; segregative biopolitics; South African apartheid; unmixing; walls

archaeology of knowledge, 115, 125, 130

Armenians: as minority in Turkey, 7, 8, 68, 122, 126, 127, 177, 184, 190, 197,

198–99, 200, 204, 205, 207, 222, 228, 299n57; genocide, 127, 223, 285n32
Armitage, David: *The History Manifesto*, 31–32
Association for Ethnology and Eugenics. *See* International Association for the Advancement of Ethnology and Eugenics
Association for the Study of the World Refugee Problem. *See* AER/AWR
Assyrians, 204–5
Atatürk, Mustafa Kemal, 180, 183, 213, 219, 290n100, 296n18, 297n33
Auerbach, Erich, 135, 141, 164, 198
Aydınlar Ocağı (Organization of Intellectuals), 141, 304n135. *See also* Safa; Turkish-Islamic synthesis

Balıkçısı, Halikarnas, 141
Balkan War, first, 44
Barthes, Roland: "The Great Family of Man," 90–94, 97, 99, 240, 279n185, 280n198; on liberal humanism, 28, 90–93, 94, 260n62
Bayar, Celal, 60
Belgian Congo, 93–94
Benjamin, Walter: on culture and power, 252–53, 254; on fascism and history, 171; on history and physical form, 173; on memory, 105; on military violence, 209; *The Origin of German Tragic Drama*, 252; relationship with Schmitt, 252; on ruins, 115, 169; "Theses on the Philosophy of History," 252–53. *See also* ruins
Berreby, Jean-Jacques: on "Oriental" Jews and eugenics, 48–49
Bhagavata-Purana, 142
biopolitics, segregative, 176, 199, 237; and AER/AWR, 34, 41, 42–43, 44, 52, 69, 71, 88, 112; as category of analysis, 11–12; defined, 11–12; as gentrification, 27–28, 194, 196, 238; Greek-Turkish population exchange as, 4, 11, 21–22, 23, 27, 35, 42, 102, 112, 114, 187, 200, 209, 229, 244, 247, 248, 254; human suffering from, 4–5, 77–78, 112; legacies of, 35, 75–76, 97, 110, 114, 115, 121, 122, 129, 168–69, 187, 202, 253; logics of, 5, 6, 11, 21, 22, 28, 41, 42–43, 46–47, 49, 50, 52, 57–72, 60, 63, 97, 114–15, 127, 128, 129, 132–33, 231, 238–39, 242, 248, 253; as regulation of categorized human bodies, 11–12, 13–14, 17, 35, 43, 45, 47, 60, 80–81, 97, 115, 124–25, 128, 157, 167, 187, 194, 241, 246, 248, 250; relationship to dispossession, 27, 35, 103, 238–39; relationship to family histories, 35, 110, 114–15, 121, 122; relationship to *Family of Man*, 79, 80, 86, 97; relationship to fascism, 11, 16, 33, 36, 68–69, 217, 246, 247, 248; relationship to historicist humanism, 31, 37, 101, 115, 129, 248; relationship to liberal approaches to culture, 26–27, 34, 36–37, 80, 86, 97, 101, 125–26, 128, 158, 162, 169, 246, 252, 254; relationship to liberal humanism, 17–20, 20, 27, 31, 34, 36–37, 73, 76–78, 80, 86, 97, 101, 102–3, 125–26, 158, 162, 169, 197, 254; relationship to peace, 4–5, 14–15, 20, 43, 47, 80, 88–89, 102–3; relationship to racialized thinking, 5, 8, 9, 11, 21, 27–28, 29, 32–33, 60, 68–69, 71–72, 73, 97, 102, 115, 200, 238, 240, 241, 243, 246, 254; relationship to securitarianism, 32–33, 50, 52, 116, 239–40, 242, 247, 249–50; role of numbers and space in, 12, 17, 60, 194, 212; ruins of, 97, 129, 168–69, 187, 202, 253; and Turkish-Islamic synthesis, 141, 157, 209. *See also* apartheid; demography; Greek-Turkish population exchange; partition; walls
Bisaha, Nancy, 144, 260n57; *Creating East and West*, 286n44. *See also* crusades
Boas, Franz, 58, 73, 158

Bonneval, Claude Alexandre, Comte de: conversion to Islam, 1, 2, 255n2; and Lady Georgina Fullerton, *La Comtesse de Bonneval*, 255n4; life of, 1–2, 255nn4,5. *See also* Fullerton; Sainte Beuve

Bonneval, Raşit Kemali: family history, 2, 3, 25, 35, 108, 183; during Greek-Turkish population exchange, 1, 9–10, 27

Bosch-Gimpera, Pere, 158–59

Bourdieu, Pierre, 210

bracketing of communities, 196–97, 198, 199, 201, 202–3, 204, 207–8

Breivik, Anders, 235, 243–45. *See also* xenophobic discourses

Brown, Wendy: on depoliticization and tolerance, 198, 201–2, 203

Browne, Edward, 141

Brown v. Board of Education, 59, 91. *See also* Gini; segregation; segregative biopolitics

Brubaker, Rogers: on categories of analysis vs. categories of practice, 11. *See also* Cooper

Bucak, Remzi, 180, 250

Bush, George W., 239, 241

Bush, Laura, 239, 240, 241

Byron, Lord, 143

Cahun, Léon, 209

canon, 95–96, 136, 142, 161, 286n48; as ancient cultural heritage, 142; Anne Frank's diary, 79, 96; Dante Alighieri as, 166; Evliya Çelebi's "Book of Travels," 79, 96, 276n136; and genius, 135, 138, 139, 140, 142, 145–46, 150, 164–65, 253, 286n48, 288n71; Homer, 135, 142, 144, 286n46, 288n76; and humanism, 132, 135, 166; Lefevere on, 95; UNESCO, 84, 96, 101, 165–66, 204, 280n190; in Turkish-Islamic Synthesis, 222; Yunus Emre as, 139. *See also* classics; historicist humanism

Capa, Robert, 78

capitalism, 29, 33, 45, 47, 92–93, 100, 237, 239, 240, 249, 264n10; accumulation of capital, 117, 235, 246; and liberal humanism, 44, 86, 90; and neoliberalism, 131. *See also* human capital

Casanova, Giovanni, 1, 255n2. *See also* Bonneval, Claude Alexandre

Celaleddin Paşa, Mustafa: *Les Turcs anciens et modernes*, 147–49, 150, 290n98. *See also* genealogy; historicist humanism; civilization; racialized thinking

Çelebi, Evliya: "Book of Travels," 79, 96

Çetin, Fethiye, 281n1; *Grandchildren: The Hidden Legacy of "Lost" Armenians in Turkey*, 122; *My Grandmother*, 122

Chamberlain, Houston Stewart: *The Foundations of the Nineteenth Century*, 145–46, 290n88; Ülken's university lectures on, 149. *See also* civilization; Gobineau; historicist humanism; racialized thinking; Ülken

Château de Clervaux: *The Family of Man* permanent exhibition in, 79–80. *See also Family of Man*

Chile: Pinochet's coup in, 24, 29, 218, 241. *See also* Cold War; fascism

Christie, John Traill, 160, 161, 163, 164, 165. *See also* Humanism and Education in the East and West (conference); cultural recognition; historicist humanism; humanities; Ülken

civilization, 134–36, 137–38, 143–47, 158–59, 166, 190, 238, 240–41, 253, 254; ancients and the moderns, 143; archaeology, 134, 136, 141, 142, 144, 221–22, 260n58, 286n46; and configurations of ancient Greece, 16, 134, 135, 142, 144, 160, 161, 165, 220, 222, 227–28, 260n57, 286n44, 289n76; and configurations of ancient Persia, 135, 142, 152; and configurations of ancient Rome, 16, 135, 144, 149, 152, 160, 165, 220, 222, 228, 260n57, 286n44;

clash of civilizations, 190–91, 295n3; classical civilizations, 16, 134, 135, 139, 142–44, 160, 161, 165, 220, 222, 227, 260n57, 286n44, 289n76; and heritage, 39, 75, 134–36, 139, 141–44, 162, 164, 200, 286n46; historicist humanism, 15–16, 132–146, 148–49, 158–169, 208, 220, 260n58; Oriental civilization and eugenics, 48–49; and origins, 15, 133, 135, 144, 152–53; Ottomans, 136–142, 146–49, 191, 200, 208, 301n81; and race, 15, 47, 133, 135, 138, 141–142, 145–47, 149, 151–52, 190, 200, 208, 240, 275n122, 285n46, 288n75, 292n116; in relation to Turks, 15, 136–142, 146–53, 191, 208, 209, 216, 220–22, 224, 229, 260n58, 264n8, 287n56; and translation, 287n56; UN Alliance of Civilizations, 184, 189–92, 200, 224, 228–29, 295n3, 297n30, 297n36; and UNESCO, 74–75, 131, 133–134, 143–144, 158–169; Western civilization, 46–47, 50, 135, 138, 142, 143, 150, 162, 220. *See also* Eurocentrism; travel literature

classics: ancients and the moderns, 143; and historicist humanism, 135, 142, 144–45, 160–64; in humanities, 144–45, 160–61, 163–64; and the figure of the national genius, 287n49; as national contribution to the archive of humanity, 135, 164; and Orientalism, 142; in relation to Humanism and Education in the East and West (conference), 160–62; as representative of different civilizations, 142, 144–45, 161–64; and tolerance, 161–63, 166; UNESCO conference translation of, 136, 138, 287n54; in world literature, 202. *See also* canon; cultural heritage; historicist humanism; tolerance

Cold War, 26, 46, 71, 102, 103, 131, 217, 239, 265n15, 266n29; against communism during, 23–24, 45, 218, 229; Berlin partitioned city of, 82; coup d'état in Chile during, 24, 29; coup d'états in Turkey during, 23–24, 29, 109–110, 116, 125, 209–18, 231, 238–39, 264n8, 264n11, 272n94, 282n14; discourses of the free world during, 23, 44–47, 57, 82, 84, 86, 90, 102, 229, 264n10; end of, 23, 108, 110, 116, 162, 169, 175, 189, 229, 235, 245–46, 247, 279n186; and *Family of Man*, 78, 81–82, 84, 85, 93, 94, 96, 98, 99; and liberal humanism, 18, 43–44, 76, 82, 86, 93, 125, 184, 247; McCarthyism, 23, 63–64, 84; Turkey during, 23–24, 29, 42, 178, 210, 241; US Atomic Energy Commission and radiation experiments during, 83, 84, 277n154; United States Information Service (USIS), 82, 93, 94

colonialism, 80, 116, 143, 145, 163, 190, 250, 256n17, 282n3; of Belgium, 45, 93–94, 240; of Britain, 240; dispossession in, 45, 241–42; and *Family of Man*, 92, 93–94; Fanon on, 17, 100, 290n86; of France, 12, 16–17, 23, 44, 87, 91, 99, 240; Gini on, 46–47; and Haiti, 100; and racialized thinking, 12; Sartre on, 289n86; Schmitt on, 171, 239, 241–42; in Turkey, 180, 250, 308n20; and United Nations, 85. *See also* Cold War; dispossession; Eurocentrism; Fanon; human rights; liberal values; Schmitt; segregative biopolitics; United Nations

Columbia University, 58

communism, 23–24, 42, 44–47, 58, 63–64, 82, 279n186; civil war in Spain, 64, 159; demography, 46, 64; House Un-American Activities Committee, 63, 82; the international, 217; Islam as a remedy of, 218, 229; McCarthyism, 23, 63–64, 84; racialist scientists and racial equality as communist conspiracy, 58. *See also* Cold War; Turkey; Turkish-Islamic synthesis

comparative literature, 142, 164
Coon, Carleton: *The Origin of Races*, 281n200; *The Story of Man*, 59
Cooper, Frederick: on categories of analysis vs. categories of practice, 11. See also Brubaker
Council of Europe, 47, 48, 49–50, 56, 167, 266n26
Crete, 107, 111–13, 122–23
cross-disciplinary analysis, 30. See also multidisciplinary analysis
crossing, 36, 57, 60, 63, 72, 86, 220; as exchange and circulation, 16, 72, 86, 220, 232, 254; *histoire croisée*, 30–31; palimpsests, 21, 254. See also palimpsests; Zimmermann
Crusades, 260n57, 286n44
cultural diversity, 132, 166, 230, 232, 238, 251; bracketing of communities, 196–97, 198, 199, 201, 202–3, 204, 207; UN Alliance of Civilizations, 189–92, 200, 224, 228–29, 295n3; UNESCO Convention on the Protection of the Diversity of Cultural Expressions, 126, 184–85, 187–89; UNESCO Universal Declaration on Cultural Diversity, 126, 131, 175, 184–87, 188, 195, 296n20; unity-in-diversity discourse, 18–19, 58, 73–74, 78, 80–81, 90, 91–92, 97, 99, 101, 125, 133, 158, 165, 175, 177, 184, 187, 197, 260n63. See also Istanbul 2010 European Capital of Culture (ECoC) project; multiculturalism; peace and coexistence; tolerance
cultural heritage: ancient heritage, 15, 16, 39, 75, 134, 135–36, 139, 142–44, 160, 161, 165, 200, 201, 203–4, 220, 222, 224, 227, 260n57, 286n44, 289n76; as common to humanity, 39, 75, 131–32, 133, 134, 188, 192; of communities, 25; contextualization of, 245; and Greek-Turkish population exchange, 3–4, 27, 111–14, 124, 178, 182–83, 191–92, 232, 247; heritage trips, 56, 111–14, 129, 141, 174; museumization of culture, 175–77, 182–83, 184, 194, 199, 201, 204, 208, 233, 234, 254, 300n60; national cultures, 133–39, 141, 150, 160, 166, 167, 168, 216–17, 220–23, 228, 229–30; of Ottoman Empire, 200, 201, 203–4, 224; relationship to family histories, 2, 3, 35, 109, 111, 115, 116, 122, 124, 129, 168, 181, 182–83, 232; relationship to historicist humanism, 75, 129, 135–36, 141–42, 161, 162, 188; relationship to segregative biopolitics, 27, 35, 169, 247–48; Ülken on, 150, 164, 294n142; UNESCO's Memory of the World project, 79, 81–82, 83, 84–85, 90, 96, 101, 204–5, 276n136; UNESCO's World Heritage list, 166–67, 246. See also civilization; heritage
cultural identification, 158, 167, 168–69, 173, 185, 186, 187, 234, 238, 248; as cultural recognition, 198–99; in EU, 193; role of family histories in, 113–14, 120, 122–24, 178–79, 181; role of genealogies and origins in, 114, 126, 128, 132–33, 141–42; as self-identification, 17, 110, 114, 120, 126, 128, 181, 233; in Turkey, 109, 113–14, 120, 122–24, 139, 140, 174–75, 178–79, 198–99, 204, 208; and UNESCO, 125–26, 131–33, 188, 247. See also Turkish-Islamic synthesis
cultural industry, 103–4, 110, 230. See also, cultural memory; literary studies; memoir boom
culturalization of violence, 239–41, 242, 245
cultural memory, 25–26, 56, 142, 169
cultural order, 245–47, 249
cultural policies, 16, 20, 27, 33–34, 129–30, 197–203, 245–48, 249; of EU, 175, 188, 189, 192–95, 205, 298n50; as managing alterity, 3–4, 6, 12, 14, 17, 18, 19, 21–22, 34, 37, 88, 176, 177, 187, 197, 200, 202, 208, 233, 238; national unity

promoted by, 211, 212–13, 216–17, 219, 220, 226; tolerance in, 162–63, 184, 185, 186, 189, 190, 205; of Turkey, 26, 35–36, 133, 165, 173–78, 184, 188, 189–92, 194–95, 196, 197–203, 204, 205, 208–35, 247–48, 264n11, 295n3, 296n20, 297n38, 302n103, 305nn140,150,151, 306n159; UN Alliance of Civilizations, 189–92, 200, 224, 228–29, 295n3; of UNESCO, 18, 19, 22, 23, 34, 35, 36, 75–76, 79–80, 97, 103, 108–9, 125, 126, 131–33, 134, 136, 143–45, 153, 155, 158–60, 161–64, 165–67, 169, 175, 176, 177, 184–88, 189–91, 192, 195, 210, 211, 219, 233, 234, 247, 250–52, 282n3, 292n110, 293n126, 302n103. *See also* European Capital of Culture; Istanbul ECoC; Turkish-Islamic synthesis

cultural recognition, 168, 176, 177, 178, 190, 200, 238, 245, 246–48, 249, 250, 252; bracketing of communities, 196–97, 198, 199, 201, 202–3, 204, 207–8; as cultural identification, 198–99; and family histories, 110, 115, 129–30; and neo-Ottomanism, 25, 224; Povinelli on, 196–97, 202–3; role of education in, 160, 169, 233–34; role of genealogies and origins in, 128, 161–62; vs. social justice, 196, 197, 232, 233–34, 246–47; and UNESCO, 76, 80, 103, 130, 133, 144, 161, 165–66, 169, 175, 185, 188, 192, 233; through visibility, 79, 80, 83, 94, 97, 175, 194, 195–97, 240, 249

cultural studies, 29, 33, 210

cultural visibility, 232–33, 234, 240, 246, 249

culture: defined, 17–18, 131, 185, 195, 210, 219; as democratized, 125–26, 129–30, 131–32, 133, 159, 161–62, 165; and neoliberalism, 104; relationship to economic development, 131, 210, 211, 235, 245–46; relationship to self-identification, 110, 114, 120, 126, 128, 181, 233; segregative biopolitics and liberal approaches to, 26–27, 34, 36–37, 80, 86, 97, 101, 125–26, 128, 158, 162, 169, 246, 252, 254; visual culture, 79, 80, 83, 97, 99, 175, 199. *See also* multiculturalism; museumization of culture

Cumhuriyet, 139–40

Curzon, Lord, 11; on Greek-Turkish population exchange as unmixing, 4, 9, 12

Cyprus partition of 1974, 6, 19, 27, 115, 231

Dante Alighieri, 135, 142, 166, 289n76

Davutoğlu, Ahmet, 190, 224, 305n151

Declaration of the Rights of Man and of the Citizen, 79; canonization of, 100–101

dehistoricization, 177, 187, 207, 247–48; bracketing of communities as, 196–97, 202–3; vs. historical contextualization, 27–28, 91–92, 93–94, 187, 190, 200–203; in museumization of culture, 176, 232, 233

democracy, 86, 132, 187, 215, 217, 218, 237–38; and *Family of Man*, 84–85, 90, 94–95, 99; role of elections in, 94–95, 279n186

demography, 11, 12, 22, 31, 44, 109, 143, 165, 180, 198, 209, 290n87, 299n56; and Alfred Sauvy, 69; and Gini, 45–47, 49, 57, 60, 66, 269n63; and *Fatih-Harbiye*, 68; Ülken on, 152, 156–57; and İskan Kanunu (1934 Settlement Law), 8, 258n38, 296n13; and land appropriation, 8, 64, 243–44; in the 1983 National Cultural Policy Report, 209, 225; and overpopulation, 50; in relation to demographics as population management, 18, 44, 48; in relation to eugenics, 10, 11, 34, 46, 49, 57, 60, 258n44; in relationship to racialized alignment, 10, 12, 48; securitarianism and control of, 6, 50, 244; and segregative biopolitics, 89, 229; as site for the management of alterity, 3, 6;

INDEX

and statistics, 60; and xenophobia, 128–29, 244. *See also* Gini; Greek-Turkish population exchange; Istanbul University; Kurds; segregative biopolitics; Turkey; Turkish-Islamic synthesis

Demokrat Party, 229, 231, 250

depoliticization, 32, 43, 77, 177, 187, 196, 231, 247–48; bracketing of communities as, 196–97, 202–3; in *Family of Man*, 93–94; in museumization of culture, 176, 208, 233; and tolerance, 198, 201–2, 203

diachronic analysis, 32–33, 168–69, 189; of cultural policies, 208, 245, 248, 252; of palimpsests, 31, 187, 189, 248. *See also* synchronic analysis.

dispossession, 14, 20, 102, 117, 128, 198, 199, 209, 213, 225; of Assyrians, 204; in colonialism, 45, 241–42; relationship to family histories, 109, 111, 168; relationship to segregative biopolitics, 27, 35, 103, 238–39; Stoler on, 116. *See also* colonialism; segregative biopolitics; Schmitt

DNA testing, 249

Dönme, 273n102; as Muslim exchangees, 7, 9–10, 25, 54, 108, 121, 123–24, 183, 257n26; Marc Baer on, 121, 257n26, 273n102; 284n24

Dostoevsky, Fyodor, 76

Durán, Gustavo, 63–65, 69, 103

Ecevit, Bülent: during Cyprus conflict, 19, 231; poem on Greek-Turkish brotherhood, 19, 231

ECOC. *See* Istanbul 2010 European Capital of Culture (ECoC) project

education, 132, 160–63, 169, 233; Bosch-Gimpera on, 159; Özal on, 210; in Turkey, 216–17, 218, 219, 221–22, 226, 227, 228, 229, 293n129, 305n151; Ülken on, 73, 157–58, 162–63, 224–25;

UNESCO on, 185, 186; in United States, 59, 91

Egyptian military coup of 2013, 29

Emigrants' Foundation. *See* Foundation of Lausanne Treaty Emigrants

Emre, Yunus, 139–40

Enlightenment, 27, 222, 280n199

Erdoğan, Recep Tayyip: ancestry and heredity, 127, 285n38; on genocide, 127; military coup attempt, 25; in relation to Menderes and Özal, 24–25; UN Alliance of Civilizations, 189, 191. *See also* Adalet ve Kalkınma Partisi (AKP)

eugenics, 9, 10–11, 17, 33, 90, 127–28, 143, 237, 242, 243, 267n39; birthrates of particular groups in, 46–47, 48, 50; eugenicists in AER/AWR, 39, 41–42, 45, 46, 48–49, 50, 51–52, 56, 57, 61, 92; and fascism, 6, 11, 34, 57, 60, 93, 254; fusion of eugenics and demographics, 11, 34, 45, 49, 57, 60; Gini as eugenicist, 34, 45, 49, 56, 57, 60; and Gobineau, 147, 149, 152; Gökay as eugenicist, 39, 56, 70; and integration, 50–52; and living organisms, 213; Müller as eugenicist, 52, 67, 127, 140; relationship to civilization, 152, 200; relationship to criminology, 7, 248; relationship to historicist humanism, 14, 21, 253, 254. *See also* demography; fascism; Gini; Müller; Ülken; segregative biopolitics

Eugenics Quarterly, 51

Eurocentrism, 15–17, 28–30, 46, 48, 88, 100, 143, 164; of historicist humanism, 135, 138, 145, 160, 161, 162; Shohat and Stam on, 15, 260n56

European Association for the Study of Refugee Problems. *See* AER/AWR

European Capital of Culture (ECOC) project. *See* Istanbul 2010 European Capital of Culture (ECoC) project

European Union, 117–18, 177, 191, 240, 298n45; Brexit, 235; cultural policies, 175, 188, 189, 192–95, 205, 298n50; economic conditions, 176; European Commission's *European Agenda for Culture*, 192; liberal multiculturalism in, 35, 36; relations with Turkey, 176; Roma in, 184, 194, 205, 298n50. *See also* Istanbul 2010 European Capital of Culture (ECoC) project

Evren, Kenan, 24, 212–14, 217, 218, 219, 221, 222, 241. *See also* Chile; fascism; *National Cultural Policy Report* of 1983; Pinochet; Turkish-Islamic synthesis

exceptionalism, 28–29

Ezine, Celaleddin: in relation to Gini's stay in Istanbul, 269n61; Mustafa Celaleddin Paşa 147; and Turkish humanism, 139, 141; 287n63. *See also* humanism

family histories, 110–14, 196; Greek-Turkish population exchange in, 1, 2, 3, 110–12, 133, 173, 176, 178, 182, 206, 230, 232; relationship to cultural heritage, 2, 3, 35, 109, 111, 115, 116, 122, 124, 129, 168, 181, 182–83, 232; relationship to dispossession, 109, 111, 168; relationship to segregative biopolitics, 35, 110, 114–15, 121, 122; role in cultural identification, 113–14, 120, 122–24, 178–79, 181; in Turkey, 2, 25, 35, 107–8, 110–12, 116, 117, 119–24, 125, 126–27, 133, 139, 147, 167, 173, 178, 181, 182, 247

Family of Man, The, 78–101, 194, 197, 202, 232; Barthes on, 90–94, 97, 99, 240, 279n185, 280n198; Belgian Congo in, 93–94; canonization of, 95–96; and Cold War, 78, 81–82, 84, 85, 93, 94, 96, 98, 99; and colonialism, 92, 93–94; and democracy, 84–85, 90, 94–95, 99; family of man trope, 42, 97–99, 128; historical contextualization of, 78, 79, 82–84, 89, 91–94, 96–97; Holocaust in, 89; and human rights, 78, 85, 279n185; in relation to the racialized tree of humankind, 99; institutions endorsed by, 82–85, 95; labor represented in, 92–94, 99; and liberal humanism, 34, 78, 79, 80, 81–82, 85, 89, 90–93, 96, 99, 231; relationship to segregative biopolitics, 79, 80, 86, 97; Steichen as curator of, 70, 78, 80, 81, 83, 89, 90, 93, 94, 99, 128, 279n185; Turkey in, 85, 94–95; UNESCO endorsement of, 34, 78, 79–80, 81, 84–85, 86, 90, 91, 94–96, 99, 101, 204; and United Nations, 89; and US Atomic Energy Commission and radiation experiments, 83, 277n154; and United States Information Service (USIS), 82, 93, 94. *See also* Chateau de Clervaux; Cold War; family tree of humankind; liberal humanism; UNESCO; segregative biopolitics

family tree of humankind, 128, 129, 134–36, 146, 153, 213; Anne McClintock on, 97–98, 129, 259n46, 280n195; and Arthur de Gobineau, 147, 149, 290n100; and Büşra Ersanlı on Afet Inan, 290n100; and Steichen's *The Family of Man*, 99; and Mustafa Celaleddin Paşa,147–149, 153, 290n100; and race, 10, 97–98, 128, 134, 136, 213; and relationship to discourses of brotherhood, 75, 213; types of, 150; Ülken on, 153, 292n116. *See also* historicist humanism; liberal humanism; *Family of Man*; racialized thinking; Orientalism

Fanon, Frantz, 99–100, 101, 138, 280n199; on colonialism, 17, 100, 290n86; on equality, 87, 100, 253; on humanism, 145, 253, 289n86; *The Wretched of Earth*, 289n86. *See also* colonialism; liberal humanism; liberal values; segregative biopolitics; racialized thinking

INDEX

fascism, 59, 62–63, 65, 68, 70–71, 93, 171, 243, 245–48, 250, 254, 273n100, 275n115; and AER/AWR, 45–46, 48, 57, 68–69, 86; in Chile, 24, 29, 218, 241; and Cold War, 217; and colonialism, 250; and eugenics, 6, 11, 34, 57, 60, 93, 254; and *Family of Man*, 89, 277n142, 277n144, 277n149, 279n177; in France, 243; fusion of demographics and eugenics, 34, 49, 57, 60; in Germany, 6, 11, 16, 34, 51, 67, 68, 73, 86, 87, 88, 89, 93, 145, 149, 154, 227–28, 237, 252, 267n35, 270n68; and historicist humanism, 16, 36, 227–28, 254; International Institute of Sociology, 66, 68, 70; in Italy, 16, 34, 45, 48, 57–58, 61, 86, 227–28, 270n70, 270n72, 304n132; neofascism, 19, 32; and production of knowledge 59–61, 63–72, 223–28, 270n72; refugees, 45; relationship to segregative biopolitics, 11, 16, 33, 36, 68–69, 217, 246, 247, 248; as a relic of the past, 86; and science, 57, 59; "Scientific Basis of Fascism," 57, 264n10, 265n14, 267n48; in Spain, 63–64, 217; Spanish National Catholicism and, 217; in Turkey, 24, 29, 36, 87, 215, 217, 304n132; Turkish-Islamic synthesis, 36. *See also* Cold War; Gini; Müller; International Institute of Sociology; *National Cultural Policy Report* of 1983; Schmitt; segregation; Turkish-Islamic synthesis
Fauriel, Claude, 142
Fichte, Johann Gottlieb, 149
Fındıkoğlu, Ziyaeddin Fahri, 104, 108, 157, 174, 266n33, 271n92; heritage trips and memory of exchangees, 54; on integration, 51, 54–56, 153, 229; research on exchangees, 54–56, 108. *See also* AER/AWR; integration; Gini; Greek-Turkish population exchange
Firdawsi's *Shahnameh*, 142, 164. *See also* canon; classics; historicist humanism

First Turkish National History Congress, 209
forced migration, 115, 162, 168, 202; advocated as promoting peace, 4, 5, 13, 47, 156–57; and AER/AWR, 53, 88, 156–57, 167; Greek-Turkish population exchange as, 4–5, 6, 10–11, 44–45, 61, 71, 103–4, 107, 112, 156, 173, 174, 178, 180; as internal, 116, 180, 198, 206, 231, 259n55. *See also* apartheid; demography; segregative biopolitics; walls
Ford Foundation, 160, 293n126
Foucault, Michel: on biopolitics, 11–12; on humanism, 28; securitarianism, 32; Stoler on, 12, 259n50
Foundation of Lausanne Treaty Emigrants, 108, 114, 122, 124, 174–75, 178, 179, 181, 183, 230
France: colonialism of, 12, 16–17, 23, 87, 91, 99; comparative literature in, 142, 164; and Algeria, 28, 44, 87, 99; *Family of Man* in Paris, 90–91; and Haiti, 100; National Front, 243; National Institute of Demography Studies, 69; and racism, 87; Revolution of 1789, 79, 100–101, 280n199; Roma in, 194, 205. *See also* Ampère; Bonneval, Claude Alexandre; colonialism; fascism; *Family of Man*
Franco, Francisco, 63, 217, 250
Frank, Anne: diary of, 79, 96. *See also* canon; UNESCO
Fraser, Nancy, 234
Freyer, Hans, 67–68. *See also* Gini; International Institute of Sociology
Fullerton, Lady Georgina: *La Comtesse de Bonneval*, 255n4. *See also* Bonneval, Claude Alexandre

Galton, Francis, 140, 149
Galvani, Luigi, 69
Gandhi, Mohandas K., 162
García Lorca, Federico, 63

Garzón Real, Baltasar, 250
genealogy, 3, 12, 26, 99, 130, 175, 247; in historicist humanism, 35, 129, 133–34, 147–48, 164, 168–69, 209, 219, 220; in racialized thinking, 10, 15, 35, 47, 71–72, 128–29, 142, 145–49, 166; role in nationalist gatekeeping, 114, 168, 228, 285n40; role in self-identification, 110, 114, 120, 126; tracing of, 111, 114, 122–23, 126–27, 128, 133–34, 137–38, 140, 141–42, 145–50, 157–58, 160, 161–62, 164, 167, 179, 180, 209, 285n40, 290n100; tree of humankind, 97–98, 128, 129, 134, 136, 146, 153, 213. *See also* civilization; cultural heritage; eugenics; family histories; fascism; origins
Genette, Gérard: on palimpsests and transtextuality, 20–21
genius. *See* national genius
gentrification, 27–28, 194, 196, 238
German nationals expelled from Central Europe, 6
German Society for Population Sciences, 52
German Sociological Association, 67
Germany: Nazism in, 6, 11, 16, 51, 67, 68, 73, 86, 87, 88, 89, 93, 145, 149, 154, 227–28, 237, 252, 267n35, 270n68; Syrian refugees in, 12, 51. *See also* eugenics; fascism
Gibb, E. J. W., 141
Gibb, H. A. R.: *Islamic Society and the West*, 301n81
Gini, Corrado, 98, 244, 266n33; and AER, 61, 62, 64, 69, 271n80; on birthrates, 46–47, 49–50, 51; on *Brown v. Board of Education*, 91; on colonialism, 46–47; *Démographie et Sociologie*, 60; as eugenicist, 34, 45, 49, 56, 57, 60; as fascist, 45–46, 57–58, 60, 61, 62–63, 65, 66, 70, 271n80; Gini coefficient, 57, 61; on Greek-Turkish population exchange, 61; on human categorization, 47; on integration of refugees, 50–51; and International Institute of Sociology, 57, 62–63, 65–66, 67, 69, 70, 71, 271n83, 275n118, 292n110; at Istanbul University, 60–61, 66, 136, 139, 268nn58,60, 269nn61,66, 292n116; on Italian emigrants, 266n28, 270n68; on low population density, 292n116; *Methodology of Statistics*, 61, 269n66; on overpopulation, 49–50, 51; on refugees as human capital, 50–51, 52, 186; *Revue Internationale de Sociologie*, 67, 101, 237, 273n99; *The Scientific Bases of the Politics of Population*, 61, 269n66; "The Scientific Basis of Fascism," 57; on security, 52; vs. Ülken, 60, 63, 65, 66, 67, 151, 291n109, 292n116; and UNESCO, 75. *See also* Istanbul University; Safa; Schmitt; segregative biopolitics; Ülken
Gobineau, Arthur de: on degeneration, 145, 146–47, 152; *Essay on the Inequality of Human Races*, 145–47, 149–50, 290nn87,90,100; and eugenics, 147, 149, 152; Ülken's university lectures on, 149; on Turks, 146–47, 149, 150, 290n100. *See also* Chamberlain; Hitler; racialized thinking; civilization; geneaology; Ülken
Gökalp, Ziya, 109. *See also* Turkish-Islamic synthesis
Gökay, Fahreddin Kerim: as eugenicist, 39, 56, 70; on human suffering, 77, 276n127; as president of AER, 34, 39, 43, 62, 264n8; during violence against Istanbul Greek Orthodox in 1955, 42, 263n7, 264n8. *See also* AER/AWR; eugenics; segregative biopolitics; Turkey
Greco-Turkish War (1919–1922), 4, 63, 143, 212
Greece: ancient civilization, 16, 134, 135, 144, 160, 161, 165, 220, 222, 227–28, 260n57, 286n44, 289n76; indepen-

dence from Ottoman Empire, 142–43; relations with Turkey, 4, 19, 63, 143, 156. *See also* Greek-Turkish population exchange

Greek Orthodox: as minority in Turkey, 4, 23, 42–43, 68, 81, 82, 87, 88, 91, 99, 150, 190, 196, 199, 200, 205, 207, 222, 228, 263nn7,8; in Ottoman Empire, 301n92

Greek Orthodox exchangees, 4, 10, 12, 103, 107, 113, 143, 173, 230; and Hellenism in Anatolia, 179; integration in Greece, 55–56, 155–56; as lacking homogeneity, 12; local Greek attitudes regarding, 2–3, 179; and multiculturalism, 181–82; occupations of, 2, 256n8; Ülken on, 155–57

Greek-Turkish brotherhood narratives, 19, 230–31. *See also* Ecevit

Greek-Turkish population exchange, 116, 212, 244, 270n75; and cultural heritage, 3–4, 27, 111–14, 124, 178, 182–83, 191–92, 232, 247; diversity of exchangees, 9–10, 55; documentaries about, 103–4, 112; ethnohistorical informants regarding, 108, 110, 111, 113, 114, 118–19, 123–24; exemptions from, 4, 42; in family histories, 1, 2, 3, 110–12, 133, 173, 176, 178, 182, 206, 230, 232; as forced migration, 4–5, 6, 10–11, 44–45, 61, 71, 103–4, 107, 112, 156, 173, 174, 178, 180; Greek Orthodox exclusions, 4, 256n12; integration of Muslims exchangees in Turkey, 54–56, 230, 267n44; as international legal precedent, 4, 6, 11, 18, 21, 22, 42, 102, 132, 173, 248; Lausanne conference/Treaty of Lausanne, 2, 4, 7–8, 13, 44–45, 85–86, 88, 143, 150, 178, 190, 256n12, 258n39; legacies, 3–4, 5, 6–11, 18, 20, 21, 22, 27, 29, 31, 34, 41, 42, 47–48, 88–89, 114, 165, 249, 253, 257n23; and liberal humanism, 19–20; Muslim exclusions from, 4, 256n12; Population Exchange Museum in Turkey, 36, 124, 173–75, 176, 178–84, 191–92, 208, 230, 232, 235, 296n18; relationship to racialized thinking, 10–12, 13, 14, 22, 35, 200; Roma during, 13; as segregative biopolitics, 4, 11, 21–22, 23, 27, 35, 42, 102, 112, 114, 187, 200, 209, 229, 244, 247, 248, 254; and Turkish-Islamic synthesis, 229–30; Ülken on, 150, 151, 155–57; as unmixing, 4, 9–10. *See also* Greek Orthodox exchangees; Muslim exchangees; segregative biopolitics; Ülken

Gül, Abdullah, 126, 204

Guldi, Jo: *The History Manifesto*, 31–32

Gülen, Fethullah, 25, 229, 306n159. *See also National Cultural Policy Report* of 1983; Turkish-Islamic synthesis

Günther, Hans F. K., 52

Güvenç, Bozkurt: *Türk-İslam Sentezi*, 304n135. *See also* Turkish-Islamic synthesis

gypsies. *See* Roma

Haley, Alex: *Roots*, 247

Hall, Stuart: on cultural studies, 29, 30, 33, 262n88

Hamle, 287n63, 288n64

Harvard University, 57

Hell, Julia: *Ruins of Modernity*, 115, 282n11, 308n27

Hemingway, Ernest: *For Whom the Bell Tolls*, 63, 103; "On the Quai at Smyrna," 270n75

heredity, 127; and heritage, 150; Hilmi Ziya Ülken on, 150, 153, 157, 291n107, 292n117; Karl Valentin Müller on, 52, 140; in relation to eugenics, 52, 140; in relation to genius, 140, 149, 288n71; and race, 52, 150, 153, 157; Sir Francis Galton on, 140, 149, 288n71. *See also* eugenics; heritage

heritage. *See* cultural heritage

heritage trips: exchangees using familial memory narratives, 56, 111–14, 129, 174; and literary classics, 135, 141–42, 288n76, 289n77. *See also* Ampère; cultural heritage; Fındıkoğlu; Greek-Turkish population exchange; Schliemann; travel literature
Hikmet, Nazım, 139, 147
historical and political contextualization, 19–20, 26, 33–35, 36–37, 88–89, 99, 116, 197, 208, 249; vs. dehistoricization and depoliticization, 27–28, 91–92, 93–94, 187, 190, 200–203; of *Family of Man*, 78, 79, 82–84, 89, 91–94, 96–97; and *histoire croisée*, 30–31; of unmixing, 21
historicist humanism, 31, 32, 35–36, 127, 216, 240, 253; defined, 10; as democratized, 114, 133, 159, 161–62, 165; as Eurocentric, 135, 138, 145, 160, 161, 162; genealogy and origins in, 35, 97, 127, 129, 133–34, 147–48, 164, 168–69, 209, 219, 220; and national classics, 135–37; and national geniuses, 140, 164, 165–66; relationship to cultural heritage, 75, 129, 141–42, 161, 188; relationship to eugenics, 14, 21, 253, 254; relationship to liberal humanism, 37, 165, 188, 254; relationship to racialized thinking, 10, 14–17, 19, 20, 21, 101, 129, 145, 149, 166, 189, 208, 227–28, 242; relationship to segregative biopolitics, 31, 37, 101, 115, 129, 248; relationship to Turkish-Islamic synthesis, 36, 109, 141, 209, 220, 221–22, 227–28; and tree of humankind, 98, 134, 136; and UNESCO, 18, 35, 97, 133, 134, 141, 143, 145, 150, 158–69, 185, 233, 251. *See also* Ampère; civilization; colonialism; eugenics; Fanon; genealogy; heritage; Mustafa Celaleddin Paşa; Orientalism; racialized thinking; Humanism and Education in the East and West; Ülken; UNESCO

history: and cultural memory, 26; democratization of, 25–26, 114, 118, 126, 128, 129, 167, 181, 283n15; and fascism, 171; *longue durée* in, 31–32, 33; as nationalist historiography, 26, 117, 119, 163, 167, 229. *See also* historical and political contextualization; historicist humanism; oral history
History Foundation, 108, 117–21, 123, 126, 167, 181, 183, 218, 229, 230; family-history competition, 120–21, 163, 294n138; Oral History Collection Project, 118–19; Ottoman language courses, 119, 123
Hitler, Adolf, 149, 154
Hoggart, Richard, 210
Holocaust, 86, 89, 248. *See also* fascism; *Family of Man*
Homer, 135, 142, 144, 289n76. *See also* Ampère; Eurocentrism; ruins; Schliemann; Troy
Hoyt, Elizabeth: "Family of Mankind: Some New Light?," 98. *See also* eugenics; segregation
human capital, 191, 266n29; refugees as, 50–51, 52, 90, 92, 186
human categorization, 13–17, 52, 101, 245; by cultural background, 48, 110, 129, 133, 143, 246; Nur on, 8–9; as racialized, 8–9, 10, 14, 22, 35, 102, 115, 129, 133, 143, 151, 153, 162, 197–98, 242; in segregative biopolitics, 12, 13–14, 17, 35, 43, 45, 47, 60, 80–81, 115, 124–25, 128, 157, 167, 187, 194, 241, 246, 248, 250; by tracing origins, 10, 97. *See also* family tree of humankind; Gini; Gobineau; historicist humanism; human capital; Müller; racialized thinking; Ülken
human dignity, 187
human essence, 81, 92, 93, 227–28, 232; in liberal humanism, 18–19, 21, 28, 58, 80; and UNESCO, 18–19, 39, 58
human evolution, 97–98
Human Genome Project, 249

humanism. *See* historicist humanism; liberal humanism
human rights, 5, 25, 187, 188, 251, 252; change regarding, 96–97; collective rights, 86, 88, 94, 117; and *Family of Man*, 78, 85, 279n185; individual rights, 86, 88, 94, 109, 110, 117; Moyn on, 89, 96–97; and United Nations, 86, 87–88, 94, 117, 263n6; Universal Declaration of Human Rights, 86, 87, 88, 96–97, 289n83; violations of, 241. *See also* Cold War; colonialism; Fanon; Orientalism; segregative biopolitics
Human Rights Association (İnsan hakları derneği), 125, 285n32
human suffering, 19–20, 53, 103–4; and AER/AWR, 43, 76, 77, 276n127; from colonialism, 93–94; and liberal humanism, 43, 77–78, 103; from segregative biopolitics, 4–5, 77–78, 112; UNESCO on, 76–77, 112
Humanism and Education in the East and West (1951 UNESCO conference in India), 159–64, 167, 185, 251, 293n126. *See also* India
Huntington, Samuel, 189–90
Hussein, Taha, 287n49; *The Future of the Culture of Egypt*, 136

IIS. *See* International Institute of Sociology
imperialism, 45, 80, 85, 145, 190. *See also* colonialism
İnan, Afet, 290n100
India: British colonialism in, 45; and Humanism and Education in the East and West (conference), 159–64, 167, 185, 251, 293n126; partition of 1947, 6, 44, 160, 162, 244, 248; population exchange in, 6
information society, 186
İnönü, İsmet, 7
İnsan (Human), 137–38, 139

integration, 20, 34, 45, 49, 50–56, 97, 193; as assimilation, 8, 14, 19, 28, 51, 53, 54–55, 69–70, 88, 109, 114, 121, 132–33, 153, 155–57, 165, 180, 187, 197, 209, 223, 225–227, 229, 230, 231, 238; and eugenics, 50–52; Fındıkoğlu on, 51, 54–56, 153, 229; Gini on, 50–51; of Greek Orthodox exchangees in Greece, 55–56, 155–56; Müller on, 51–52; of Muslim exchangees in Turkey, 54–56, 109, 156–57, 183, 200, 206, 208, 230, 267n44; of "Oriental" Jews in Israel, 48; role of economic productivity in, 51–52, 156, 157–58; and Turkish-Islamic synthesis, 133, 209, 223, 225, 227, 229
International Association for the Advancement of Ethnology and Eugenics (IAAEE), 57, 58–60, 91, 98
International Institute of Diplomatic Study and Research, 48
International Institute of Sociology (IIS), 65–68, 69–71, 273n100; congress of 1950, 61–62, 63, 66, 69–70; congress of 1952, 67–68, 70; and Gini, 57, 62–63, 65–66, 67, 69, 70, 71, 271n83, 275n118, 292n110; and Ülken, 63, 66, 70–71, 292n110
International Monetary Fund, 12, 23, 51, 210, 218, 249, 283n14
International Red Cross, 56, 263n5
International Sociological Association (ISA), 68, 270n80, 275n114; and Ülken, 65, 66–67, 275n118, 292n110; and UNESCO, 62, 63, 64–65, 66, 69, 70, 71, 144, 271n80
Iraq: Kurds in, 198; United States intervention in, 239
ISA. *See* International Sociological Association
İskan Kanunu (1934 Settlement Law), 8, 258n38, 296n13. *See also* Settlement Law; Kurds
Islamic State (ISIS), 245

Israel, 143; Alfred Sauvy on, 70; Jean-Jacques Berreby on, 48, 265n22; transfer of Arab Jews to, 6, 48–49; Ülken on, 154. *See also* demography; integration; United Nations

Istanbul: AER 1954 convention in, 41, 43, 46, 49, 51, 53, 61, 62, 71, 77, 99; anti-Greek pogrom of 1955, 23, 42–43, 82, 87, 88, 91, 99, 150, 263nn7,8; Armenians in, 68; Çatalca, 173, 183–84; exchangees in, 54–55, 206; Greek Orthodox in, 4, 23, 42–43, 68, 81, 82, 87, 88, 91, 99, 150, 196, 263nn7,8; Greek winehouses, 196, 300n60; International Institute of Sociology congress of 1952, 67–68, 70; Municipality, 173–74; Pandora Bookshop, 283n15; Sulukule neighborhood, 194

Istanbul 2010 European Capital of Culture (ECoC) project, 179, 197–98, 203, 224, 228–29, 295n3, 298n45; diversity and multiculturalism celebrated by, 84, 173–74, 175–77, 184, 189, 190, 191–95, 201, 205–8, 232, 298n40, 299n57; funding of, 189, 192, 297n38; Population Exchange Museum as part of, 36, 173, 174–75, 180, 182, 191–92, 230, 232, 235

Istanbul University: Faculty of Letters, 292n116; Gini at, 60–61, 66, 136, 139, 268nn58,60, 269nn61,66, 292n116; Institute of Statistics, 57, 60–61, 268n58; School of Economics, 77, 276n131; Ülken at, 136–37, 149. *See also* Gini; Ülken

Italy: Central Institute of Statistics, 57; fascism in, 16, 34, 45, 48, 57–58, 61, 86, 227–28, 270n72, 304n132; Manifesto of Fascist Intellectuals, 57; Society of Genetics and Eugenics, 57. *See also* Gini; fascism

Jews: Arab Jews transferred to Israel, 6, 48–49; as minority in Turkey, 177, 184, 190, 199, 200, 204, 205, 207; in Ottoman Empire, 301n92

Jyllands-Posten: Muhammad cartoons in, 244

Kafesoğlu, İbrahim, 219, 220, 304n135. *See also* Turkish-Islamic synthesis

Kaplan, Mehmet, 211; *Dream of a Grand Turkey*, 227, 306n159. *See also* National Cultural Policy Report of 1983

Kemal, Namık, 201

Kemalism, 190, 204, 208, 216, 219, 295n5, 297n33

Khalili, Laleh, 26, 87; on colonialism, 16–17

Kıptî. *See* Roma

knowledge-based economy, 185–86, 187, 191

Köprülü, Mehmet Fuat: and Gini, 61, 131; and the 1955 anti-Greek pogrom, 264nn7,8; on origins of Turkish culture and canonization, 136, 139–40, 287nn49,51; and Taha Hussein, 126 139–40, 287nn49,51

Kornrumpf, Martin, 257n23

Kuran, Ercüment, 302n103

Kurds: "Eastern provinces" in the parliament, 180, 250; Kurdistan Workers Party (PKK), 19, 116, 198, 212, 214–15, 308n20; as minority in Turkey, 8, 9, 19, 24, 36, 116, 125, 180, 197, 198, 205, 206, 213, 218, 225, 228, 234, 246, 259n55, 296n15, 303n118; and state of emergency, 24. *See also* colonialism; Nur; segregative biopolitics; Settlement Law; Turkish-Islamic synthesis

labor capacity, 12

labor unions, 117, 218, 228, 241, 283nn14,18

Lahy, Bernard, 69

Lamarck, Jean-Baptiste, 291n109

Lambert, Léopold: *Weaponized Architecture*, 238

INDEX   323

Latin language, 152
Lausanne conference/Treaty of Lausanne: and Greek-Turkish population exchange, 2, 4, 7–8, 13, 44–45, 85–86, 88, 143, 150, 178, 190, 256n12, 258n39; minorities recognized by, 199, 204
League of Nations, 4, 47, 85–86, 89, 258n39
Lebanon: civil war of 1975–1990, 5
Lefevere, André, 95–96, 280n289
Leibniz, Gottfried Wilhelm, 257n19
Le Monde, 90
Le Pen, Marine, 243
lesser evils, 5, 36–37, 80, 234, 246, 247, 250
Lévi-Strauss, Claude, 73
liberal humanism, 32, 98, 238, 248–49; Barthes on, 28, 90–93, 94, 260n62; brotherhood of man in, 58, 59, 74, 75, 81, 101, 175, 199; and Cold War, 18, 43–44, 76, 82, 86, 93, 125, 184, 247; and *Family of Man*, 34, 78, 79, 80, 81–82, 85, 89, 90, 91–92, 231; human essence in, 18–19, 21, 28, 58, 80; and human suffering, 43, 77–78, 103; limits of, 20, 34–35, 36–37, 76, 93–94, 97, 102–3, 231; peace and coexistence in, 18, 20, 34, 74–75, 80, 81, 96, 125, 158, 171, 177, 181, 247, 251; relationship to historicist humanism, 37, 165, 188, 254; relationship to segregative biopolitics, 17–20, 27, 31, 34, 36–37, 73, 76–78, 80, 86, 97, 101, 102–3, 125–26, 158, 162, 169, 197, 254; and social justice, 20, 37, 101, 102, 169; in Turkey, 19–20, 21, 25, 35–36; and UNESCO, 18–19, 22, 23, 58, 73–76, 79, 80–81, 97, 125, 133, 158, 169, 184, 188, 233, 247, 251; unity in diversity in, 18–19, 58, 73–74, 78, 80–81, 90, 91–92, 97, 99, 101, 125, 133, 158, 165, 175, 177, 184, 187, 197, 260n63. *See also* multiculturalism
liberal values, 26–27, 29, 36, 37, 110. *See also* colonialism; Eurocentrism;

Fanon; human rights; liberal humanism; liberal multiculturalism; segregative biopolitics; tolerance
linearity of progress, 135, 138, 159, 237
literary studies, 30, 286n48, 288n76; and civilization, 134–145; and heritage 134–145; and historicist humanism, 134–145, 160–163, 167, 185, 251, 293n126, 293n135; and translation of classics, 202. *See also* canon; classics; comparative literature; civilization; multidisciplinary analysis

Macedonians, 108
Mahabharata, 164
Malkki, Liisa: on humanism, 28, 78; 260n62; 262n84; 282n8; 294n147; on national genealogy, 167; on radical historicization, 28, 78, 97. *See also* Barthes; liberal humanism; *Family of Man*
Mankind Quarterly, 58, 98
Maraş massacre, 214–15, 217, 225. *See also* Evren
Mardin, Şerif, 211, 305n 150. *See also National Cultural Policy Report* of 1983
Marxism, 210, 212, 213, 217, 218, 221, 228, 244
Mazower, Mark: on Schechtman, 278n172; on United Nations, 18, 85–86, 88, 89, 263n6
McClintock, Anne, 97–98, 129, 280n199
Mehring, Reinhard, 273n99
memoir boom, 25, 108–9, 110
Menderes, Adnan, 56, 60, 85, 87, 95, 221, 229, 304n132; and anti-Greek pogrom, 23–24, 42, 43, 87, 264nn7,8; overthrown by 1960 coup, 215, 264n8; policies on Sunni Islam, 23
Mérimée, Prosper, 142, 149. *See also* Ampère
Meskell, Lynn, 252
Milliyet, 118
Montagu, Ashley, 39, 58, 73, 275n119

Montesquieu, 1
Muhsam, Helmut Victor, 266n32; on integration and economic absorption, 51
Muhteşem Yüzyıl–The Magnificent Century, 286n40
Muller, Jerry Z., 267n35, 270n80
Müller, Karl Valentin, 69; as eugenicist, 52, 67, 127, 140; on refugee integration, 51–52
multiculturalism, 173, 192, 196–97, 244; and bracketing of communities, 196, 198; liberal mode of, 17, 19, 21, 22, 25, 35–36, 37, 108, 132, 169, 176–77, 189–90, 196, 198, 199, 202–3, 208, 214, 218, 232–35, 238, 248; in Turkey, 181–82, 189, 190, 194, 195, 199–201, 203–8, 214, 218, 231–32, 298n40, 299n57
multidisciplinary analysis, 22, 27, 29, 31–33
Munich: AER 1952 convention in, 62, 71
museumization of culture, 175–77, 194, 199, 201, 204, 234, 254, 300n60; dehistoricization in, 176, 232, 233; depoliticization in, 176, 208, 233; in Population Exchange Museum, 176, 182–83, 184
Museum of Modern Art (MoMA), 78, 81. See also *Family of Man*
Muslim exchangees, 4, 6, 107–8, 122–24, 143, 173, 295n6; attitudes of local Turks regarding, 3, 13, 123, 183; descendants of, 183–84; Dönme, 7, 9–10, 25, 54, 108, 121, 123–24, 183, 257n26; integration in Turkey, 54–56, 109, 156–57, 183, 200, 206, 208, 230, 267n44; as lacking homogeneity, 10–11, 12–13, 181, 183–84, 200, 206, 208, 230; occupations of, 2, 256n8. See also Foundation of Lausanne Treaty Emigrants
Mussolini, Benito, 34, 57, 58, 86, 304n132. See also fascism; Gini
Mustafa Celaleddin Paşa (Mustapha Djelaleddin Pasha), 147, 149, 152, 290n100; Deringil on, 147; Ülken on, 150. See also historicist humanism; Gobineau

national classics, 135–37. See also canon; classics; literary studies
National Cultural Policy Report of 1983 (1983 Milli Kültür Özel İhtisas Raporu), 19, 133, 141, 165, 209–13, 216, 218, 219–29, 231, 264n11. See also Cold War; colonialism; communism; Evren; fascism; Özal; Safa; Turkish-Islamic synthesis
national essences, 15–16, 154, 168, 216–17, 221, 225, 226, 227
national geniuses, 135, 139–41, 164, 165–66, 286n48, 287n49. See also Galton; genius; heredity; historicist humanism; racialized thinking
national identity, 133, 140, 141, 179, 200, 298n50, 299n57
nationalism, 16, 162, 163, 213; Kemalism, 190, 204, 208, 216, 219, 295n5, 297n33; nationalist gatekeeping, 114, 168, 228, 285n40
national refugees, 47–49, 54, 132, 153, 293n120
national security. See securitarianism
national unity, 119, 237; promoted by cultural policies, 211, 212–13, 216–17, 219, 220, 226. See also Turkish-Islamic synthesis
Navaro, Yael, 263n92; on ruination, 27, 115, 262n80
neoliberalism, 108, 131, 238, 246; culture in, 104; in Turkey, 24, 25, 116, 117, 191, 196, 198, 199, 201
New Delhi: Humanism and Education in the East and West (conference) in, 159–64, 167, 185, 251, 293n126
Nixon, Richard, 82
Norway: Breivik killings, 235, 243–45
nostalgia for lost homelands, 54, 55–56, 104

nuclear weapons, 78, 83, 98
numbers and space, 8–9, 64, 243–44; and AER/AWR, 45, 47–49, 129; birthrates of particular groups, 46–47, 48, 50; role in Greek-Turkish population exchange, 6, 10, 11; role in segregative biopolitics, 12, 17, 60, 194, 212
Nur, Rıza, 11, 222, 258n38; on minorities in Turkey, 7–9, 88, 180, 190; on population management policies, 8–9, 12; racialized thinking of, 7–9. *See also* racialized thinking; segregative biopolitics; unmixing

oral history, 103–4, 110–14, 117, 174; ethnohistorical informants, 108, 110, 111, 113, 114, 118–19, 123–24; Oral History Collection Project, 118–19
Organisation for Economic Co-operation and Development (OECD): *The Knowledge-Based Economy*, 185–86, 187
Orientalism, 28–30, 209, 241, 249; Ampère and, 142, 164; Oriental Jews, 48
origins, 2, 3, 6, 8, 9, 12, 19, 26, 52, 99, 130, 175; of civilizations, 15, 133, 135, 144, 152–53; countries of origin, 47, 48, 50–51, 53; in historicist humanism, 35, 97, 127, 129, 133–34, 147–48, 164, 168–69, 209, 219, 220; in racialized thinking, 15, 35, 127–29, 208; relationship to territorial claims, 143, 167, 286n45; role in nationalist gatekeeping, 114, 168, 228; role in self-identification, 110, 114, 126; tracing of, 10, 15–16, 97, 111, 114, 121, 122, 126–27, 128, 133–34, 135, 137–38, 141–42, 146–50, 151, 160, 161–62, 164, 165, 167, 180, 209, 249, 260n57, 286n45. *See also* family histories; genealogy
Ottoman Empire, 4, 79, 108, 136, 142–43, 148, 183, 222, 243, 248; Armenian genocide, 127, 223, 285n32; capture of Constantinople, 260n57, 286n44; and Crete, 122, 123; cultural heritage of, 200, 201, 203–4, 224; *millet* system, 207–8, 301n92; minorities in, 22, 195, 198–99, 301n92; neo-Ottomanism, 25, 36, 177, 189, 190–91, 199–204, 207–8, 218, 220, 223–24, 229, 232, 234, 285n40, 295n5; texts from, 2, 119–20, 123; tolerance in, 189, 191, 199, 201, 202, 203–4, 220, 224, 299n57; vs. Turkey, 8, 15, 19, 22
overpopulation and refugee problems, 49–50, 51
Özal, Turgut, 24, 210, 211–12, 216, 304n132. See also *National Cultural Policy Report of 1983*; Turkish-Islamic synthesis

Pakistan: population exchange in, 6
Palestine: partition of, 44, 154, 244
palimpsests, 72, 102, 193; of cultural policy, 29, 193, 208, 238; diachronic analysis of, 31, 187, 189, 248; Genette on, 20–21; of humanism, 30–31, 101, 133; of language and policies, 20–22, 28, 31, 33–34; of liberal multiculturalism, 35–36, 177, 195; regarding Population Exchange Museum, 173, 175, 176, 177, 184; of racialized thinking, 73; ruins as palimpsest, 114; of scholarly activities and institutions, 63; of segregative biopolitics, 29, 43, 63, 73, 75–76, 101, 248, 252, 253–54; synchronic analysis of, 31, 187, 189, 248; and transtextuality, 20–21; Turkish-Islamic synthesis as palimpsest, 141, 220, 229
partitions, 87–88, 102, 163; partition of Cyprus, 6, 19, 27, 115, 231; partition of India, 6, 44, 160, 162, 244, 248; partition of Palestine, 44, 154, 244, 248. *See also* apartheid; segregative biopolitics; walls
peace and coexistence, 14, 43, 68, 104, 173, 174, 181–82, 190, 198, 207; EU's promotion of, 192, 193; in liberal humanism, 18, 20, 34, 74–75, 80, 81, 96, 125, 158, 171,

177, 181, 247, 251; in neo-Ottomanism, 101, 191, 199, 200, 201, 202; UNESCO's promotion of, 44, 62, 69–70, 74–75, 76–77, 80, 81, 84–85, 99, 103, 125, 131, 158, 166, 185, 186, 247, 251
Peker, Mehmet Recep, 13
Persia, ancient, 135, 142, 152
Pinochet, Augusto, 24, 29, 218, 241, 250. *See also* Cold War; fascism
Pittard, Eugène, 290n100
PKK (Kurdistan Workers Party), 19, 116, 198, 212, 214–15
politics of expertise: after 1980 military coup, 223, 228; and race, 59–60; and the social, 63–72, 270n72
politics of visibility, 195–96
Potsdam agreement of 1945, 6, 44–45, 248
Povinelli, Elizabeth, 13, 26, 262n78; on bracketing communities, 196–97, 202–3; on cultural recognition, 196–97, 202–3
Prévost, Jean-Guy: on politics of expertise, 270n72

racial equality, 58–59, 62, 74, 91, 98, 99–100, 101, 158, 281n200
racialized thinking, 26, 33, 35, 136, 138, 143, 187, 213, 257n26, 281n200, 293n120; bloodlines in, 6, 7, 8, 9, 10, 12, 15, 16, 47, 71, 126, 127, 128, 140, 154, 180, 232; of Breivik, 235, 243–45; and colonialism, 12; and cultural diversity, 188; as gentrification, 27–28; Gobineau on degeneration, 145, 146–47, 152; and national geniuses, 166; of Nur, 7–9; and poverty, 238, 241; racial hierarchization, 10, 13, 15, 16–17, 71, 97, 98, 99, 115, 128, 129, 133, 134–35, 145–49; racialized genealogy, 10, 15, 35, 47, 71–72, 128–29, 142, 145–49, 166; relationship to Greek-Turkish population exchange, 10–12, 13, 14, 22, 35, 200; relationship to historicist humanism, 10, 14–17, 19, 20, 21, 101, 129, 145, 149, 166, 189, 208, 227–28, 242; relationship to segregative biopolitics, 5, 8, 9, 11, 21, 27–28, 29, 32–33, 60, 68–69, 71–72, 73, 97, 102, 115, 200, 238, 240, 241, 243, 246, 254; relationship to unmixing, 9, 21, 167, 227–28; as resilient, 68–69, 126, 130, 151, 247, 252; scientific racialism, 10, 12, 14, 15, 17, 18, 20, 21, 58–59, 62, 67, 73, 81, 98, 127; of Ülken, 151–52, 153, 155, 158. *See also* Chamberlain; civilization; demography; eugenics; Galton; genealogy; Gini; Gobineau; origins; segregation; segregative biopolitics; Ülken
Ramayana, 142
refugee crises, 3, 6, 12, 14, 42, 44–45, 265n15
Renaissance, 260n57, 286n44. *See also* civilization; historicist humanism; translation; Ülken
Republican People's Party (CHP), 87, 103, 126
Revue Internationale de Sociologie: Carl Schmitt in, 101, 237, 273n99; revival by Gini, 67
Rodríguez Zapatero, José Luis, 189
Roma, 13, 108, 196–97, 259n53; in EU, 184, 194, 205, 298n50
Rome: AER 1954 convention in, 47; International Institute of Sociology congress of 1950 in, 61–62, 63, 66, 69–70
Royal Central African Museum, 240
ruins, 82, 140, 167, 186, 195, 222; ancient ruins, 152, 179; Ann Stoler on, 262n80, 282n12, 300n71; Benjamin on, 115–16, 282n11; heritage trips to, 111–14, 135; historicist humanism, 135, 152; Hell and Schönle on, 115, 282n11, 308n27; and liberal humanism, 37, 97, 169; and memory, 169; of modernity, 254, 282n11, 308n27; as palimpsest, 114; photography of, 89; and the population exchange, 1–3, 5, 107, 111–14; and segregative bio-

politics, 5, 35–36, 97, 125, 129, 168, 187, 248; of violence, 234, 246, 252; of war, 6, 27, 89, 251, 257n18. *See also* Ampère; cultural heritage; heritage; ruination; Schliemann; trips; travel literature
ruination, 28, 35, 119, 125, 167–69, 196–97, 202, 252; excavation of ruins, 115–16, 169; Navaro on, 27, 115, 262n80; Stoler on, 27, 28, 115, 116, 200, 262n80

Safa, Peyami: on being human, 220, 249; *East-West Synthesis*, 68, 137, 139, 141, 220, 287n63; *Fatih-Harbiye*, 68, 139, 141; impact on Turkish-Islamic synthesis, 288n73; and humanism, 287n63; "Sociology and the Novel," 68, 103; as substitute member of the executive board of the 1949 UNESCO Turkish National Commission, 141, 288n73; as Vice President of Turkish Sociological Society, 68, 136, 273n103; 109, 136, 249, 273n102, 304n137
Sainte Beuve, Charles-Augustin, 289n76; correspondence with Ampère, 288; "Le Comte-Pacha Bonneval," 1, 255n4. *See also* Ampère; Bonneval, Claude Alexandre; historicist humanism
Salonika: A Family Cookbook, 123–24
Sandburg, Carl: "There is One Man in the World, and His Name Is All Men," 80
Sarc, Ömer Celâl, 268n58
Sarkozy, Nicolas, 194
Sarol, Mükekerrem, 263n7
Sartre, Jean-Paul, 289n86
Sauvy, Alfred, 69; Shohat and Stam on, 274n110
Saygun, Adnan, 288n73
Schätzel, Walter: on assimilation, 53–54; on immigrants vs. refugees, 53–54; on undesirable refugees, 51, 53
Schechtman, Joseph, 278n172. *See also* Mazower

Schliemann, Heinrich, 135, 141, 142
Schmieden, Werner von, 48, 266n26
Schmitt, Carl, 67, 241, 246, 248; on appropriation as progress, 249, 253, 254; "Appropriation/Distribution/Production," 101–2, 104, 242–43, 245, 273n99, 281nn201,204; on colonialism, 171, 239, 241–42; *The Concept of the Political*, 242; on humanitarianism, 239; on liberal democracy, 237; in *Revue Internationale de Sociologie*, 101, 237, 273n99; relationship with Benjamin, 252. *See also* Gini; *Revue Internationale de Sociologie*
Schönle, Andreas: *Ruins of Modernity*, 115, 282n111, 308n27
Schremmer, Ernst, 77
securitarianism, 37, 232, 245; and Foucault, 32, 263n94; relationship to segregative biopolitics, 32–33, 50, 52, 116, 239–40, 242, 247, 249–50; in Turkey, 36, 213, 230, 234, 246; in United States, 243
segregation, 168, 174, 202, 238, 259n44, 267n48, 275n120; apartheid in South Africa, 85; *Brown v. Board of Education*, 59, 91; Emmett Till, 91; Gini, 58, 71, 91; justified as peace and stability, 5; as illiberal policy, 23; and infrastructure, 27; the International Association for the Advancement of Ethnology and Eugenics, 58, 91; Jan Smuts, 85; *Mankind Quarterly*, 58; and mass displacement, 4; population management, 9, 11, 21; racialized thinking, 9, 11; reproducing segregation, 232, 265n12; in the United States, 23, 44, 58, 59, 71, 91, 232, 259n44. *See also* The International Association for the Advancement of Ethnology and Eugenics; Till; segregative biopolitics
segregative biopolitics. *See* biopolitics, segregative. *See also* apartheid; eugenics; historicist humanism; Greek-

Turkish population exchange; liberal humanism; partition; ruins; walls
self-determination, 89, 102, 131
self-identification, 17, 110, 114, 120, 126, 128, 181, 233
September 11th attacks, 33, 189, 239, 279n186, 295n3
Settlement Law. *See* İskan Kanunu
Sewell, William H., Jr., 282n3
Shabbatai Zvi, 7, 183
Shohat, Ella: on Alfred Sauvy, 274n110; on Arab Jews, 48, 265n21; on Eurocentrism, 15, 260n56; *Race in Translation*, 274n110; on Wacquant, 306n166. *See also* Stam
Sicard, Émile, 267n39
Simpson, George Gaylord, 98
Smith, Adam, 266n29; on the relationship between economy and peace, 102, 247
Smuts, Jan, 85, 96
social justice, 95, 188, 198, 203, 213, 219, 226, 235; vs. cultural recognition, 196, 197, 232, 233–34, 246–47; and liberal humanism, 20, 37, 101, 102, 169
social order and stability, 4, 5, 102, 116, 211–13, 215–16, 242, 265n11, 283n14
social sciences, 57, 221, 222–23, 270n72; big data in, 33; and UNESCO, 62, 63, 64–65, 69–70, 73–75, 98
Sotiriou, Dido: *Farewell Anatolia*, 230–31
South African apartheid, 44, 85, 259n55
Spanish Civil War, 63–64, 78, 103, 159. *See also* fascism
Stam, Robert: on Eurocentrism, 15, 260n56; *Race in Translation*, 274n110; on Wacquant, 306n166
Steichen, Edward: as curator of *Family of Man*, 70, 78, 80, 81, 83, 89, 90, 93, 94, 99, 128, 279n185
Stoler, Ann: on dispossession, 116; on Foucault and race, 12, 259n50; on racialism in French colonial histories,

12; on ruination, 27, 28, 115, 116, 200, 262n80
Suleiman the Magnificent, 286n40
Sunni Islam, 8, 15, 23, 190, 213, 214, 229; as melting pot, 208; in Turkish education, 218, 224–25, 305n151; and Turkish-Islamic synthesis, 25, 109, 200, 226–27, 228
synchronic analysis, 32–33, 35, 76, 79, 117, 168; of cultural policies, 208, 245, 248, 252; of palimpsests, 31, 187, 189, 248. *See also* diachronic analysis
Syrian refugees, 4, 12, 51, 107, 206, 235, 261n63

Tanzimat reforms, 221
Taylor, Charles: "The Politics of Recognition," 233–34
Thatcher, Margaret: on Pinochet, 29, 218
Till, Emmett, 91
Time magazine, 64
Tocqueville, Alexis de, 142, 149
tolerance, 161, 166, 207, 224–25, 235; Bilgin Ayata on, 299n57; Brown on depoliticization and, 198, 201–2, 203, 300n68; Ceren Özgül on, 284n19; and civilizations, 190, 295n3; and classics, 161–63, 166; in cultural policies, 162–63, 184, 185, 186, 189, 190, 205; and dehistoricization of alterity, 200; and diversity, 184–86, 190–91, 199; and humanism, 162–63, 166; in humanities education, 161, 163, 166; and Islamic education to remedy crime, 226; Istanbul European Capital of Culture, 174, 184, 189–91, 205–7; Mustafa Celaleddin Paşa on, 148; and neo-Ottomanism, 199, 201, 220, 224; in relation to liberal discourses, 27, 188, 202; in relation to *Family of Man*, 202; and the Ottoman Empire, 189, 191, 199, 201, 202, 203–4, 220, 224, 299n57; and the Turkish-Islamic synthesis, 220; and

UNESCO, 162–63, 166, 184–86, 189, 205. *See also* classics; coexistence; cultural policy; peace
Torres Bodet, Jaime, 166
translation, 95, 202, 286n46; attributed role in cultural renaissance, 137–38, 287n52; *Race in Translation*, 274n110, 275n122; as rewriting, 95, 230, 280n189, 286n48; Turkish Translation Bureau, 136, 161; and Ülken, 136–38; UNESCO's Translation Bureau, 161, 287n54
travel literature, 118, 142; Ampère, 142, 288n76, 289n77; Schliemann using Homer, 142; using classics as a map for heritage travels in pursuit of designated civilizational origins, 135, 141–42, 288n76, 289n77
tree of humankind. *See* family tree of humankind
Troy, 135, 142. *See also* Ampère; historicist humanism; Schliemann
Trump, Donald, 235, 243. *See also* demography; securitarianism; xenographic discourses
Turkey: as case study, 22; civil war of 1970s, 211, 214–15, 221; during Cold War, 23–24, 29, 42, 178, 210, 241; criminalization in, 226; cultural identification in, 109, 113–14, 120, 122–24, 139, 140, 174–75, 178–79, 198–99, 204, 208; cultural policies, 26, 35–36, 133, 165, 173–78, 184, 188, 189–92, 194–95, 196, 197–203, 204, 205, 208–35, 247–48, 264n11, 295n3, 296n20, 297n38, 302n103, 305nn140,150,151, 306n159; Directorate of Religious Affairs, 204; economic conditions, 117, 209, 210, 221; education in, 216–17, 218, 219, 221–22, 226, 227, 228, 229, 293n129, 305n151; family histories in, 2, 25, 35, 107–8, 110–12, 116, 117, 119–24, 125, 126–27, 133, 139, 147, 167, 173, 178, 181, 182, 247; in *Family of Man*, 85, 94–95; gentrification in, 28,

194; High Council of Atatürk Culture, Language, and History, 223–24; historicist humanism in, 35–36; human rights in, 25, 117, 119, 214; integration of Muslim exchangees in, 54–56, 183, 200, 206, 230, 267n44; during Korean War, 23; liberal humanism in, 19–20, 21, 25, 35–36; liberal multiculturalism in, 35–36; military coup of 1960, 23–24, 215, 264n8, 272n92, 272n94; military coup of 1980, 19, 24, 29, 35, 36, 109–10, 116, 119, 125, 128, 141, 175, 181, 208, 209–10, 212, 214, 215–18, 220, 229–30, 231, 237–38, 241, 264n11, 282n14, 304n132; Ministry of Culture and Tourism, 173–74, 195; Ministry of Foreign Affairs, 271n92; minorities in, 7–9, 13, 19, 25, 28, 121, 177, 180, 184, 190, 194, 196, 197–99, 199, 203–4, 205–8, 214–15, 222–23, 226–27, 305n151; multiculturalism in, 181–82, 189, 190, 194, 195, 199–201, 203–8, 214, 218, 231–32, 298n40, 299n57; *National Cultural Policy Report*, 133, 165, 209–13, 216, 218, 219–29, 231, 264n11, 302n103, 305nn140,150, 306n159; national essence, 15–16, 221, 225, 226, 227; national identity, 200, 299n57; National Security Council, 212, 219, 222, 282n14; NATO membership, 23; neoliberalism in, 24, 25, 116, 117, 191, 196, 198, 199, 201; neo-Ottomanism in, 25, 36, 177, 189, 190–91, 199–204, 207–8, 218, 220, 223–24, 229, 232, 234, 285n40, 295n5; Penal Code, 304n132; population growth, 225; privatization policies in, 23, 24; referendum of 2017, 25; relations with EU, 176; relations with Greece, 4, 19, 63, 143, 156; relations with Syria, 224; securitarianism in, 36, 213, 230, 234, 246; Settlement Law of 1934, 8–9, 180, 258n38; Translation Bureau, 136, 161; Zonguldak, 13. *See also* Greek-Turkish population exchange; Turkish-Islamic synthesis

Turkish Airlines, 241. *See also* Orientalism
Turkish Higher Education Council, 216
Turkish Historical Society, 223
Turkish-Islamic synthesis, 19, 24, 35, 55, 68, 178, 189, 208–35, 267n44, 304n135, 304n136, 304n138; and assimilation, 133, 209, 223, 225, 227, 229; and dispossession, 209; and demography, 109, 165, 209, 225, 229; and Greek-Turkish population exchange, 229–30; and integration, 133, 209, 223, 225, 227, 229; and military coup of 1980, 36, 109, 141, 208, 209–10, 212, 215–16, 217, 218, 220, 229–30; and *National Cultural Policy Report*, 133, 165, 209–13, 216, 218, 219–29, 264n11; and neo-Ottomanism, 200, 201, 208, 218, 220, 223–24, 229, 232, 285n40; as palimpsest, 141, 220, 229; and Peyami Safa, 68, 109, 137, 141, 220, 274n104, 288n72; and relationship to historicist humanism, 36, 109, 141, 209, 220, 221–22, 227–28; and segregative biopolitics, 141, 157, 209; Sunni Islam as norm, 25, 109, 200, 226–27, 228, 302n94. *See also* cultural policy; fascism; Gökalp; Greek-Turkish population exchange; Safa
Turkish Sociological Society, 60, 68, 136, 274n103

Ülken, Hilmi Ziya, 139, 143, 160, 263n2, 272nn92–94, 273n100, 291n106; and AER, 35, 41, 56, 60, 63, 70, 150, 156–57, 158, 292nn110,116; on assimilation, 153, 155–57, 292n120, 293n121; on civilizations, 137–38, 152, 153; on degeneration vs. mixedness, 151; on education, 73, 157–58, 162–63, 224–25; on family of Turks, 153, 292n116; on forced migrations, 156; vs. Gini, 60, 63, 65, 66, 67, 151, 291n109, 292n116; on Gobineau, 149–50; on Greek-Turkish population exchange, 150, 151, 155–57; on heredity; 150, 153, 157, 291n107, 292n117; on heritage of humanity, 150, 164, 294n142; on hierarchized civilizations, 137–38; on Houston Sewart Chamberlain, 149; *İçtimai Doktrinler Tarihi* (History of social thought), 149–50; *İnsani Vatanperverlik* (Humanist patriotism), 163; and International Institute of Sociology (IIS), 63, 66, 70–71, 292n110; and International Sociological Association (ISA), 65, 66–67, 275n118, 292n110; at Istanbul University, 136–37, 149, 272n94; on Jews, 154; on low population density, 292n116; on national refugees, 292n120; on origin of Turks, 151, 152; on partition of Palestine, 154; on patriotic humanism, 163–65, 251, 294n141; racialized thinking of, 151–52, 153, 155, 158; on social life and nature, 138; on social race, 150–55, 158, 162, 220, 291n110; on social types, 150–51, 152–55, 157, 162; *Toplum Yapısı ve Soyaçekim* (The structure of society and heredity), 153; on translation, 137, 138, 161; on Turkish civilization, 137–38; *Veraset ve Cemiyet* (Heredity and society), 150–58, 291n110; on Western civilization, 137–38. *See also* historicist humanism; Istanbul University; Gini; Greek-Turkish population exchange; racialized thinking; Safa; segregative biopolitics; Turkish Sociological Society
Ulusu, Bülend, 215–16
UNESCO: vs. AER/AWR, 76, 77, 132, 153; Convention on the Protection of the Diversity of Cultural Expressions, 126, 184–85, 187–89; and cultural identification, 125–26, 131–33, 188, 247; cultural policies of, 18, 19, 22, 23, 34, 35, 36, 75–76, 79–80, 97, 103, 108–9, 125, 126, 131–34, 136, 143–45, 153, 155, 158–60, 161–

67, 169, 175–177, 184–88, 192, 195, 210, 211, 219, 233, 234, 247, 250–52, 282n3, 292n110, 293n126, 302n103; *Cultural Policy: A Preliminary Study*, 210, 211; and cultural recognition, 76, 80, 103, 130, 133, 144, 161, 165–66, 169, 175, 185, 188, 192, 233; *Family of Man* endorsed by, 34, 78, 79–80, 81, 84–85, 86, 90, 91, 94–96, 99, 101, 204; founding of, 43, 57, 248; and historicist humanism, 18, 35, 97, 133, 134, 141, 143, 145, 150, 158–69, 185, 233, 251; and human collaboration, 74, 75, 83; and human essence, 18–19, 39, 58; Humanism and Education in the East and West (conference), 159–64, 167, 185, 251, 293n126; on human suffering, 76–77, 112; *International Social Science Bulletin*, 74–75; and International Sociological Association (ISA), 62, 63, 64–65, 66, 69, 70, 71, 144, 271n80; on knowledge-based economy, 185–86, 187; and liberal humanism, 18–19, 22, 23, 58, 73–76, 79, 80–81, 97, 125, 133, 158, 169, 184, 188, 233, 247, 251; Memory of the World project, 79, 81–82, 83, 84–85, 90, 96, 101, 204–5, 276n136; peace and coexistence promoted by, 44, 62, 69–70, 74–75, 76–77, 80, 81, 84–85, 99, 103, 125, 131, 158, 166, 185, 186, 247, 251; polices on education, 185, 186; relations with France, 87; and social sciences, 62, 63, 64–65, 69–70, 73–75, 98; Statement on Race (1950), 23, 39, 57, 71, 73–74, 81, 91, 94, 98, 99, 139, 158, 281n200; Translation Bureau, 161; *UNESCO Courier*, 76, 80, 81, 95, 136, 144, 158, 250–51; Universal Declaration on Cultural Diversity, 126, 131, 175, 184–87, 188, 195, 296n20; Universal Declaration on Cultural Policies, 125, 126, 131–33, 161, 175, 176; Turkish National Commission of 1949, 288n73; World Conference on Cultural Policies, 302n103; *World Culture Report 2000*, 234; World Heritage Committee, 246; World Heritage list, 166–67, 246; world kinship emphasized by, 75. *See also* Gini; liberal humanism; ISA; IIS; Montagu; Strauss; *Family of Man*; Ülken

United Nations: Alliance of Civilizations, 189–92, 200, 224, 228–29, 295n3; Charter, 78, 85, 96; and demographic management, 6; and *Family of Man*, 83, 84–85; founding of, 43, 248; Genocide Convention, 86, 88; High Commissioner for Refugees (UNHCR), 56; and human rights, 86, 87–88, 94, 117, 263n6; Mazower on, 18, 85–86, 88, 89, 263n6; and minority rights, 88, 89; mission, 27; national self-determination endorsed by, 89; and refugee crisis, 6, 12; and status quo, 18; Universal Declaration of Human Rights, 86, 87, 88, 96–97, 289n83. *See also* UNESCO

United States: Atomic Energy Commission, 83, 84, 277n154; *Brown v. Board of Education*, 59, 91; civil rights movement, 58–59, 71, 249; Cold War policies, 29; comparative literature in, 164; distribution of wealth in, 243; Donald Trump, 235, 243; intervention in Afghanistan, 239, 240, 241; intervention in Iraq, 239; McCarthyism in, 23, 63–64, 84; Muslim ban in, 235; poverty in, 232–33; radiation experiments, 83, 277n154; securitarianism in, 243; segregation in, 23, 44, 58, 59, 86, 91, 232–33, 259n55; September 11th attacks, 33, 189, 239, 279n186, 295n3; Supreme Court, 59, 91; white supremicists in, 245. *See also* Cold War; United States Information Service (USIS)/United States Information Agency

United States Information Service (USIS)/United States Information

Agency, 82, 93, 94. *See also* Cold War; *Family of Man*
unmixing, 4, 9–10, 12, 16; apartheid and segregation, 5, 9, 76, 102, 202; as category of analysis, 9–10; and eugenics, 9, 16, 21; and partition, 5, 76; population exchange and transfers, 4, 9, 21, 256n14, 257n21, 258n39; in relationship to racialized thinking, 9, 21, 167, 227–28; segregative biopolitics, 32; as spatial population management, 9–10. *See also* segregative biopolitics; walls; segregation
Ustaoğlu, Yeşim: *Waiting for the Clouds*, 122

Voltaire, 1, 257n19

Wacquant, Loïc, 232–33, 238; Shohat and Stam on, 305n166. *See also* segregative biopolitics
Wagner, Richard, 145, 149. *See also* Chamberlain; fascism; Gobineau
walls, 5, 32–33, 235, 238. *See also* segregative biopolitcs; apartheid; securitarianism; partition
Wall Street Journal: on Egyptian coup of 2013, 29

Weizman, Eyal, 26; on human rights regime, 5; *The Least of All Possible Evils*, 257n20; on lesser evils, 5, 234, 246, 257nn19,20
Werner, Michael: on *histoire croisée*, 30–31. *See also* crossing; Zimmermann
Wiese, Leopold von, 64–65, 69
Wirth, Louis, 70, 275nn114,118
World Bank, 23, 24, 249; *World Development Report*, 210

xenophobic discourses, 128–29, 144, 222. *See also* fascism; Orientalism; racialized thinking

Yalçın, Kemal: *The Entrusted Trousseau*, 103, 179, 182
Yalman, Ahmet Emin, 273n102
Yeni Sabah, 60, 66–67, 272nn93,94, 291n109, 292n116
Yücel, 139
Yunus Emre Society, 140

Zekâi Apaydın, Aziz, 7
Zimmermann, Bénédicte: on *histoire croisée*, 30–31. *See also* crossing; palimpsests; Werner

The authorized representative in the EU for product safety and compliance is:
Mare Nostrum Group
B.V Doelen 72
4831 GR Breda
The Netherlands

www.ingramcontent.com/pod-product-compliance
Lightning Source LLC
Chambersburg PA
CBHW031857220426
43663CB00006B/659